D0687557

TENDER GEOGRAPHIES

GENDER AND CULTURE

Carolyn G. Heilbrun and Nancy K. Miller, editors

Tender Geographies

Women and the Origins of the Novel in France

Joan DeJean

COLUMBIA UNIVERSITY PRESS

NEW YORK

Columbia University Press
New York   Oxford

Library of Congress Cataloging-in-Publication Data
DeJean, Joan.
    Tender geographies : women and the origins of the novel in France
    / Joan DeJean.
        p.   cm.—(Gender and culture)
    Includes bibliographical references and index.
    ISBN 0-231-06230-3
    1. French fiction—Women authors—History and criticism.
2. French fiction—17th century—History and criticism.   3. French
fiction—18th century—History and criticism.   4. Women and
literature—France—History—17th century.   5. Women and literature—
France—History—18th century.   I. Title.   II. Series.
PQ637.W64D4 1991
843.009′9287—dc20   91-28239
                                                                                      CIP

Casebound editions of Columbia University Press books are Smyth-sewn and printed on
permanent and durable acid-free paper.

Printed in the United States of America

c 10 9 8 7 6 5 4 3 2 1

For Natalie Zemon Davis
with gratitude for her example

Contents

Illustrations

Acknowledgments

THIS BOOK has been a long time in the making. When it was in its initial phase I became fascinated with the frequent references to Sappho in early modern women's writing: that fascination eventually set me off on a detour that led, some five years later, to my *Fictions of Sappho.* I don't know that I would have been able to return to the material in *Tender Geographies* without Nancy K. Miller's encouragement: she made me feel that, despite the radical ways in which our critical landscape has shifted since I began to articulate my thinking about early women writers, there was reason to revive my original project. Although I am now a very different reader from the person who began this study and would not always make the same choices, either of exclusion or of inclusion, I am glad that Nancy, and subsequently Jennifer Crewe of Columbia University Press, wouldn't let me give up when I became bogged down in the task of blending my earlier interests and my current ones. Despite all that has changed, my devotion to the writers I discuss here remains real.

That devotion began long ago, when I was growing up in Louisiana in a milieu whose vision of French culture was, I now realize, a product of Louisiana's eccentric position, isolated not only from France but also from the French educational system. The French in Louisiana had, of course, continued to read Molière and Racine: those were the first books my maternal grandmother gave me. They also remembered another canon, composed of works that had been widely influential in seventeenth- and eighteenth-century France (before the main periods of immigration to Louisiana) but that had subsequently been excluded from the canon imposed when the French national educational system was established in the nineteenth century. French readers in Louisiana kept alive the memory of works that have largely been ignored by modern readers in metropolitan France. When I was growing up I took the novel for the central genre in early modern literature and such women novelists as Germaine de Staël and Madeleine de Scudéry for major figures in the French national tradition. How could I have done otherwise, when my best friend was named Clélie, for her mother's best friend, who had in turn been named, everyone still remembered, for *her* mother's favorite novel. *Clélie,* or so my friends in that little corner of New France long forgotten by Old France still believed, was surely one of the most famous French novels.

The week of my arrival in New Haven as a graduate student, I rushed to Sterling Library: faced with the sight of no fewer than three complete editions of *Clélie, histoire romaine,* I sank to the floor in admiration. Scudéry's novels are perhaps not as exciting for a twentieth-century reader as the buildup had led me to believe, but I have never regretted my long association with early women's fiction. I am grateful to the long line of Clélies without whom it might never have begun.

I am also grateful to friends and colleagues closer to what has now become home. The students who attended the seminars I gave on early women's writing at Princeton kept the subject vital for me during its initial phases. Without the friendship of Faith Beasley, Kathleen Woodward, and Herbert Blau I would never have survived the months when I was ending the project. Steve Ferguson from Princeton's Firestone Library tracked down material. Erica Harth offered a generously detailed reading of the final version of my manuscript. My interpretation of *La Princesse de Clèves* was enriched through dialogue with John Lyons. Georges May provided help with references; his example was always there, since my work has never been more closely related to that of the person I will always think of as "my" teacher. Tim Reiss sent references and shared his own work on early constructions of gender with me. Jamie Rohrer provided important assistance in compiling the bibliography of early women writers. Natalie Zemon Davis—I'll take the "z" as alphabetical authorization for Natalie's placement in this list—was, as always, able to suggest just the right reference and to pinpoint the moment when my argument needed correction. Natalie proves that it is possible to live up to the highest human and scholarly standards at the same time: her example is a constant source of inspiration.

A fellowship from the John Simon Guggenheim Memorial Foundation made possible early work on this project. The last revisions were completed in the haven of the University of California Humanities Research Institute.

TENDER GEOGRAPHIES

Introduction

In its August 6, 1984, issue *Newsweek* trumpeted "Headline Equality Comes to the Times." Until Geraldine Ferraro's nomination as Walter Mondale's running mate, the article explained, *The New York Times*

> had stubbornly stuck by its rule that a title—Mrs., Miss or Rep. (but never Ms.)—always precede the last name of a woman in a headline, although male subjects were exempt from the code. But after a couple of weeks of constantly pairing "Rep. Ferraro" with just plain "Mondale," the requirement was quietly dropped . . . , and the Queens congress-woman became simply "Ferraro."

Would that the wheels of French literary history could turn as quickly and as quietly.

The *American Heritage Dictionary* contains two entries for "Lafayette." The first manages to be both correct and faithful to the French code:

> Lafayette, Comtesse de. Called "Madame de Lafayette."

XVIIe/XVIIIe Madame de...

The dictionary's formulation is apt. The writer is *called* "Madame de . . . ," even though there is no logical reason why this should be the case. The second Lafayette identified there, a Marquis, is never called "Monsieur de . . ."—nor is this custom followed in speaking of the male writers who were "Madame de" Lafayette's contemporaries: the Duc de La Rochefoucauld today has become simply "La Rochefoucauld." For other periods roughly parallel codes are employed for male and female writers: Chrétien de Troyes and Marie de France, Louise Labé and

Clément Marot, Jean-Paul Sartre and Simone de Beauvoir. In the nineteenth century, women writers' use of male pseudonyms makes this parallelism seem deceptively simple (George Sand and Gustave Flaubert), whereas initially these pseudonyms must have been adopted in part to break the code enforced whenever women writers of the seventeenth and eighteenth centuries are spoken of: by the early nineteenth century, the practice was in place from which we have yet to deviate, whereby these women writers, bourgeoises and aristocrats alike, are *only* identified as "Mademoiselle de . . ." or "Madame de. . . ."[1]

As a result of this practice, first names of women writers are not easy to locate, and have sometimes even been lost: in the indexes of standard reference works such as Antoine Adam's *Histoire de la littérature française au XVIIe siècle* and Henri Coulet's *Le Roman jusqu'à la Révolution*, women are identified only as "Mme de" or "Mlle de." The consequences of this practice can be serious; for example, how many scholars working in the Bibliothèque Nationale would think to consult entries for both "Charrière, Madame de" and "Charrière, Isabelle"? Somehow, books have been divided up between the two; unsuspecting readers would miss a good number of the library's holdings.[2]

→ missing library holdings

The majority of women writers in the seventeenth century were aristocrats: we could never fashion a handy double name for someone whose correct full title is "Marie-Madeleine Pioche de La Vergne, Comtesse de Lafayette."[3] The only convenient solution is to refer to aristocratic women solely by the family name associated with their title, in this case, "Lafayette." Those who resist a policy of standardization maintain that the current double standard recreates the practice of ancien régime noblemen, who referred to each other by a family name alone. If precedent must be established, here are two examples showing that women intellectuals of the French classical age also spoke of each other in this way: in the anonymous novel *Le Triomphe de l'indifférence* (1650s?), when discussing the sister of the writer's husband, the characters call her only "Lafayette"; in the body of *L'Apothéose de Mademoiselle de Scudéry* (1702), Marie-Jeanne L'Héritier deviates from the code followed in her title and consistently refers to her subject as "Scudéry," a practice she adopts when speaking of any woman intellectual.

Until today's students of French Studies begin to follow this lead we will continue to transmit a sense of what Sandra Gilbert and Susan Gubar term "the social dependency, the matrimonial respectability or vulnerable virginity, of women [writers]" (562). For the ideological baggage transmitted along with "Madame de" and "Mademoiselle de" is far from negligible. In all Western traditions, great writers are known by a family name alone; dominant usage in French suggests that women writers are ladies first.

In addition, as long as we cling to this familiar code, we cannot properly evaluate women writers' complex relation to what is today considered the foundation of modern authorial identity, the signature. In the sense of Michel Foucault's *nom d'auteur,* the signature is a public gesture that signifies an individual's desire to be identified as the author of a literary corpus.[4] In the following pages I will on several occasions raise the vexed question of the anonymous publication of much early women's writing. Such apparent disregard for the authorial signature has often been treated as proof of women's disregard for literary authority, proof that they did not see themselves as authors. My position in general is that this issue is far too complex to be resolved simply. There is much evidence to suggest that, during the period to which we now trace the birth of modern authorial identity, women writers had a more ambivalent response to the signature than did their male counterparts.

This ambivalence can be explained in different ways. It is sometimes evident that ancien régime women writers wished to maintain a distinction between personal identity and authorial identity, that they sought to have the quality of their works judged independently of preconceived ideas associated with their person. The notion of the separation between public and private identities is well illustrated by a passage in *Le Pour et le contre* (1733) by the Abbé Prévost, among the eighteenth-century male writers most preoccupied with constructions of the feminine. A dialogue between the narrator and a female interlocutor culminates in an attempt to define just what makes an author, via a discussion of the signature and the importance of an established authorial identity. The interlocutor's position is that a work should be read because it is "good," a judgment made according to "the pleasure produced by the reading." In such a context, nothing could be "more useless" than "to know ... the name of [its] author" (99). In his "astonishment," the narrator at first takes this position for a personal "mania," until the woman explains to him that "she had more than one friend who felt as she did" (100). "Friend" is in the feminine to indicate Prévost's point in this passage: the notion that judgments of literary merit should be situated beyond authorial identity was linked to literary women.

The most nuanced vision of the early woman writer's complex relation to the *nom d'auteur* is in the autobiography of George Sand, who, especially in *Indiana,* her first novel written without collaboration, seems the last true inheritor of this politics of female authorship:

> A family whose name I had found good enough for me found this name of Dudevant ... too illustrious ... to be compromised in the republic of arts. I was baptized ... between the manuscript of *Indiana* ... and a 1000–franc bill. ... It was a contract, a new marriage between the poor apprentice poet that I was and the humble muse who had consoled me in my misfortune. (1:140)

Her ancien régime precursors predicted in various ways Sand's conclusion: for the woman writer the *nom d'auteur* marks the troubled boundary between public and private. If she is married, the authorial signature seals a contract into which she cannot legally enter. She has no name of her own to attach to her corpus, simply that of her husband's family, which she is only entitled to use by her marriage contract. The woman writer might therefore fashion her own name, "rebaptize" herself as Sand did, in the manner of her precursors—"M. de Villedieu," for example. Or she might, in the manner of other precursors, choose anonymity as a way of keeping private and public apart. In either case, she was aware that the signature was, in Sand's words, "a contract, a new marriage." For the woman writer, especially the woman writer of the ancien régime, as we will see on numerous occasions, a literary life and a traditional marriage proved incompatible.[5]

Unlike their male counterparts, women writers of the ancien régime seem to have been unable to forget the fine line between their private unions and the more public "new marriages" they contracted when they became authors. This difference in attitude seems logical if we bear in mind that female authorship as a major phenomenon in the French tradition begins at the same period as the modern notion of authorship; women writers would therefore have been doubly self-conscious about the potential effects on their person of a professional phenomenon in a state of transition. This awareness explains the political placement of what I am calling their tender geographies, the fact that in their novels affairs of the heart are portrayed as indissociable from affairs of state. Their persistent connection of private (the romantic) and public (the political) explains in turn the existence of the code dictating that they be known only as "Madame" or "Mademoiselle."

The limits of this study are those within which this onomastic curiosity is implemented, the seventeenth and eighteenth centuries, and in particular the period for which it was initially put in place, roughly 1640–1715.[6] At no other time have women writers played a more influential role in the French tradition: we therefore portray women writers as least equal onomastically precisely when they were most powerful literarily. As must by now be evident, I find this naming annoying.[7] However, I realize that it is only a by-product of a complex and multifaceted process, at the end of which a vastly simplified view of women writers' involvement in the shaping of classical French literature was written into the literary history that has been passed down from the late seventeenth century to the present day. I will in due course consider aspects of this process; for the moment, I would like to suggest briefly the extent and the nature of the contribution thus obscured.

In France, the novel was a feminist creation. Historians and literary historians for some time have asserted that the earliest forms of prose fiction important in seventeenth-century France played a central role "in the development and diffusion of feminist ideas" (Maclean 201; see also Magendie, *Le Roman français ... de "l'Astrée" au "Grand Cyrus"*). The prose narrative that inspired this claim was initially developed by male writers such as Gomberville and La Calprenède and is usually called the *roman héroïque,* in English, "romance." However, if the relation between prose fiction and an ideology that can be qualified as feminist is linked to the history of women writers' involvement with the creation of what came to be known as the modern novel, it becomes possible to claim a more central role for feminism in the shaping of that genre. Without exception, the strains of prose fiction that today's readers would identify with the novel were the creation of women writers. In addition, the fictional forms devised by seventeenth-century women writers were both feminocentric and the product of an ideology that sought to promote equality between the sexes. (Consider, for example, the final shape given to the *roman* by Scudéry in *Artamène,* the variant of the *histoire* developed by Scudéry [*Clélie, histoire romaine*] and continued by Lafayette [*Zayde, histoire espagnole*], and the miniaturization of that form known at the period as the *nouvelle.*) In the following pages I hope to go beyond the assertion that the early novel was a vehicle for feminism to demonstrate that feminist ideas played a crucial role in the development of the French novel.[8] This second claim is based both on the evolution of political activity undertaken by seventeenth-century women and on the intentional bond repeatedly forged in this activity between the making of history and the making of literature. Because of the existence of this bond, activity in the public domain of court politics and activity in the more private literary sphere can ultimately be seen as functionally equivalent.

In this context, the terms "feminist" and "feminism" are, of course, anachronistic. As Joan Kelly notes, the first feminists did not develop a vocabulary to characterize their philosophy: "If [the early feminists] had applied any name to themselves, it would have been something like defenders or advocates of women." However, I subscribe to her conclusion that "it is fair to call this long line of prowomen writers that runs from Christine de Pisan to Mary Wollstonecraft by the name we use for their nineteenth- and twentieth-century descendants" (5). At the beginning of the twentieth century, at the time of a more recent flowering of feminist ideology, Léon Abensour and Georges Ascoli, among others, examined the early history in France of written defenses of women's rights and abilities. Kelly's definition of feminist is derived from a consideration of those same defenses, but only those written by women.

I have in mind still a third view of this history of proto-feminist thought: I will consider the possible relations between these defenses and the activities, both political and literary, through which women exerted influence at the time when they were written. I will use "feminist" to describe two related enterprises: governmental and military endeavors undertaken by women who considered themselves and were considered by others the equals of their male counterparts—the historical equivalent of what Ellen Moers, speaking of forceful novelistic portrayals of women, calls "heroism"; and creative writing that either glorifies female political daring or attempts to translate political activity into literary terms. The process by which the first female literary *tradition* in France was conceived as the continuation of women's activity in the public sphere generated what I would term, in a deliberate historicization of our current avant-garde, an *écriture féminine,* writing not the body but the body politic and women's involvement in it. From this perspective, striking parallels between political and literary heroism become apparent, parallels too frequent and too close to be fortuitous: in seventeenth-century France, the strength of prowoman sentiment generated repeatedly, in a space where history and literature meet, what can be termed a feminist textuality.[9]

To date, women's literary achievements in France have almost always been discussed, implicitly if not explicitly, as though the English tradition contributed a generally valid model. Moreover, the history of the English female tradition was for too long written as though women's writing had only come into existence just prior to its maturity in the nineteenth century. Thus the pioneering studies of women writers— Sandra Gilbert and Susan Gubar's *Madwoman in the Attic,* Ellen Moers' *Literary Women,* and Elaine Showalter's *A Literature of Their Own,* to cite but the most prominent examples—begin their accounts of the development of a female literary tradition at the turn of the nineteenth century. Only in recent years have studies appeared—I think, for example, of Jane Spencer's *The Rise of the Woman Novelist: From Aphra Behn to Jane Austen,* Dale Spender's *Mothers of the Novel: 100 Good Women Authors before Jane Austen,* Moira Ferguson's *First Feminists: British Women Writers, 1578–1799,* and Margaret Doody's *Frances Burney: The Life in the Works*—to fill in the prehistory of English women's writing and expose the foundation on which the extraordinary nineteenth-century flowering was constructed.[10]

Ultimately, however, these studies may prove misleading for students of other traditions: their lessons cannot often be translated into French terms. Now that its full history is being explored, the overall course of English women's writing appears readily comprehensible, perhaps because it so nearly duplicates that of the novel, the form that has so often served as the model for the history of genres. After an initial rise, the English female tradition reached what is generally presented as its moment of greatest prominence in the nineteenth century, before knowing something of a decline. French women's writing has a very different, and a far less easily comprehensible, history. It came very quickly and fully into its own, so that we can speak of a veritable tradition of French women's writing as early as the 1660s, when across the Channel there is far less evidence of literary community. In addition, the French tradition produced its masterpieces so early that by the turn of the eighteenth century, when English women's writing was becoming more organized, it was already less forceful—even though women writers continued to play a major role in the novel's development until just after the Revolution.[11] The French tradition is characterized by a final phenomenon, easily the most difficult to explain: in the nineteenth century, when both the novel and English women's writing reach what from today's perspective is considered their fullest expression, the French female literary presence is, with an occasional exception, most notably that of George Sand, at its nadir.

In France, in other words, the female tradition has a history incomprehensible through reference to either that of the novel or that of English women's writing—and this despite the fact that French women writers were no more likely than their English counterparts to explore forms other than the novel. It is as if the French female tradition had come into existence in order to create the modern novel. Once the genre had acquired the full range of its expression and the way had been paved for it to achieve in the nineteenth century what is now considered its canonical formulation, women writers became far less prominent in its history. This atypical involvement with a genre's formation might be written off as the co-opting of a form by male writers as soon as it was perceived to be a locus of literary power, but such an explanation cannot begin to account for the complexities of the rise, let alone the fall, of the French women's novel.

We must instead try to understand the circumstances in which a genre had women as its principal architects, was read and prized equally by male and female readers, and, initially at least, was granted official status by an important faction in the largely male critical establishment. Two closely interrelated questions must be kept in mind: first, to what degree may this extraordinary, probably unprecedented, level of sustained female literary prominence have been possible only under the ancien régime? second, to what degree may the far earlier rise to prominence of the French tradition as opposed to its English variant be explained by the predominantly aristocratic status of the majority of the women writers of the first generation in France, by the greater independence they may have enjoyed over their English counterparts, far more often bourgeois, by their closer proximity to centers of power?[12] We must also be mindful of the factors that would lead both to the tradition's decline after the Revolution and to its virtual elimination from the pages of modern French literary history. For even though women's writing flourished under the ancien régime, it does not follow that the female tradition enjoyed a relation of complicity with the reigning political system. On the contrary, unlike the contemporary literary expressions of the art of civility that Norbert Elias has analyzed as reinforcing the ancien régime's power, women's writing far more often than not provides at least a subtle contestation of the political structure under which it reached its most impressive development.

The English model's unquestioned authority over the history of women's writing undoubtedly accounts in part for the fact that French *écriture féminine* has, to date, generally been presented as derived or stolen from dominant masculine discourse. This is the view of Claudine Herrmann's influential *Les Voleuses de langue*. In order to challenge it, we must keep in mind that playing a founding role in genre formation is a literary enterprise far less submissive than contributing to a genre whose rules have already been established. The terms in which French women's writing has often been presented are inadequate to chronicle a period during which women played a dominant, rather than a subordinate, role.

Nina Auerbach uses as an epigraph to *Woman and the Demon* Maxine Hong Kingston's meditation: "Perhaps women were once so dangerous that they had to have their feet bound." I believe, as Auerbach does, that commentators have concentrated so much on the footbinding that they have obscured the "danger at its source" (187). It is too often assumed that women are, in Susan Gubar's terms, "somebody in the nowhere of utopia" but "nobody in the somewhere of patriarchy" ("She in Herland" 140). For a brief time in seventeenth-century France, women walked with unbound feet, first through the "somewhere of patriarchy," and only then through the "nowhere of utopia"—but a "nowhere" given a more precise topography as a result of their earlier march through history. Their triumphant procession, I contend, constituted the "danger" at the origin of women's subsequent "footbinding" in eighteenth- and nineteenth-century France.

My presentation of certain moments as instances of female political influence, in particular women's often spectacular participation in the French civil war known as the Fronde, would be contested by those commentators who consistently maintain that women had no real power, but only the appearance of power (see, for example, Jean-Michel Pelous 94–100). In general, I waste little energy countering this skeptical view: the degree to which individual accounts are faithful to ancien régime political reality cannot be accurately measured today. We can only recreate with confidence a history of constructions of gender, a succession of images whose possible historical validity is far less important than the very fact of their widespread usefulness at a particular period. These constructions tell the story of what women were believed/hoped/feared to be capable of accomplishing.

I will deal in particular with the construction of two successive images, which correspond to the two phases of women's influence during the period 1640–1715. Beginning early in the seventeenth century and culminating in the midcentury decade of political insurrection, the dominant female icon was the Amazon. The possible reality of this image—were women actually responsible for the Fronde? did their military daring attain truly Amazonian proportions?—is less crucial to the pattern that concerns me here than the dual realization that it was considered possible for women to play decisive political, and even military, roles, and that this belief was so widespread that it marked the political pamphlets that are the nearest approximation available to us of the contemporary popular consciousness. All facets of this image, negative as well as positive, teach us that women were considered capable of threatening the stability of the State.

This myth proved so durable that it remained entrenched long after women had shifted the center of their political involvement from the public arena to the republic of letters. After this shift, women writers made marriage their central literary preoccupation. In the final decades of the seventeenth century, a new female icon replaced the Amazon, an image still firmly in place well into the following century, woman as home-wrecker, once again as threat to State security, but this time in the State's very foundation, the family. In this instance again, the image's possible reality—were women (not just women in the novel, but women) really threatening the institution of marriage? was State security truly at risk because great families were no longer able to guarantee the transmission of their estates?—was overshadowed by the common perception that women were playing this destabilizing role, and that the novel was the chosen arm in their struggle, the signal sent out to their fellow conspirators.

Since this second image was based in part on a textual legacy, we are able to evaluate its accuracy with some precision. We thus realize that French women writers radically politicized the novel's then standard plots. Contemporary readers believed that they had broadened literature's interior range. Their novels were considered to have claimed, each in its own way, new territory for the genre by describing with increased precision the life of the heart and what Scudéry termed the geography of tenderness, the range of plots open to the literary couple. However, it is hard to imagine that any reader would have considered that the new narratives had implications only for literature. From the desire of Scudéry's heroines to live their affective lives unconstrained by marriage, to Lafayette's suggestion that women win increased control over the legalities of that institution, to the call by writers as different as

---

Margin annotations (handwritten):

early-mid: dominant icon = Amazon

♀'s political role = possible

even threatening

- - - - -

later in century literary women: ♀ as threat to institution of marriage

(? of transmission of estates)

plots = politicized

geography of tenderness = range of plots open to literary couple

eg— affective lives divorced from marriage

control over legality of marriage

Murat and Graffigny for woman's right to terminate unhappy unions
—to varying degrees each key text in this tradition gives a feminocentric
perspective on issues of concern as immediate to women outside the
novels, their readers, as to their heroines.

In an effort to display the full actuality in which these tender geographies were charted, I include several incursions into the contemporary
legal context. The period in which this female tradition flourished is
also the period to which recent family historians trace the birth of
modern conceptions of the family unit, of marriage, and of the affective
bond between husband and wife. The novels I will discuss here indicate
that this conceptual shift was under way in France long before historians
establish its beginning; it may even be that these novels played a role in
inciting its development. The particular French chronology of these
private debates (and perhaps of the woman's novel as well) can be
explained by the fact that, from the late sixteenth century to the early
nineteenth century, the country was actively involved in highly public
debate on the nature of marriage, debate that pitted Church against
State in a struggle to define the institution (as contract or as sacrament)
and to obtain authority over its jurisdiction.

In such a context, to write about shifting conceptions of love and
marriage was hardly an innocent gesture. In ancien régime France, a
woman became an author when she made the novel the site of speculation on questions as essential to the organization of society as the right
of individuals to choose their marriage partners rather than have their
lives directed by the interests of the family and the State. In this
tradition, female authorship was a political act: these novels are never
solely about love, but always stress the political and social implication of
affective choices.

The flowering of women's writing under the most absolute monarchy
elicited commentary as early as Germaine de Staël's *De la Littérature*
(1800). The easy explanation for the relationship between the female
literary tradition and absolutism portrays its complicity: these women
were either aristocrats or bourgeoises who frequented aristocratic milieus; they had no wish to disturb the political order that guaranteed
their privileges. Such was not Staël's view. She pointed out, as we will
see, that absolute monarchies felt threatened by all forms of difference,
and that women who openly displayed their intellectual gifts displayed
at the same time their difference (*De la Littérature* 2:333). While agreeing with Staël's view of the incompatibility between absolute monarchy

and women's writing, I would suggest the following justification for the simultaneous rise of Louis XIV's absolutism and of the female tradition: the official policy of assimilation then being put into place denied women writers the possibility of complacency about their own difference and inspired in them an unparalleled awareness of (the exclusion of) otherness.

In France, the rise of the modern novel was rigorously contemporaneous with the establishment of an intricate, official system for determining difference—cultural, religious, social, sexual, racial—in order more effectively to control it. I take as the founding date in this practice 1661, a year which often appears in the following pages: it marks the beginning of Louis XIV's absolute reign and the end of the salons' feminocentric cultural dominance. The Sun King's reign changed course in 1661 because of the death of the individual with whom he had shared power until then, his prime minister, Cardinal Mazarin. In his will, Mazarin provided a vast sum for the construction of the Collège des Quatre Nations, a school for the instruction of sixty male students. The cardinal, whose foreign birth explains to a great extent the public animosity directed against him during the Fronde, well understood the political importance of cultural assimilation. Despite a name that suggests ethnic diversity ("nation" is used in its then dominant sense, as a synonym for "peuple"), the school endowed by the cardinal had as its mission the elimination of all forces that remained foreign and, therefore, potentially threatening to the State. Its students were to be chosen from the four provinces France had most recently annexed. The *collège* was designed to make these new citizens culturally French, so that they would continue this civilizing mission upon their return to their "nations."[13]

Mazarin's project is typical of one strain of French absolutism's policy with respect to the foreign other, assimilation to Frenchness. In the collective memory of Louis XIV's reign, assimilation is generally overshadowed by its companion policy, the often violent exclusion of the threatening other. The revocation of the Edict of Nantes in 1685, the most visible exercise of this policy, was also the culmination of a process gradually amplified during Louis XIV's reign whereby the persecution of Protestants and Jews taught the members of the dominant religion both to recognize the religious other and to close ranks behind their own sameness.

Religious purity was but one strain of enforced national identity: in

January of 1685, the French were forbidden to marry abroad without royal authorization, a step taken, according to René Pillorget (40), to prepare the way for the revocation. The official attempt to limit the contamination of French bloodlines was extended two months later, when the French in the colonies were forbidden to marry blacks (*code noir,* article 6). The effect of curtailing what could hardly have been a frequent occurrence was surely overshadowed by the measure's more important effect: it served as an officially decreed demarcation of racial difference.

[margin note: no contamination of bloodlines by non-French marriages]

These laws for the protection of racial purity are but two symptoms of a broad cultural vision, an officially decreed cultural nationalism.[14] The novel receives its modern expression against the grain of the official policy of racial and cultural purity and assimilation. In 1670 the theoretician Pierre-Daniel Huet defined the modern novel as the creation of women writers and "the origin of novels" as the exposure of enforced conversion to an official (French) system and the establishment of an alternative system designed to undermine dominant social codes and demarcations.[15]

[margin note: novel ⇒ alternative system designed to undermine dominant social codes]

The women of privilege who "originate" the modern novel never ratify the policy of domination through exclusion and assimilation. On the contrary, they all highlight the possible subversion of bloodlines by playing on contemporary fears similar to the modern anxiety about miscegenation, the dread of misalliance and the fear that aristocratic bloodlines could be contaminated with the children of adultery. These writers use gender as a vehicle for introducing issues of class (and even at times of race, although this is always a far less visible concern in ancien régime France).[16]

[margin note: subversion = highlighted]

An important role in the vast cultural project at the foundation of Louis XIV's absolutism was reserved for literature. The origins of the canon on which the French educational system still stands can be traced to the late seventeenth century. For the first architects of this canon, women novelists played the part of literary history's foreign other and were dealt with according to the two policies developed by the State to guarantee French ethnic supremacy, assimilation and exclusion.

[margin note: in XVIIth c. development of canon - ♀ = exclue as lit's foreign other]

In the rhetoric of assimilation that dictated the reception of those women writers who were allowed into the annals of French literary history, they were not threatening because their novels were concerned *only* with affairs of the heart. The early critical judgments on which this vision of women's writing rests consistently mock the plots proposed for

the radical
dénouements
of P's affairs
of the heart
ridiculed as
outlandish

these heroines as too incredible to be true. Thus, Valincour, the first opponent of *La Princesse de Clèves,* ridiculed both the rejection of marriage that Scudéry chose for one of her heroines and the end point of Lafayette's fiction: "Madame de Clèves should have, following the example of [Scudéry's Sapho in *Le Grand Cyrus*], proposed to Monsieur de Nemours to go with her to her estate near the Pyrenees to spend the rest of his days, having first received his word that he would never press her to marry him" (275–76). Valincour dismissed their plots as "outlandish" (*invraisemblable*), out of this world—ridiculous fantasies that could only be imagined in a novel and never in real life.[17]

', sentimental
tale w/o
serious
content

Because of this line of reasoning, the first French women novelists were written into literary history as the creators of sentimental tales without serious content. This assimilation is nowhere more evident than in the case of Lafayette's masterpiece, the only work of French women's writing ever to receive true canonic status. *La Princesse de Clèves* was accepted as a masterpiece when her novel's subversiveness had been erased.[18] The serious content of these works has been so carefully obscured that the reader familiar with them only in the pages of literary history would have difficulty imagining that they could ever have been controversial, that anyone would have bothered to attack them.

nb. J
nonetheless
intense
critical
hostility
directed
against P's
novels

Initially, however, they were attacked, and with a violence that would startle readers trained to think of them as mere escapist fiction. It was the intensity of this critical hostility that initially set me on the trail of this project: I could not believe that real fires had not been necessary to generate so much smoke. The first practitioners of literary exclusionism had little use for critical indirection. Following the lead of Nicolas Boileau, the individual who, with royal backing, imposed his authority as supreme arbiter of French literary taste, commentators displaced all the fictional content of women's writing onto reality. They refused to grant these novels any subtlety, denied them any role in the creation of constructions of gender. According to the argument thus promoted, these novels had to be suppressed because they propagated a socially and politically subversive vision: women's writing constituted a threat to the

P's writing
seen as a
threat to the
state, family,
man'

foundations of the nation-state, the family, and manly, virile virtue.[19] For over three-quarters of a century, this view was so vociferously proclaimed—on one occasion it was even trumpeted, with fire-and-brimstone, from the pulpit and in Latin, in Father Porée's 1736 harangue against the novelistic "plague"—that one would think women writers had been battering the gates of fortress France.[20]

In short, those who now say that French women novelists have only written about love are guilty, at the very least, of wishful thinking. At most, they may be guilty of a desire to impose this critical cliché to distract modern readers from the political content of the novels.

Throughout this study I speak of "women's writing," "women novelists," and so forth, as though this were not a controversial gesture.[21] I do not intend to imply by this usage that women's literary achievements can be neatly isolated from the broader contemporary context. However, while I contrast women novelists with their male contemporaries (Scudéry and d'Urfé, for example), I am unable to include many potentially useful comparisons (Lafayette and Saint-Réal, for instance). I have devoted three prior studies to other traditions of early prose fiction: in each case, space constraints forced me to omit comparisons with contemporary production that would have been useful in establishing the specificity of the tradition I was defining. In the present case, these omissions are more likely to trouble readers: I have often noticed that the standard first response to studies of women writers is to ask why male writers were excluded. However, no reader has ever inquired about the absence of women writers from, for example, my study of seventeenth-century libertine fiction.

Nor is my use of "women's writing" intended to convey belief in a literary production *essentially* different from men's writing. I maintain this terminology despite my sense of its limitations to reflect my belief that women authors of the ancien régime wrote from a vantage point inevitably defined in part by the fact that their contemporaries responded to them not only as writers but as women writers. (The clearest evidence of this is provided by the numerous seventeenth- and eighteenth-century literary histories devoted exclusively to women writers.)

However, I do not take this sign of their originally separate status to signify inferior status as well. When I first read Ellen Moers' judgment in *Literary Women* that "to be a woman writer long meant . . . belonging to a literary movement apart from but hardly subordinate to the mainstream" (42), I felt that this image was close to my evaluation of the ancien régime tradition. I have since come to modify that stance as I have become increasingly convinced both that the literary mainstream was not defined at that time as clearly as we imagine today (a point to which I return in my concluding chapter) and that it is unnecessary to apologize for the contributions of these women writers as in any way subordinate.[22]

When I speak of women's writing in this study, I do not mean literature composed exclusively by women. Many of the works I will examine were published anonymously; they are attributed to women writers but were in fact produced by literary collectives directed by a woman writer. Within these collectives, male and female intellectuals worked together on the research and the stylistic revision of novels, but, in each case, all collaborators allowed a woman to play the dominant role of principal author. The original model for French women's writing has much in common with a configuration evident in this country today, one of whose more visible components within the academy is known as "men in feminism." In the ancien régime, long-term gains in the republic of letters were possible for women because so many men supported women's causes and worked for the advancement of women —a situation that might well be reestablished in our time. Numerous male writers contributed to the creation of the literary voices that I refer to with a term from our modernity, "women's writing," and therefore to the creation of the process of literary survival that I refer to as the French female tradition.[23]

I
❧

Women's Places, Women's Spaces

THIS CHAPTER is a conscious blend of history and literary history. Both the modern French novel and the French tradition of women's writing came into existence during and just after a period of the kind of extreme political turbulence in which extraordinary things become possible. My argument about the development of literary tradition cannot, therefore, be separated from a precise historical context. However, because this study is primarily concerned with literary rather than political or social history, my presentation of the public sphere will of necessity at times be distorted by the need to accent events and tendencies that had a more permanent effect on literary tradition than on French society or the French State.

In addition, I will at times appear to be presenting a vision of the French State under the absolute monarchy of Louis XIV that I know to be insufficiently nuanced.[1] However, when I speak of the official repression of women, I do not intend to imply a monolithic view either of the functioning of power or of its repartition in Louis XIV's France. I do wish to suggest that the terms in which we view the seventeenth-century French State are significantly altered when we reconfigure its history to include the politics of gender. Throughout France's so-called Great Century, it is clear that the principal architects of public policy promoted the belief that female rebellion posed a particular threat to the body politic. It is equally clear that women were not allowed equal participation in the collaboration with absolutism in which their male counterparts were involved. Throughout the period of the creation of the modern novel, Woman and the State were intertwined in a relation

propaganda
re threatening
♀ behavior
↑   ↓
behavior

whose complexity makes it nearly impossible to determine cause and effect. Did propaganda regarding threatening female behavior predate actual behavior? Did women shift the arena in which they challenged societal structures in response to concrete political pressure or in response to the kind of propaganda now termed a "construction of gender"? This ultimately undecidable dialogic situation is what I have in mind when I speak both of official repression and of female unruliness.

Despite such obvious and important methodological disadvantages as these, I chose not to disentangle the particular set of problems that converges here. This choice reflects my dissatisfaction with the compartmentalization of discourses normally operative today, as well as my belief that the choices currently standard cannot satisfactorily account for the developments that interest me. Absolute distinctions between word and event, between history and literature, between public and private (history), between domestic economy and political life cannot be maintained to account for situations that developed in violation of these traditional boundaries.[2]

The status of both the ideas and the places I evoke in this chapter is often ambiguous, even disconcertingly so. At times, modest, apparently private spaces, such as the area between a woman's bed and the wall of her bedroom, clearly had true ideological status: by this I mean that, from them, women were able to alter conduct and disrupt the existing order. The same ideological power may even be attributed to certain spaces that probably never attained anything but utopian status, such as *projected* learned societies that *would have* included women after the Académie Française refused to do so. At times, even places with an existence no more "real" than in the pages of a book—I think in particular of Madeleine de Scudéry's project in *Clélie* for a new affective topography—were far from socially impotent. Seventeenth-century French women often refused the places traditionally assigned them; from the new vantage points they inhabited, they were able permanently to reconfigure the shape of French culture.

♀'s refusal of
places
traditionally
assigned to
them

In the Public Domain
SALON POLITICS

Rendez-vous, Amants et Guerriers,
Craignez ses attraits et ses armes;

Sa Valeur égale à ses charmes
Unit les myrthes aux lauriers:
Miracle d'Amour et de Guerre,
Tu vas domter toute la terre.

> Corneille, liminary verses for
> André Mareschal's *La Soeur*
> *valeureuse* (1634)

IN FRANCE, for several centuries prior to the early seventeenth century, debate about issues as basic to feminism at any period as women's political activity and female education had taken place in the context of what is known as the *Querelle des femmes*. The early years of the seventeenth century still witnessed the publication of documents defined by the familiar discourses of the *Querelle* (Maclean 62–63). The beginning of the seventeenth century, however, marks a decisive turning point in the history of French feminism, an evolution that generates innovative types of writing about women that reflect new realities and mark an important departure from the treatises produced in conjunction with the *Querelle*. To the nearly simultaneous inceptions of the regency of Marie de' Medici (1610) and the equally absolute reign in the socio-literary sphere of another Italian, Catherine de Vivonne, Marquise de Rambouillet, founder of the French salon tradition, may be traced the origin of a golden age of activity that is not only feminocentric but also feminist.[3] The double origin of female influence over the Splendid Century sets a pattern consistently reenacted during the next seventy years: the most striking manifestations of classical French feminism have a dual nature, jointly political and literary.

Under Salic law, according to customs that had acquired the power of law, women could not inherit the crown, although they could serve as regent. On two occasions during the first half of the seventeenth century, France was ruled by a dowager queen and experienced, therefore, a sort of legally sanctioned foreign rule, a period during which final authority was confided to a woman French only by adoption. Both regencies were authentic transitional times, periods during which new options were explored and rival authorities tested the limits of official power. A similar atmosphere of political polyphony may be characteristic of all regencies, as it certainly was, for example, of the period that followed Louis XIV's death in 1715, when no legitimate dowager queen survived to serve as regent. The seventeenth-century regencies are nevertheless remarkable because, during them, women exercised an exceptional degree of influence in zones ranging from literary arbitrage to political sedition.

Marie de' Medici's

The extraordinary pictorial gallery of the life of Marie de' Medici executed by Rubens between 1622 and 1625 provides images that suggest the tone of what may be termed the prehistory of the alliance between women's political activity and the modern French novel. Rubens' canvases are gigantic, and the interpretation of events in the Queen Regent's life that they provide—an interpretation for which Marie de' Medici was herself responsible (Thuillier 27)—was correspondingly larger-than-life. The Queen Regent chose to have her life, from the escape to Blois through the battle of Juliers, portrayed as a series of novelistic adventures, over which she presided, in Maclean's words, "more as a

of images of Marie as heroine (vs. as Queen)

∴ novelistic aspirations

heroine than as a queen" (209). In fact, this vision of the bold, martial ruler is often mythic—Marie de' Medici is shown, for example, on horseback in the canvas of the battle of Juliers, whereas she was not present at the confrontation. This royal fiction is no less fantastic than the vision of the liberating power of transvestism conveyed by *Astrée,* a novel that played a central role in the fantasy life of the Marquise de Rambouillet's salon.[4]

By stressing the novelistic aspirations of the women who ruled over France's political and intellectual life in the early years of the seventeenth century, I do not intend to minimize historical precedent for their feminocentric activities.[5] However, the conjunction between the novel and the feminization of political activity can explain the crucial tactical shift in prowoman activity in the early seventeenth century. Whereas, as Georges Ascoli (40) and others stress, sixteenth-century feminism was largely passive and limited to the defense of women's abilities in the face of often virulent attacks, its seventeenth-century

feminism on the offensive

reincarnation takes the offensive. In this evolution the novel played a complex and not easily defined role—part model, part inspiration,

novel as outlet for newly aggressive activity

eventually outlet for the newly aggressive energy.

Much has been made of the civilizing influence exercised by the Marquise de Rambouillet's *chambre bleue* on the rough manners of the French court. Her salon played at least an equally decisive role in the feminization of political and literary activity in France. The woman

SALON

widely known as the "divine Arthénice" gave definitive form to the salon, the structure that more than any other explains the social and

↳ social/intellectual freedom

intellectual freedom enjoyed under the ancien régime by both women of aristocratic birth and those, like Scudéry, whose intellectual merits won for them a share in the privileges of aristocracy. The marquise served as her own architect when she had the Hôtel de Rambouillet rebuilt so that it would contain rooms more suitable for entertaining, in particular, a series of reception rooms, leading one into the other, in the style invented in her native Italy. Such high-ceilinged rooms, open to all visitors, were known in the seventeenth century as "salons," the only usage of the term attested in contemporary dictionaries. When we use "salon" to refer both to the rooms in which cultural assemblies took place and to the assemblies themselves, we are following a usage introduced, ironically, only at the time when the tradition of such assemblies, and the tradition of French women's writing as well, was dying out: the first instances documented are in the works of Germaine de Staël (*Robert Dictionary*).

In the seventeenth century, salon gatherings were generally referred to either by the day on which they took place—the *samedis* of Madeleine de Scudéry, for example—or by one of the architectural terms then used to designate the more intimate space in which the public salons culminated, an inner sanctum first conceived for the Hôtel de Rambouillet and subsequently widely imitated in classical architecture. The marquise received her guests while reclining on her bed and had them seated in the narrow corridor or recess between bed and wall. She delimited a space within her private space, her *chambre,* a space first referred to as a *ruelle,* later by a variety of terms from *alcôve* to *réduit.* The modesty of the *ruelle* should not blind us to the importance of the activities undertaken there. The marquise defined the salon as a zone over which women served as arbiters as they sought to impose behavioral codes that gave women greater freedom over their fates.

All too often, commentators stress only the more exaggerated aspects of this new program for male/female relations. They thus overlook the serious consequences of a rebellion against marriage as a legal prison and too frequent childbirth as a health hazard—the ways in which positions initially formulated at the Hôtel de Rambouillet instilled in women throughout the century the belief that they had a right to what would be termed today greater control over their own bodies. Mockery of what has been thought of since Molière as the "ridiculousness" of the women known as *précieuses* always originates in the threat to a patriarchal society's traditional functioning posed by women who not only refused to make the passage through marriage to motherhood but who encouraged others to follow their example.[6] The women of the Hôtel de Rambouillet thus can be seen as one origin of the Amazon myth that seventeenth-century commentators used to characterize activities of contemporary women once they had invaded the military domain.

The contribution of the Hôtel de Rambouillet to the development of seventeenth-century literature has been systematically undervalued. Yet this devaluation cannot be explained solely by the threat that a female *prise de parole* represented for the male writers like Molière whose parodic accounts have been accepted as the truth about *préciosité*. This early assertion of female literary authority remained timid: the task of developing new literary forms was still confided to male writers like Voiture. Nevertheless, the Marquise de Rambouillet's decision to turn the attention of her literary assembly to the creation of a new literary language would influence decisively the development of French literature. The way had been paved for the creation of a female literary tradition in the 1650s, a tradition whose creators shared both the marquise's belief in the necessity of a separate space for women and her conviction that the art of conversation should be the foundation of women's literary authority.

Although Marie de' Medici continued to exercise influence until 1630, her regency was officially over with the majority of Louis XIII in 1614. To this transition from female to male rule may be traced the first of the transfers of energy from political to literary life that punctuate the seventeenth century and always signal a redefinition of prose fiction. At the time of the initial waning of the Queen Regent's power, one of her closest confidants, Louise-Marguerite de Lorraine, Princesse de Conti, left the court, in the company of a group of friends all loyal to the regent, for her château at Eu. There she created a salon-in-exile in which her group's principal activity was literary. According to Alexandre Cioranescu's reconstruction of the complex process by which the princesse became an author, she initially composed an urtext, now lost, a fictionalization of her memories of the court of Henri IV in which she had spent her youth (50). The princesse then read her text to the members of her literary circle, integrating, as virtually all the women novelists of her century would after her, the salon discussions into her creative process. Then, inaugurating another pattern crucial to the early history of the French novel, she handed over her revised manuscript to various writers in her circle, asking them to rewrite it for publication as a novel. Her request produced no fewer than three novels, seemingly unrelated, to judge by their titles, but in fact recounting the same fictionalized tale of the loves of Henri IV: the *Romant royal* (1621), the *Advantures de la cour de Perse* (1629), and finally, the *Histoire des amours du grand Alcandre,* published only in 1651, twenty years after the princesse's death. Each of these novels opens with a preface in which the writer under whose name it was published explains that he or she is not the author of this fiction, but, in the words of the "scribe" of the *Romant royal,* Piloust, merely its "adjuster" ("j'ai ôsé le dresser").[7]

The Princesse de Conti's novels provide an early illustration of a particular variant of the process Hélène Cixous terms "coming to writing" often encountered in the classical French tradition of women's writing. When women from the highest ranks of the aristocracy had literary aspirations, they turned to men possessing literary talent and expertise. These men, often called secretaries (today we might call them literary assistants), played a role in the composition of their work, as did other members of their salons, to an extent that we can no longer evaluate. Too often, literary history has simply given all credit to the literary assistants, whereas aristocratic women like the Princesse de Conti should be considered authors when the idea of writing a novel as well as the idea for the type of novel to be written originated with them, and when they directed the various aspects of the work's composition. This type of collective effort should not be confused with the more familiar associations entered into by literary women, such as the phenomenon known as "writing couples," in which a woman writer forges a long-term partnership, personal as well as professional, with a man of letters. The group effort that may be called "salon writing" played a very different role for the powerful women who orchestrated these activities: it allowed them to fulfill their own literary aspirations at the same time that it served as the founding gesture of their salons by involving the members of their circle in literary activity.

Salon writing provided an authorization, from the highest rank of court society, for women's writing. The salon writing that was a product of the Princesse de Conti's exile indicated the path most frequently chosen for early French women's writing: the novels created at Eu elect a historical setting to develop a plot composed in equal parts of political and amorous adventures. This would remain, until the mid-eighteenth century, the stock formula for French women writers recording women's involvement in the body politic.[8] The next stage in the development of a female literary tradition, the key literary flowering, would take

[handwritten marginalia:]
men became "literary assistants" of aristocratic ♀s w/literary aspirations

group effort w/powerful ♀ as orchestrator

Salon writing = authorization for ♀ writing

stock formula: historical setting, plot w/ equal parts political + amorous adventure place only after women writers moved back out of the salons into the public sphere and Marie de' Medici's mythonovelistic dream had been realized in fact and in fiction, France having very nearly become the legendary country of the Amazons.

STRONG WOMEN

> La postérité, malgré ce que je fais,
> Répondra mal peut-être à mes justes souhaits,
>
> .   .   .
>
> Et qu'enfin à l'avenir, contraire à vos attentes,
> Ait peine à rencontrer quatre femmes savantes.
>
> Jean de La Forge, *Le Cercle des*
> *femmes savantes* (1663)

THE MODERN reign of amazons began in literature. In the 1620s, 30s, and 40s, fictions of female heroinism proliferated in romances by male authors. Maurice Magendie provides an impressive list of characters who are portrayed fighting, hunting, shooting, and riding, and who dress as men while engaged in these pursuits (47–48). His examples range from the heroines of Du Verdier's *Roman des dames* (1629, reprinted in 1632 as *Les Amazones de la cour*), who turn to bloody military exploits when they become bored with their sheltered lives, to Amazons and other professional warriors such as Le Maire's Sémiramis who, dressed as a soldier, opposes Ninus in individual combat and later fights beside him in the Armenian war (*La Prazimène,* 1638), and Gomberville's Télésmane, who in *Polexandre* (1632) lays siege to King Quasmez's capital with an army of 200,000 women.

These male fantasies of female militarism found a contemporary parallel in the exploits of at least the woman known as the warrior poet or the Christian amazon, Barbe d'Ernecourt, Comtesse de Saint-Baslemont.[9] When the French and the house of Austria were devastating Lorraine, her husband was away fighting under the Duc de Lorraine. On horseback and dressed as a man, she organized the defense of her property—and she was so successful in her efforts that her neighbors asked her to protect their lands as well. She seems to have fought constantly in the late 1630s and early 1640s.[10] Her contemporary biographer, Jean-Marie de Vernon, praises her in daunting terms: "Whoever looks attentively at the conduct of Barbe d'Ernecourt will find her the equal of the heroes of antiquity and will be able to suggest her as a

[handwritten margin notes: 1620's-40's / fictions of female heroism in romances by men; Contemporary example: Saint-Baslemont]

model . . . for the most courageous [men]. The only difference lies in the diversity of opportunities: she accomplished in individual encounters what the most famous generals do in large-scale confrontations and sieges" (203). At the same time, Vernon seeks to render her exploits less threatening. Unlike her legendary precursors, Saint-Baslemont was a "Christian amazon," and her daring, extraordinary though it may have been, never violated "the laws of propriety" (298). Subsequently, following what was by then the example of such celebrated amazons of the Fronde as the Duchesse de Longueville, in 1659 the amazon comtesse underwent a formal conversion and withdrew from armed confrontation to take up a life in religious retreat.

Before her conversion, however, Barbe d'Ernecourt entered the retreat practiced by prominent early women writers from the Princesse de Conti to Germaine de Staël: she turned away from affairs of state and took up a literary career. Unlike most other literary women, she composed not novels but tragedies, the literary form preferred by contemporary men of letters to express their vision of heroism. In both her published *Les Jumeaux martyrs* (1650) and the play she left in manuscript, *La Fille généreuse* (also 1650), Saint-Baslemont provides a subtle questioning of the nature of heroic action. She suggests that heroism is a space for transvestism, an arena in which constructions of gender can be freely exchanged. Her vision only becomes comprehensible in light of both her own military prowess and that of her amazon successors at the time of the French civil war that began shortly before she composed her plays.

Barbe d'Ernecourt is the archetypal figure of the heroic woman as defined in the mid-seventeenth century, a woman whose life was positioned at the intersection of military and literary daring. There are even indications that she was not unique in her day. If the *Mémoires de Madame de La Guette* is an authentic biographical account, as Micheline Cuénin believes, at least one other woman began a military career in the 1630s.[11] Like Saint-Baslemont, Catherine Meurdrac de La Guette crossdressed and lived a soldier's life during a series of armed conflicts. Like her, she gave up the sword to become a literary amazon: her memoirs provide the only extended account, from a woman's perspective, of the invasion of the male military preserve that we encounter repeatedly from the 1630s to the 50s.

Men of letters were far more inclined to leave accounts of female military transvestism. For example, a letter addressed in 1628 by the celebrated epistolary stylist, Guez de Balzac, to a female correspondent indicates precedent for Saint-Baslemont's conduct. Above all, Balzac indicates that men are fascinated with female militarism because they are threatened by it. Balzac praises his correspondent (Madame Desloges) because she is not like those women of their acquaintance "who want to act like horsemen" (*faire les cavaliers*) (1636 ed. *Lettres* 237). His condemnation of such behavior is violent: "I am opposed, Madame, to these usurpations of one sex on the other ... and count the Amazons not as women but as monsters" (238). Balzac even calls upon divine authority for his position: "Moses included in God's commandments the distinction between your dress and ours, and you know he expressly forbids us to cross-dress" (238). Balzac's (over)reaction to this female "usurpation" may be the first clear indication of a construction of gender encountered with increasing frequency as the seventeenth century unfolds: male writers become so obsessed with exceptional female behavior in any domain that they are quick to imagine its proliferation, in order to condemn that behavior in the strongest possible terms as a danger to the continued orderly functioning of Church and State.

Subsequent seventeenth-century incarnations of the amazon became increasingly flamboyant and therefore increasingly threatening. In 1643 France once again knew a period of political experimentation during the rule of another foreign Queen Regent. The early years of Anne of Austria's regency witnessed the century's most glorious officially authorized exercise of political influence by a woman. New portrayals of female power were developed, as if to document women's capacity to govern. Note, in particular, Claude Deruet's representation of amazons, both his drawings of obviously fanciful figures and his portraits of the real-life amazon, Saint-Baslemont, as conquering heroine, in a naïve mode appropriate for the plain style of this military woman (figures 1 and 2). Deruet's baroque amazons have been described as prefigurations of female military daring in the early 1650s (Pariset 168), but they can be more accurately evaluated in the tradition of male fascination with Woman's amazonian potential that began long before this historical realization.[12] Deruet was obviously influenced by the example of Saint-Baslemont. He must also have been aware of the commentaries on female political power that became increasingly numerous as the regency progressed, commentary centered on a new figure of heroinism, the *femme forte,* the strong or the heroic woman.

Compilations of biographies of famous women, the tradition of what

FIGURE I

cʌɔ

Claude Deruet, *Mounted Amazon with a Spear* (1620? 1640?). Reprinted
by permission of the Pierpont Morgan Library, New York. Purchased as
gift of the Fellows.

FIGURE 2

ぐ♪

Claude Deruet, *Alberte d'Ernecourt, dame de Saint-Baslemont, défendant son château de Neuville* (c. 1640). Reprinted by permission of the Musée Carnavalet, Paris. Photo. Musées de la Ville de Paris.

Natalie Zemon Davis calls the "collective memorials of 'Women Worthies' " (83), had previously been published in France, but the early 1640s saw a veritable outpouring of portrait books of women referred to as "illustrious," "generous," "heroic," or "strong" (see Maclean's listing of titles, 76–77). The collected biographies of women through the ages distinguished by their capacity for political or military leadership served as emblems for a new age of heroism. Even in collections whose examples of female courage were exclusively taken from antiquity, the desired link with contemporary France was usually made explicit through dedications to women currently exercising political power (most often the Queen Regent, but occasionally the Duchesse de Montpensier, called the Grande Mademoiselle, the daughter of Louis XIV's uncle, Gaston d'Orléans, a woman who plays a series of roles in the drama of seven-

[margin handwritten note: early 1640's portraits of heroic women]

teenth-century female influence). Furthermore, as is true of the contemporary image of the amazon, the tradition of literary portrait galleries developed in tandem with a pictorial tradition: numbers of contemporary French châteaux contained picture galleries of illustrious women (Maclean 210–11). During the 1640s the cultivated French public was virtually bombarded with images of heroinism.

Most literary glorifications of Woman's place in history were composed by men.[13] Carolyn Lougee contends that few of them provide an overt challenge to the status quo. Ian Maclean, concentrating primarily on their extravagant iconography, proposes a reading directly opposed to Lougee's, with the volumes as icons for a feminist age. Such interpretive diversity seems inevitable when we consider both the political complexity of the period during which these volumes were composed and their differences in content and in tone. *¿Icons for a feminist age?*

Witness the example of the best-known compilation, Father Pierre Le Moyne's 1647 *La Gallerie des femmes fortes*. Le Moyne makes it clear that he is not necessarily giving historical examples in order to provide inspiration for contemporary women: "My question concerns only what they are capable of, and not what they should do in the present state of affairs" (251). However, every portrait collection contributed to an atmosphere in which women's heroic potential was lavishly displayed for public recognition. The interpretive conflict between Lougee and Maclean originates in the ambiguous nature of the recognition thus called for. Maclean's feminist reading seems justified, initially at least, by the illustrations of Claude Vignon to Le Moyne's collection and by those of François Chauveau to Jacques Du Bosc's 1645 *La Femme héroïque*. For example, Vignon's portrayal of Zénobie, queen of the Palmyrians (figure 3),[14] merits Maclean's evaluation: "The traditional passive and frontal depiction of women is here replaced with a profile of a heroine in movement" (225).

Other illustrations are less easily interpreted. Consider the example of Vignon's Jaël (figure 4). The dynamism of his Amazon queen is also evident here. However, whereas the backdrop vignette makes plain that Zénobie intends to turn her weapon only against a wild animal, the companion scene in Jaël's portrait reveals that her "military virtue" (225) will be used to drive a nail into the head of a military man (Sisera); in the distance, we see a group of warriors horrified by her action. This portrayal of heroism cannot be taken for an unproblematic feminist statement—it recalls contemporary male fantasies, such as Guez de Balzac's, about the public menace of female "usurpation" of military

FIGURE 3

Engraved by Abraham Bosse after Claude Vignon, *Zénobie,* illustration,
Le Moyne, La Gallerie des femmes fortes (1647). Collection of
the author.

FIGURE 4

∽

Engraved by Abraham Bosse after Claude Vignon, *Jaël,* illustration, Le
Moyne, *La Gallerie des femmes fortes* (1647). Collection of the author.

garb. In the final analysis, these alleged glorifications of women's place in history remain ambiguous: in these calls for female military action an occasional note of misogyny (or at least of a male counterresponse to female daring) can be detected.[15] The problematic nature of this early instance of what has recently been termed "men in feminism" becomes clearer still when a volume like Le Moyne's is compared with the only contribution to the genre by a woman writer, Madeleine de Scudéry's 1642 *Femmes illustres*.

Scudéry devises the formula subsequently repeated by Le Moyne. The narrative mix she invents for her collection is, however, more complex than anything used by her followers. Scudéry's volume illustrates perfectly the problem I wish to foreground in this overview of seventeenth-century feminocentric activity, for it is poised on the frontier between history and literature. All of her heroines are historical figures—a certain number, such as Artémise and Clélie, reappear in Le Moyne's volume—yet Scudéry does not present them primarily in their historicity. Rather than creating the third-person biographies of illustrious women later characteristic of this tradition, Scudéry imagines the first-person "autobiographical" accounts of those she views as having been neglected by previous chroniclers. Scudéry surrounds each of these accounts with brief liminal texts—a presentation of the argument, a prefatory and a concluding poem, a moral ("the effect of this speech") —that transform her portrait book into an at times virulently action-oriented call to contemporary women to repeat the glorious exploits of their predecessors.[16]

Scudéry and other creators of the "strong" or the "illustrious" woman mounted the original challenge to a key rule of seventeenth-century literary esthetics. They created the model for a confrontation between authors and critics that was reenacted in the early history of French women's writing whenever a formal breakthrough took place. The *femme forte* openly violated the standards for acceptable female behavior proposed by contemporary critics. Thus, in his *Poétique* (1640), Jules de La Mesnardière decrees that "with regard to the decency of conduct (*propriété des moeurs*), the poet must consider that one should never introduce without absolute necessity either a valiant girl or a learned woman." To avoid "shocking normal plausibility" (*vraisemblance*), the poet should keep "generosity" a male preserve and create only "gentle and modest women" (137, 140). The "illustrious" or "strong" heroine was thus both a moral transgression, a "sin" against propriety (what La

Mesnardière terms "propriété" and subsequent critics "bienséance"), and a literary infraction against the limits fixed to determine the "real-seeming."[17] La Mesnardière justifies his interdiction by asserting that in real life one "seldom" encounters bravery and learning in women (137).

The attempts in the 1640s to script a history featuring female courage and erudition set the stage for a virtual revolution, if not in the standards proposed for acceptable female behavior by critics, in two more essential areas: actual female behavior and female behavior as it was portrayed in literary texts. Thus, in 1678—when the second generation of women novelists was already creating a less mythically proportioned vision of heroism—the first biographer of the original French literary amazon, Saint-Baslemont, declares that "we no longer have to search in foreign kingdoms" to locate a *femme forte;* "France is now rich in generous women" (Vernon 2). The events of the late 1640s and the 1650s had made possible this transfer of a vocabulary ("forte," "généreuse") created to characterize a nearly legendary foreign past to the depiction of contemporary French women. By 1678, we can infer, commentators no longer considered actual female bravery and learning "random" occurrences. According to the terms of La Mesnardière's decree, therefore, *femmes fortes* could no longer be excluded from the domain of literary representation. This representational transfer was initiated shortly after the appearance of Le Moyne's volume with a large-scale female invasion of the political arena.

THE NEW AMAZONS

Tout arrive en France.
La Rochefoucauld to Mazarin,
October 1650

THE MONUMENT that serves as a visual representation of women's prestige during the years of Anne of Austria's regency is the ceiling painting that Mazarin commissioned from the Italian, Romanelli, in 1646–1647 for a newly built (by F. Mansart in 1645) gallery in his palace (figure 5).[18] The subject depicted is a classic of this genre, Apollo surrounded by the muses. But the variant executed for Mazarin transforms this visual cliché into a testimonial to the influence of seventeenth-century women in the intellectual domain. Rubens mythologized the story of Marie de' Medici; Romanelli (working with another Italian,

FIGURE 5

Gian Francesco Romanelli, *Les Précieuses parisiennes entourant Apollon*
(1646–1647). Reprinted by permission of the Bibliothèque Nationale,
Paris. Photo. Bibl. Nat., Paris.

Gismondi) anchored mythology in the contemporary context. The ceiling of what is today called the Galerie Mazarine was known as "The Parisian *précieuses* surrounding Apollo." While its central figure is not a portrait, each of the muses has the face of an intellectual woman prominent at the court—a *femme savante,* as seventeenth-century women called themselves before, and after, Molière attempted to make a mockery of the term.[19] No certain attributions have come down to us; however, it is not important for my view of the painting's centrality to establish that the muses actually were portraits, but simply that they were thought to be so at the time of the gallery's completion. *Galerie mazarine—apotheosis of salon Ps*

We do not know if the artist himself decided to integrate actuality into his interpretation or if the idea was suggested to him by his patron. However, if we attribute the responsibility to Mazarin, the following political reading of the canvas becomes possible. In 1646–1647 the Queen Regent's most trusted adviser must have been acutely aware of the mounting resistance to his influence, and especially of the role played by prominent women in organizing this resistance—a movement that would culminate the year after the ceiling's completion in the outbreak of the civil war known as the Fronde. By having notable *précieuses* prominently depicted in his palace, Mazarin could have hoped to win the approval of an influential, but hostile, group. He could also have been issuing thereby a subtle warning to these women. If they would confine their interventions to the intellectual sphere, they would be rewarded with official recognition and a place in the literary hierarchy. However, since seventeenth-century women did not initially limit their authoritative incursion to Apollo's world, I will return to this hypothetical reading of the painting's significance against the backdrop of subsequent events. *Mazarin hoping to win over Ps hostile to his influence*

The apotheosis of the salon woman in the Galerie Mazarine is a perfect dramatization of the constant intermingling of fact and fantasy that in effect makes it impossible to trace the genealogy of the *femme forte* from the 1640s to the 1670s and to determine when history modeled itself on literature and when the opposite was true. Yet the question of origin ultimately seems uninteresting in comparison with what can be determined regarding this development. In the first half of the seventeenth century, it became increasingly unnecessary to argue the question of women's equality, for women's intellectual prestige was progressively greater.[20] The first goal these newly enfranchised citizens of the republic of letters set for themselves was to demonstrate that *history ? litt* *1st ½ of XVII less nec to argue Q equality* women were capable of full participation in the business of government, that they could lead armies as well as councils. At the end of the 1640s, the *femme forte* was surpassed in history, and amazons actually did seem to walk the earth in France. During the Fronde, women acted out the most extreme iconography imagined for heroism during the preceding two decades. Like the most audacious heroines of Corneille's plays of the 1640s and early 1650s, they took power into their own hands and revolted against the laws governing the kingdom of France.[21] When they brought legend to life, seventeenth-century French women helped to alter permanently both the course of the French monarchy and the course of French literature.

The question of the primacy of history or of literature in the genealogy of the *femme forte* is therefore ultimately less important than the fact of their complex and continuous intermingling throughout the seventeenth-century development of heroism. The most extreme manifestations of female daring during the French civil wars of the mid-seventeenth century defy characterization according to normally operative distinctions between history and literature. The most notable women's writing of the day can be seen as a type of political "event," literature as call to action, in the way that Christian Jouhaud has presented the contemporary political pamphlets known as *mazarinades*. Inversely, the most influential political activity performed by women was always surrounded by an aura of mythmaking that can clearly be termed literary.

For centuries, historians have debated the seriousness of the threat to the monarchy posed by the Fronde, the name used to characterize a series of popular uprisings that took place between 1648 and 1653 with the backing of an almost constantly shifting alliance of parliamentarians and nobility from the highest ranks. (The *frondeurs* were often led by one of the outstanding military geniuses in French history, the so-called great Condé, a prince of royal Bourbon blood and therefore potentially an appropriate substitute for his young cousin, Louis XIV.) The conflict originated at least in part with the rebels' desire to limit the influence of Anne of Austria's prime minister, Cardinal Mazarin. Ultimately, the *frondeurs* offered a sustained challenge to France's legitimate rulers and kept most of the nation in an almost continuous state of siege for months on end, often controlling sizable portions of French territory, including for a time Paris. While the Prince de Condé led their dominant faction, he was imprisoned along with the other rebel princes by order of the

Queen Regent between January 1650 and February 1651, among the most agitated months of the war. During that time the command of rebel troops and the defense of *frondeur* outposts was largely in the hands of aristocratic women, most notably Condé's sister, the Duchesse de Longueville. The Fronde offers both a striking confirmation of women's political influence over the century and the most convincing explanation for the short duration of their direct rule. More than any other conflict in French history, the Fronde can be seen as a woman's war.[22] For once women had taken command, the resistance to absolutism remained, even after the princes' liberation, a domain in which female rule was prominently displayed.[23]

The exploits of the female leaders of the Fronde are truly the stuff of escapist fiction. If their story had been invented by a man, it would undoubtedly be interpreted as an inscription of the threat of female sexuality: the *frondeuses* in a sense reinvented themselves as a male phantasm.[24] Even though they never brought their utopian scenario to a successful conclusion, they nevertheless created a tear in the fabric of history in whose gaping can be glimpsed the potential for political change that could be wielded by militaristic women who refused to be bound by sexual conventions. The great, now incredible, images of the Fronde are centered on the women who were its principal instigators. The Princesse de Condé marches on Bordeaux and convinces its citizens to defend the *frondeurs* against their king—even at the risk of losing the grape harvest for that year. The Duchesse de Longueville leads the Spanish army on the road to Paris, manipulates all the great rebel leaders from Condé to La Rochefoucauld—and when Anne of Austria and Mazarin try to imprison her to put an end to her intrigues, disguised as a man she rides for days on end and sleeps in barns and haystacks along the English Channel until she is able to bribe a fisherman to take her to Holland, whence she immediately rides back to France to rejoin her forces. The Duchesse de Chevreuse also carries off her most daring flights from royal justice while in male garb and rides distances considered extraordinary and under conditions deemed harsh even by the men who accompany her.

The Grande Mademoiselle adopts a modified male costume for her role as heroine of two of the Fronde's finest hours. When she gains entrance into Orleans by breaking down the only gate no one had thought to fortify, her persistence wins the city over to her cause. To her also belongs the credit for the last victory won by the *frondeurs*. The gates of Paris are closed to all troops, and Louis XIV and Mazarin have the rebel army, led by Condé, trapped just outside the barrier. The apparently inevitable massacre is avoided when Montpensier issues orders first to open the gates and let the rebels in and then to turn the cannon of the Bastille against the royal army. This scene is emblematic of the theatricality that is the signature of the great female exploits of the Fronde years. The Grande Mademoiselle, the amazonian *femme forte* come to life, her large hat and long plumes supplementing her naturally impressive stature, dominates the scene from the towers of the Bastille. Not only does she control the outcome of the confrontation, but in the exercise of her authority over her male counterparts with official titles she is constantly visible to—and seen by, for the two leaders' impressions of her actions are recorded—both king and rebel prince even as they do battle.[25]

The great *frondeuses* brought Rubens' depiction of Marie de' Medici to life. For nearly six years, they dominated French political life in heroic style, forcing a suspension of the ancien régime's normal hierarchy of authority. They threw their world upside down, made the early years of Louis XIV's majority the equivalent of Bakhtin's carnivalized world, and thereby won by conquest a territory where women could live as men when they chose to.[26] For a brief time, women in effect governed France on major occasions, and those who negotiated with them, from princes to parliamentarians, recognized their authority as legitimate (Abensour ix). The political pamphlets that proliferated during those years offer proof of the widespread popular perception of female political rule. The vocabulary used earlier in the decade to characterize the famous queens from antiquity who were the model for the figure of the heroic woman—"illustre," "généreuse," "héroïque," "forte"—was now associated with the women accepted as the modern reincarnations of this type: *L'Illustre conquérante ou la généreuse constance de Madame de Chevreuse* is the title of a 1649 anti-Mazarin pamphlet, whose author compares the duchesse to female military leaders such as Tomiris and Jeanne d'Arc (6–7). The titles of other *mazarinades*—for example, *L'Amazonne françoise au secours des Parisiens, ou l'aproche des troupes de Madame la Duchesse de Chevreuse* (also 1649)—reveal that in the popular imagination the chief *frondeuses* were also seen as fulfilling the recent plots of novelistic heroism.

As has often been pointed out, the *frondeuses* were so concerned with self-promotion that they lost touch with the harsh economic reality that

(handwritten margin notes:)
frondeuses dominate Fr political life in heroic style

? live as men when they choose to

nb. they lost contact w/harsh economic reality

sparked the peasant revolts at the origin of the Fronde. However, this objection should not make us forget the power possessed by, for example, a Montpensier to galvanize the masses. In Gelbart's words, "*Frondeur* rhetoric evoked the memory of a republican past and promised, however vaguely, the recovery of lost liberties in a better future. Not until 1789 would male and female, capital and provinces, high and lowborn share such energies and hopes again" (19).

yet it was women who galvanized the masses

Nor did the association between the *frondeuses* and women's capacity for political sedition disappear from the popular imagination at the end of the civil war that brought women to prominence. That the memory of their exploits was still fresh two and a half centuries later is demonstrated by an engraving of the Grande Mademoiselle undoubtedly part of the iconography of the Revolution's centennial (figure 6). To illustrate an analogy commonly evoked at the time of the Revolution—the events of the Fronde as a prefiguration of those of 1789—the engraver, Pierre-Vincent Gilbert, selects key icons of each conflict. Thus, the Revolution is represented by the fall of the Bastille, and the Fronde by the battle of Saint-Antoine, during which the Bastille's cannon was used against Louis XIV. The central figure in this iconography of civil war is the Grande Mademoiselle: her portrait is presented next to the Bastille in the engraving's upper frame; in its lower half, in full amazonian regalia, she is depicted commanding the battle of Saint-Antoine.

were models during revolution

Gilbert's engraving testifies to the survival of the Fronde's fantasmatic importance and to the content of that representation: the Fronde was a fundamental moment in French history, and, for once, the history of France was shaped by women. It is easy, of course, to dismiss popular representations as being of no true historical significance. In general, to do so is to deny the mythic afterlife in which events central to any nation's self-fashioning live on. In the case of the Fronde, this gesture of dismissal is fundamental to all accounts that seek to minimize the significance of female political involvement.

nb female political involvement often dismissed

Accounts of the Fronde—from the contemporary pamphlets, to the memoirs composed by participants and eyewitnesses in the several decades that followed the events, to the tradition of historical commentary that has accrued during the last two centuries—have always presented opposing visions. The first takes female achievements seriously and grants them a central role in the civil war's unfolding. The second consistently downplays these same actions, portraying them as empty histrionics. It is impossible to mediate between these two views, since

FIGURE 6

ᏟᏉ

Pierre-Vincent Gilbert, *Mademoiselle de Montpensier*, chromolithograph
(c. 1880). Collection of the author.

they are based on radically different definitions of what counts as evidence of historical importance. Indeed, by its very content the Fronde seems to have been designed to provoke just such an interpretive conflict: in particular, the manner in which the modern amazons made war goes a long way to explain their subsequent dismissal. It is not easy to know how to interpret their theatricality: such an (by modern standards) unconventional self-fashioning in what we too lightly call the theater of war makes it difficult to measure the degree to which participants were taking themselves and their actions seriously. *[margin notes: posterity hasn't taken them very seriously - of in part their conspicuous theatricality]*

But this question has only become central because of the Fronde's failure to achieve the victory it seemed on several occasions close to winning. Once the uprising had been crushed, its leaders were immediately sent into exile, and the royal propaganda machine was set into motion to stamp out any trace of the recent events. The long public repression that surrounded what Molière—in one of the first references in literature, some sixteen years after the uprising's end—dubbed "our troubles" (*Le Tartuffe,* 1669), a silence that delayed for decades the publication of eyewitness accounts, virtually guaranteed that subsequent generations would be locked in conflict over the significance of the events. And debate on this issue has continued to forestall discussion of the particular character of the most intense participation in political and military affairs by women at any time during the ancien régime. *[margin notes: but nb. Fronde failed + propaganda stamped out memory]*

One aspect of that participation cannot be overemphasized: it is feminocentric without ever becoming what we now call feminist. The *frondeuses* never seem to have realized that, in order to make permanent gains, it would have been necessary to forge a union *in their lives* between the two visions of female heroism, literary and historical, consistently intermingled in the first half of the seventeenth century. If the heroines of the Fronde had made the amazon a *femme forte,* the future of female influence at the French court might have been different. The *frondeuses* were amazons only according to the meaning that name had acquired in seventeenth-century France, a woman daring enough to engage in military exploits. The so-called heroic woman, however, is always depicted as belonging to a community of women. She is portrayed not alone but as part of a gallery or a collection of portraits, and a sense of female solidarity that transcends historical obstacles is central to this vision, as though the women singled out for their heroism had never worked in isolation but were always conscious of belonging to a community. Witness Le Moyne's presentation *[margin notes: nb. not feminist, but feminocentric; ⇓ women engaging in military exploits]* of his *Gallerie des femmes fortes* to Anne of Austria: "The heroic women assembled in this gallery have come from all places in History to put their crown at Your Majesty's feet and rejoice at the honor that you bring to your sex" (dedication n. pag.).

The portrait of the amazon developed in seventeenth-century France runs counter both to the contemporary vision of female solidarity across the centuries and to the classical fiction of the Amazons, the prototypical community of women.[27] The Amazons were seen as a persistent threat to classical civilization because of their rejection of male domination and their assumption of male roles, and perhaps above all because this systematic reversal was the result of a female conspiracy, the decision on the part of a group of women to submerge individual daring in a collective struggle and to preserve their difference by living apart from societies governed according to traditional hierarchies. However, the French neoclassical amazon belonged to no community; her heroinism was antihierarchical, but it was also solitary, self-serving, and acted out in the very society she sought to undermine. The extraordinary military maneuvers of the *frondeuses,* demonstrating the desire for sexual equality in the political arena, cannot be thought of as feminist in a larger sense, as the effect of self-conscious participation in a united effort. The heroines of the Fronde never joined forces. They were most successful when their individual efforts were complementary, but they were capable of sacrificing the common cause to personal vanity, as happened during the last act of the Fronde when the Duchesse de Longueville's intrigues became more a confirmation of her personal magnetism than an attempt to retain powerful men in the service of the rebel cause.

P. G. Lorris, Moote, and other recent historians of the Fronde stress how close the Fronde came to altering permanently the development of the French monarchy. The lack of solidarity among *frondeuses* is surely one explanation for the Fronde's failure. It may also help explain the abrupt and definitive cessation of women's direct official participation in French political life for the remainder of the ancien régime. After the Fronde, women come closest to political action when they return to the most traditional (within the French tradition at least) manner of exercising influence, as royal mistresses. Had the *frondeuses* who directed their revolution recreated the legendary state of the amazons, the most absolute of French monarchies, that of Louis XIV, might have been avoided.

The Rise of Female Authorship
AFTER THE REVOLUTION

[Les femmes] sont si essentielles [aux révolutions et aux conspirations]
que souvent elles en sont l'âme et le mobile. Cette manoeuvre délicate...,
si nécessaire dans les affaires secretes, les y fait conduire avec plus
d'adresse que les hommes.

Lenglet-Dufresnoy,
De l'usage des romans (1734)

THE EVOLUTION of feminocentric activity during the Fronde's final
act suggests that at least some *frondeuses* may have understood both the
source and the consequences of their failure. The energy that for five
years had been exclusively devoted to political endeavors was rechan-
neled into literary affairs. With this change of focus, the sense of
community absent from women's political activity came into being. The
literary forms initially developed by seventeenth-century French women
writers are without exception, first, the product of a collective effort
and, second, an attempt to recreate or provide a textual equivalent of
the shared experience of female communities.

The Fronde had a great impact on the general development of
French literature: two of its central participants, the Coadjuteur de
Gondi and the Prince de Marsillac, were destined to reign—under their
definitive titles, the Cardinal de Retz and the Duc de La Rochefoucauld
—as undisputed early masters of French prose. Yet neither of them
turned to literature as an immediate substitute for sedition; their textual
production belongs, along with works we will examine shortly, such as
the Montpensier-Motteville correspondence, to the second generation of
works brought about by the Fronde's failure. Nor are their works
marked by a sense of tradition or community: the *Mémoires* is centered
on the glorification and justification of Retz's magisterial "I," while all
trace of its collaborative composition has been erased from the *Maximes*
by its authorial vantage point of disdainful detachment.

In addition, all ties have been broken between this writing by men
and the literary form that, by their own admission, sets the stage for the
Fronde. For example, January 11, 1649, marked a summit of *frondeur*
glory: the Duchesse de Longueville, every inch a queen and a heroic

woman, displayed herself to the people from the steps of the Hôtel de Ville; her infant son by La Rochefoucauld, patriotically christened Paris, was in her arms; the future Cardinal de Retz threw coins to the mob from the window. In his account, Retz characterizes the scene at the Duchesse de Longueville's later that day as a novel (*roman* or romance) come to life: "The mixture of the blue scarves, the women, the cuirasses, and violins that were in the room, and the trumpets that were outside, produced a spectacle seen more often in novels (*romans*) than elsewhere" (153).[28] He does not, however, attempt to recreate the narrative form that had presided over his youthful exploits. For Retz, as for La Rochefoucauld, emotional detachment is also literary detachment from the textual naïveté of pastoral and heroic fiction.

In contemporary women's writing, the relationship between the making of history and its recreation in literature is decidedly more complicated. During the early years of the regency and the beginning of the Fronde, heroinism is a favorite subject for male writers but women themselves seldom do more than talk about writing in the salons. With the outbreak of the Fronde, however, two major traditions of women's writing are inaugurated. The first of these, memoirs, would eventually include important accounts from both *frondeur* and royalist positions, the *Mémoires* of Montpensier and those of Motteville. The second literary form elaborated in the shadow of political revolt is the keystone of the bond between feminism and the modern (French) novel.

On January 7, 1649, just four days before the heroic drama at the Hôtel de Ville that was for Retz *Astrée* come to life, the first two volumes of a new *roman* were printed. *Artamène, ou le Grand Cyrus* would fire the collective imagination of the contemporary reading public as no prose fiction since d'Urfé's magnum opus had done. The heroines and heroes of the Fronde were self-conscious, novelistic actors on the stage of history; *Artamène* is in a sense a literary recreation of the living-out of a novel. Yet this is not to say that *Artamène* is merely a novelistic mirror of the Fronde years. Such was the position of Victor Cousin, who devoted his *La Société française au XVIIe siècle d'après "Le Grand Cyrus"* to establishing the "key" to the novel's characters, out of a conviction that the work's popularity could only be explained by the aristocratic public's desire to recognize familiar faces in a ten-volume, 14,000–page novelistic mirror. The reading Cousin inaugurated has successfully obscured the more intricate bond between history and fiction in Scudéry's work, in particular the parallelism between its literary evolution and the contemporary evolution of feminist activity.

Under the ancien régime, in order to publish a book it was necessary first to obtain a *privilège,* the permission to publish granted by the royal censor. Novelists often requested a *privilège* as soon as a subject was sufficiently formulated to give it a title, so the permission also functioned as an informal copyright. By comparing the date of the *privilège* for a volume and the date of that volume's publication, it is possible to calculate with some precision the period devoted to its composition. This task is greatly facilitated in the case of a prolific writer, and Madeleine de Scudéry was among the most prolific authors of her century: the volumes of a given project appeared with remarkable rapidity and regularity.

"Nothing is as contrary to wit (*bel esprit*) as civil war," Scudéry's friend Sarasin wrote her at the end of the explosive year 1650 (Rathery and Boutron 429). This maxim was borne out by the contemporary literary climate, for the years of the Fronde, as Maurice Lever's bibliography of seventeenth-century narrative fiction attests, were hardly conducive to the publication of novels. Their output is reduced for the duration of the upheaval, and the years 1652 and 1653 were the only time in the seventeenth century when no novels appeared (Lever 520–21)—with one exception, that is. The *privilège* for the first two volumes of *Artamène* was granted in July 1648, when the principal actors in the Fronde—Longueville, Condé, Marsillac, and Gondi—were plotting the active phase of their rebellion, which was launched the following month. Since the initial volumes of *Artamène* were published just six months later, they were composed precisely during the first days of the war against the monarchy.[29] Throughout this time of political upheaval, volumes of *Artamène* continued to appear at regular intervals, and the final volumes (volume 10 was printed in mid-September 1653) were the unique novelistic production during the months that nearly marked the downfall of the absolute monarchy. All the volumes of *Artamène* were dedicated to the Duchesse de Longueville, and the novel's central couple, Cyrus and Mandane, were seen from the beginning as the fictional counterparts of the great Condé and his sister, the Duchesse de Longueville. The bond forged thereby between prose fiction and political subversion marks the origin of the modern French novel; it is the founding gesture that makes *Artamène,* rather than *Astrée,* the earliest indication of prose fiction's definitive early modern tradition. However, only a reader insensitive to the formal evolution of Scudéry's novel could conclude from this that *Artamène* is an unambivalent eulogy of political sedition. Rather *Le Grand Cyrus* is initially a celebration of the vitality of these years during which the making of history was approached as a literary enterprise, and especially a commemoration of woman's power to inspire military heroism.

Scudéry's correspondence from the period reveals a seemingly paradoxical simultaneous loyalty to the house of Condé and to the monarchy (if not to the actual monarch).[30] Her admiration and sympathy lie with the rebel princes, but at the same time she never doubts that the royal forces will ultimately be victorious and, furthermore, she predicts, all too accurately, the long-term consequences of this temporary reversal of the established order. As early as March 1651 she compares the young monarch to "those little birds who sing so well and rejoice, even though they are prisoners in their cages, for at present this poor young King is really more a prisoner than they." She understands that "the King seems to hate all those who seek to abuse his authority and in all likelihood he will remember for a long time everything that is done to him today" (Rathery and Boutron 244–45). She sees more clearly than other contemporary commentators, or at least records more openly than they, that Louis XIV would never forget this threat to his absolute reign and that when the old order returned its rules and hierarchies would be enforced, literally with a vengeance. Those who had the most to lose when the world was again turned right side up were of course those who had profited most dramatically from the tear in the fabric of history, the women who had risen first to legitimate and then to illegitimate prominence during Anne of Austria's regency.

Scudéry's understanding that women must prepare to exercise power in a radically different arena is evident from the dramatic evolution of *Artamène*. The novel's sixth volume appeared the month after the letter describing Louis XIV's imprisonment in the gilded cage. By the time the next volume was published just seven months later, Scudéry had made a major change in her novelistic formula, the first indication of the central evolution in her fiction. She introduced one of the two fixed forms that came to be seen as the signature of her *roman,* the conversation (the second form, the portrait, was codified later in *Clélie* [Godenne 191]). The conversation, in which characters gather together to debate different views on a given subject (usually a fine point of amorous conduct related only tangentially to the action of the novel), can be viewed diachronically as a female variant of the philosophical dialogue. Scudéry's introduction of the conversation in 1651 can be more precisely interpreted as a gesture of homage to the power women had exercised before the outbreak of heroism and to the art of conversation in which they had excelled in the salons. The interpolation of conversations marked the first step in Scudéry's rejection of the action-oriented model for romance that she had inherited from her precursors and exploited in her first novel *Ibrahim* and earlier in *Artamène*.

Salon activity was in suspension during the last years of the Fronde. Scudéry's progressive turning from action to dialogue in the final volumes of *Artamène* ensured, therefore, that the other feminist tradition would be kept alive. It was an indication that in the aftermath of the Fronde, when the king's long memory would once again close the public sector to all but officially sanctioned participants, another preserve would still belong to women, a domain outside the jurisdiction of the former prisoner in the gilded cage. With hindsight, the prescience of Scudéry's decision is evident: as commentators (most famously, Ferdinand Brunetière in the late nineteenth century) repeat, the conversational style (*esprit de conversation*) is the cornerstone of French literary modernity. And this style, as Brunetière still admits and as Scudéry is the first to explain, is originally a female concept, invented in the salons and reinscribed in prose fiction when, following Scudéry's example, women found a new power base in the republic of letters.

Maclean ends his monumental study with the majority of Louis XIV on September 7, 1651, because he feels that feminist activity, both political and literary, either disappears or declines in originality at this point: "Louis XIV's majority and the depreciation of the 'morale héroïque' herald the return of the traditional moral order, and with it an attachment to firm divisions and the rule of common sense" (265, see also 118). It was evident at the majority of Louis XIV that the reign of the amazons had effected no permanent political change. Yet just at this time Scudéry was putting the final touches to volume 7 of *Artamène,* and the changes in her novelistic model she made there, as well as other contemporary textual signals, can be read as indications that, within their separate communities, women still intended to reign supreme. In the salons, women would actualize the link between women's political prowess and female literary collectives that Guez de Balzac suspected as early as 1638, when he wrote to Chapelain that women who write books

Handwritten marginalia:
conversation = f variant of philosophical dialogue

" homage to salons

action-oriented model ↓

conversational style → Cornerstone of French literary modernity

Balzac: P's who write books use their minds to cross dress

"use their minds to cross-dress" (1661 ed. *Lettres* 139). The literary
women of this generation would prove him right by becoming the
amazons of the intellect. The conversational style, the literary counterpart of the art of conversation, was the signal of this new *prise de
pouvoir*, the female arena that, at least until the Revolution, would be
opposed to what was considered the quintessentially male literary preserve, the classical style.

The final volumes of Scudéry's immense commemoration and eventually critique of heroic action were contemporaneous with the last act
and epilogue to the Fronde. The nine months that elapsed between
volumes 7 and 8 witnessed some of the Fronde's most violent activity.[31]
Volume 8 appeared in August 1652, the month after the crucial battle
when the *frondeurs* took Paris and forced Louis into semi-exile because
the Grande Mademoiselle opened the city to the rebels and opened fire
on her monarch. Condé, the rebel "king," withdrew from Paris and the
legitimate ruler was invited back in October of that year; Mazarin
returned to the city in February 1653, the month that saw the publication of *Artamène*'s penultimate volume. The novel's ninth volume, composed even as the rebellion was going down in defeat, commemorates
both that defeat and the end of an age for the French novel, since it is
the last tome in which action-oriented fiction predominates. The novel's
final volume, published in September 1653 and the only part written
entirely under the uncontested rule of the monarchy, presented Scudéry's initial public with much more than the conclusion to the adventures of Cyrus and Mandane. *Artamène*'s tenth volume signals the death
of the *roman* (romance) and the inauguration of a new model for French
prose fiction, feminocentric in content and oblique in narrative stance.

Scudéry's rejection of action in *Artamène*'s last volume is coupled
with a turning away from her central characters, Cyrus and Mandane.
Scudéry sacrificed the narrative economy of her final volume to devote
its central and longest section to a character who had not previously
figured in its action, but one who allowed her to end her novel's
association with heroic adventure. "The Story of Sapho" is the most
important of the numerous intercalated tales that are the basic building
blocks of Scudéry's immense novels: it is nothing less than an accurate
prediction of life after heroism. Scudéry had filled nine volumes with
characters who fight battles and cross continents—always driven by a
desire for the form of closure traditional to the early novel, marriage.

She devotes the heart of her final volume to a character who as a writer is concerned with matters not usually the stuff of fiction, from the proper subject matter for poetry to the kind of space required for creative activity. Scudéry's Sapho is the first sure indicator that the former (and future) salon organizers realized early in 1653 that in the aftermath of the Fronde women would once again exercise their talents only on private stages and only in matters intellectual.

Artamène's ultimate heroine also shows that this new form of commitment could be as subversive as political sedition. Through the character of Sapho, Scudéry advocates a number of the archetypal feminist causes of the post-Fronde decades. Sapho pronounces marriage legally "a long slavery" for women (10:343) and declares that "in order to love each other forever with no loss of ardor, it is necessary never to marry" (10:607). Since she feels that their society will not accept such a union, Sapho obliges her beloved to "retire" with her to the land of the Sauromates, according to Herodotus the home of the Amazons. Not only is this the first of a series of celebrated "retreats" in French women's fiction; it also foreshadows the equally celebrated official "retreats" (the euphemism used for "exile") of the amazon rebels whose inception was nearly simultaneous with the volume's publication—for example, the Grande Mademoiselle received the order to leave Paris on October 19, 1653, less than a month after volume 10 appeared. (To indicate that this correspondence between fiction and reality is intentional, Scudéry declares that the society of the new Sauromates had been founded by a group exiled after a civil war [10:572–73].) Furthermore, in Scudéry's portrayal the land of the Sauromates becomes the first of a series of post-Fronde feminist utopias: it is a domain governed by a queen, in which courts of love both regulate the economy of desire and give legal status to unions outside of marriage.

For this female community, independence from the great world signifies no loss of status: Scudéry's society is portrayed as separate but equal. Since the Sauromates wished to avoid potential contamination from "foreign customs" (10:567), they made their country self-sufficient. They created the geographical self-containment necessary for peaceful political autonomy, first by winning from the Greeks sufficient territory to form "a small state in the middle of their [state]," and then by further isolating their territory by surrounding it with an immense no-man's-land. They laid waste to the land surrounding them, turning it into a "desert" so vast that, to reach their political oasis, "one must spend at least three long days crossing the desert, no matter what side one comes from" (10:569). Thus isolated in their "state within a desert" (10:570), the Sauromates enjoy a world in which intellectual occupations and a proto-*précieuse* code of love flourish. Scudéry's vocabulary reveals her prescience: "retreat" and "desert" were destined to remain, virtually until the end of the century, synonymous with the disaffection of an intelligentsia that was never again to come as close to the source of political power as it had during the Fronde years.

In addition, Scudéry provided a prototype for the new type of literary woman who would rise to prominence in the salons virtually as soon as the hostilities ceased, the *précieuse*. Safe within the confines of utopia, Sapho "writes every day" (10:608). Financially independent, she presides over "the most agreeable lodging in the world," three rooms of her own, culminating in the space that seventeenth-century French literary women portray as essential to the making of a woman writer, the inner sanctum referred to in *Artamène* as a *cabinet* (10:355).[32] In addition, Scudéry uses Sapho to defend—appropriately, in one of the conversations that become a set piece in *Artamène*'s last volumes—the art of conversation, the conversational style. She stresses that the spontaneity and improvisation that were essential qualities of salon literature were not to be confused with the lack of craft or effort: "[Sapho] did not work by accident, ... without taking the trouble to search out the ultimate perfection; everything she wrote was precise and polished" (10:356).

By the time *Artamène*'s final volume appeared, the literary world it predicts was very nearly in place. The rejection inside the realm of the Sauromates of marriage and the legal status it confers in favor of the status conferred by literary talent parallels the demands that inspire post-Fronde feminist activity. It simultaneously signifies the creation of a feminist model for prose fiction: Sapho's rejection of marriage indicates her creator's rejection of the closure and the order that had previously governed the novel. In Scudéry's wake, French women writers from Lafayette, to Staël, to Sand, to Colette bring their novels to an end by calling into question marriage's function to regulate the social order. This repeated rejection of fictional and civil closure, coupled with the simultaneous inscription of literary and legal disorder, can be seen as the founding gesture of the tradition of French women's writing.

REGROUPING

Mais Rome veut un maître, et non une maîtresse.

Racine, *Britannicus* (1669)

THE YEAR 1653 is *the* crucial year in the history of seventeenth-century French feminism; it is also a major date in the annals of French women's literature. In the capital, activity in the salons resumed and quickly took on greater importance than before the war. The solitary political action of the modern-day amazons was replaced by a renewed atmosphere of female solidarity. At the forefront of this rechanneling of female energy were the gatherings, known as *samedis*, presided over by Madeleine de Scudéry at her home on the rue de Beauce.[33] Thus began what Dorothy Backer terms the "precious decade," the years from 1653 to 1660 that marked the flowering of *préciosité* as a literary-linguistic model and a code to govern male-female relations. As Maclean points out (119–20), after the Fronde the *femme forte,* a creation of male writers, was reinvented, rescripted, as the *précieuse* by women intellectuals.[34] Whereas the strong woman was proposed as an ideal because of her ability to govern and her military genius, intellectual qualities determined the status of the *précieuse* as model. The vocabulary of generosity, heroism, and strength used to characterize both literary and historical amazons was replaced by a new series of adjectives to which writers turned again and again to suggest the intellectual brilliance of the great *précieuses:* "incomparable," "nonpareille," "sans exemple."

Michel de Pure, among the first chroniclers of salon activity, defined the *précieuse* as the product of Louis's *pax romana:* "The first fine days that peace gave us created this happy production [*la précieuse*] and enriched our conversations" (1:66).[35] De Pure did not realize that *préciosité* influenced more than oral forms of expression, and that even as his novel was being published in 1655–1658, two women writers were composing their accounts of the power still open to women in time of peace. In addition to the *précieuse* as de Pure defined her, the advent of peace "created" women writers who realized the need to develop a literary portrayal of strong women that was more than two-dimensional.[36] One of these writers introduced the most important formal innovation in seventeenth-century prose fiction.

Rôle of Mademoiselle de Montpensier

The woman often known simply as "Mademoiselle" realized perhaps better than anyone that life after the aborted revolution reserved a harsher fate for *frondeuses* than for *frondeurs*. The king chose to make peace, or at least a simulacrum of peace, with many of the *frondeurs*.

king: peace w/ frondeurs

Barely a year after the cessation of hostilities, for example, Conti was married to one of Mazarin's nieces, a social humiliation easily deciphered as a gesture of complicity with the absolute monarchy. In general, former male rebels continued to play political roles during and after Louis XIV's self-transformation into the Sun King. Thus occupied,

but frondeuses → polit non-existence

they had no need to move precipitously into new occupations.[37] However, women returned to political nonexistence during the Sun King's increasingly absolute reign. When her royal cousin sent the Grande Mademoiselle into exile in October 1653, she turned the energy previously devoted to rebellion to literature instead.[38] When she did so, the former solitary amazon portrayed herself not as a unique heroine but in a circle of women.

her Nouvelles françaises attributed to Segrais "scribe"

Or rather she had herself thus portrayed: Montpensier, like many other seventeenth-century French women writers, used a male writer as literary assistant. The collection of tales called the *Nouvelles françaises* (1657) was signed by Segrais, and he is today accepted as its author. But Segrais himself presents a more complex interpretation of the production of literature at the conclusion of the work's prologue. He distinguishes between storytelling as oral creation and as written recreation and describes himself as the scribe of Montpensier (portrayed under the name of the Princesse Aurélie): "I was very attentive to her discourse and some time later I wrote this story as much in conformity as I could with what I had heard her tell.... Even though I tried not to omit a single one of her words and to add nothing, nevertheless only she herself could have written this story (*nouvelle*) with all the perfection and charm with which she recounted it" (1:23–24).[39]

king's majority of Ps must forge life elsewhere

The prologue to the *Nouvelles françaises* presents the king's majority as the signal to women that they must forge a life for themselves away from the official center of power: "The first year of the majority of the Prince who by a thousand handsome qualities merited the epithet of Louis the Great was hardly over when a great Princesse having withdrawn (*s'étant retirée*) from Paris came to live in one of her most beautiful country houses" (1:1). The elegant compliment paid to the king against whom she had ordered his own cannons to fire is no more misleading than the rescripting of her enforced exile in her château,

Saint-Fargeau: of her own free will, the great princesse (clearly the great prince's equal) leaves Paris, the royal preserve, to live in "retirement" in a geography totally under her control. No more than the retreat by Scudéry's Sapho to the land of the Sauromates can this retirement be understood as life in seclusion. The princesse has been joined by a company exclusively female and with a common political past—"having found themselves agitated in the disorders that had just tormented France" (1:11).[40] This community has no occasion to regret the pleasures of life at court: they eat well, converse, and in short "ha[ve] a good deal of pleasure in their solitude" (1:11, 22).

Within this separate space, the main activity is literary. The women meet every day to tell stories to the assembled company. Montpensier reproduces the structure of a collection of tales in open homage to the most illustrious French practitioner of that form, Marguerite de Navarre. The company is discussing their precursors in the *Heptaméron* when the princesse defines the special importance those stories have for her: "They are my grandmother's stories (*des contes de ma grand'mère*), said the Princesse, laughing at the application she was making of such a vulgar expression (*d'une chose qui se dit si vulgairement*), ... and I am obliged therefore to defend them" (1:22). The princesse laughs because a slight substitution allows her to make a proverbial expression literal, therefore translating it from the public to the personal linguistic domain and erasing its "vulgarity." Her definition of the *Heptaméron* as "my grandmother's stories" is a correct, if foreshortened, genealogical reference: the Grande Mademoiselle was the great-great-granddaughter of the author of the *Heptaméron*. However, when she puts her great-great-grandmother in her grandmother's place, Montpensier imitates the paternal grandmother she thereby displaces, Marie de' Medici, by reinventing her life. When she renounces descent from her century's original heroic woman, in favor of the age's Scheherazade figure, her substitution is a sign of the times: the new home of the amazons is situated in the republic of letters.

Furthermore, her phrase is also, as she says, an "application": in "des contes de ma grand'mère" her audience recognizes the proverbial expression "des contes de ma mère l'oie" (Mother Goose tales). For Montpensier, Marguerite de Navarre was in a sense a mythical origin, a fictional individual whose name had become synonymous, one hundred years after the publication of her work, with the legendary past of women's storytelling, just as that of Mother Goose was already in the

seventeenth century synonymous with the traditional collections of nurs-
ery rhymes. In Montpensier's evocation, the possessive adjective that
usually sounds a strange note in "contes de *ma* mère l'oie" is for once
pertinent. It also serves as a commentary on the narrative situation of
the *Nouvelles françaises,* on the limit between oral and written. Marguerite de Navarre's art was in part a written record of the assemblies of
her day. At the time of the composition of the *Nouvelles françaises,* the
tales of my mother the goose were still a part of oral tradition, still the
property of the substitute mothers, the nurses, who recounted them to
their charges. But the tales were destined shortly (1697) to be transcribed, like the stories told by women in the *Nouvelles françaises,* by a
man, Charles Perrault.[41]

*of oral tradition
of mother
Goose
stories*

In the prologue, the ties to actual and fictional female literary precursors authorize a decisive break with novelistic tradition: Montpensier
shared Scudéry's belief that after the Fronde it was no longer possible to
make fiction as before. Her program proved so revolutionary that the
prologue has been commonly referred to as the first manifesto of the
modern French novel and considered—along with the preface (often
attributed to Georges de Scudéry) to Madeleine de Scudéry's *Ibrahim*
and Huet's preface to *Zayde*—one of the three major seventeenth-
century theoretical statements on prose fiction. The most frequently
cited passage occurs in Princesse Aurélie's commentary on the story she
has just recounted to her friends: "It seems to me that this is the
difference between romance (*roman*) and novel (*nouvelle*), that romance
describes these things according to the rules of propriety (*comme la
bienséance le veut*) and as a poet would, but that the novel must remain
closer to history and strive more to give images of things as we ordi-
narily see them happen than as our imagination conceives of them"
(1:146). This statement merits the interpretation it usually receives, as a
condemnation of the wildly improbable, extravagant fictions created
until the end of the Fronde, and as a defense of the sort of carefully
documented historical fiction that practitioners like Lafayette would
develop some ten to twenty years later into the modern French novel.
For this fiction born after political sedition, love stories would be of
interest, as the example of Lafayette's novels proves, only in the context
of war and political intrigue.

*prologue of
Nouvelles =
prose fiction
manifesto*

*novel must
remain
closer to
history*

Yet the story on which this passage allegedly serves as commentary
has nothing in common with the novel (*nouvelle*) whose superiority it
proclaims. In fact, Aurélie's story of a German gentleman disguised as a

*but n.b.
Montpensier
doesn't exactly
practice what
she preaches*

lady-in-waiting to his mistress, while it is brief and has a contemporary setting, is as incredible as any tale from *Artamène*. The Grande Mademoiselle would not break away from the larger-than-life scenarios of action-oriented, heroic fiction.[42] Nevertheless, the fiction produced during her exile at Saint-Fargeau introduces elements that eventually help complete the transition from romance to novel: a radically abbreviated format and a prominent use of the conversational model, both explicitly linked to the tradition of women's fiction. It was also during her exile that Montpensier began work on her memoirs—by her own account, only months after her "retreat" began (2:383–84)—the clearest indication of her intention to replace the making of history with the writing of history.

*but her work →
radically
abbreviated
fiction;
use of
conversational
model*

*later, →
memoirs
=)
making of
history
eclipsed by
writing of
history*

While the *Nouvelles françaises* was not published until 1657, the work's incipit shows that it was begun early in Montpensier's exile, at the time when Scudéry was working on the final volume of *Artamène*, in which Sapho's entrance signals the death of the action-oriented model for fiction and in which the new amazons owe their independence to the power of the word rather than the power of the sword. In Scudéry's new model for prose fiction, as in the courts in exile like Montpensier's, the making of history is eclipsed by the writing of history. This deferred, deflected perspective on action is a vision that, while fatal to romance, generates what can be seen as the great French tradition of the novel, the novel as saga of voyeurism and oblique action, progressing inexorably toward the *livre sur rien*.

Scudéry brings what many consider her finest work to a close by sounding the death knell of the heroic fiction that made her famous. However, in the original edition of *Artamène* the final volume opens with a foreword announcing the impending publication of her next novel. True to form and just as announced, a mere eleven months later the first volume of *Clélie, histoire romaine* appeared. *Clélie* fulfills perfectly the promise of *Artamène*. First, Scudéry broadens her rejection of action-oriented fiction, turning increasingly to an oblique presentation of events and continuing to slow down the pace of her narrative.[43] At the same time, she continues, and eventually completes, her transformation of the novel into a chronicle of salon life: she allots more and more space to conversations and begins to interpolate other set pieces, all of which have a parallel in contemporary salon creations. The best known of these is the often cited (generally by those who have not looked at it) *Carte de Tendre*, actually invented in Scudéry's salon.[44]

*Scudéry's
Clélie
fulfils promise
of Artamène --
histoire*

*narrative =
slower;
chronicle of
salon life*

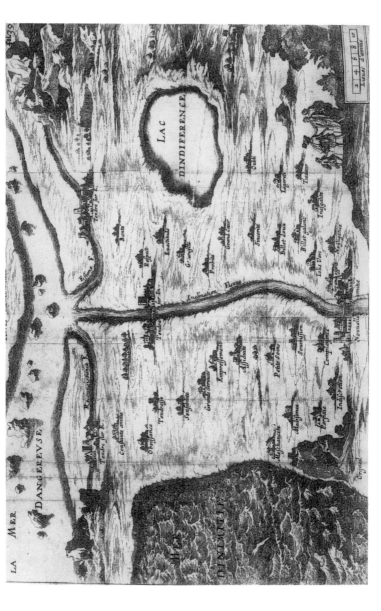

FIGURE 7
&

La Carte de Tendre, illustration, Madeleine de Scudéry, *Clélie, histoire romaine* (1654). Reprinted by permission of Princeton University Libraries.

The *Carte de Tendre,* centerpiece of *Clélie*'s first volume and the most *Carte de Tendre* celebrated document in salon literature, functions on a number of levels (figure 7). Allegorically, it is a map of an imaginary land called Tenderness. As the novel's heroine teaches her audience how to read it, the *map = course* map is revealed to be a course in gallantry, giving men the woman's *on gallantry,* perspective on both the ways to win her heart (for example, a stop in *ways to win* Pretty Verse and a visit to Sincerity eventually lead to the town of *♀'s hearts* Tenderness-on-the-Esteem) and the ways to lose it (a wrong turn at Negligence puts a suitor on the road to Obliteration). Scudéry's map is an ancestor of board games such as Monopoly, and it was just as *≈ board game* successful in its day: at least fifteen imitations and parodies appeared in the next decade to capitalize on the success of the game of love. The *Carte de Tendre* also acts to lay claim definitively for women writers to *claim to new* the new literary territory in which its tender geography would play a *literary* central role. Novelists like Lafayette and Villedieu would soon begin to *territory =* develop what Scudéry first mapped out, a novel dominated by conver- *conversation,* sation instead of action and by an ever more intricate analysis of the *analysis of* human heart. As Ferdinand Brunetière remarked in 1889, French "nov- *human heart* elists have never ceased traversing the *Carte de Tendre*" (56). At the onset of the decade before Louis XIV's marriage, during which *préciosité* and the salons reigned supreme, Scudéry offered a mapping of a territory situated simultaneously in the domain of literature and in that of human relations, a place in which men were consigned to the margins while women set the course. It may have been the last time in the *= ♀'s prise* French tradition that a woman dared suggest such a forthright *prise de* *de pouvoir* *pouvoir.*

Most examples of salon creativity translated into *Clélie*'s pages are, *also: intro* like the *Carte de Tendre,* unique occurrences. However, one form, the *of portrait* portrait, plays an increasingly important role as the novel progresses, until in the novel's second half it rivals the conversation in frequency. Scudéry introduced portraits as early as volume 7 of *Artaméne,* the volume that initiated the conversation, but began to realize the form's potential only much later, in volume 5 of *Clélie,* composed in late 1655 and 1656 (Godenne 191, 235). The explanation for this delayed reaction to formal innovation surely lies with Scudéry's desire to have her fiction evolve in tandem with the salon style. Thus, even though she conceived of the portrait's usefulness much earlier, she truly exploited it only once the portrait, as both an oral and a written exercise, was in vogue in the salons.

galleries
of portraits

Again, the chronology of the Grande Mademoiselle's literary evolution parallels Scudéry's almost exactly, for, according to Montpensier's memoirs, members of her court-in-exile began a collective exploration of word portraiture in 1656. The following year she began to collect the products of her friends' *bel spirit* for publication (*Mémoires* 1:364). Montpensier was slower to get her efforts into print than Scudéry, however, for of the two collections of portraits for which she was responsible, the first, *Divers portraits,* did not appear until January 1659 and the far more comprehensive *Recueil des portraits et éloges* not until a few months later. It is generally assumed that the written portrait was inspired by the painted portrait (Lafond 141), so it is not surprising that the two examples that open the *Divers portraits* and that are characterized by Montpensier as the origin of the genre are identified as having been composed while their authors were in Holland, a country with a strong tradition of painted portraiture. For its 1663 reedition, the second collection was retitled *La Galerie des portraits de Mademoiselle de Montpensier,* in a reminder of the French artistic tradition most closely related to the new society amusement. The salon portraitists could look back to the portrait galleries of famous women popular during Anne of Austria's regency in conjunction with the *femmes fortes* collections. They might also have been inspired by the portrait galleries then being created by a series of nobles exiled to their châteaux. Both Montpensier herself and Sévigné's cousin, Bussy-Rabutin, to cite but the most striking examples,

importance of
order of
portraits, of
architecture of
Recueil

manipulated such possibilities as the order in which portraits were positioned and the juxtaposition of portraits to infuse their portrait galleries with a subversive political message, to create, as it were, the exile's eye view of the relative rank of the major personages of the day.

Similar techniques and a similarly subversive intention are quietly evident in Montpensier's verbal portrait galleries. In *Divers portraits,* 42 of 58 portraits are by women and 41 are of women. The collection is so unmistakably under female control that the king's portrait ("under the name of Tirsis") figures only as number 33. This initial volume was

King, eg,=
#33,
high # of women's
portraits

published privately (through the efforts of Huet and perhaps those of Segrais as well), and only 60 copies were printed. The *Recueil des portraits,* on the other hand, was made available to the general public. It is not surprising, therefore, that it opens with a gesture of homage to Louis XIV, in this case with two portraits of the monarch. After this initial gesture, however, the volume suggests that the court-in-exile is a more powerful model than the actual court by once again according a preponderant place to women's portraits.[45] Of the 104 portraits it contains, 85 are of women and 38 are by women—and the lower total in this second category can undoubtedly be explained by the far higher number of unsigned portraits in this volume (62 in contrast with only 8 in the *Divers portraits*). From the end of the Fronde to the death of Louis XIV, women were more likely than men to resort to anonymity for any public literary endeavor.[46]

These word portraits provide additional evidence of the attempt to present a more complex view of character that is evident throughout post-Fronde writing. "The pen has a great advantage over the brush," declares Segrais in his (unsigned) preface to the second volume. "[Our painters] discover the interior and devote themselves to the soul. They reveal if we have intelligence (*esprit*), judgment, and memory. . . . [These portraits] can be called . . . a kind of general confession" (ii-iii).[47] The word portrait as devised in the assemblies of the mid-1650s is a perfect vehicle for the aspirations of the new ideal woman. The sum total of its two obligatory parts—physical sketch followed by psychological study—is invariably the model salon figure, a woman whose attributes are shown to their best advantage in a female assembly. When Scudéry interpolates portraits into her novel's plot, she recreates their collective origin and preserves their status as both oral and written creations; the portrait she develops is a quite different creation from the more limited form used earlier by d'Urfé and La Calprenède.[48] One character presents the portrait of another character to an assembled audience. The members of the audience then intervene to comment on the presentation. As a result, the final portrait is explicitly, just as those in Montpensier's collections are implicitly, a written text both born in the art of conversation and recreating its origin in its form. The desire evident throughout Scudéry's fiction to commemorate its conversational origin makes us aware of a literary value of the precious decade no longer prized in our canon. Protoliterary histories, in particular Marguerite Buffet's *Eloge des illustres savantes* (1668), demonstrate that in the salon era conversational brilliance was just as likely to be rewarded with literary status as the written production that is today the sole measure of talent. Those known as literary women during the precious decade were by no means all writers.

At the same time, the pressure of more traditional literary values was also evident. In de Pure's 1655 compendium of *préciosité*, only oral artistry is considered: "[*Alcôve* and *ruelle*] compose a single sphere and are in the same circle, [the circle] of conversation" (1:66). By the end of the precious decade, however, female artistry receives a more conventional definition. Somaize, in his *Dictionnaire des prétieuses* (1660–1661), gives a brief history of the phenomenon he seeks to circumscribe: first the *précieuses* passed judgment on literary matters in private; next they began to make their opinions public; finally they became writers themselves. By the end of its reign, *préciosité* was portrayed as a literary movement and no longer as a uniquely ephemeral display of conversational talent (*esprit*). "I realize very well that I will be asked if all intellectual women (*femmes d'esprit*) are *prétieuses*," Somaize reasons. "To that question I answer no, that [the *prétieuses*] are only those who get involved in writing or correcting what others write" (1:23).

Somaize gave in 1660 the clearest indication of the prominence that public literary production had acquired by the end of the precious decade, the proof that for the ex-*frondeurs* reassembled in the salons literature had become, according to Segrais's 1659 pronouncement, a "general confession," the collective signature of a generation (*Recueil des portraits* iii). In the decade following the Fronde, literature had become the site for political subversion. In the course of the precious decade, woman's sphere, the circle of conversation, had extended its limits to include a public space, that of the novel. When the *précieuses* went public, however, they did not adopt conventional literary values. They privileged a concept I will define in the following chapter, "salon writing," a collective style prized precisely because of the absence of individual personality. True salon writing is without an internal authorial signature, somehow beyond personality, the collective style of a literary assembly—or of a politically disabused generation.

However, even as the spokesmen for the *précieuses* were announcing the rechanneling of *frondeur* energy, the political climate surrounding the creation of women's fiction was once again being radically altered. A new "retreat" became necessary, a retreat that completed the withdrawal from the political scene initiated at the end of the Fronde.

FROM *RUELLE* TO *RÉDUIT*

Toutes les conversations que l'on avait avec [mon père] ... finissaient toujours par des souhaits d'être en repos à Blois, et par le bonheur des

gens qui ne se mêlent de rien. . . . Je jugeais par là qu'à la suite du temps
cette affaire [la Fronde] irait à rien, et qu'on se verrait réduit comme on
a été, chacun chez soi.

Montpensier, *Mémoires*

SCUDÉRY'S *ARTAMÈNE* ends with a coronation. At the close of a
volume centered on the archetypal woman writer, Sapho, Scudéry chooses
as her final image the ascent to the throne of Cyrus the Great. The
volume was published on the second anniversary of Loüis XIV's majority, shortly before the first anniversary of his return to Paris to resume
his kingly role. Cyrus' ascent must have seemed to some the sort of
homage that the young king was already receiving from many quarters
and that would become an obligatory gesture as his monarchy became
more absolute.[49] However, this royal apotheosis can no more be taken at
face value than the eulogy of the great prince that opens Montpensier's
Nouvelles françaises. Louis XIV, only fifteen at the end of the Fronde,
was not yet worthy of the epithet "le Grand" that would later be
assigned him, no more than the French kingdom could have been seen
as having attained the totally secure borders and perfect order that
Scudéry describes as the hallmark of Cyrus' domain (10:849–50). Indeed, throughout the precious decade the young king was in no way a
threatening figure. His greatest conquests were amorous, and the French
court knew a reign of pleasure, spectacles, and *galanterie* that formed an
ideal backdrop for Scudéry's most frivolous fiction, *Clélie, histoire romaine.* Just as the publication of *Artamène* coincides with the time of
political revolt, so *Clélie,* which appeared between August 1654 and
March 1660, overlaps with the period of royal innocence.

The young monarch's unthreatening frivolity was already coming to
a close when Scudéry ended her monumental contribution to the literary
influence of female assemblies and the privileges enjoyed by women
within their separate spaces. *Clélie*'s final volume appeared when Louis
XIV and the important members of his court were sojourning in Aix,
preparing for the final stage of the journey to Saint-Jean-de-Luz, where
the king was to be married. The last installment of Scudéry's *histoire
romaine,* unlike that of *Artamène,* does not indicate that the unfolding of
seventeenth-century political life was once again in the process of rede-
fining women's sphere of influence. Indeed the volume contains Scudéry's eulogy of Louis's minister, Fouquet (under the name of Cléon-
ime), and her description of his château at Vaux (called Valterre in the

novel), as though the *précieuses* would reign forever. But by this time the *samedis,* like all the most public salons of the century, were almost over—as was the unofficial reign of Fouquet, friend to the *précieuses* and protector of Scudéry's dear friend Pellisson. Within a year of Louis's return to Paris with his new bride, his *surintendant des finances* and Fouquet's secretary Pellisson would be imprisoned in the Bastille.

The death knell of the separate but equal space of the female assemblies is sounded in a correspondence authored by the other ubiquitous performer on the seventeenth-century female stage, the Grande Mademoiselle. Two months after *Clélie* was brought to a close, Montpensier found herself in Saint-Jean-de-Luz, waiting, along with the rest of the court, for the royal marriage. That she never alludes to her surroundings or the reason for her absence in the letters she addresses to her friend Françoise de Motteville is significant, for the letters propose a simultaneous rejection of marriage and life in the world. The correspondence opens with a reference to a recent conversation between them on "the happiness of life in retirement" (3) that seems to echo two key moments in the transition from political to literary activity after the Fronde, the conclusion of Scudéry's revision of the Sapho legend and the incipit of the *Nouvelles françaises* describing Montpensier's own "retreat" to Saint-Fargeau. Subsequent letters make inevitable the comparison with the life Scudéry's Sapho builds for herself in the land of the Sauromates. Together Montpensier and Motteville create a plan for women's conduct: renunciation of the world of the court with its intrigues and its *galanterie* and rejection of marriage, "that which has given men the upper hand" (35), will give them the freedom to create "a corner of the world where women are their own mistresses" (35).[50]

But their ideal community differs from Scudéry's in a crucial way. Sapho's life with the Sauromates is a blueprint for an already beginning future, Scudéry's tribute to the inception of the salon's golden age. Montpensier, on the other hand, writes the script for her projected community at a time when such assemblies are about to become smaller, more informal, less official: Louis XIV would ensure that only one powerful community would exist, and that that community would assemble around him and would be markedly androcentric. With her career as an amazon long behind her, Montpensier "dreamed so sweetly, as [she] walked by the sea" at Saint-Jean-de-Luz (4), and she dreamed a dream she knew had become impossible, for never again would nobles gather together out of their monarch's sight. In Saint-Jean-de-Luz, in

[marginal notes:]
death-knell of salons / female assembly (1660)

marriage of king vs. Montpensier's rejection of marriage (as an institution) in her letters

renunciation of world of court; retreat

Scudéry had described inception of salon life; Montpensier its demise

Montpensier realized that nobles would assemble only around the king

the midst of the festivities for the approaching marriage, the Grande
Mademoiselle apparently saw more clearly than anyone how brutally
still another of her feminocentric worlds would be transformed by her
ever more self-assured cousin with the long memory. The lack of
temporal and geographic precision in her letters is therefore appropriate:
the former heroine of the Fronde, the former organizer of the pleasures
of storytelling, can now dream only of a truly utopian space, a space
outside of time and topography.

Since only the first letter of the Montpensier-Motteville correspondence is dated, the chronology of their exchange cannot be determined.
But on May 14, 1660, in Saint-Jean-de-Luz, the broad outline of the
future must already have been clear. Indeed the next year brought a
rapidly unfolding chain of events that solidified the young monarch's
power and initiated what many consider the true seventeenth century,
what Voltaire termed the century of Louis XIV. In August, Louis and
his new bride Marie-Thérèse returned to Paris in triumph. The following year, Mazarin died and Louis began his absolute reign. He celebrated his expanded powers by beginning construction on the new
wings at Versailles, the palace designed to keep the French aristocracy
together in one community and under one roof, and to keep its principal
members permanently under the king's surveillance. In this way, he
could protect himself against all forms of subversion, from political
sedition to feminocentric academies. As he transformed himself into
Louis le Grand, the king turned his palace into the unique center of
French political and intellectual life. With this single decision, he made
Paris a shadow of its former self. During the Versailles era, seventeenth-
century feminism could never again manifest itself as openly as before.
The tradition of feminist moralistic writing almost ceases, as Maclean
has documented. The absolute reign of Louis XIV marks, in Abensour's
words, "the triumph of other doctrines, all hostile to women's emanci-
pation" (xx).

Despite this context, Montpensier's dream of a female utopia should
be seen not as a nostalgic reminder of a past definitively lost but as a
final revision of the plot for women's history imagined by this infinitely
resourceful and protean woman. In the new city of women she imagines, female plots will be far calmer and less heroic than in the earlier
amazon empires. "Passions are banished" (18) from their "solitude" (28),
their "desert" (13)—thus is joined to the vocabulary of "retreat" and
"retirement" inherited from the literature of the precious decade what

solitude,
desert
retraite
repos...
cabinet

was destined to become the key vocabulary of the next phase of women's writing, the language of inaction, of *repos*. "I want . . . every one of us to have a closet (*un cabinet*) . . . where we would learn . . . to delight in that tranquillity (*repos*) that we will have chosen over the turbulent agitation of the court and the world" (20–21). In an age of absolute monarchy when all assemblies are viewed with suspicion, the new female utopia will be a room of one's own.[51]

≠ inglorious

It is essential to note that this continuing retrenchment, this turning aside and away from the outside world and its activities, is never portrayed as an inglorious alternative. On the contrary, Motteville teases Montpensier that she has "found the means of ornamenting our deserts with pomp and grandeur" (16). And the former amazon worries only that "I will be very bored" when obliged to go to court or the city on business (10). Montpensier sums up her attitude toward this empire for those now deprived of actual estates in a phrase that could serve as the epigraph for the entire seventeenth-century feminist tradition: "Let us celebrate ourselves in the centuries to come by means of a life that will make us live forever" (35). The sentence's impossible temporality reveals the goal of this desert retreat. Montpensier's memoirs testify eloquently to her discovery in her post-Fronde exile of textual pleasures; her correspondence reveals her desire to have those who share her political fate learn "to delight in [their] tranquillity" as she had, by becoming writers. For Montpensier in 1660, just as for Virginia Woolf nearly three centuries later, the closet, the *cabinet,* the room of one's own would allow women to control their own destinies in the present and to leave a legacy for the future—and that legacy, the product of their freedom and their leisure, would be a permanent, written one, the "works that will be brought to light" (9).

tranquillity →
+
writing =
legacy for
future

The last new frontier conquered by women in seventeenth-century France was a separate space intentionally divorced from direct historical or political impact and with purely literary dimensions. In the 1660s and 1670s, while the Sun King was making an ordinary palace into an art form, the next generation of women writers set the novel on a new course. The novel as extended conversation, as written recreation of salon activities, disappears. From a narrative striving to maintain the primacy of an oral tradition and constantly to reenact the passage from oral to written, under the direction of Lafayette, heir apparent to *préciosité* and its chronicler Scudéry, the new novel increasingly divorced itself from traditional oral forms.

w/Lafayette :
↓ oral tradition

In the simplified view of her oeuvre that currently prevails, Lafayette is too often known simply as the author of *La Princesse de Clèves.* In the seventeenth and eighteenth centuries, literary history referred to the enigmatic comtesse as the author of both *La Princesse de Clèves* and *Zayde, histoire espagnole. Zayde* was written in collaboration with Segrais, whose previous collaborative effort with Montpensier, the *Nouvelles françaises,* had heralded the inception of the literature celebrating a female communal existence. Interestingly, however, *Zayde* resembles neither the stories that resulted from the Montpensier-Segrais collaboration nor the new type of fiction called for in the prologue to the *Nouvelles françaises. Zayde, histoire espagnole* is Lafayette's *Clélie, histoire romaine. Clélie* kills the *roman* by depriving it of the action that was its lifeblood; in *Zayde,* Lafayette builds her own funerary monument to the fiction that had dominated the literary horizon during her reign as a young *précieuse. Zayde* is an intentionally retrograde work. When it was published in 1670, less spacious forms—most prominently, Lafayette's own 1662 *La Princesse de Montpensier,* a short fiction that seems cut from the pattern provided by Montpensier-Segrais in the *Nouvelles françaises* —were already displacing Scudéry's longer, more complicated fictional model, and the modern novel was in the process of being created.

Yet *Zayde* is not a new old novel. It is rather an extended narrative echo-chamber, a patchwork of devices and plot twists familiar from the fictions of more heroic days. In its very excessiveness, *Zayde* is intentionally implausible, although not in the manner of a parody. *Zayde* is an exploration of the future for women's fiction at a time when women had lost, first, their official power, and then their independent domains and all but their most private spaces. In the writings that mark the last stage of Scudéry's career, the collections of conversations published in the 1680s, she explains the redefinition of representation under the absolute monarchy. In *Zayde,* Lafayette prefigures her demonstration by exploring alternative inscriptions of women's writing. Lafayette's homage to her precursors is an extended meditation on the interpretation of women's plots and the value of women's stories. In *Zayde,* Lafayette transforms the standard devices of *précieuse* fiction—the conversation, the recital of a life story, the portrait—when she takes them out of the feminocentric setting in which Scudéry showcases them in *Clélie* and illustrates their translation into an androcentric literary universe more closely related to the political context taking shape in Lafayette's day.

The lesson of *Zayde,* this crucial shift of focus, reveals Lafayette as the first writer able to take the woman's novel as a given, an already constituted literary entity. In the interval between *Zayde* and *La Princesse de Clèves,* Louis XIV was undergoing an elaborate process of self-transformation, making himself into the Sun King, a dazzling representation of the systematic mechanization of power that was the hallmark of his reign. Historians of Louis's monarchy from Voltaire to Ferrier-Caverivière see 1678 as the turning point in his monarchy: after the peace of Nimwegen it became increasingly evident that Louis the Great's thirst for conquest would not be checked by a desire to bring prosperity and security to his subjects.

The year 1678 also saw the publication of the text generally referred to as the first modern novel. *La Princesse de Clèves* is the culmination of a feminist tradition nearly a century old. The novel closes just as the regency of Catherine de' Medici is beginning, allowing Lafayette's princesse to take up her life in retirement during a period of official female political rule. Furthermore, the princesse has read the stories of Marguerite de Navarre (89), so the prehistory of seventeenth-century women's literature is also evoked. Lafayette, heir to the splendid century of women's accomplishments, situates her most famous fiction at the dawn of that era. She portrays her title character's initiation into the plots of women's fiction and the process by which she seeks control over her own story. In the context of seventeenth-century women's writing, Lafayette's masterpiece can be seen as both a miniaturization of Scudéry's *précieuse* epic and a continuation of the recurrent debates of the salon era—on, for example, marriage, inconstancy, the necessity of a lover's discretion. Lafayette demonstrated that if women no longer ruled over armed camps and fortified places, or even over their private fortresses in the salons, they had won definitive control over a literary territory. The ultimate women's space in seventeenth-century France is the modern novel, a construct, as the theoretician Huet saw as early as 1670, entirely of their creation, a product of the determination of several generations of *femmes fortes* to conquer a permanent domain. Lafayette brought the woman's novel out of the closed circle of the female academy and into the claustrophobia of the male-dominated political arena, and in so doing she won for the predecessors whose work lives on in hers a measure of the more permanent glory that was the Grande Mademoiselle's utopian dream.

LA COUR ET LA VILLE

Pour la propriété des moeurs, le poète doit considérer qu'il ne faut jamais
introduire sans nécessité absolue, ni une fille vaillante, ni une femme
savante, ni un valet judicieux. Car encore que ces parties se recontrent
quelquefois en ce sexe et dans ce métier, il est néanmoins véritable qu'il
y a peu de Sapphos, encore aussi peu d'Amazones.

Jules de La Mesnardière,
Poétique (1640)

AT THE beginning of this history of women's spaces, I noted that in
1646–1647, in a central gallery in Mazarin's palace, Apollo was portrayed surrounded by Parisian *précieuses* occupying the muses' places.
During his rule as prime minister, Mazarin had fulfilled many of the
functions in the republic of letters formerly carried out by his predecessor, Richelieu. He was, for example, a collector of paintings and art
objects, many of which were displayed in his palace. One of the former
prime minister's roles not continued by his successor, however, was that
of patron of the Académie Française. Upon Richelieu's death, the Académie's meetings were transferred from Richelieu's palace to the hôtel of
the Chancelier Séguier, where they were held until Louis XIV brought
the Académie under direct royal control by giving it a home in the
Louvre. Had Mazarin taken over the protection of the Académie Française from Richelieu, in all likelihood its assemblies would have taken
place in the palais Mazarin, the palace crowned, as it were, by the
apotheosis of contemporary female, not male, intellectuals. No setting
could have been more appropriate for the change in that august assembly's composition that almost took place shortly after Mazarin's palace
was endowed with a visual encomium to female intellectual influence.

We know that sometime in the 1650s two prominent literary figures,
Ménage, Lafayette's and Sévigné's teacher and Scudéry's friend, and
Charpentier, a close friend of Scudéry's lifelong companion, Pellisson,
nominated a number of women intellectuals for admission to that
body.[52] Their list was headed by Madeleine de Scudéry, who (as a
consolation prize?) was in 1671 the recipient of the Académie's first
prize for eloquence for her "Discours de la gloire."[53] Antoinette Deshoulières was almost certainly nominated at the same time. (She became the only woman admitted to a seventeenth-century French academy when she was elected to the Académie d'Arles in 1689.)[54] Further-

more, the idea that women deserved membership in the Académie Française did not die with the failure of the Ménage-Charpentier proposal. In 1695, when La Bruyère's turn to vote on a vacancy came, he is reported to have given his vote to André Dacier (a noted classicist), while adding, "I would prefer his wife [Anne Dacier, perhaps the most celebrated Hellenist of the day], if you admitted to your ranks persons of her sex" (d'Ortigue 1194). Given the apparently genuine support for female intellectual achievements that many male intellectuals of the period frequently demonstrated, the early members surely must not have determined the exclusion of the first female candidates as simply as subsequent generations of academicians rejected future women intellectuals over the course of the next three centuries. During the early years of the Académie Française, women—not just a handful of "exceptional" women, but significant numbers of women—had defied the traditionally accepted behavioral code given an extreme expression in the epigraph to this section and had become first-class citizens in the republic of letters.

Contemporary Italian learned societies admitted women intellectuals to their ranks as a matter of course—in the words of one of their early French female members to her colleagues in the Academy of the Ricovrati in Padua, "You do not assume a distinction that heaven and nature never had the intention of making between men and us" (Salvan de Saliez, cited in Vertron 1:145–46).[55] Scudéry was the first "illustrious French lady" admitted to the Paduan academy, but a number of others eventually shared this distinction with her.

Furthermore, as Frances Yates has shown, women were also allowed admission to the sixteenth-century French assemblies that provided, in her words, "the first sketch for the French Academy."[56] Yates lists numbers of assemblies in which women participated and cites D'Aubigné's tribute to the quality of female participation (32). Her thesis is that the academic movement of the Renaissance was brought to an end when the country was torn apart by wars of religion; she maintains that "the academies, nevertheless, managed to hand on their tradition to the seventeenth century" (35).

If this is so, why was the practice of admitting women not a part of the tradition "handed on"? Yates seems to suggest that women were excluded when the subject matter for academic discussion was redefined. In her presentation of the women admitted to perhaps the most noted Renaissance assembly, the Palace Assembly, she quotes D'Aubigné's account of the participation of Madame de Retz and Madame de Lignerolles: "These two gave proof that they understood things better than words" (32). According to Yates, the seventeenth-century French academic tradition is devoted above all to a linguistic function, "the study and refinement of the French language": from this point on, the study of "words" is divorced from the study of "things" or "ideas" (291). Although Yates never says so directly, she implies that women were better suited to the earlier academic mode, which she obviously sees as superior to its later variant (291, n.1).

However, it seems more likely that this exclusion was a conscious *[XVIIe s. / exclusion / probably / conscious]* decision on the part of those who in 1634 designed the model seven- *[probably / conscious]* teenth-century academy—the academy they designated as eponymous with the French nation rather than, according to previous practice, with a city alone. Women had plotted actively against its founder, Cardinal Richelieu. Undoubtedly influenced by this personal political history, Richelieu inscribed this maxim in his *Testament politique:* "A woman *[by Richelieu / in part]* caused the world's fall; nothing is more capable of harming the State *[in part]* than this sex" (301). Such an individual would not have been inclined to give women a new power base, especially not a *droit de cité* in the assembly designed to be the foundation of the absolute monarchy's intellectual glory. And Richelieu's reasoning would have been even more strictly applied in the aftermath of the Fronde, the most spectacu- lar upheaval in the French body politic ever inspired by women. The cardinal's *Testament politique* also contains this evaluation of what he presented as the indissoluble bond between women and cabals: "Most unsettling factions come into being because of women's hard work (*industrie*)" (370).

Subsequent histories of what became known as France's Golden Age prove that Richelieu's design was realized. When, for example, Charles *[Perrault's / history starts / w/ Académie / française / excludes ?]* Perrault prepared his overview of the age just as the Splendid Century *[history starts]* came to an end, he started the practice of beginning what Voltaire called *[w/ Académie / française]* "the century of Louis XIV" with the foundation of the Académie *[excludes ?]* Française. Perrault called his compilation *Les Hommes illustres* (1700, 1701), proving that the exclusionary gesture of the century's founding intellectual body would be ratified by the official histories of the Golden Age, in which no women would figure in the ranks of its most illus- trious citizens. At the same time as the offical histories were erasing female intellectual accomplishments, by the end of the century, as we will see, an abundant critical discourse had been drawn up to demonstrate that, just as women had proved a political threat during the reign of the *frondeuse* amazons, so women writers posed a continuing threat to the integrity of the French state.

Perhaps it was the outbreak of the Fronde the year after Romanelli completed his ceiling painting of the *précieuse* muses that, by temporarily allowing women extraordinary political power, cost them official literary recognition. Had Madeleine de Scudéry been allowed to flourish in still another assembly, and women therefore been a part of the Académie Française almost from its origin, the future course of French letters would have been profoundly and radically altered. French women writers might have continued to know the exceptional situation they enjoyed initially, that of belonging not to a separate tradition but simply to the tradition of writing not otherwise or against dominant male discourse but of writing still as women, but somehow "samewise." Three centuries after the original exclusion, in 1981, Marguerite Yourcenar would simply have entered the Académie Française as a matter of course and would not have begun her reception speech by describing herself as "accompanied by an invisible troop of women who should perhaps have received this honor sooner, to the extent that I am tempted to stand aside to let their shades go first" (10). Had Yourcenar been standing in the palace Mazarin built during his own lifetime, rather than in one whose construction was provided for by his will, she could have pointed to the faces of her anonymous seventeenth-century precursors as representations of the shades of her not yet forgotten ancestors.[57]

2
ಞ
The Politics of Tenderness: Madeleine de Scudéry and the Generation of 1640–1660

"Naming the Unnameable"

This nameless mode of naming the unnameable is rather
good.   Mary Shelley[1]

La réalité de l'île ... est désignée par un nom qui s'annule
lui-même comme appellation propre. La négation ne porte
pas sur le référent du nom, mais sur le nom lui-même
qui, du même coup, désigne un référent "autre."
                                        Louis Marin,
                                        Utopiques

IN THE course of a meeting to discuss my progress on this book, my
editor at Columbia University Press, Jennifer Crewe, described a conversation she had overheard in an elevator: one undergraduate student
was asking another if she knew that *La Princesse de Clèves* (recently
added to the syllabus for the required undergraduate course, Masterpieces of European Literature and Philosophy) had really been written
by a man, La Rochefoucauld. The anecdote is to my mind a fitting
reminder of what, in its broadest definition, may well be the major
obstacle to a proper appreciation of seventeenth-century women's writing, the problem of literary collaboration.

Critics have only recently become attentive to collaborative literary
ventures, to the politics, and in particular the erotics, of the act of
making books together.[2] To date, only modern literary partnerships

[margin note: ? of literary collaboration]

[margin note: politics/erotics]

have been studied, collaborations that are well documented and in which the limits of each partner's participation are at least fairly clearly understood. However, when we consider collaborative creation in the early modern period, it quickly becomes apparent that, in the absence of elaborate documentation, critics simply have no generally accepted standard for assigning value to an individual author's reputation on account of his or her participation in a literary partnership. When in doubt, critics have always taken the easy way out and simply given full credit to one author, generally the better known of the partners—in most cases, the male collaborator. Thus, Segrais is said to be the author of the *Nouvelles françaises,* rather than Montpensier, and the rumor that La Rochefoucauld was really *the* author of *La Princesse de Clèves* has persistently recurred through the centuries.

All such attributions are based on a modern conception not only of literary collaboration but of authorship and authorial identity as well. However, everything we know about the actual production of every important model for early French prose fiction indicates that these collaborations are far more complex than the ventures now associated with that term. Already in the sixteenth century, in the circle of the poets known as the Dames des Roches, for example, the foundations for the practice I call salon writing were established when members of a literary assembly participated actively in the elaboration of each other's creations: a work was initially circulated only among the members, who proposed suggestions for revision.[3] Then, when the work was finally made available to the public at large, the preferred vehicle was the collective volume or anthology, a format in which individual authorial identity was subordinated to an aggregate presence.

In the course of the seventeenth century, the influence of the collective on literary production became ever more pronounced. The quintessential French literary côterie, the salon, was codified as a feminocentric and politically active assembly just when the French tradition of literary collaboration dramatically shifted course: during the seventeenth century, for the only time in their history, French côteries were far less likely to collaborate on poetry, the literary production most readily adaptable to collective creation. On the contrary, seventeenth-century salons most often generated prose fiction. This production on a more expansive scale necessitated literary partnerships far more intricate than those formed around verse creations such as the Hôtel de Rambouillet's "Guirlande de Julie."

Madeleine de Scüdéry's novels provide the clearest illustration of this phenomenon. Because of their vast scale and their tight production schedule (between 1200 and 1500 pages appeared approximately every six months in the case of *Artamène*), it is difficult to imagine that one *Scüdéry's prolixity, eq — how much < Georges?* person could have created every aspect of these gigantic novels. The traditional view of Scudéry as collaborator depicts her in partnership with her brother Georges; for centuries, critics have assigned shares in the enterprise and pronounced, for example, Georges the principal author, or Madeleine the sole author, or indicated fixed limits to the brother's collaboration—the first seven volumes of *Artamène,* or the first five, and so on.[4] Critics have no surviving documentary evidence to support their views; only rarely do they offer stylistic analyses to back up their claims, and, even then, only superficial ones. Their theories appear to be based solely on either their sense of the subjects that only a man would be competent to treat (battle scenes are the classic example) or their opinion of the relative authorial merits of brother and sister.

Literary scholars have almost never considered the possibility of a broader, less definable collaboration.[5] However, if one considers the range of subjects and settings included in each immense novel, and if one thinks of the research necessary for the level of documentation maintained throughout, the participation of numbers of individuals in *logically, huge novels => participation of numbers of individuals* this vast literary enterprise seems an inevitable conclusion.[6] The members of Scudéry's salon included a number of the most prominent contemporary scholars, in particular, Huet, Ménage, and Pellisson. Collaboration on her fiction would have been a logical extension of their literary discussions in her salon. Huet, to cite but one example, was perhaps the finest Hellenist of the century; he also possessed particular expertise in ancient military history, especially naval history.[7] Scudéry's vast novels are the most elaborate product of seventeenth-century French salon writing: they could only have been completed with the collaboration of writers responsible for specific questions. We cannot be certain that the actual writing was also a joint venture. However, in all the seventeenth-century côteries from which novels were generated it was common to circulate manuscripts for suggested rewrites.

Salon writing was always women's writing. A few seventeenth-century male novelists, Paul Scarron, for example, opened their homes *# men who preside either over a salon or over literary collaboration* to literary gatherings. However, no salon was ever presided over by a man, nor were novels such as Scarron's *Roman comique* collaborative ventures. Contemporary male writers, for instance Gautier de Costes de

La Calprenède, also authored *romans fleuves,* but not in conjunction with literary collectives. Only the women writers who also presided over salons combined these dual literary functions to produce salon writing.

The earliest instance of salon writing occurred at the Princesse de Conti's court-in-exile at her château, Eu. The three novels that resulted from this collaboration were published under the names of different authors. There has never been a consensus about their attribution: some critics give credit for all production to the aristocratic lady who was the center of the court, while others portray the men of lesser rank who call themselves her scribes as the novels' authors. However, because of what they perceive as the need to identify a single author, critics may well be missing the point.

In 1701 Charlotte-Rose Caumont de La Force composed *Les Jeux d'Esprit,* subtitled *La Promenade de la Princesse de Conti à Eu,* a self-conscious exploration of the process of making novels together.[8] La Force depicts the members of the princesse's salon-in-exile participating in a series of literary pastimes that culminates in "the game of the novel": La Force's fiction about the making of fiction is the only contemporary account of salon writing. The participants decide to compose a historical novel. After having first selected Piloust (often credited with authorship of the actual novels created at Eu) to write up the proceedings "in an organized fashion" (73), they jointly choose a period and the principal characters. The friends then participate in the communal oral creation of a novel: one takes up where the other leaves off, each in turn "authoring" a segment of their tale. With the exception of occasional interruptions to fine-tune a twist of plot or to decide who should take over the storytelling, the novel unfolds seamlessly, as though it had been invented, rather than merely being transcribed, by a single writer. When she blends one author's voice into the next, La Force reproduces the most uncanny aspect of salon writing, its devalorization of individual creativity. Instead the personal is made subservient to the collective literary will, the collaborative project that celebrates the shared life in the salon.

In 1683 Du Plaisir (undoubtedly thinking in particular of *La Princesse de Clèves*) provided the first critical assessment of the stylistic ideal that had been imposed by salon writing, what he termed "writing nobly" (*écrire noblement*). In such collaborative efforts, "one style would be less different from another; several people could undertake the same work together, and some would finish easily that which others had begun"

(99). Du Plaisir's modern editor, Hourcade, dismisses what he terms a "uniform style" as an "illusion of the age" (99, n.74), but this is to refuse to recognize the reality of salon writing. The taste for collaborative writing prevalent in seventeenth-century literary assemblies thwarts the twentieth-century desire to classify classical French prose fiction, to attribute each text to one author and to assign limits to the participation of collaborators. Neither La Force's description nor Du Plaisir's can be considered an exact account of these joint endeavors, but each suggests reasons why, for example, it is impossible to decide when the Princesse de Conti should be given sole responsibility for a novel rather than her salon's official secretary, Piloust, or to distinguish Madeleine de Scudéry's style from that of her brother—or to stamp out the rumor that La Rochefoucauld "really" authored *La Princesse de Clèves*.

Seventeenth-century writers often began their careers by publishing, in most cases anonymously, in the collective volumes—of portraits, of letters, of assorted prose fragments—that were their century's equivalent of the previous century's verse compilations.[9] This collective initiation into writing fostered a lack of concern with individual authorial privileges, an undermining of the importance of the signature, and finally a definition of the author as director or animator of a creative enterprise. When considering anonymous publication, modern critics assume that "Anon," to borrow Virginia Woolf's expression, is always a single author and, furthermore, that the absence of a signature generally signals an aristocratic author, since aristocrats, or so the dominant line of reasoning goes, would have felt shame at being associated with an activity unworthy of their rank.[10]

But if this perception were correct, how can we explain the fact that so many aristocrats participated with vigor in the production of the novels that came out of seventeenth-century salons? Critics who promote the view of literature as déclassé never imagine that aristocrats might have considered literary activity as very much of their class and still have been unwilling to advertise their association with it. The time for the extensive salon collaboration essential to the production of novels rather than poems was most often the result of political exile.[11] In particular, the vogue of collective writing in the late 1650s and early 1660s that proved vital to the French literary tradition resulted from the leisure forced on ex-*frondeurs*. Segrais described the 1659 *Recueil des portraits et éloges* as the "general confession" of "our" painters (iii). When these literary painters laid bare their souls, the sins revealed were

THE POLITICS OF TENDERNESS

exile =>

Salon-writing = soul-bearing

political. Salon writing is the collective soul-baring of the concerns of a generation, in seventeenth-century France most often that of the ex-*frondeurs*. Its collective signature provided them with a means of protection, a convenient camouflage for the identities of individuals recently punished for their exposure on the political scene. Both the collective

anonymous =) no one person responsible

volumes and the novels published from manuscripts revised throughout their circulation were in effect beyond individual authorial identity— and responsibility.

In addition, the assumption that literary activity was considered a déclassé activity is based on the belief that aristocrats wished to prevent outsiders from enjoying the privileges of their rank. However, evidence (most prominently, Lougee's) about the seventeenth-century salons indicates that the nobles who participated in these assemblies were not

Salon as equalizing force — bourgeois on par with aristocrats

driven by this obsession: on the contrary, they frequently used the salon as a medium to enable bourgeois to pass to higher rank. (Sometimes this passage was formal, as a result of the marriages between bourgeois and aristocrats that Lougee documents; sometimes it meant the informal freedom granted the writer to treat social superiors as intellectual equals, or even inferiors.) The most active salons such as Scudéry's operated in effect as social levelers to blur the demarcations of a normally rigid class system: because of shared literary and political views, the members of a salon functioned as though they constituted a socially homogeneous group.[12] Everything known about the behavior of the aristocrats who chose to function in seventeenth-century literary assemblies indicates that many of them were willing to accord the privileges of aristocracy to the artist. They thereby participated in an enterprise evident in the political fabric of the Sun King's reign whenever reformers attempted to transform the French class system along the lines of a meritocracy.

subversive

The salon enabled rebellious aristocrats to continue their politics of subversion in less visible ways.

In these circumstances, the authorial signature does not have the meaning we are accustomed to grant it. "Mr de Scudéry," the controversial mark found on every volume of the novels and always interpreted simply as the signature of either the brother or the sister, represents instead the collective signature of the salon presided over by Madeleine.

"author" => the woman who presided over salon where work was composed

In instances of salon writing, I take the signature to stand for a particular woman—Princesse de Conti, Comtesse de Lafayette, and so forth— not as sole author of the entire work, but in a sense of the term that disappeared along with the salons: the "author" is the woman who presided over the salon in which the novel developed, she who dictated the style of the salon, the style that lives on in each of these extended exercises in writing the politics of a salon.[13]

By introducing the concept of salon writing, I am in effect arguing that seventeenth-century France witnessed the appearance of two very different types of writers. To date, critics—most prominently, Alain Viala in *La Naissance de l'écrivain*—have concentrated on those writers whose motivations and careers are most readily comprehensible in twentieth-century terms. The second type of author, authors who came to writing as part of a collective, is far more elusive. Clearly the existence of this second category facilitated the advancement of women writers, although not for the reason generally accepted (they were too modest to write on their own). Explanations of salon writing's particular usefulness for women will become evident throughout the following chapters, but I will suggest two very different reasons now. Throughout the seventeenth century, women intellectuals were among those most seriously compromised in political conspiracies, among those, therefore, who would find the protection afforded by the collective most appealing. In addition, since women had only limited opportunities for formal education, they often needed the resources the collective put at the disposal of the writer who directed it.

Both the amount of control over the entire enterprise and the type of participation requested from others varied enormously from author to author. In the following pages, rather than attempt a detailed account of the vast literary production that can be assembled under the name Madeleine de Scudéry, I pursue a more modest goal: to characterize Scudéry's salon writing, especially those elements that combined to make her such an essential figure for subsequent women writers, and also those elements (often the same) that early critics of the novel found so threatening.[14]

In particular, I want to define the factor that made Madeleine de Scudéry a major literary force for several generations of writers, her ability to give the novel an interiority that readers found both new and accurate. In the domain in which Scudéry's accuracy was recognized, that of interpersonal relations and especially of love, she can be said to have initiated a new strain of what would come to be known as realism, a realism with which women writers of the ancien régime would continue to maintain a close association. I will refer to this realism as "psychological" or "affective" in order to avoid the pejorative connotations associated with "sentimental," the vocabulary coined in the early eighteenth century when critics were trying to account for the prominence of *sensibilité*.[15] Psychological realism is the net result of Scudéry's vast literary project, of her allegorical mapping of the land she called Tenderness (figure 7).

Scudéry's tender geography has been enshrined in literary history as a mere bagatelle, the frivolous pastime of idle aristocrats. This recollection is founded on a deliberate forgetting, that of the political content of Scudéry's Tenderness, the content that would have appealed to aristocrats idle only because their attempted revolution had come so close to success. Scudéry's tender geography is simultaneously a mapping of emotions and affective choices and a demonstration of the politics of tenderness, the inscription of the affective realm on the political map.

"SISTER OF THE AUTHOR WITH THE SAME NAME"

> Personne ne sait mieux que moi ce que [Madeleine de Scudéry] vaut, car je l'ai faite ce qu'elle est.
>
> Georges de Scudéry,
> letter to Anne de Rohan-Soubise,
> abbesse de Caen, April 7, 1660

IF ANYTHING "made" the writer whom Boileau scornfully referred to as "the sister of the author with the same name" (*O.c.* 444), it was surely nothing so simple as a partnership with a single male writer whose greater experience enabled her authorial rite of passage. There is no evidence whatsoever of timidity in Madeleine de Scudéry's "coming to writing"; the early works, on the contrary, are remarkable for their impressive range and bold innovativeness. During the initial phase of her career (1641 to approximately 1649), prior to the years of salon writing with the aid of an extended support system, Scudéry composed small-scale works dominated by a single creative impulse, the desire to offer an alternative to the traditional literary vision of female conduct. A brief consideration of two early works reveals tendencies evident throughout her vast production.

When Ellen Moers traces the origin of the phenomenon she terms "heroinism," the telling of "the woman's side of the love story in her own words," she declares that "the letter form is central" (160, 147). She has in mind what may well be the most influential fiction of female desire in modern times, the foundation of both the epistolary novel and the vision of women's writing that the letter novel succeeded in imposing, for nearly a century and a half, as the archetypal image of the female literary style. This fiction, established in the seventeenth and eighteenth centuries by epistolary writers inspired by their tradition's canonical text, Ovid's *Heroides,* promoted a formula whose success can only mean that contemporary readers found in it a convincing construction of gender: the equation of Woman in love with Woman seduced and abandoned. In this founding vision of heroism, when Woman writes, when she tells her "side of the love story in her own words," it is always a tale of lamentation, the litany of the woes of one forsaken addressed to the man who has left her behind.

Scudéry inaugurated her literary career with a forceful response to the Ovidian model. The 1641 collection, *Lettres amoureuses de divers auteurs de ce temps,* marks an intermediate stage between the letter manuals that proliferated during the first half of the seventeenth century and the epistolary novels whose vogue began only when the popularity of the manuals began to abate. Her collection is composed of seven series of epistles, each addressed by an abandoned lover to the agent of betrayal—who offers no reply to the pleading missives. Rather than repeat the already familiar tale of female amorous suffering, however, Scudéry reverses the Ovidian model: the unhappy speaking subjects are all men, while women play the role of the absent agents of their humiliation.

Just a year later she offered a renewed attack on the epistolary model identifying women's writing with complaining abandonment that was her century's most popular fiction of female desire. *Les Femmes illustres, ou les harangues héroïques* (1642) is a collection of first-person accounts that are almost identical to the allegedly spontaneous outpourings of the then dominant epistolary model. Scudéry's illustrious women, however, pour out their passion not to win back a delinquent lover who would take pity on their suffering but in order to provide their side of tales already told by others, to supply that which has been left out of traditional historical accounts. Like Ovid, Scudéry presents the stories of female figures from antiquity, including some of the same women, notably Sappho, already fictionalized by Ovid. She gives them voice for one of two reasons: first, to allow them to stand outside the shadows cast by their more celebrated husbands or lovers (thus Scudéry's Arté-

[margin notes:]
form = often letters

Lettres amoureuses

Scudéry reverses: MEN speak of their humiliation in love via letters

Femmes illustres

to tell their part to fill in faulty historical accounts

mise is presented as the widow of King Mausole, who had built for himself a mausoleum so magnificent that it became known as one of the seven wonders of the world and forged the association between his name and such enterprises—Artémise desires to speak in order to create her own type of funerary monument); second, to allow them to set aside previous historical accounts (thus her Mariamne is able to defend herself against the accusation of infidelity by revealing all that was omitted by historians attempting to "flatter" her husband Hérodes [18]). When they are given the opportunity to speak for themselves, Scudéry's heroines protest the slanders of history and attempt to vindicate themselves. Their collective testimonies demonstrate resoundingly that female auto-biographical speech could be far removed from the pitiful cries of abandonment: in one of the most memorable harangues, Cloelia (later, newly Gallicized as "Clélie," the heroine of Scudéry's salon epic) defends her exploits through a comparison of female and male heroism in which she concludes that posterity will judge them equal.

That judgment is the message of this volume, the only one of Scudéry's works to contain the adjective "heroic" in its title. This epithet is frequently associated with Scudéry's prose, more often than with that of any other writer of her century. However, critics never follow Scudéry's own placement of heroic: they elide the feminocentric heroic of *Les Femmes illustres* and speak only of Scudéry's "heroic novels" (*romans héroïques*). They thereby eliminate her initial literary efforts in order to present a streamlined image of her production according to which Scudéry is remembered in literary history only as the author of works both epic in proportion and, initially at least, homocentric.[16]

Scudéry must have begun her first "heroic" novel, *Ibrahim, ou l'il-lustre bassa,* while completing the *Lettres amoureuses,* since it was pub-lished less than four months after the epistolary collection (and thus a year before *Les Femmes illustres*). In the early 1640s, therefore, Scudéry came to writing with a period of intense activity that was also a period of literary experimentation: the writer who, more than any other, made the historical novel the dominant seventeenth-century form initially hesitated between the epistolary and the historical mode. Scudéry began her career by trying out three very distinctive prototypes for the fledg-ling French tradition of prose fiction. Of the three, the initial audience clearly preferred the work with the most familiar format and the only work without a feminist perspective, *Ibrahim.* However, *Ibrahim* is not yet really a typical Scudéry novel: it is relatively short (four volumes of

THE POLITICS OF TENDERNESS

portrait,
conversation ⟩ ⟹ *anti-*
narrative
stance

400–500 pages each, making it approximately a sixth as long as *Artamène*) and does not contain the set pieces (the portrait, the conversation)
that are the foundation of the antinarrative stance that is her contribution to the genre. *Ibrahim* offers fast-paced, action-oriented adventures
set in exotic locales—evidently the escapist formula that the public was
hungry for, to judge from the numerous reeditions and translations that
quickly followed. It is, both from a seventeenth-century perspective and
from today's, the most traditional of Scudéry's novels, the work considered by a recent critic her best-organized and most readable novel
(Godenne 40). After the creative flurry of 1640–1642, Scudéry entered
the only prolonged silence of her career. Some seven years later she
returned to the literary scene amid the political turmoil of the nascent
Fronde. From that political crisis was generated her mature literary
voice, her particular mode of salon writing.

early writings,
silence,
Fronde,
salon writing

Another tradition refers to Scudéry's novels as *romans de longue
haleine.*[17] Both designations, "heroic novel" and "long-winded" novel,
indicate above all the work that literary history has pronounced Scudéry's archetypal production, *Artamène, ou le Grand Cyrus* (1649–1653).
In *Artamène,* more intricately than in any other work, Scudéry develops
her model for historical fiction. The novel is historical in that its setting
in antiquity is based on extensive research. It is also historical because it
is an *à clef* work, in which complex correspondences have been worked
out to identify figures from antiquity with the principal participants in
the central drama of the time of its composition, the Fronde. This
double historical focus was the enabling structure for the dual purpose
Scudéry assigned her novels. Extensive use of classical sources made her
fiction pedagogical (*Correspondance* 295). The parallels with contemporary history guaranteed that, in the highly charged atmosphere of a
period of civil war, the work would be read as a political allegory on
history in the making. In the wake of *Artamène,* until well into the
eighteenth century, the decision to write historical fiction almost invariably was accompanied by the desire to have the fictional setting decoded
as a reference to contemporary political events.

Artamène —
historical
fiction
setting research:
novel = à clef

dual purpose:
1) pedagogical
2) fictional
setting →
contemp
politics

Artamène established a second standard for prose fiction. The reader
attentive to the narrative unfolding of this immense novel witnesses
Scudéry's gradual discovery of the ways in which she could modify the
form now known as the heroic novel by introducing techniques borrowed from her initial formulation of a female heroic. In form and in
content, *Ibrahim* closely resembles the production of the leading contem-

During the
writing of it:
constant
modification
of techniques

porary male novelists, La Calprenède and Marin Le Roy de Gomber-ville. It is action-oriented, centered on the exploits of its hero and his doubles; the only major departure from this active focus is Scudéry's more extensive use of intercalated stories, the retrospective accounts of characters' lives that are a legacy of the epic tradition. Yet these accounts are almost indistinguishable from the frame narrative: the content and the narrative organization of the novel's two components are essentially the same.

Initially, Scudéry does not alter this successful formula for *Artamène*. In the course of the novel's unfolding, however, she introduces with increasing frequency two new forms, the portrait and the conversation, intended to produce a radical disruption of the narrative flow. As we have seen, these forms no longer equate character development with the recital of exploits and achievements: they replace the pure exteriority of the traditional heroic format with an increased emphasis on interiority —certainly not in the fullness to which more recent fiction has accustomed us, but to a then unprecedented degree. Rather than simply moving from one adventure to the next, characters begin to reveal their thoughts on various subjects, what they value in other human beings, their codes and rules of personal conduct. When, in *Artamène*'s final volumes, Scudéry shifts the spotlight from the life of the warrior-king Cyrus to that of the woman writer Sapho, all the elements are in place for the redefinition of the traditional heroic novel she completes in *Clélie*.

Scudéry's realignment of prose fiction parallels the gradual extinction of the aristocratic hopes for political reform during the collapse of the Fronde. Her decision to privilege a female heroic and a sphere of action in which Cloelia's prophecy in *Les Femmes illustres* could be realized and female exploits judged the equal of male marks a return to her initial literary impulse, the determination to force fictional models to accommodate a fiction of the feminine based on female accomplishments rather than on complaining abandonment. Scudéry's revision of her age's stereotype of heroic action explains the violent attacks critics leveled first against her and subsequently against French women writers in general for nearly a century after *Artamène*'s publication. It also prepared the way for *Clélie, histoire romaine*.

Clélie (1654–1660) is Scudéry's most original work. It is also the clearest illustration ever of salon writing as a collective literary expression, writing beyond any individual authorial voice. In *Clélie,* Scudéry makes the two nonnarrative components found in *Artamène,* the conversation and the portrait, her fictional staples until, in sections of the novel, characters seem to live in order to converse, and action is virtually limited to the displacement from the setting for one conversation to the next. It is at these moments, when the novel is least novelistic, that the time-honored critique of what Boileau in its initial formulation termed Scudéry's "endless empty talk about love" (*O.c.* 445) seems most comprehensible. However, it is also possible to evaluate the narrative mode of *Clélie* as another facet of Scudéry's complex political project.

Jean Rousset made readers sensitive to Scudéry's elaborately staged avoidance of first-person narration, the convoluted excuses invented to explain why characters are never able to tell their own stories. If we highlight the distrust of the first person most prominently displayed in a passage from *Clélie*—"When one tells one's own story, everything that one says to one's advantage is suspicious to those who are listening; ... so that it is a thousand times more reasonable to have a third person do the telling than to tell oneself" (2:1378)—Scudéry could be seen as foreshadowing the Jansenist condemnation of self-representation on moral grounds.[18] However, the description does not suit Scudéry's literary project.

Clélie has been widely hailed as the central monument of *préciosité:* Backer considers the six years during which it was published coextensive with the golden age of the French salon tradition. Two years into that publication, another document that has been referred to as "a manifesto of the *précieux*" (Adam, "Ecole de 1650" 147) appeared, a forty-page preface to an edition of the poetry of Jean-François Sarasin dedicated to Scudéry by her companion and collaborator for more than forty years, Paul Pellisson. Pellisson is explicitly paying tribute to Sarasin's genius, but the terms of his dedication to Scudéry—he wants to honor her "publicly" for her "extraordinary learning and accomplishments"— invite the reader to include her in the eulogy. Certainly, the qualities Pellisson values in Sarasin—protean facility, the ability to move easily from prose to verse, an emphasis on urbanity (34–35)—also qualify Scudéry's style.

In particular, Pellisson contends that, while literature that strives for "sublimity" should of course be highly prized, there should be room for a second literary ideal, creations on a more "human" scale designed to distract a worldly readership from its day-to-day cares. The model writer in this mode is simultaneously a prodigy in the ways of literature and in those of the world. Pellisson departs from the standard critical practice of privileging literary timelessness over timeliness when he defends the seriousness of worldly creations: they can "distract the Prince and his minister from the cares of state"; they can serve the "public good" and help ensure that "citizens can live together in virtue, peace, and contentment" (38). Given his status as privileged observer, it seems likely that Pellisson's eulogy of salon writing as an extended lesson in civic virtue represents an authorized version of Scudéry's literary project.

The dominant feature of Scudéry's vast novelistic enterprise is the erasure of the identity of the individual literary subject. In *Artamène,* this process concerns exclusively the third person. The sidestepping of autobiographical accounts—as well as such devices as the replacement of proper names with pronouns whenever possible and the multiplication of intercalated tales, each of which introduces a new possible referent for every pronoun without a proper name—creates a narrative surface dominated by often unclearly defined "he's" and "she's." In *Clélie,* the situation is stranger still. Scudéry makes what may well be the major stylistic innovation in the early development of the novel when she introduces conversations on a large scale. However, Scudéry's conversations seem almost to undermine the form's normal functioning. Since speaking styles are generally not differentiated, the demarcations among characters are rarely precise; the reader is confronted once again with a mass of referentially unbound, nearly free-floating pronouns, this time in the first person.

Modern readers, accustomed to the easy identification of character, have a tendency to dismiss this style as characteristic of the prehistory of the modern novel, when novelists had not yet learned how to create distinct speaking styles. In Scudéry's case, however, the effacement of individual character identity inevitably calls to mind the erasure of individual authorial identity in salon writing and suggests that the at times bewildering multiplication of unbound pronouns may be an intentional strategy rather than a sign of literary naïveté. For example, the same intentional severing of the pronoun-referent bond and the resulting lack of individual identity are also evident in *La Princesse de Clèves,* a novel now valued for its stylistic sophistication.[19] In the case of *La Princesse de Clèves,* modern readers readily view the court of Henri II as a transparent reference to the "magnificence and gallantry" of that of the Sun King and thus are quick to admit that devices such as the elimination of pronouns may be intentionally bewildering in order to imply an ideological message so threatening that it could not be directly expressed. If we view Lafayette as following Scudéry's example, we might understand both the anxious impatience with which Scudéry's seventeenth-century readers awaited each installment of her novels and Pellisson's assessment of salon writing as an incitement to civic virtue.[20]

In *Artamène,* the accumulation of third-person pronouns suggests that characters may be divided into categories—great warriors, untrustworthy ministers, rebel princes—and that the actions of any character in a given category may have implications for his or her doubles. When thus reconfigured, so that, for example, the actions of all the rebel princes add up to a complex central type, *Artamène* can be seen as an indirect commentary on the politics of civil war. In *Clélie,* conversation increasingly dominates action, indicating that the scene of aristocratic power has shifted from the battlefield to the salon. The concomitant domination of the printed page by first-person pronouns almost beyond individual identity suggests that Scudéry blends worldly issues and literary ones, according to Pellisson's formula, in order to create a novel narrative voice, a collective first-person singular in which "I" projects the concerns of her salon's members, the generation that had made the transition from civil war to a life of civility. When Cloelia reenters Scudéry's fiction as Clélie, she no longer calls for women to engage in military activity. But the return of the first person to Scudéry's salon writing revives the feminist militancy of the *Femmes illustres.*

"THE ANATOMY OF THE HUMAN HEART"

Les bons romans sont l'histoire du coeur humain.

Jean de La Harpe, *Lycée*

Le but [de Restif de La Bretonne] n'est pas, comme celui d'Augustin et de Jean-Jacques Rousseau, de *s'historier* lui-même, mais l'espèce humaine, et son dessein, dans cette *anatomie morale,* est d'enseigner aux pères, et surtout aux mères de famille at aux véritables instituteurs, à former leurs élèves.

Poster displayed on the
walls of Paris in the Year IV

FROM MOLIÈRE's day (the *Précieuses ridicules* was staged in 1659, while *Clélie* was still being published) to ours, the leaders of seventeenth-century salon society have generally been portrayed as silly, frivolous women who frittered away their time and that of the male aristocrats who, in the post-Fronde years of Louis XIV's rising absolutism, found themselves increasingly idle. According to this vision, all products of salon culture are only social games, shallow amusements of the idle rich. What if, however, the *précieuse* salons were thus ridiculed precisely because they were far more than a superficial pastime? Their pronouncements in literature could have no legal status, but they were nevertheless widely perceived as a threat to what one eighteenth-century commentator on the novel termed "the laws most necessary to preserve society" (Jacquin 339), in particular, the legal and social code that governed woman's status in marriage.[21] In *Clélie*, Scudéry follows the political subversiveness of *Artamène* with a novel of social subversion.

It is easy to underestimate her project because her new subversiveness depends on an element in which the nonliterary implications are hardly evident, what early commentators saw as "her intimate knowledge of the human heart" (Alletz 323). From the beginning, even those critics who find fault with the "implausibility" of her narrative or with the "excessiveness" of her stylistic *préciosité* praise the "natural" quality of her portrayal of sentiments.[22] If even Scudéry's detractors consider *Clélie* psychologically realistic, that judgment deserves our attention. Not only is *Clélie* the first novel in the French tradition to be so praised, but, in addition, that critical praise is confirmed by the intensely personal reaction of early readers like Lafayette, who seem to have found in the novel a mirror for their own feelings, much like Rousseau's readers a century later.[23]

I evoke *Julie* in this context because the psychological realism perfected by Scudéry in *Clélie* is of a variety still highly prized in the eighteenth century, when it remained a rival to the more exterior and more physical realism developed in other novelistic strains.[24] Witness Diderot's justification for his "Eulogy of Richardson" (1762): he chastises (with "impatience") those who speak of the "excessive length" of Richardson's novels; they fail to understand that "it is upon this multitude of little things that the illusion depends" (34–35). Diderot distinguishes between two types of elements capable of creating "the illusion" of reality: "there are *moral* phenomena as well as *physical* phenomena" (35, my emphasis). Richardson merits his eulogy as a master of moral effects, of an interior or a psychological realism.

Diderot's defense of Richardson is compatible with contemporary descriptions of Scudéry's novels, with Pellisson's defense of salon writing, and with Scudéry's own statements about her production. Diderot contends that Richardson's novels are real-seeming because of their perfectly observed pronouncements about "the human heart" (40). Such realism can turn a novel into "maxims put into action" (29), a practical guide to morality for a worldly public (38). By and large, twentieth-century critics have forgotten this other realism. In their readings of the early novel, they reaffirm the influential judgment formulated by Ian Watt in *The Rise of the Novel* (1957): they privilege the physical over the psychological, and they denigrate its psychology, in Watt's terms, as "elegant" but "[in]authentic" (30).[25]

perfectly observed pronouncements about the human heart → practical guide

Nowhere in Scudéry's oeuvre does the confrontation between these divergent opinions seem more comprehensible than in *Clélie,* in which Scudéry privileges conversation to display "her intimate knowledge of the human heart." No document in the history of the early French novel has received more attention than the *Carte de Tendre* in the novel's first volume (figure 7). On the surface, nothing could seem more "ridiculous" (in Molière's language), less "realistic" (in Watt's), than Scudéry's board game of the ways to a woman's heart. However, if the map's prodigious success can initially be explained by its novelty, the strange format that almost invites these criticisms, this cannot account for its enduring influence, the product, it would appear, of Scudéry's ability, on the one hand, to categorize amorous experience in a manner identified as accurate by generations of readers and, on the other, to formulate a radically new politics to govern the land she called Tenderness.

nb. accuracy of the Carte de Tendre!

The *Carte de Tendre* forces us to confront the central interpretive dilemma posed by *préciosité:* the conjunction it stages between a rhetoric that is by today's standards overblown virtually to the point of being no longer readable and the hard-hitting vindication of the rights of women that is couched in this rhetoric. The *Carte de Tendre* features the concept in which the accuracy of Scudéry's psychological realism was most apparent to generations of readers, what she termed *inclination,* a term that may be translated as "penchant" or "propensity," and is clearly related to, but not to be confused with, love at first sight.[26] Whereas love at first sight emphasizes the spontaneous birth of a passion that suddenly and violently transforms the lives of those it strikes, the power of *inclination* manifests itself otherwise. As indicated by the expression "mariage d'inclination"—which seems only to have entered the French

préciosité: overblown rhetoric → vindication of Pt. rights. hidden therein

eg. INCLINATION

language in the nineteenth century and which may well be the long-term legacy of Scudéry's influential concept—*inclination,* like *préciosité,* is a strange hybrid, a psychological force whose impact is felt primarily in the legal domain.[27] In *Clélie, inclination* is defined as a force of attraction that works against prearranged marriages and encourages women to rebel against the authority and the values of the patriarchal system. (Unlike love at first sight, which strikes both partners simultaneously, *inclination* is consistently described from the woman's perspective as the force that makes her lean in the direction of one suitor over all others.)

Shortly after Clélie maps out Tenderness, *inclination* receives a practical illustration that makes these implications clear. Scudéry's heroine turns to her mother, Sulpicie, for advice: she is torn between two suitors, her father's choice, the noble and Roman-born Horace, and Aronce, to whom she personally "inclines," even though he is of unknown birth and therefore expressly forbidden to her by her father's dictate that she can only marry a Roman. Sulpicie appears unmoved by either the paternal concern for pure lineage or the paternal definition of marriage as political alliance: she unhesitatingly encourages her daughter to "give over her heart to her inclination for Aronce" (1:424). Sulpicie explains that, like her daughter, she has an "aversion" for Horace but is drawn to Aronce who, "even if he was not born in Rome, has at least the heart of a Roman" (1:425). The mother declares her preference in the rhetoric of the *Carte de Tendre:* Sulpicie explains that she "loves [Aronce] tenderly" (*l'aimait tendrement* [1:424]). With these words, Sulpicie makes explicit the simultaneous double focus of the key concepts of the *Carte de Tendre:* "inclination," "tender love," and so forth illustrate both Scudéry's psychological realism and her feminist project. It is easy, for modern readers at least, to overlook the political implications of Clélie's tender geography, but the mother's discourse reminds us that Scudéry is asserting such fundamental concepts as a woman's right to choose for herself and merit rather than family status as the measure of an individual's worth.

Recent readings of the *Carte de Tendre* by Alain-Marie Bassy and Claude Filteau point to a reevaluation of Scudéry's project: they replace the traditional vision of *Clélie* as affected, otherworldly novel with the image of a fictional economy solidly grounded in economic and legal realities. Both critics stress Scudéry's originality and her subversiveness. Bassy emphasizes in particular her radical departure from a tradition

cf Don Sanche d'Aragon

with which the *Carte de Tendre* has often been compared, that of courtly love speculation: for the courtly notion of a unique, predestined, irreversible passion, Scudéry substitutes the idea of choice, of multiple amorous trajectories; in *Clélie,* courtly love's fatality is replaced by codes of behavior that an individual can be taught to master (30–31). Filteau emphasizes the practicality of Scudéry's goals: "All speculations about tenderness . . . aim at the formulation of a contract" (41). The nature of that contract explains why generations of critics and commentators responded instinctively to *Clélie* as a menace to the social order. *Clélie* develops the notion already introduced in *Artamène*'s "Story of Sapho" of private contracts that offer an alternative to the official marriage contract. These private contracts are all designed to reverse the imbalance inherent to the marriage contract, which, according to the women of *Clélie,* delivers all control over the institution into the hands of men: Scudéry maps out the land of Tenderness in order to suggest that individual contracts could be recognized as equally binding alternatives that would return to women control over their own destinies.

According to Filteau, this desire to offer a personal legal code as an alternative to official laws also explains Scudéry's bizarre choice of format: her topographical design guaranteed, as the explosion of allegorical maps published in *Clélie*'s wake demonstrates, that her project would be compared with the contemporary tradition of utopian speculation.[28] The invited comparison highlights Scudéry's subversiveness: Filteau's reading of the Abbé d'Aubignac's contemporary critique of her map reveals that her tender geography was immediately perceived as a reversal of the conventional utopian order, which, like the legal contracts that managed the official distribution of women in marriage, could only be patriarchal. For d'Aubignac, because the *Carte de Tendre* did not represent a proper state, it was an anti-utopia, an attempt to replace princely authority with a personal code of conduct (Filteau 58–60).[29]

The *Carte de Tendre* is the most visible sign of Scudéry's social project, a demonstration that aims at nothing less than the justification of private contracts as a legitimate counterforce to the officially sanctioned legal and political order. Statements culled throughout the vast novel can be assembled to form a protosocial contract. I will give but two brief examples that illustrate the categories I have in mind. First, there are eulogies of female communities such as the extended discussion in volume 2 between the two Princesses Tullie regarding the Vestal

Virgins, eulogies that praise these communities because of the exceptional *legal* status they guarantee to their members: the Vestal Virgins
are the only women who enjoy rank and its privileges in their own
name and *as women*—"unmarried [women] are esteemed according to
their father's rank; those who have a husband are honored in proportion
to his status" (2:873). Second, there are persistent calls for what we
would term a meritocracy, always pointing out that such a system would
give women greater control over their marital destiny—"Between two
people of quite different status, only extraordinary merit can make the
match" (*faire la liaison*) (8:269). And, consistent throughout Scudéry's
proposed social contract runs the argument that women must wrest
from the patriarchal system—from the king, from their fathers, from
their suitors—the power to control their own rank and to govern the
bestowal of rank.[30]

It is obviously impossible to use *Clélie*'s politics of tenderness as
evidence from which to draw conclusions about the reality of social
practice in seventeenth-century France. I agree with Joan Kelly's position (formulated with respect to the courtly love tradition) that it is
"fruitless" to raise "the question of whether such love relationships
actually existed or if they were merely literary conventions. The real
issue regarding ideology is, rather, what kind of society could posit *as a
social ideal* a love relation . . . that women freely entered and that, despite
its reciprocity, made women the gift givers while men did the service"
(*Women, History* 26). From Carolyn Lougee's research, we know that
the salon women did encourage marriage based on inclination and
merit, and that they became thereby a force promoting the mixing of
ranks when those who frequented the salon, influenced by the ideals
expressed in *Clélie,* entered into misalliances with non-noble spouses,
affording them thereby passage into aristocratic milieus (138–70). But
more important even than this knowledge is the realization that part of
mid-seventeenth-century French society was able, in Kelly's words, "to
posit *as a social ideal* [such] love relations." From this perspective, *Clélie*
must be seen as the first salvo in the post-Fronde women's war, a
literary war that sought to win for women new status within marriage
and outside it, ultimately to redefine marriage as an institution in
France. In this, as in so many ways, Scudéry was ahead of her time: as
will be seen in my discussion of *La Princesse de Clèves,* legal commentary
on marriage caught up with Scudéry's speculation in literature only two
decades after *Clélie*'s publication.

Readers can also learn from *Clélie* that the society that had simultaneously dreaded and empowered the amazon in the early 1650s now dreaded, at least as much as it made into "a social ideal," the woman aware of her legal rights and responsibilities, the figure that Scudéry codified for French fiction. The particularly violent response provoked by *Clélie* may be partially explained by Scudéry's choice, in Boileau's words, of "the new-born Roman republic" ("Dialogue" 445) for the setting of her most feminocentric fiction. As she surely realized, the Augustan age was already being promoted as the model for France's self-designated Golden Age, an era dawning as *Clélie* drew to a close. By making *Clélie* a *histoire romaine*, Scudéry was taking on the newly appointed architects of classicism on their own turf. Boileau naturally fought back, characterizing, for example, the "geographic maps of love" as "completely opposed to the character and to the heroic soberness of the first Romans" ("Dialogue" 445). He set the mold for future attacks on Scudéry's fiction by pronouncing it a double threat to the foundation of the French State: first, her novels promote *embourgeoisement*, the rise of the bourgeoisie (both in the direction of aristocrats who declass themselves by marrying beneath their status and in that of bourgeois who practice intermarriage with aristocrats); second, they glorify female usurpation of the male prerogative to rule over the domestic space and thereby encourage what Boileau and his followers term male "mollesse" (lack of vigor, flabbiness).[31]

This same attack was repeated, and amplified, for decades, proving with each reformulation that French society was still able to conceive of Scudéry's new woman as a social ideal. Some of the most extreme arguments were advanced by Father Porée in the harangue against novels that he delivered and then published in 1736. (It was so successful that it was reprinted the following year, surely no mean achievement for a work in Latin at that time!) Porée seems primarily alarmed by the proliferation of novels in Scudéry's wake—he speaks of the "corruption" of novels as spreading "by contagion" (8)—but he clearly still has Scudéry's example in mind.[32] In particular, he continues—over eighty years after its publication—to cite the *Carte de Tendre* as the symbol of the danger of novels: "What do we see [in novels]? a daughter in her father's house busy drawing up the map of her infamous exploits" (20, 108). The danger of novels, according to Porée, is the blame they bear for the social unrest and societal transformation that those who share his beliefs in the late nineteenth century term degeneration:

What are [women] in civil society? a part of society, but a subordinate part that must receive the law and not give it. . . . Novels reverse the natural order; they make woman independent from man; they make her the supreme lawgiver. (20, 108)

[Novels] corrupt [men's] hearts . . . with the examples they propose: thus the indolence, and the lack of vigor on the part of our young men . . . which are so detrimental to the Republic. (16, 100, 106)

"What are women in civil society?" "What are women in a man's world" (*parmi les hommes*)? Ironically, what the cleric-critic, like the master critic Boileau before him, presents as a violent diatribe can also be seen as an accurate formulation of *Clélie*'s fundamental concerns, the questions that made Scudéry's novel a founding work for the early modern French tradition of women's writing. I subscribe to Ferdinand Brunetière's 1889 assessment that "novelists have never ceased traversing the *Carte de Tendre*" (56) with the dual meaning that I ascribe to Scudéry's tender geography in mind. An intricate analysis of the human heart formulated in tandem with a questioning of basic assumptions regarding woman's social and legal status—that combination is the foundation of the psychological realism that is Scudéry's contribution to the French novel's development. In *Clélie,* Scudéry blurs the demarcations among individual speaking subjects in order to celebrate the dominant salon ideology of the precious decade, in particular the desire to challenge all institutions that limited women's control over their fates.[33]

Scudéry's career is marked by her increasing mastery of salon writing, in the double sense of her ability to direct an intellectual collective and her ability to forge a collective literary voice. A bourgeoise, she began, in Du Plaisir's terms, to "write nobly" when she created a uniform style beyond individual authorial identity. She defined a model for female authorship in France that would remain a standard until shortly after the end of the ancien régime under which this literary subversion of the social order flourished: in her wake, women writers from Lafayette to Sand strove to create an *écriture* that was beyond person and beyond class, but not beyond gender. Under the ancien régime, French women's writing is composed by individual authors who translate the collective desire of a group of intellectuals male and female, aristocratic and bourgeois, for new social and legal freedom for women. The new realism Scudéry developed in the aftermath of the Fronde translates the military feminocentrism of those tumultuous years into a less heroic but more enduring mode. Scudéry's salon writing was the first indication of the new politics of marriage and married life that would be the dominant concern of French women's fiction until the 1820s.[34]

3

"What Is an Author?": Lafayette and the Generation of 1660–1680

SALON WRITING IN THE LITERARY MARKETPLACE

auteur => imprimé

fauteur => elle a fait qq livre

AUTEUR, en fait de littérature, se dit de tous ceux qui ont mis en lumière quelque livre. Maintenant on ne le dit que de ceux qui en ont fait imprimer. . . . Cet homme s'est enfin érigé en *auteur,* s'est fait imprimer. . . . On dit aussi d'une femme, qu'elle s'est érigée en *auteur,* quand elle a fait quelque livre ou pièce de théâtre.

Antoine Furetière, *Dictionnaire universel* (1690)

Madame de Lafayette, disait Monsieur de La Rochefoucauld, m'a donné de l'esprit, mais j'ai transformé son coeur. Jean Renauld de Segrais[1]

Il faut des lumières très grandes pour pénétrer jusqu'au fond de [l']abîme [du coeur], pour ne point s'égarer parmi tant de diversités, pour toucher vivement des matières si imperceptibles, et pour expliquer avec netteté des choses qui, par le peu de connaissance qu'on en a eu jusqu'ici, n'ont presque point encore de termes propres.

Du Plaisir, *Sentiments sur les lettres et sur l'histoire* (1683)

commonplace Lafay=> egg of human emotions

DU PLAISIR may well have first formulated the original critical commonplace concerning *La Princesse de Clèves:* Lafayette had revealed to her contemporary readers a more finely tuned language of human emotions; she had followed in Scudéry's footsteps by retracing the

"anatomy of the amorous heart" (52). Yet, according to La Rochefoucauld (at least as remembered by the century's ubiquitous amanuensis
Segrais), it was he who "had transformed [Lafayette's] heart," he, therefore, who had taught the author of *La Princesse de Clèves* everything she
knew about "the abyss of the heart." We return, as always it seems, to
the question of whether the author of the *Maximes* was also in some
way responsible for *La Princesse de Clèves*.[2]

Add to this configuration the fact that, in the same text in which he
proclaims Lafayette's "striking" understanding of "almost imperceptible
matters" (52), Du Plaisir also becomes the first theoretician of salon
writing when he discusses collaborations designed to produce a uniform
style—"One style would be less different from another" (99)—and we
reach the explanation for my title borrowed from Foucault's classic
essay. In "Qu'est-ce qu'un auteur?" he argued that authorial status is an
affair of recognition: an author exists from the moment at which the
public can recognize a name as an author's name (*nom d'auteur*), as the
signature that has already appeared on the title page of a book. More
recently, scholars—for the French tradition, Alain Viala in particular
—have analyzed the material conditions, from copyright laws to pensions, in which the modern conception of authorial status evolved during the second half of the seventeenth century.

To date, as I have indicated, studies of the rise of authorial status
have ignored the often anonymous collective publications, thereby passing over the women writers who directed them. In addition, these
studies have often avoided the production of aristocrats: in an argument
that parallels the reasoning that women did not sign their works out of
modesty, it is commonly accepted that aristocrats did not wish to be
associated with the economic aspects of literary activity. It has been
assumed, in effect, that an author in the modern sense of the term could
only have been male and bourgeois.

The process I am calling salon writing allows us to reevaluate both
women's writing and collective productions, to introduce a concept of
authorship not based on a signature with a unique, stable referent. The
class politics of the salons, and in particular the mixing of ranks that
they promoted, should be reason enough to encourage us to reconsider
the class assumptions commonly associated with the birth of modern
authorial status. In the following pages I will feature Marie-Madeleine
Pioche de La Vergne, Comtesse de Lafayette's *La Princesse de Clèves* as
the centerpiece for a revised view of the participation of aristocrats in
the creation of modern authorial status: Lafayette's novel demonstrates

that the aristocrats involved in salon writing were aware that literary production was acquiring greater status in the second half of the seventeenth century; that they intended to share in the increased profits; and that any failure to participate openly in the new system can, like female anonymity, be understood as an attempt to manipulate changing conditions of production from a position of collective strength, rather than as an avoidance of déclassé activity.

La Princesse de Clèves is the product of both a second wave of salon writing and the radically different political climate in which this writing was produced. The originally anonymous corpus that is today unified behind Lafayette's *nom d'auteur* was composed during the period in which the French monarchy was rising to a never equaled degree of absolutism. One of the numerous spheres of activity over which the Sun King and the architects of his absolutism sought greater control was the republic of letters: no French regime had a more acute understanding of literature's power to serve the State. The end of the precious decade coincides with the rise of classicism, the literary style officially sanctioned by Louis XIV's monarchy. Unlike the tumultuous years of the Fronde and the early years of the Sun King's reign, the next three decades were a high-risk environment for those who sought a literary career. Literary form and content were then the subject of intense critical debate, a debate with strong political underpinnings: as I will show in this study's final chapter, these decades initiated the most influential moment of canon formation in French history; only literature useful to the absolute monarchy was promoted by the critics who worked in collaboration with the State.

In this highly politicized climate, salon writing had the same appeal as in the Fronde's aftermath, especially for intellectuals, like many in Lafayette's circle, directly or indirectly compromised in that rebellion — even more so for writers like Lafayette who continued to make women's writing a political activity.[3] Lafayette revealed the influence of the *précieuse* milieu in which she had come of age intellectually and of Scudéry's fiction when she centered her novels on a meditation of woman's rights within the institution of marriage. In *La Princesse de Clèves,* she proposes a new model for the historical novel in which affairs of state are dominated by marital politics.

At the same time, Lafayette's oeuvre also reveals a sense of the limits and the limitations of a collective literary style. I center my reading on *La Princesse de Clèves* because the heroine's saga is simultaneously a lesson in the politics of marriage and a coming to authority, the process by which the princesse becomes in a sense an author. The novel thus reveals both its creator's definition of women's writing as political act and her awareness of the writer's new status in the age of absolutism.

Lafayette's novel can be seen as an extended meditation on the powerful attraction of originality that was a necessary correlate of the establishment of modern authorial identity. However, it proposes an equally powerful reflection on the dangers of life in the public domain and on the personal price to the author who writes to establish a *nom d'auteur*. *La Princesse de Clèves* draws a conclusion borne out by the early novel's fate in French literary history: when writers acquire greater status, women writers rarely gain from this public exposure. Lafayette witnessed the decline of salon writing's domination of French women's writing. In the new high-stakes literary market, it was inevitable that women writers would decide to work outside of a collective (as the next generation would do). It was also inevitable during a moment of canon formation that collective writing would be publicly assigned to individual authors (this was already happening when Lafayette was creating her novels). The salon house thus put in order was perhaps the ultimate divide-and-conquer project, the final victory of absolutism over the disruption produced by the Fronde's feminocentrism. By the early eighteenth century, Lafayette had been given a *nom d'auteur* and her works accepted into the canon of the newly proclaimed Golden Age of French letters, but on two conditions: first, the political content of her fiction was dismissed from critical discussion; second, her bond with a female tradition was severed. Her oeuvre thus recontoured, Lafayette was enshrined as the unique woman novelist of her age. Lafayette's *nom d'auteur* was acquired at a high price, the effacement of the politics of female authorship.

[margin notes: w writers rarely gain from public exposure; but- collective writing would (eventually) be ascribed to individual authors; conditions for acceptance of Lafayette: dismissed political content from discussion + bond w/ tradition = severed; LF = THE unique ♀ novelist...]

℃

La petite de La Vergne, fille de La Vergne gouverneur de Monsieur de Brezé, qui, dit-on, ressemble à Madame de l'Esdiguières, dit un jour à Roquelaure, comme il se mettait auprès d'elle: "Monsieur, prenez garde à la ressemblance." "Mademoiselle," répondit-il, "prenez-y garde vous-même." Tallement des Réaux, *Historiettes*

In the utopias of Scudéry's generation, heroines redefine marriage as easily as they dictate new laws of love. After the novelistic revolution twentieth-century readers have come to associate far too exclusively with Lafayette, heroines seem to have lost the power magically to transform legal and social realities.[4] The new heroines created by the second generation of salon writers are women struggling for self-definition within a society that punishes originality threatening to the status quo by exposing it to public ridicule.[5]

Lafayette signed none of her works—common practice at a time when an anonymous publication was not defined as it is today, as a work "bearing no author's name" (*OED*), but as a work with an author "whose name was not known" (see both Richelet's 1680 and Furetière's 1690 dictionaries). Very few works published in the seventeenth century without an author's name were anonymous in the period's sense of the term; various people's letters prove that authors' identities were widely known, at least within that relatively small circle of well-connected and generally well-born Parisian intellectuals who then formed the essence of the public for literary works.[6] At a time when all kinds of literary partnerships were standard occurrences, it was never considered necessary that an author work without collaborators, only that he or she direct the enterprise. La Rochefoucauld's correspondence, for example, reveals authorial conduct identical to Lafayette's. He thanks his various "consultants" for their contributions, even recognizing that some of them were important enough to make the notion of authorship problematic. Witness this 1663 letter to Scudéry: "You so improved some of my last maxims that they belong to you far more than to me" (533).

Lafayette's correspondence provides ample evidence to the effect that, in the privacy of her intellectual circle, she demonstrated behavior typical of a salon author (circulating manuscripts with requests for corrections [*Correspondance* 2:22–23]), even typical of an author at any period (dictating how many copies of a work should be bound in leather and overseeing their distribution; complaining bitterly about a printing error). She also sought to maintain absolute control over the circulation of her production, on one occasion roundly chastising her frequent collaborator Huet after he had written to compliment her on a text that he had read in an unauthorized copy (*Correspondance* 1:192–94): she clearly understood that, as the definition in Furetière's 1690 *Dictionnaire universel* stresses, one becomes an author by "bringing [one's work] to light."

However, this behavior is in direct contradiction with the ostentatious self-effacement characteristic of Lafayette's pronouncements about her authorship.[7] A month after the publication of *La Princesse de Clèves,* for example, presumably after she had been questioned about the rumors assigning the wildly successful novel to a team of collaborators,[8] Lafayette "assured" her frequent correspondent, the Chevalier de Lescheraine, "that I have no [part] in it and that M. de La Rochefoucauld, to whom people have also tried to attribute it, has as little [a part] as I; he has taken so many oaths to that effect that it is impossible not to believe him, especially for a thing that can be admitted without shame" (*Correspondance* 2:63). Had she wanted simply to end the discussion, the letter would have been over here. But it goes on: "For myself, I am flattered that people suspect me and I believe I would acknowledge the book, if I were assured that the author would never ask for it back." The coy formulation — she would accept the attribution if she were sure that the book wouldn't be taken away from her — is a denial that opens up the possibility of an affirmation, a possibility that becomes more evident as the letter concludes with lavish praise of the repudiated novel:

> I find it very pleasing, well written without being extremely polished, full of things that are admirably delicate and that one must even reread more than once. And above all I find it a perfect imitation of the world of the court and the way people live there. There is nothing either farfetched (*romanesque*) or laborious about it; in fact it is not a novel: it is more properly a memoir, and that was, according to what I have been told, the title of the book, but it was changed. (*Correspondance* 2:63)

Far from distancing Lafayette from this creation, a stance the initial "assurance" seems to indicate, the letter in the end establishes its author in an inside position — both with regard to "the world of the court" and with regard to the novel made more desirable as a result of this evaluation.

Lafayette operated in a similar fashion in 1691, when a lifelong friend and former teacher with whom she had recently been out of touch, Giles Ménage, begged for written confirmation of her authorship of *La Princesse de Clèves.* He was writing as a close friend, but also as a professional historian, who planned to refer to *La Princesse de Montpensier* and *La Princesse de Clèves* in one of his histories: "Having had the honor of knowing you since you were born, ... I would be ashamed to have been misinformed of this circumstance, and to have misinformed the public" (Lafayette, *Correspondance* 2:181). Even such a personal appeal is denied a straightforward response. Lafayette begins, as before, with a denial: "You can speak, in your *Histoire de Sablé,* about the two little stories (*histoires*) . . . but I entreat you to name no one in conjunction with either of them." As before, the denial is immediately complicated by the addition of inside information: "I do not believe that the two individuals [La Rochefoucauld and Segrais] that you named played any part, other than a little correction." By the end, the denial has become, as in the psychoanalytic sense of the term, simultaneously affirmation and negation: "People who are your friends do not admit having played any role, but to you what wouldn't they admit?" (2:182). Given that, in 1691, Lafayette had been in bad health for some time and had only two years to live, Ménage may have sensed that he could ill afford to wait. He asked for a confirmation of Lafayette's authorship that could be used as historical evidence. The woman he had known since 1653, when he had sponsored her entry into salon society, was willing to give an account—"the two individuals that you named" provided only "a little correction"—on the condition that no author's name be given. "Je vous demande en grâce de ne nommer personne."

That withholding has traditionally been seen as a sign of the "modesty" of a woman also an aristocrat. As Roger Duchêne's recent biography proves, however, Lafayette's conduct should not be confused with modesty: she turned indirection into the fine art of camouflage, working behind the scenes but using a full range of legal and political manipulations to protect what she termed "my estate" (*ma maison*) (*Correspondance* 2:208). It is unlikely that a woman so absorbed by questions of property and inheritance would have detached herself from the economic aspects of highly profitable literary production. It seems far more likely that her denials—always accompanied by attempts to promote the novels attributed to her—were connected to, rather than dissociated from, the economy of literature.

Lafayette's career is marked by her experimentation with the forms of salon writing. In *Zayde* (1669–1670), her longest novel and her most complex collective venture, we know that she worked with her collaborators (some of whom were also Scudéry's collaborators) to create a style reminiscent of Scudéry's salon writing, yet not identical to it (Niderst, "Traits" 825). The story itself turns on a plot of mistaken identities and uncanny resemblances in which techniques borrowed from her precursor, notably the replacement of proper names with pronouns, are exaggerated to produce an extended meditation on the dangers of representation for the viewer innocent of the deceptions of mimesis.[9] "Beware of resemblance," as Gaston de Roquelaure and the young Lafayette are reported to have said to each other (Tallement, ed. Adam 2:382).

In her two tales of princesses (1662 and 1678), Lafayette crafts the finest examples of the second style of salon writing, the excessively neutral *écriture blanche* produced by a generation of intellectuals disabused by political repression. In the white writing of such cautious authors as La Rochefoucauld and Sévigné, political content is always ambiguous: in the end, these texts seem to lack a personal voice, as Du Plaisir first noted; rather than expressing individual wisdom, their authors convey a sense of the doxa—collective wisdom, the set of prejudices and received ideas about conduct—that governed courtly life in the late seventeenth century.

In *La Princesse de Clèves,* Lafayette exposes the complex dynamics of literary collaboration in an age of political absolutism. Her most extended exercise in salon writing reveals the advantages and the risks to the individual of a literary style that is both the voice of the author and that of a collective. The princesse's struggle can be seen as the equivalent, for a woman writer, of the process Viala terms "the birth of the author": from her greater understanding of the accepted codes of conduct, what Peter Brooks calls "worldliness," she comes to see the importance of an individual voice, both in the sense of a personal style of one's own invention and in the sense of a literary property, a story to which the author holds the rights and controls access. However, the novel also reveals a sense of the limitations of the new authorial status, for the princesse's birth to authority is far from an uncomplicated process. By the end of the novel, she stands as an illustration of the dangers of resemblance and therefore of salon writing (one has no claim to originality, no absolute right to one's story). At the same time, her story represents the attractions of collaborative ventures (the individual is protected by the collective from personal attacks and is not the object of the desire to contain all efforts at originality that, the novel teaches us, is a seemingly spontaneous reaction to difference on the part of a highly organized social collective). Rather than a straightforward progression toward individuation, the princesse's saga reveals a profound hesitation between the desire for originality, for authorial status, and the fear of reproduction, of becoming a (literary) cliché and thereby without identity.

Lafayette's strangely ambiguous self-portrait as author may well reflect a similar hesitation between the attraction of authorial identity and the security of collective anonymity. How could she have remained unaware of the increasingly personal and the increasingly malevolent nature of the gossip about her authorial status that appeared in correspondence even before the success of *La Princesse de Clèves* was guaranteed? Thus, three months *before* the novel's publication, Bussy-Rabutin asked Scudéry's sister-in-law to inform him as soon as the novel was published "so that I can order it; I would be most unhappy if [M. de La Rochefoucauld and Mme de Lafayette] were any younger, because they would do other things together that would not distract us as much as their books" (*Correspondance* 3:435).[10] As soon as he had read the novel, Bussy suggested to his cousin Sévigné that, if they were to collaborate "in the composition or the correction of a little story," their characters would be "more natural" than those in *La Princesse de Clèves* (*Correspondance* 3:465). How could Lafayette not have felt that such envy of her literary originality was aggravated by her personal originality, the determination to control the plot of her own life demonstrated by her concern (to a degree totally without parallel in the history of French women's writing) for legally authorized spatial autonomy?

Thus, at a time when it was a husband's prerogative to govern his wife's access to geography (in what city she was to live and under whose roof), Lafayette managed the extraordinary feat of spending virtually all of her life very squarely on her own turf. For example, all the major religious ceremonies (baptism, marriage, funeral) were celebrated at her family's parish church (Saint-Sulpice in Paris), the church in which her parents had been married. After her marriage, she spent only two and a half years in the fashion customary for a woman marrying another landed aristocrat, on property belonging to her husband's family. After this brief fling with conventionality, upon her return to Paris with her husband they took up residence in a house built by *her* father.[11] And the comtesse remained under her own roof from her husband's return to his family estate four years later until her death some thirty-three years later. For the greater part of her marriage (twenty-two years), she and her husband lived apart. Their arrangement cannot be confused with the numerous ancien régime "marriages of convenience": they appear to have remained on good terms (Beaunier, *Jeunesse* 269–75); rather than sexual independence, each appears to have wanted the way of life possible only on his or her native soil.[12]

My incursion into biography at the close of a section devoted to authorship and literary style should by no means be taken for a portrayal of Lafayette's novel as literal reflection of reality. I agree with Nancy K. Miller's conclusion that the novel is concerned with received ideas of female conduct, rather than with " 'life' and solutions in any therapeutic sense."[13] My emphasis on the practical conditions in which Lafayette carried out her literary career and her family life is intended, as will be my discussion of the changing conception of marriage in seventeenth-century France, to countermand readings of *La Princesse de Clèves* as a historical novel in name only, in reality a timeless work concerned with affairs of the heart and merely superficially with affairs of state.[14] The most important consequence of Lafayette's reception into the canon to replace the female tradition has been the evacuation of the political and social content of her fiction. No more than Scudéry's, however, Lafayette's tender geographies cannot be removed from the context of their creation. It is only by restoring a sense of its timeliness to our reading of *La Princesse de Clèves* that we can understand Lafayette's relation to the seventeenth-century tradition of women's writing and the attacks of the novel's early critics, who (correctly) saw the novel as a renewal of Scudéry's threat to civic well-being.

Lands Known and Unknown

> Nous vous souhaiterons bien quelquefois derrière une pallisade pour entendre certains discours de certaines terres inconnues que nous croyons avoir découvertes.
>
> Sévigné to her daughter, May 30, 1672

NEARLY TWENTY years after the publication of *Clélie*'s first volume, Marie de Rabutin-Chantal, Marquise de Sévigné, among the most astute chroniclers of her age, demonstrated that the key concepts of Scudéry's tender geography were still common currency: for the group gathered in Lafayette's garden that summer evening (Lafayette, Sévigné, La Rochefoucauld), to speak of *terres inconnues* was to evoke *Clélie*'s warning about passion's threatening ability to lead women into situations over which they have no control. In addition, Scudéry was no museum artifact for them: they were still enlarging her topography, trying to "discover" situations not yet codified by her courts of law.

They had their work cut out for them: in the years between the *Carte de Tendre* and 1672, a great deal had changed. In particular, the heroic élan with which the literary amazons, from Scudéry to Montpensier, had set about reinventing women's writing after the Fronde, the optimism with which they had portrayed retreat and retirement as positive concepts, as the conquest of new domains over which women could rule, and within which they could write—all these utopian concepts of which Montpensier still "dreamed so sweetly" in Saint-Jean-de-Luz in 1660 were no longer defined so gloriously in 1672. A new pessimism had set in.

Or perhaps it had been there for some time, as far back as the aftermath of the Fronde. It is less visible for us now because it is associated with a younger generation of writers, women like Lafayette who were too young to have participated in the Fronde and were not yet authors in the 1650s.[15] Lafayette's correspondence begins with a series of letters written to Ménage from her family's post-Fronde exile in 1653. The most striking of the nineteen-year-old Mademoiselle de La Vergne's pronouncements is her categorical rejection of love: "I am so convinced that love is an inconvenient thing that I am overjoyed that my friends and I are exempted from it" (1:34).[16] The language in which her bravado is couched, "exempted" (*exemptés*), suggests the state-of-siege mentality of a country emerging from civil war: the future novelist writes as if she had been spared the travails of love by official decree. Her only emotion ("j'ai de la joie") is reserved for the absence of emotion, freedom from the "inconvenience" of love.

One could hardly imagine a more appropriate entrance onto the stage of posterity for the woman who as an adult is reported to have been fond of saying "it is enough just to be," a phrase glossed by its recorder (Segrais) as "to be happy it is necessary to live without ambition and without ... violent passion."[17] In the code of this inconvenience-free existence, as during the Fronde years, affairs of state ("ambition") and affairs of the heart ("passion") are inseparable. To live without political ambition, as the rebels would now be forced to do, would simultaneously make it necessary, Lafayette's adult maxim makes clear, to live without love.

André Beaunier presents these phrases as defining the cynicism of one young woman, the future "amie" of the century's professional cynic, La Rochefoucauld. However, the maxim takes the form of a collective manifesto, "mes amis et moi." The youthful declaration represents the decision of a generation to create a code for social conduct based on self-domination and the absence of spontaneity. It was only thus, with an "officially" decreed ideal of self-mastery, that these aristocrats still in the process of assimilating public political humiliation seem to have been able to reconcile themselves to defeat, and even to imagine themselves somehow *victorious*. Rather than continuing to fantasize utopian places in which women reigned triumphant, the women writers of the first post-Fronde generation began to impose as the signature theme of their salon writing the image of the political centrality of perfect social conduct and, along with this image, the belief that women, because of their "natural" role as social arbiters, had always wielded vital political influence.

No document better illustrates the usefulness of (the fiction of) social influence as a substitute for political action than a text initially attributed to Lafayette by Beaunier, her editor and one of the most perceptive scholars of her work. *Le Triomphe de l'indifférence,* an anonymous dialogue between two young women recounted by a third that appears to have been written in the mid-1650s, may well be the earliest illustration of the new situation for Scudéry's tender geography imagined by the first women writing in her wake.[18] This self-described "combat between love and indifference" (157) recounts a collective coming to terms with woman's life in the world enacted by three young unmarried women. They have assimilated Scudéry's lesson about the incompatibility of marriage and happiness, but they refuse the optimism of the extramarital, private agreements that she proposes as an alternative. The young women condemn love in general and conclude that "the justice that we owe ourselves and the love that we have for ourselves oblige us to choose that which is most advantageous for us, ... *generous* indifference" (175; my emphasis). Thus, the code word for female military and political activism, even equality, during the decade prior to the end of the Fronde, when generosity was the essential attribute of the *femme forte,* is revived to signify the "triumph" of (affective, at least) inactivity: "the heart is almost dead ..., [but] this state, sad though it may seem, is infinitely preferable to the agitations ... and unhappiness that love causes"; "indifference is a languishing state, but the peace and the rest (*repos*) that accompany it make it infinitely preferable to love's bitter suffering" (175, 204). They reason that the loss of affective life is more than compensated for by the permanent control indifference affords over one's actions and one's emotions (204).

Since it portrays a group of young women reaching a collective decision about their fates, *Le Triomphe de l'indifférence* seems the ideal signature piece for a generation of women (writers) committed to the "exemption" from love vaunted by the one destined to become its spokesperson: "it is enough just to be." The novel also illustrates the shift of geographic focus that was the mark of the new generation: its protagonists no longer imagine escape to utopian spaces; they seek instead an accommodation for women, in fiction at least, between self-determination and *terres connues,* life in the society of their own day. *Le Triomphe de l'indifférence* is the first seventeenth-century women's novel with a contemporary setting, a shift in locale that Marie-Madeleine de La Vergne may already have been contemplating herself at the time she decided (rather abruptly, to judge by her correspondence) to make a marriage that could not be taken for a love match.

Lafayette seems to have deferred authorship during the first years of her marriage and motherhood;[19] she began her literary career only when she was in control of her life. The mature woman had not modified her adolescent stance on love: within months of the publication of *La Princesse de Montpensier* in 1662, she composed (in a salon competition with Sévigné's great confidant, Jean Corbinelli) "a case against love" (Beaunier, *L'Amie* 9; *Correspondance* 1:192–94). In her first novel she immediately defined her contribution to her generation's "war" against love, the choice of a setting and a plot from recent history that allowed her to illustrate the major post-Fronde construction of gender invented by women writers, the notion that historical events cannot be understood independently of women's affective choices.[20] Because of its treatment of marriage, *La Princesse de Montpensier*—published in 1662, just at the end of the precious decade and the publication of *Clélie* and just after Louis XIV's marriage—can be said to usher in a new era in French women's writing.

When we place Lafayette, as literary history has long since accustomed us to doing, at the origin of the modern novel, then we must face up to a major consequence of this positioning: the modern novel is thereby defined as the novel of adultery.[21] Lafayette's most important departure from previous novelistic convention concerns the role she assigns marriage. Unlike contemporary novelists, who follow romance technique and make marriage the goal of the plot's unfolding, Lafayette dispenses with the union between protagonists at her fiction's incipit.[22] Rather than the elaborate dance of deferral culminating in a utopian union, simultaneously a love match and the fulfillment of both families' desires, to which the reader of early fiction is accustomed, Lafayette instead proposes marriages much closer to the institution as it existed in her day, marriages that serve the best interest of the family and not the individual. She then defines the novel's plot as the unraveling of a political match. Lafayette uses the story of that dissolution as the keystone from which she builds in two directions: outward, in an illustration of the intersection between love and national politics; and inward, in an illustration of "personal" politics, the shifting politics of marriage. Lafayette brings this conception to its fullest development in *La Princesse de Clèves,* but the essential elements are already evident in *La Princesse de Montpensier.*

Lafayette's first heroine initially commands attention primarily because of her elaborately detailed *financial* charms: she is an "only daughter" and a "very considerable heiress both because of her own great wealth and because she was a descendant of the illustrious house of Anjou" (43). Her personal charms are amply illustrated as the story unfolds, but both her marriage (to the Prince de Montpensier) and her extramarital attraction (for the Duc de Guise) originate in her unparalleled status as *héritière.*[23] In a universe in which marriage is an affair between houses (estates), it is natural that individual happiness will lose out to landed interests. And so it does. Three years after her political match, the Princesse and the Duc de Guise meet as adults; their passion is rekindled; a series of events convinces her of his sincerity, and she allows him to visit her one night in her apartment. This symbolic adultery is swiftly punished: the duc flees to Paris, where he soon falls in love with someone else; the princesse falls ill and dies (from the knowledge of the duc's betrayal as much as from her guilt); the Comte de Chabannes, her confidant and the go-between for their affair (himself guilty of loving the princesse, his best friend's wife), also flees to Paris, just in time to be a victim of the Saint-Barthélemy massacre. The disorder passion generates explains not only each character's intersection with major events (thus, Chabannes is in Paris at the time of the massacre because he was fleeing the scene of the princesse's passion) but even the actual shape of History itself. (For example, Lafayette indicates the jealousy between the Duc de Guise and the Duc d'Anjou over the Princesse de Montpensier as one explanation for the creation of the Ligue nearly twenty years later [75].)

However, the ideological implications of *La Princesse de Montpensier* are far more intricate than those explicit, but incidental, reminders of crimes whose status, whether real or imaginary, was no longer threatening since they were nearly a century old at the time of the story's publication.[24] The novel's prefatory text, "The Publisher to the Reader," in an interesting twist on the subsequently standard formula ("only the names have been changed to protect the innocent"). It explains—out of "consideration for the eminent descendants of [those who bore the illustrious name on the cover of this book]" (32)—that the story is a pure fabrication and unable therefore "to harm the reputation of Madame de Montpensier."[25] I take this as a subtle signal that the novel's ideological placement involves an "eminent descendant" of the Montpensier name—and fortune.

In 1659, when Lafayette began her literary career by contributing to a collaboration directed by the Grande Mademoiselle, the former amazon was just emerging from her post-Fronde disgrace. Also in her recent history was a triumph, her victory after a lengthy lawsuit against Richelieu's heirs for the restitution of a château that had long been the property of the Montpensier line (it was built by Louis I and Louis II de Bourbon, the father and the grandfather of the Prince de Montpensier in Lafayette's story). Champigny-sur-Veude (the château in which Lafayette situates the scene of symbolic adultery) had been confiscated by the cardinal, razed, and its stones used for the construction of his château at nearby Richelieu, the city planned as a monument to his power and to his house's elevation to unrivaled prominence in the region.[26] Lafayette's story is the symbolic reenactment of Montpensier's legal victory: she reconstructs the château (in detail so accurate that it proves, as Cuénin has demonstrated, that she had access to architectural drawings or some other record of the destroyed property ["Châteaux" 114–15]). This restoration in fiction of an estate leveled by the first architect of the absolutism that, in 1662, Louis XIV was beginning to emulate could not have failed to call to mind in a more general way the question of resistance to an empire-building royal minister.[27]

Lafayette's reconstruction of the razed château at Champigny also permits an exploration of the personal politics of marriage (as opposed to the official marital politics of the French state). The estate was not included in the dowry of her heroine, Madame de Montpensier; the property was in her husband's family. When the prince orders her there after her indiscreet behavior toward the Duc de Guise has aroused his jealousy, his order, therefore, recalls the power, officially recognized and increasingly used by husbands in the course of the seventeenth century, to confine wives they believed adulterous to a form of house arrest: "He *ordered* the Princesse *his wife* to leave for Champigny" (82; my emphasis). Had "the Princesse his wife" been confined instead to Saint-Fargeau, the domain from which the Grande Mademoiselle had fought the battle in defense of her estate, she would have enjoyed a certain degree *and in HIS property, not hers* of freedom, since that property belonged to her family. However, at Champigny even one of the great heiresses of France is without authority. Thus her continued commerce with the Duc de Guise is more than a violation of marital fidelity: especially at the moment when she "orders" her lady-in-waiting to lower the drawbridge that gives the duc direct access to her apartment (90), she is violating her husband's legal *there she violates his laws* rights as well; without his consent, she cannot give orders concerning his property.

Like the Grande Mademoiselle during her official confinement, Lafayette in the course of her "exile" on her husband's estate was working at the intersection of women's writing, the great actions that founded the French State, and the private history of women's legal rights in marriage. In *La Princesse de Clèves,* she made a fuller revelation both of her post-Fronde generation's wisdom, the "triumph of [its] indifference," and of its new vision of salon writing and female authorship.

THE SOCIAL CONTRACT

Les premières femmes qui écrivent, si elles sont mariées,
sont presque toutes veuves ou séparées.

Claudine Herrmann,
Les Voleuses de langue[28]

is writing < out of wedlock

AT LEAST from the time of the widow Sévigné to that of the divorcée George Sand, with (to include but the better-known names) Marie-Jeanne Riccoboni (separated), Françoise de Graffigny (separated), and Germaine de Staël (divorced) in between, French women's writing has most often been conceived out of wedlock. Can we infer from this checkered marital history any concrete lesson about the incompatibility, at least under the ancien régime, between marriage and women's writing? Any theory of the early modern fiction of marriage, or of the history of literary women's relation to that institution, must originate with *La Princesse de Clèves,* the most intricate early modern representation of marriage, the first text to direct our attention to an issue that was perhaps the final political fallout of the Fronde: the public confrontation

between Church and State, doubled by the more private struggle between husband-family and wife, for control over marriage, and therefore over property. During the 1670s, marriage was in crisis in France:
this crisis becomes visible in the intense debate regarding its dissolution.[29]

The problem that finally erupted in the 1670s originated in the
previous century with a broken promise of marriage remarkably similar
to that which opens *La Princesse de Montpensier.* This case was nearly
contemporaneous with the events of *La Princesse de Clèves,* and Lafayette
characterizes it in the novel's prologue as a founding moment in the
rivalry between the houses of Montmorency and Guise. Some eighteen
months before the novel's action begins, Henri II had issued an edict on
clandestine marriages (marriages contracted by minors without their
parents' consent): the edict had a precise goal, the dissolution of a
promise of marriage so that a marriage more advantageous to the royal
house could take place.[30] The edict of February 1556 marked a crucial
moment in the history of marriage in France: it was the first attempt
since the Middle Ages by the State to usurp the power that it had
allowed the Church to exercise over marriage; it was the beginning of
the Church-State marriage controversy that culminated in the legaliza-
tion of divorce on September 20, 1792.[31] The conflict underwent several
moments of crisis, each of which led to a major redefinition of marriage.
Collectively, these new interpretations created a sense of the institution
unique to the last centuries of ancien régime France. The years 1556–
1563 (from Henri II's edict to the Council of Trent) mark a preparatory
phase, the period that first set the Gallican Church on a separate course,
leading it to redefine traditional canon law distinctions in order to give
parents greater control over their children's marriages, and therefore
over the inheritance of their estates.[32]

In the incipit to *La Princesse de Montpensier,* the work that made her
an author, Lafayette singles out "the house of Bourbon" (45) for its
desire to rewrite the laws governing marriage so as to guarantee the
distribution of property most favorable to the Crown.[33] Her choice of
starting point for her oeuvre immediately reveals the basic technique of
her historical fiction, the telescoping of two courts so that the sixteenth-
century precursor court inevitably evokes the assembly gathered around
the Sun King. Lafayette's authorial incipit also establishes a bond between marriage and authorship: these were the two institutions over
which women of her generation sought increased economic control, a

desire that put them in conflict with "the house of Bourbon." When she used marriage to contextualize the confrontation between national politics and personal politics, and in particular the personal politics of women (like herself) who wished to influence the legal conditions for their marriages, Lafayette revealed extraordinary prescience: in the years (1662–1678) between the publication of her two fictions of princesses *mal mariées,* the simultaneous evolution of royal absolutism and the French economy made the issue of marriage, especially its dissolution, a central preoccupation of the French State for the first time since the crisis contemporaneous with the events described in the novels. It was only logical that the major salon writer of her generation would center her most developed fiction on this controversial territory that was both a tender geography and an affair of state.

The heart of the matter, just as *La Princesse de Montpensier* predicts, was the Crown's power to terminate a union. On the surface, the issue seems minor: should the authority to pronounce invalid a small number of marriages in precisely defined categories lie with civic or with religious courts? From the beginning, however, the question of what we would term "annulment" (contemporary documents always consider cause rather than effect, and speak of "obstacles to marriage," that is, preexisting conditions such as diversity of religion that render marriage invalid) is never clearly dissociated from issues of "separation" (that is, obstacles to the continued successful functioning of a marriage, such as domestic violence, that are a result of the union). And the legislation of "separation" is inevitably the first step on the road to the legal existence of "divorce" (the dissolution of a marriage that, unlike separation, allows both partners to remarry), as seventeenth-century terminology indicates: early treatises frequently use "divorce" to designate what we would call "separation." This means that officially initiated debate on annulment inevitably led, as it does in *La Princesse de Clèves,* to debate on issues central to salon politics, such as a woman's right to financial and personal security in marriage.[34] This debate was in reality never limited to a few clearly defined cases. On the contrary, the conflict eventually put into question the nature of marriage and the successful cooperation of Church and State. In effect, the separation of Church and State that necessarily preexists divorce in the modern sense of the term was already partly operational by the time Lafayette composed her masterpiece: the Sun King and his female subjects prepared in different ways the Revolution's divorce decree.[35]

The most important official realignment of marriage in French history begins with the post-Fronde desire to centralize power in order to limit the influence of individual nobles. No document reveals more clearly the political prominence marriage acquires during the decade of *La Princesse de Clèves* than the treatise drawn up on Colbert's orders by the lawyers Abraham and Gomont in April 1670:

> The society composed of families is the source and the summary of the public society of states. Just as the well-being and the orderly functioning (*le bon ordre*) of the State result from the well-being and the orderly functioning of individual families, so the control over families depends on the establishment of marriages. It is for this reason that the Prince must have sovereign authority over marriages: they are individual societies, which are the pillars of his state.[36]

In the official vision promoted by the Sun King's propaganda machine, just as in the historical fiction written by women during the final decades of his reign, marriage was the foundation of the Prince's state. Only the unswerving belief that absolutism depended on control over this institution could explain the treatise's conclusion. "Ecclesiastical courts have been infringing on secular jurisdiction"; "the accommodativeness of ecclesiastical jurisdiction has multiplied the already too frequent abuse of marriage" (60): the State must intervene to end the independence encouraged by the Church and correctly govern "the pillars of state," for the very structure of society was threatened.

Colbert's men present as a simple righting of wrongs—the Church has been "infringing" on the State's jurisdiction—what was in fact a major realignment of power, based on a complete redefinition of a founding institution: "The substance of this sacrament is a civil contract, which is only raised to the dignity of a sacrament when it is perfect. . . . [A marriage] is a sacrament only insofar as it is legitimate, and is not a marriage unless it is contracted according to the laws of civil society" (61). The architects of royal absolutism were preparing for a period of territorial expansion during which all the wealth of French subjects would be needed; they decided simply to confront the Church head-on in order to obtain control over the property exchanged through marriage contracts. According to this new reasoning, the Church in effect no longer had jurisdiction over marriage, for the sacrament only began if and when all legal issues were properly settled.[37]

The reasoning of this document intended for internal circulation was soon made public: the régime's spokesperson was one of the foremost legal scholars of the day, Jean de Launoy. To give his argument weight, Launoy wrote in Latin, and he marshaled an impressive array of authorities: his 1674 *Regia in matrimonium potestas* is less a treatise than a vast compendium; Launoy states each element of his argument briefly, then offers numerous examples of two kinds of precedent, citations from authorities and examples of French kings exercising their power. His thesis is unswerving: since marriage is a secular contract, the king alone has power over it. The Crown's position had no sooner been made public than it came under heavy fire, first from Rome, where Bishop Dominique Galesius published his *Ecclesiastica in matrimonium potestas* in 1674, then locally, with the appearance two years later of an anonymous volume (attributed to L'Huillier), *In Librum Launoii ... observationes*. Both books attack Launoy violently; both defend marriage first and foremost as a sacrament; both grant the Church all power over it.

We will see the consequences of this war—for it was a war, with impressive stakes—only with the next generation of women writers. For the moment, its very existence is of the essence: no other decade prior to the Revolution witnessed such a production on the subject of marital law. Marriage was literally redefined as a result of this decade of speculation: the first definition in Furetière's 1690 dictionary reads "civil contract by which a man is joined to a woman."[38] Marriage was also rendered more fragile as an institution. All these treatises claim to be about marriage and about jurisdiction over it. Yet there is never discussion of jurisdiction over its formulation, never anything like the logical solution to this crisis in authority represented by the modern French double-marriage ceremony. These treatises are concerned solely with the *dissolution* of marriage, with establishing lists of the conditions that serve as obstacles to the continuation of marriages already celebrated, and with deciding which authority could pronounce a marriage nul.

With *La Princesse de Clèves*, Lafayette created a new formula for the historical novel: she portrays the events of history as dominated by the institution of marriage. The peace negotiations with which the novel's political frame opens are shaped by marriage propositions: "The principal stipulations were the marriage of Mme Elisabeth of France with Don Carlos, Infant of Spain, and that of Madame, sister of the King, with M. de Savoie" (40). The frame action ends with the accomplishment of the first of these unions (127, 175). In between, marriage is the measure of political favor and the instrument of political alliances. Lafayette could have been illustrating the definition of the institution being proposed by contemporary legal scholars: rather than a sacrament obeying eternal laws, they defined it as a contract obeying its own individual laws, an exchange of property that had to be well drawn up. A good marriage was in essence a good contract.[39]

good marriage= good contract

In addition, Lafayette portrays this new official definition of marriage as doubled by a new private conception of the institution: *La Princesse de Clèves* provides the earliest testimony in literature to the desire for what James Traer terms a "modern" marriage, that is, a union founded on "equality and sentiment" (16). Evidence of this desire is provided by both members of the novel's central couple: the prince, for example, speaks of his great appreciation for "sincerity" between man and wife (76); he frequently mentions his belief that marriage should be a means to personal "happiness" (50, 52); his wife realizes that marriage without "inclination" is not what marriage should be (50).[40] When she places her modern couple in a political context dictated by the new politics of marriage, Lafayette implies that, by focusing attention on the dissolution of unions, the State had contributed to a situation in which individuals were beginning to feel that the institution was not immutable, and that they therefore could renegotiate unsuccessful unions.[41] The two simultaneously nascent views of marriage were inevitably on a collision course. The Prince de Clèves (conveniently aided by his father's death) sacrifices his family's best interest to his "inclination" for the princesse's "dazzling" beauty (49). And his wife is encouraged to believe—prematurely—that the context for marriage was evolving more rapidly than was the case.

new private conception of marriage => equality + sentiment

State's attn to dissolution led indivi to question the immutability of institution

WHAT DO WOMEN WANT?

AUTEUR, en termes de Palais, on appelle *Auteurs,* ceux dont on a acquis le droit de posséder quelque héritage par vente, échange, donation, ou autre contrat.... Ce mot en ce sens vient du Latin *auctor,* qui signifie le maître d'une chose, qui peut prouver que le domaine et la possession lui en appartiennent.

Furetière, *Dictionnaire universel* (1690)

SCUDÉRY'S HEROINES proved controversial because they either re- *[margin note: Scudéry on marriage: — reject — insist on inclination]*
jected marriage outright (Sapho) or accepted marriage only on their
own terms (*Clélie* teaches women that rank is less important than
sentiment, that they have a right to contract *mariages d'inclination,* even
if this means braving a paternal interdiction). The menace of this
wisdom becomes clear only if we think of the marriage treatises of the
1670s and remember that, in its official reconception by "the house of
Bourbon," the institution was defined not in terms of individuals but in
terms of families and the politics of inheritance. By following her *[margin note: but nb inclination could really screw up inheritances + honor]*
inclination, a young noblewoman like Clélie threatened to hand her
family's estate over to an undesirable family, or even to a non (that is, a
non-Roman) family. At least all her wild schemes were embroidered in
ancient Rome, in *terres inconnues.* However, the Princesse de Clèves was
very much of her creator's world: all the families in the novel were still
transmitting estates in 1678. Lafayette's fictional mother never suggests
that her daughter should follow her heart, and her young noblewoman
never considers doing so: both women recognize that hers is a marriage *[margin note: princesse's marriage + of inclination; all recognize this]*
without *inclination.* However, since it is the most advantageous match
possible after the failure of the mother's initial marital strategies, the
contract is drawn up ("les articles furent conclus," 50).[42]

Scudéry's heroines also proved controversial because of their decisive
prise de parole: when Sapho and Clélie turn to the first person, it is to *[margin note: Scudéry = prise de parole; Clèves = silence]*
preach their doctrine of a new life for women. Lafayette's heroine is the
opposite of what Marguerite Duras and Xavière Gauthier call a "par-
leuse": her habitual response to situations that affect her fate is silence.
Readers today often find her silence irritating, but *La Princesse de
Clèves*'s first critic, a man of letters named Valincour (who, barely six
months after the novel's appearance, published a booklength attack of *[margin note: which, nb, gains reader's sympathy]*
the new work), felt that the princesse's silence wins the reader's sympa-
thy, whereas a (more overtly) strong heroine would have had the opposite effect:

> Many people defend the character of Madame de Clèves. They say . . .
> that the author was right to avoid giving her great intelligence and wit
> (*esprit*); that that would not have been appropriate for the role she had to
> play, which only requires sweetness and weakness; . . . that this is why
> the reader is concerned about Madame de Clèves, . . . while he would
> only have had repulsion, and perhaps scorn, for a woman who, with
> great intelligence and resolution, would have found herself in the same
> predicament. (127–28)[43]

What exactly was "the role she had to play," and why has it proved even more controversial than the rebellion of the outspoken Clélie? We probably have more evidence about the critical reception of *La Princesse de Clèves* than about that of any other seventeenth-century work. Valincour scornfully alludes to the first public's enthusiasm: "Never has a work made me more curious. It had been announced long before its birth; enlightened people . . . had praised it as a masterpiece. . . . There are few books which have enjoyed . . . such widespread approval . . . before they have even been seen by the public" (2).[44] For the first time in the history of French letters, a work's arrival on the literary scene had been staged. The central moment of prepublication publicity involved the appearance in a public paper edited by Donneau de Visé, *Le Mercure galant* (January 1678), of an anonymous short story, "La Vertu malheureuse," with a plot so similar to part of *La Princesse de Clèves* that its author must have had access to the novel in manuscript. Maurice Laugaa calls the story an "advance reproduction of the masterpiece" (26) and its publication two months before the novel "a veritable preconditioning of the public" (25). The scene featured in the advance copy clearly indicates "the role [the princesse] had to play": it defines the future novel's particular focus as life after marriage. The marriage is "unhappy," the wife "virtuous": in the case of the story, as in the novel to come, that not particularly enticing foundation is made controversial because of the way the wife handles the situation. In both instances she speaks her mind ("avouer") and attempts to work out with her husband's cooperation a solution to their dilemma that would keep her from adultery. The princesse's conduct, still hotly debated more than three hundred years after the novel's publication, guaranteed that neither the novel nor the institution of marriage would be the same once Lafayette's initially "sweet and weak" heroine had found her own voice.

I am referring, of course, to the *aveu*, the scene in which the princesse veers off the path traced by her precursor bearing the Montpensier name, who attempted an unauthorized takeover of her husband's property. Lafayette's heroine for the 1670s confronts her husband directly and tells him of her attraction to another man. The month after the novel's publication, Donneau de Visé turned *Le Mercure galant* into a public forum on the novel when he published the first of a series of *questions galantes* asking his readers whether a virtuous woman, who has all the esteem possible for her husband, ... and who is nonetheless combated by a very great passion for a lover ... does better to confide her passion to this husband than to say nothing of it, at the risk of the battles she will continually be forced to concede because of the unavoidable opportunities to see this lover, from whom she has no other means of distancing herself than the confidence in question. (298–300)

When he directed (presumably with Lafayette's authorization, and even at her suggestion) the reader's attention to what he presented as the innovation of this marital plot, Visé hoped to provoke a collision between reality and fiction. The question is phrased with respect to "a virtuous woman," rather than to the Princesse de Clèves in particular, and readers (who answered in droves, and many of whose responses were printed in subsequent issues) responded to that opening up of the issue by relating the novel to their own lives. Bernard Pingaud completely misreads the debate when he concludes (a conclusion also subscribed to by Gerard Genette) that the readers were "hostile" to an action they considered "the last word in bourgeois behavior" (*du dernier bourgeois*) (Pingaud 145; Genette 72, n.2).

There is no hostility in the readers' responses, nor do they dismiss the "virtuous woman's" conduct as déclassé. Their responses are marked above all by a sense of the *novelty* of such behavior: one reader, for example, contrasts "husbands of today" with their precursors (*Le Mercure galant*, "Extraordinaire," July 1678, 40). Other readers are taken aback by what they consider an excess of honesty. One after another, they repeat that undue sincerity is bound to be misinterpreted (for example, the princesse's husband may think that she wants to remain in the country because her "retreat" would shelter her rendezvous with her lover [July, 334]). A reader from Grenoble expresses this collective bewilderment best: "We have to admit that marriage has its laws, and that it is dangerous for those embarked on it not to follow them" (July, 306). In the opinion of this man named Bouchet, the princesse broke the law with her honesty and with her desire for life in "retirement." Responses are also marked by a sense of *irresolution*. Letters are always collective (with the speaker representing the views of others), and within each collective there is dissent. Nowhere is this more evident than in the case of a provincial couple who meet in the company of family and friends to sign their marriage contract. Discussion turns to the princesse's behavior, and the couple quickly discover their opposing views: their quarrel is so heated that only mediation persuades them to go ahead with their union (October 1678, 317–21).

On reading certain of these letters, especially the one just cited, it is hard to take them for authentic documents. If they are a fiction, it is likely that they were generated by the collective directing the novel's publicity campaign. This would mean that Lafayette had imagined this scenario in which her novel forced a postponement of a marriage contract until the partners had debated issues such as the value of sincerity and the limits of a husband's influence. The Prince and Princesse de Clèves are less fortunate: they take up their discussion of these issues only long after the formal contract uniting their houses has been signed.

could attribute all this to publicity campaign

When interpreting their confrontation, commentators usually translate its key word, *aveu,* as "confession," thereby understanding this occurrence in terms of contemporary literary usage. For male writers of Lafayette's day, *aveu* signifies the admission, on the part of the woman whose undecidability gives her power over male characters, of the secret she withholds, the name of the man she loves. Thus (among the first instances of this meaning cited in modern historical dictionaries) in Molière's *Misanthrope* (1666) her admirers press Célimène to reveal her intended's name (2:2:506, 3:1:833, 5:3:1630). *Aveu* in this sense signifies the ritual by which men attempt to regain control over a situation by forcing women to collaborate in the public exposure of their criminality, their desire to dictate the laws of courtship.

aveu = admission

to power & name she withholds

This usage of *aveu* is related to the judicial procedure whose refinement in the seventeenth century Michel Foucault traces in *Surveiller et punir.* According to Foucault's analysis, the complex machinery for disciplining criminality then put into place aimed at the production of the perfect account of criminal activity. For the account to be perfect, the accused had to confirm its accuracy: the victory of the system was complete when he repeated the prefabricated story of his crime and signed and authenticated this confession, thereby "agreeing" to the official version of his guilt: "*Avouer,* confess and recognize that something is true, to agree" (*Académie Française Dictionary,* 1694). This legal exchange became essential to the criminal justice system; any means, even torture, could be used to obtain the confession. A related sense of urgency drives Molière's heroes to force Célimène to admit what they believe they already know.[45]

legal status of an aveu — agreeing to account of crime => she is criminal

The princesse's use of *aveu* does not, however, correspond to this contemporary neologism. No one forces her to speak; her *prise de parole* is freely elected. Nor is the text of her avowal prearranged; it is because her husband and Nemours know only what she chooses to reveal that their curiosity drives them to try to learn more. Finally, the princesse does not speak as a criminal: she stresses that "the innocence of my conduct and my intentions gives me the courage [to do this]" (122). For the avowal scene, Lafayette imagined a new function in the novel for the first person and for conversation.[46] She has every character acknowledge this formal innovation: the princesse announces "an *aveu* that no one has ever made to her husband" (122); the prince refers to "the greatest mark of fidelity that a woman has ever given to her husband" (123); Nemours pronounces the scene "extraordinary" (124).

Lafayette also defines the nature of such "extraordinariness."[47] Shortly before the *aveu,* the Queen Dauphine snaps at Madame de Clèves that she is "the only woman in the world who confides everything she knows to her husband" (116). During the scene itself, the princesse explains that "in order to do what [she] is doing, it is necessary to have more friendship and more esteem for a husband than anyone has ever had before" (122)—"friendship" and "esteem" are situated by today's historians of the family at the foundation of the so-called modern marriage. These qualities define the conduct that the prince—in a passage usually cited as an illustration of his lack of self-awareness but that could be more accurately described as proof of his awareness that husbands can be divided into two categories, what one of *Le Mercure galant*'s reader's called "husbands of today" and "husbands of before"—feels that the wife of a modern husband should demonstrate in this kind of situation: "Sincerity touches me so profoundly that I believe that if my mistress, and even my wife, revealed to me (*m'avouait*) that someone attracted her, I would be saddened without being bitter" (76).

It is hardly surprising that the princesse—who, as critics have often pointed out, spends the better part of the novel absorbing the wisdom thrust at her from all sides[48]—would understand that "friendship" and "esteem" are based on "sincerity," and that sincerity requires a kind of first-person self-revelation still an innovation in 1678 (and a total anachronism in 1559). Nor is it surprising that her sincere "revelation" (*aveu*) would be shaped by the other lesson in modern marriage that the novel teaches all its readers, the wisdom contained in the historical sound track that forms a backdrop to the heroine's marital misadventures.

From Lafayette's vision of court politics, we can predict the confrontation of the 1670s between Church and State for control over marriage: for the great houses vying for supremacy, marriage is a contract exchanging land and wealth for influence; the king, as head of the most powerful house, must have the last word about the repartition of parcels of his national estate.

The princesse's *aveu* reveals her creator's attempt to forge a compromise between the two modern views of marriage—the sentimental view (*mariage d'inclination*) that is the legacy of the *précieuses*'s protestations against marital "slavery" and the economic view of marriage as well-wrought political contract. Lafayette portrays a couple trapped in the confrontation between these irreconcilable visions of the event that constituted them as adults, and totally without precedent for resolving this fundamental conflict. Her heroine's *aveu* is the equivalent of Clélie's *Carte de Tendre* for Lafayette's generation: it is an attempt to draft a private agreement that reconciles sentimental and economic demands.[49] When she speaks with the requested sincerity of her fear that she will betray her "weakness" (for a man she refuses to name) if she remains "exposed" at the court (122), she wants something in exchange, control over her geography. She wants her husband's permission to remain at Coulommiers, a property Lafayette defines (with unusual precision) as "a beautiful house that they were having constructed with care" (120).[50] The estate is thus defined as community property; nevertheless, the princesse needs her husband's authorization if she is to be mistress there without him. She is requesting in effect the equivalent of the *procuration générale,* the document authorizing her to take legal action concerning his property in his name, that the Comte de Lafayette signed for his wife when they parted ways. The princesse is asking for an unofficial *séparation de corps et de biens* (the legal term for a separation, often referred to at the time as a *divorce*)—unofficial, but with an official air nevertheless.

The princesse's use of *aveu* evokes the earliest legal sense of the term: "the acknowledgment for a fief that [a vassal] is obliged to give to his Lord forty days after he swears loyalty to him, containing an enumeration of the property that he admits having received from him" (Furetière, 1690). In return, the lord "signed" and "sealed" the charter granting the estate. In the contractual agreement that founds the feudal (patriarchal) order, the exchange of authority was initially verbal, confirmed only subsequently with a document.[51] The prince, as though recognizing his wife's intention of transforming her speech of sincerity into a proper contract, says that she has given him a "mark of fidelity" (123), a sign or signature of homage. His wife realizes that such negotiations are unorthodox: "The singularity of such an *aveu*, for which she could find no precedent, made her aware of its peril" (125). Nevertheless, her desire for a new type of marriage has caused her to internalize the modern conventions: "Elle trouvait qu'elle s'y était engagée sans en avoir presque eu le dessein" (she realized that she had pledged herself almost without having had the intention of doing so) (125). In her formulation, *dessein* denotes her "intention," but it also contains "design," the equivalent of her husband's "mark," the *sein*, "mark" or "signature," that could validate such a "pledge" and transform their verbal exchange into the equivalent of a written document.[52] Brian Stock stresses the necessity of an oral component to make legal acts such as property transfers valid in the Middle Ages: "performance ... created the legal act" (45). The princesse's "design" is to act out symbolically a transfer of possessions in order to enjoy a male prerogative, to rule as lord over an estate.

And so she does, in two different ways, the first entirely symbolic. *Avouer* in another sense signified "reconnaître une chose pour sienne" (to admit one's ownership of or responsibility for something). The two examples given by the 1694 *Académie Française Dictionary* to illustrate this definition indicate the transfer that takes place in *La Princesse de Clèves*: "No one knew the author of the play, but someone recognized it" (*l'a avouée*); "he recognized him as his son." The princesse's gesture is positioned at the intersection between ownership (possession) and creation (legitimation).[53] It reminds us, as does Furetière's 1690 *Dictionnaire universel*, of the proximity between *aveu* and *auteur*:

AUTHOR, in legal terms, are called *authors*, those from whom one has acquired the right to possess an inheritance by sale, exchange, gift, or some other contract. ... The word in this sense comes from the Latin *auctor*, which signifies the master of a thing, [he] who can prove that the domain and its possession belong to him.

The princesse asks for recognition as "master of a thing," with the male's right to profit from paternal estates. She becomes instead an author in the sense of an inventor of a script and acquires authority through the originality of her desire.[54]

In a more concrete sense the *aveu* seems a failure: her husband quickly reassumes his full authority and "informed her in writing (*lui manda*) that he desired absolutely for her to return to Paris. She returned as he ordered" (127).[55] But this may be a hasty reading of the scene's consequences: Nemours overhears the scene; he repeats the story, putting it thereby into circulation, so that it gets back to the principals in the drama—unleashing the force that drives the prince to an untimely death, leaving his wife a very young widow and free to make a new marriage, this time of *inclination*. But was she?

If Lafayette's contemporaries responded most forcefully to the princesse's attempt to redefine the terms of her marriage, their twentieth-century counterparts are more often drawn to her second controversial act, her refusal to remarry after her husband's death.[56] The end point to which Lafayette moves the princesse's plot—unmarried, spending half her life in "retirement" in a "religious house" (*une maison religieuse*) (179), and the other half also in "retirement" but on "a large estate that she owned near the Pyrenees" (178)—is generally read solely with reference to her putative emotions—she loves Nemours; she feels guilt about her husband—even though the novel makes little use of interiority to elucidate her final decisions. From all we know of the princesse's emotions at her life's final juncture, they seem a true "triumph of indifference": "the heart is almost dead"; "it is enough just to be."

But not "just to be" in some ill-defined no-man's-land, *terres inconnues*. What little we do know about the princesse's life after fiction concerns the surroundings in which she will live out her life—the division of her time between two places, her ownership of the estate to which she retires, the fact that she finally obtains what she requested of her late husband, the right to live "chez elle," in her own house (180). From the beginning of the seventeenth-century women's tradition, the interests of "retirement" and "repos" (tranquillity, the absence of agitation) are linked to the choice of private space over the space of public exposure, the court, and this choice is seen (logically) as possible for a noblewoman only if she refuses marriage and a place in the landed order.[57] The princesse's refusal to marry Nemours grafts a new legal precision onto the tradition to which Lafayette subscribes: it is only by *not* marrying Nemours that she, as a woman and widowed, can truly have a "chez elle."

A seventeenth-century noblewoman who obtained the right to remain single denied her family the possibility of enriching its estate through her union. Once she was no longer a minor, she had a good deal of control over her fate. If she married, however, she lost freedom because she became an object of concern for the two families whose legal fates had become intertwined. This dual tutelage did not cease if her husband died, but was intensified. Jean Portemer notes the existence of a law decreeing that widows under twenty-five were to be treated as minors ("La Femme dans la législation royale" 443)—a sure indication of the fear that, if allowed to act as adults, widows might act on their own, without seeking familial consent, and attempt, through a new union, to transfer one family's property to an undesirable family. When the princesse becomes a widow, she has long years as a minor ahead of her: a decision to remarry would have been strenuously negotiated among three families—and would have left her movements once again dependent on a husband's permission.[58] Her rejection of Nemours is a triumph of indifference, and a legal triumph as well.

nb. widows <25 = minors!

; princesse = legal triumph

Almost from the beginning, her decision has been taken for a sad defeat. Witness Jean de La Croix in 1769: "Madame de Clèves, filled with the deepest sorrow, retires to a religious house, where she spent the few days that she lived after the sad event [her husband's death]" (1:480). La Croix originates the various misinterpretations that are still repeated: she was sad (whereas all we know, as the author of *Le Triomphe de l'indifférence* warns us, is that such a gesture "appears" sad); she locks herself up in a convent (whereas, for a noblewoman wishing to live independently, this was a choice of respectable but nonrestrictive surroundings); she dies shortly after the novel ends (whereas Lafayette calls her life "fairly short," which for an eighteen-year-old could easily have meant living another twenty years). And the key, final error: she lived out her days in the convent—whereas the essential gain for the princesse is that she becomes, at last, "master of [an estate]," an author.[59]

not sad defeat

she becomes an owner, ie. an author

I am not suggesting that the princesse, like her creator, begins to write once she has won control over her life. But through the trajectory from avowal to retreat she recreates herself as the owner of a family plot, in the double sense of an ancestral estate and of a family romance. Her abrupt fade-out, in the novel's famous last words, into "inimitable examples of virtue" signifies a movement outside of narration. Lafayette makes Woman in control of her life into that which cannot be narrated, deliberately distancing her heroine from all the examples of virtue (Marie Stuart) and its lack (Diane de Poitiers) that circulate so promiscuously in her novel. The princesse's plot suggests a solution to a

her life cannot be narrated!

dilemma created by the desire for modern authorial status: how to be
held up as an example, to gain reputation, without being reproduced ad
infinitum and turned into a literary cliché, thereby losing authority?
Lafayette proposes that the writer, the woman writer at least, is born
not simply from the movement into the public sphere that recent
historians have traced but only once the writer understands the negative
as well as the positive aspects of such exposure. The strange nature of
salon writing, in which every personal voice is the voice of a collective,
makes it logical that one of its practitioners would understand that a
successful author may guarantee his or her originality or inimitability
by careful management of his or her estate, limiting that which is put
into public circulation.

understanding
+ and -
aspects of
public exposure

☙

> There must come after me some other Madame de Lafayette who will
> do that which I was not able to accomplish. She will not do badly, if only
> she does as much as I. (*Correspondance* 2:208)

In context, Lafayette's self-appraisal is not startling: she writes her old
friend Ménage eighteen months before her death to assess her study of
the Lafayette family history: she hopes that the women who continue to
marry into the family will learn more about its genealogy.[60] However,
her evaluation recreates the paradox in the ending of her most famous
novel. The novelist makes her identity and her author's name, just as
she does for her princesse, synonymous with control over her place in
the patriarchal order. This letter is the completion of the earlier missive
in which she refuses Ménage the public "acknowledgment" of her two
novels.[61] To be a successful author, a woman had to think first of the
legitimacy of her estate; literary property was best legitimated behind
closed doors.[62]

lit property best
legitimated
behind closed
doors

Lafayette's self-acknowledgment also highlights the paradoxical position in which posterity placed her, much as she had positioned her
heroine. "Inimitable," "another Madame de Lafayette"—does her
greatness inspire future authors to "do as much as I"—tantalize with
the prospect of imitability? Or does it radiate the threat of inimitability,
absolute and isolating uniqueness? In 1768 Marie-Jeanne Riccoboni
"quarreled" with one of the numerous eighteenth-century historians of
French women's writing who had categorized her as the new Madame
de Lafayette: "I do not have the vanity . . . to adopt the title of Lafay-

paradox:
she becomes
inimitable

ette's rival." Riccoboni is willing to accept second place: "Madame de Lafayette was always my mistress and my guide; the honor ... of following her, even at a certain distance, is the praise I want to merit" (cited by Mouligneau 93). Riccoboni responded with another denial to Choderlos de Laclos's attempt to establish solidarity between them: "I am hardly [an author]" (Laclos 759).

"I am not really an author"; "I am not the new Lafayette." Riccoboni understood Lafayette's lesson about the vulnerability of the woman who ventured alone onto the literary scene. She was undoubtedly also responding to the work of literary history, which, a century after Lafayette's death, had either accepted her into the canon as the woman who drove all others out or, if even this limited intrusion was threatening, had integrated only *La Princesse de Clèves*—but attributed to La Rochefoucauld. Riccoboni, who was writing in the last decades of the ancien régime and the female literary tradition it had involuntarily sheltered, confirms the victory of the official story of the seventeenth century promoted by the architects of political absolutism: she is no longer sensitive to the note in Lafayette that a woman writer a century earlier would have understood as an invitation to become that "other Madame de Lafayette."

In Lafayette's last letter to Scudéry, not long before they both died, she pronounced: "You are still ... inimitable" (*Correspondance* 2:153). Such praise must have been instinctive to Lafayette: throughout her literary life she was known as "incomparable," "nonpareil."[63] Moreover, from the time of her debut in *précieuse* society just after the Fronde, the future Madame de Lafayette also bestowed these superlatives on other salon literati. In his first letter to her, Pierre Costar explains, "When you call me *Incomparable,* I receive, thanks to your courtesy, a quality that belongs to you, one that the just dispensers of reputation and esteem have assigned you, one that defines you as much as your name" (cited by Mouligneau 11–12). It was thus an accepted maxim of salon society that someone whose incomparability was a "reputation justly dispensed" could in turn assign a share in this status to others. It was also accepted that incomparability defined someone's essence, that it functioned as a *nom (d'auteur).* "Incomparable" and "inimitable" were thus the collective names of salon writers, signatures that identified a particular conception of originality by acknowledging that the individual voice was also a collaborative production. An "author" wrote with a single voice; salon writing was "inimitable" because it resulted from the combined forces of collaborators. When at the end of their careers Lafayette called Scudéry "still inimitable," she both took her place as Scudéry's successor and gave Scudéry her due.[64] When she pronounced her princesse "inimitable," she acknowledged the collectivity of that work's production and issued an invitation to collaborators to come, the Mesdames de Lafayette who would inherit her literary estate. As early as Riccoboni's day, once the myth of Lafayette's uniqueness had been propagated, the collective inscription was invisible: Lafayette became the confirmation of a new maxim of female conduct (one perhaps first properly fulfilled by Germaine de Staël), the extraordinary woman isolated from any community.

However, the collective message of La Princesse de Clèves was not lost on Lafayette's first critics. Valincour, for example, considered the work proof that there existed "a secret conspiracy" against the Académie [Française], and called the novel "the signal sent out to the conspirators" (339).[65] Subsequent commentators were more specific as to the result of that conspiracy. In the section of his Entretiens sur les romans entitled "The Dangers of Novels," Jacquin reviews the intellectual glories of Louis XIV's reign, during which "great men devoted themselves to the noblest accomplishments" (283), as a prelude to a condemnation of the work of Lafayette and Villedieu. Their novels are the cause of the subsequent "decadence of belles-lettres." Their stylistic "gracefulness" and the "conduct" they portray had incited literary "fatigue" and intellectual "languor" (285). For Jacquin, this feminization of literature had seduced writers from their true calling.[66] La Princesse de Clèves, in other words, had launched an attack on the Académie Française that ended the Golden Age of French letters. We will learn the nature of the conspiracy critics believed that Lafayette had launched, identify the conspirators who heeded her "signal," and understand why literary historians felt Lafayette had to be isolated as a single extraordinary woman when we discuss the last generation of seventeenth-century women writers. These scandalous women carried her exploration of the politics of marriage to its logical conclusion: marriage would really be redefined and women become truly "masters of their estates" when they obtained the right to terminate the marriage contract. Lafayette's fellow conspirators heeded her signal so well that they gave her plot for a new marriage a more public forum in "novels" set squarely on the frontier between literature and autobiography.

4

❧

Divorce, Desire, and the Novel:
The Notorious Women
of 1690–1715

THE MARRIAGE PLOT

La plupart des femmes qui écrivaient ces oeuvres édi-
fiantes étaient, dans la vie, d'effrontées aventurières.
Antoine Adam, *Histoire de la littérature française
au XVIIe siècle*

THE FIRST critic of *La Princesse de Clèves*, Valincour, mocked the *Valincour's alternative ending to Clèves* novel's ending: "Madame de Clèves should have, following the example of [Scudéry's heroine, Sapho, in *Artamène*], proposed to Monsieur de Nemours to go with her to her estate near the Pyrenees to spend the rest of his days, having first received his word that he would never press her to marry him" (275–76). The man who termed the novel "a signal sent out to conspirators" (339) may have sensed that this conspiracy was both a literary and a legal affair. But he does not seem to have taken any of this very seriously: his tone suggests that he found it ludicrous *"ludicrous", impossible soln* that a fiction devised for a character from classical antiquity might be applied to characters and a context both modern and authentically French; a French princesse could never have managed to enjoy both the man and the land on her own terms.

However, had Valincour composed his attack two decades later, he might have realized how badly he had underestimated the situation: by the final years of the seventeenth century, his conspiracy theory might no longer have seemed a laughing matter. Literary women became

128

DIVORCE, DESIRE, AND THE NOVEL

increasingly numerous as the century advanced; the final fifteen years
witnessed a veritable explosion in their ranks—to the extent that in this
chapter I will consider for the first time a group of writers of virtually
equal status, rather than organize the discussion of a generation around
its dominant figure. Moreover, the women who followed Lafayette onto
the literary scene were far more radical in their attack on marriage and
the family plot. Indeed they were so graphic in their condemnation of
the abuses of women both past and present that literary history reserved
for them a fate unique in the French tradition: they were labeled, in
Antoine Adam's pithy phrase, "brazen adventuresses" (*Histoire* 5:315),
women whose *personal* lives were so absolutely scandalous that this alone
was sufficient to deny them a place in literary history. Literary historians
have done their work so well that, at present, it is truly impossible, first,
to distinguish "fact" (accusations at least based on documents from the
period) from fiction (allegations that merely repeat early gossip); and,
second, to tell when commentators are speaking about documentable
facts of a woman writer's life and when alleged facts are merely a
literalized reading of her works. Their cover-up cannot obscure the
statistics: it is still possible to realize what a major force women represented in the production of novels at the end of the seventeenth century,
during the period when classical theater and poetry were on the wane
and the novel was on its rise to the apex of the French tradition.

Maurice Lever's *La Fiction narrative en prose au XVIIe siècle* is the
most reliable barometer of the novel's production during this crucial
period. If we consult his lists—and even if we eliminate the significant
percentage of novels whose author is still unknown today[1]—for the
period 1687 (twenty years after *La Princesse de Clèves*) to 1699 alone, 33
percent of the novels included by Lever are by women. For certain
years, especially in the early 1690s, the percentage is even higher. Surely
these are statistics on female participation rarely encountered in the
history of any genre in any country. And this output is not simply the
result of two or three prolific novelists: no fewer than nineteen women
novelists were publishing. These include well known authors such as
Villedieu, Catherine Bernard, Charlotte Caumont de La Force, and the
Comtesse d'Aulnoy; novelists less known today but very prolific and
celebrated in their time, such as Anne Ferrand, Marie-Jeanne L'Héritier, and Anne de La Roche-Guilhem; novelists who never escaped
obscurity, the mother-daughter team of Geneviève Gomes de Vasconcellos and Louise-Geneviève de Saintonge, for example; and even authors

of only one novel, such as Madame de Tenain, so obscure that her first name now appears lost. Anyone so inclined could well have believed that there really was a female conspiracy to take over this literary estate.

The conspirators, furthermore, trafficked in all the subgenres, from voyage novels to pseudomemoirs, that were then the preferred shelters for subversive political and social commentary. A number of them were closely connected to that group of male writers who were helping prepare the ultimate subversion from within the French tradition, the Enlightenment: L'Héritier was the niece of Boileau's archenemy, Charles Perrault, Catherine Bernard either the niece or the protégée of Bernard Le Bovier de Fontenelle. Others were part of the brain drain that left France after the revocation of the Edict of Nantes in 1685; the intellectuals who thus blended into the Protestant diaspora often followed Pierre Bayle's lead in denouncing the French system.[2]

The conspirators were also the first French women *writers,* in the modern sense of the term. (They worked alone or, if they had collaborators, they did not participate in the type of intensely symbiotic collective that earlier women writers had directed; they were for the most part only marginally connected to salon society; they were more likely than their precursors to sign their production.) Their example proves that, as French women moved away from the assemblies through which salon writing was generated and into the republic of letters on the same terms as their male counterparts, they did not shy away from controversy, in their lives or in their work. These women writers were both so public, and so publicly controversial, that their threat forced the arbiters of public taste (who, without them, might simply have allowed salon writing to die out naturally as the salons were displaced by the academies) to take action. In particular, the threat of their proliferation explains Boileau's decision to return to and then to publish two works that he had begun in the 1660s but abandoned, the *Dialogue des héros de roman* and the tenth satire, diatribes against women intellectuals and women's writing that set the standard for future attacks. I will return in conclusion to the construction of a case against their literary production. Before presenting their work, however, I would like to consider the origins, insofar as they can be retrieved, of their transformation into notoriety, the process by which their biographies acquired the trappings of scandal, in order to understand their exclusion from literary history as dangerous acquaintances.

It is easiest to illustrate this development with the woman generally

Original notorious= Villedieu

presented as the original notorious woman, Villedieu, because her biography is by far the best known.[3] Villedieu, it is true, seems seldom to have adhered to generally accepted maxims of female conduct. This is already evident in her contribution to the ultimate salon compendium, the *Recueil des portraits:* whereas the vast majority of contributors compose the portrait of someone else, the young woman (she was only between sixteen and nineteen years old at the time) submitted a selfportrait, a gesture whose forthrightness is magnified by the text's directness, its nonconformity with the conventions of the genre, and its bold confrontation of such controversial issues as class.[4] The boldness of

bold prise de parole at young age

Villedieu's *prise de parole* is less surprising when one considers that the next year the young woman would leave her provincial family and begin living alone in Paris "on her own reconnoissance" (*sous sa bonne foi*), which meant that she lived "without *aveu*" (an expression used for vagabonds, those who in legal terms owed loyalty to no one), answering to no man for her acts. She had a rented room, where she received

lived alone in Paris

friends (Cuénin 33, n.37). This situation, still unusual for young women as recently as earlier this century, was unheard-of for a minor of any social status in her day. Once on her own, Villedieu became with Scudéry one of the first French women writers to support herself with

supported self

her production.[5] She continued to act out marital scenarios that are the stuff of fantasy for Lafayette's heroine. When a young man of superior rank who had promised to marry her (once again secretly) refused to do so, she simply took his name: in the late 1660s she began to be known

took another man's name just upon his promise (unfulfilled) to marry her!

as "Madame de Villedieu."[6] This assumption of a name to which she had no legal right had two possible advantages for the young woman: it gave her the appearance of a regularized marital situation (rather like a settlement from the man who had refused to honor his word); and it also gave her a true *nom d'auteur,* a public signature for her literary production. The career of the writer today listed in card catalogues as "Madame de Villedieu [Marie-Catherine Desjardins]" really began when she adopted, "sous sa bonne foi" and with the authority (*aveu*) of no man, a new family name: all her major publications feature this name —even after the ersatz widow had (re)married and taken on in her private life another man's name.

Such defiance of custom could hardly have passed unnoticed. Indeed, the presentation of Villedieu's biography is a litmus test of the position with regard to women writers of any early literary historian. Thus, prowoman commentators like La Forge (writing in 1663 before her rebirth as Villedieu) and Vertron (writing in 1698 long afterwards) speak only of her literary accomplishments and make no reference whatsoever to her private life. However, toward the end of the century a tradition was inaugurated, in the process of making "Villedieu" synonymous with a life of sexual scandal, that made it virtually impossible ever again to understand the private life of the woman behind the author called Villedieu.

NB: only at end of century does her name acquire notoriety

The first sign of Marie-Catherine Desjardins's second rebirth, this time as notorious woman—and also an early indication of the vast campaign against the "scandal" of the generation of literary women who had followed her—is the brief biography included by Pierre Richelet in the 1699 reedition of his letter manual, *Les Plus Belles Lettres françaises.*[7] Despite the fact that at that time the female domination of the epistolary form was generally acknowledged, Villedieu is the only woman included in Richelet's "Vies des auteurs français." Furthermore, her inclusion can hardly be taken for a sign of admiration. It is appropriate that she be listed under her private name, "Desjardins," for Richelet privileges the woman at the expense of her work. He transforms her biography into one of the eighteenth century's standard fictions, the merry widow. Richelet portrays her life as inspired by a desire to escape poverty: to this end, she marries twice, Villedieu and (the novelist's actual husband) Chate. When she is widowed for the second time, "she renounced marriage entirely and resolved to devote the rest of her days to sexual intrigue" (*galanterie,* a word whose complicated history we will soon retrace) (lix). Richelet displaces the scandal of Villedieu's private life: the woman whose conduct was independent but not immoral has her initial marital situation regularized, only to become sexually notorious. In addition, her notorious conduct is postdated, so that it is contemporaneous not with her own entry onto the literary scene but with that of a far more personally audacious generation of women writers.

Richelet's biography of her discounts her work; privileges her person -- merry widow

2 marriages widowed, renounces + moves on to galanterie

ie. scandal of later, which associates her w/ later notorious writers

Proof that Richelet knew better, and therefore that his *biographie romancée* is an intentional construction, is supplied by Pierre Bayle.[8] From Bayle, we learn that Richelet "omitted many things" (333), that his account is erroneous—"many people assured me that this woman's sexual intrigue was far less important than he claimed and did not take place when he said it did" (332)—and that he could easily have given a more accurate one: "Since he was living in Paris and did not lead a sedentary life, he could easily have informed himself about ... many things" (333). Bayle's account, unlike his precursor's, is centered on Villedieu's literary accomplishments. In particular, Bayle shifts the accent on her audacity back to what was certainly the origin of Richelet's accusation, her work: "It is regrettable that Mademoiselle Desjardins opened the door to a *license* that is growing every day, that of attributing invented sexual liaisons (*intrigues galantes*) to the greatest men of the last centuries, and of blending them in with facts founded in history" (332–33; my emphasis).

None of her early commentators takes public notice of the woman writer's real crimes against patriarchal authority, in particular, her taking a name without license; instead, Bayle focuses on her literary license, the liberties she took with the leaders of the state, and Richelet invents a tale of her personal licentiousness. Predictably, Richelet's more quotable version won out, despite Bayle's proof that Richelet's account of Villedieu's life had no foundation in reality. ("We can believe the narrative of Richelet, who knew her" [Adam 3:173].) Indeed, the only basis for Richelet's vision of sexual scandal is in her fiction, both her propensity to dwell on male sexual indiscretions, noted by Bayle, and her authorship of the original French fiction of female sexual notoriety, her *Mémoires de la vie de Henriette-Sylvie de Molière* (1671–1674).

When early commentators like Bayle praise Villedieu's innovativeness (even when they do so, like Bayle, the better to attack a genre whose success they find alarming), they credit her only with the invention of the type of historical novel critics today more readily associate with Lafayette. However, Villedieu deserves credit for a second type of novel, one whose existence literary history generally prefers not to recognize, the pseudomemoirs of an adventuress. Her *Mémoires de la vie de Henriette-Sylvie de Molière* shares the bravado and the passion for action characteristic of the early female autobiographical tradition whose best-known representative is Montpensier.[9] Henriette-Sylvie rides off for many of her finest exploits dressed "en amazone," that is, as a man. Like her precursor amazons, she flirts with danger in her attempts to take on roles traditionally defined as male. However, in this domain Henriette-Sylvie far surpasses her real-life counterparts: Villedieu's most striking enlargement of the fictional space reserved for heroinism is her decision to imagine the story of a sexual adventuress, a full half-century before such a plot seems to have been conceivable in French literature.

Thus, whereas the amazons of the Fronde turned to cross-dressing to facilitate their invasion of the military sphere, Henriette-Sylvie adopts amazon garb for a more delicate invasion: she dresses as a man to make love to women. Most notable is the sequence in which the cross-dressed heroine courts a marquise by day, and arranges that she be replaced for the crucial nighttime sequences by her lover who (conveniently) looks like her (106–8). Henriette-Sylvie's amorous life as a man ends only when the marquis, in order to "punish" the man with whom his wife has been betraying him, has her "stripped," and discovers "that I was only a woman" (109). Rather than being a proto-Freudian confirmation of woman's castration, however, the scene functions as a potent reminder of (this) woman's ability to confound the established order: Henriette-Sylvie shows how powerful she still is when "only a woman" by immediately seducing the husband who had hoped to castrate her.

Villedieu's novel is simultaneously a celebration of women bold enough to challenge a repressive social order and a defense of those it presents as victims of this system. Henriette-Sylvie's travels are a complex variation on the picaresque theme: hers is less the tale of one woman's social ascension than an extended meditation on the variety of threatening situations that any formal tie with the familial order creates for women. Villedieu matches encounters with fictional characters with references to historical figures of her day. Thus, on the one hand, Henriette-Sylvie meets a fictional Comtesse de Cardonnoy who is "fleeing, dressed as a man, the house of a husband because of his inhuman treatment" (121) and, on the other hand, she explains her own cross-dressing by borrowing the identity of a woman who had just met in real life the tragic fate the fictional comtesse was trying to avoid: "I said that I was that Marquise de Castellane who has since had such a tragic end, and that I was trying to flee the persecution of my husband's brothers who were looking for me in order to assassinate me" (111).[10] The novel dwells in particular on the fate of women pronounced "scandalous" because their conduct threatens in different ways the institution of marriage: Henriette-Sylvie discusses the practice of locking them up and catalogues the places commonly chosen for their confinement. Because of her involvement with a young nobleman who wishes to marry her despite his family's interdiction, Henriette-Sylvie herself enters this category of women who try to brave the family: the lion's share of Sylvie's memoirs is devoted to the persecutions of the Englesac family, who lock up their son to keep him from marrying her (157), and who seem endlessly on the trail of Villedieu's heroine to confine her to a convent (see, for example, 285).

The *Mémoires de la vie de Henriette-Sylvie de Molière* marks a crucial moment in the history of French women's writing. Furthermore, because, like the monuments of that tradition, it allows the reality of women's lives to invade its fiction, the novel cannot be divorced from the history of women's legal status under the ancien régime. In both those histories it is a troubling document. In fiction, it heralds the advent of explosive texts in which characters male and female break out of the confinement of the roles previously dictated by fiction. In reality, it offers additional evidence of the crisis in marriage that inspires Lafayette's historical fiction. The novel may also help explain why the monarchy decided, at the very moment of its publication, to take control over marriage, to assume the power to decide who could marry, and to determine the grounds for separation.

Finally, Villedieu's novel, with its return to the amazonian spirit of the Fronde years, forces its readers to confront for the first time interrelated issues that become unavoidable when considering women's writing at the end of Louis XIV's reign. At the conclusion of the novel's original edition (book 2), Henriette-Sylvie declares: "I will always be ready to acknowledge (*avouer*) my most secret follies; whatever the fashion in which my enemies have chosen to interpret them, appearances, which are often deceiving, are the only crime of my conduct" (117). What is a scandalous woman, and where does her scandal lie? Should we believe the outsider's version of her story ("appearances"), or her own "acknowledgment" of her daring? With this novel, Villedieu inaugurated what proved to be a long and complicated saga of guilt (the official story) and self-defense (the woman's tale), of condemnation (Richelet) and defense (Bayle). By the time it was over a half-century later, all the scandalous women had lost any claim to literary history and many innocent bystanders had been dragged into oblivion with them.[11]

THE HISTORY OF PRIVATE LIFE

Ceux qui écrivent l'histoire générale n'étudient point le particulier de la vie des hommes qui ont joué un grand rôle: cependant c'est ce particulier ... qui fait connaître le caractère de leurs inclinations, et par lequel on voit s'ils sont dignes d'estime ou de blâme. Voilà pourquoi le lecteur a plus de curiosité de le connaître que ce qui se passe

devant tout le monde, où les hommes ... se tiennent
toujours sur leurs gardes.

Françoise de Motteville,
Mémoires[12]

IT WAS some twenty years before writers took up the challenge to the
family plot offered by the saga of Henriette-Sylvie de Molière. However,
the year after its last volume appeared, Villedieu began her involvement
with the type of novel generally considered the modernization of Scudéry's historical fiction, the *histoire*. In *Les Désordres de l'amour* (1675),
she presented the new novel as a challenge to France's official story,
especially with her emphasis on the sexual indiscretions of the nation's
great men.[13] The new model for historical fiction imagined simultaneously by Villedieu and by Lafayette had a powerful influence on the
immediate development of French prose: from the late 1680s until the
dawn of the Enlightenment (1715), historical fiction was the dominant
mode.

The historical fiction of women writers is almost always faithful to
the Lafayette-Villedieu model. In their struggle to decide whether wom-
en's writing should be praised or banned, early commentators effectively
define this object of controversy. For example, in his defense of *La
Princesse de Clèves* against Valincour's attack, the Abbé de Charnes
includes a detailed explanation of Lafayette's project.[14] In his formulation, what he terms the "histoire galante" is a form entirely without
precedent in antiquity (130), a recent invention created as a literary rival
to history. Charnes thus explains the generic marker chosen by its
creators, *histoire,* which means "story" and is usually translated "short
story," even though this effacement of the word's other meaning, "history," also effaces the creators' decision to establish themselves as authors
by challenging the authority of a genre celebrated by ancients and
moderns. According to Charnes, the subjects of *histoires galantes* are
partially or entirely historical (130); more important, these new "stories"
are crafted to seem better than the real thing: "They are faithful copies
of real history, often so similar that they are taken for history itself"
(135).

However, the new histories did not lay claim to history's full scope:
rather than "considering kings in the highly visible (*éclatantes*) actions
that are the subject of history," they portray kings as "private" individuals "considered only in their domesticity" (139). These self-proclaimed
precursors of today's historians of private life reveal, their first theoreti-

cian contends, "certain things that authors of true history do not" (140). Charnes' description confirms the lesson of Lafayette's two private histories of royal princesses, in which the great events of French history are shown to be the result of unrequited love or broken marriage contracts: according to these histories, in their "unofficial capacity" (*état privé*) kings are concerned above all with "sexual intrigue" (*galanterie*) (135, 139).

In his authorized version of a nascent literary genre, Charnes acts as if he were accounting for many *histoires galantes*. His description may have functioned instead as a prescription for success: two decades later the form had become so common that in his *Dictionnaire* Bayle attacked "a problem growing more important every day" because of the success of what he termed "the new novels" (*les nouveaux romans*) (article "Nidhard," n.C, 1720 ed., 3:2091). The "new novelists" have been so successful in simulating history that "they have thrown a shadow over real history": readers cannot "separate fiction from true fact" in their intrigues.[15] So outraged was Bayle by what he considered an undermining of history's authority that, even though sympathetic to Villedieu because she had been wronged by an unscrupulous biographer, he chastised her for having invented "sexual liaisons" that she blended in with historical facts about great men (333). So outraged was he that, in his more general attack on the history of private life, he suggests that "the authorities may have to force these new novelists either to decide to write pure history or pure fiction, or at least to use brackets to separate truth and lies [in their work]" (3:2091).[16]

To comprehend Bayle's outrage, we have to remember that Lafayette and Villedieu conceived (apparently independently) their common project at the beginning of what came to be known as the "quarrel of history," a long-term critique of history as it had traditionally been practiced in France that was testimony to a widespread discontent with a genre considered no longer worthy of confidence.[17] The rise in the *histoire galante*'s fortunes was simultaneous with the fall from grace of "true history." During the same period, new historical genres and new approaches to history were developed in an attempt to win back history's traditional public. Bayle worried that the new novel, because it was "poison[ing] Modern History so flagrantly" (*Nouvelles* 317), might make it more difficult for pure history to reestablish its credibility.

His concern would have been more acute had he lived to see the whole trajectory of the *histoire galante*'s influence. By 1734, Lenglet-Dufresnoy entitled a long chapter of *On the Usefulness of Novels* "The Imperfection of History Causes Us to Esteem Novels." In it, he proclaims the superiority of novels to pure history, which has for too long neglected women's role as the prime movers of history (115). Such theories, coupled with the genre's credibility at a time when history was in disfavor, explain the Abbé Jacquin's attack on "The Dangers of Novels": these works are dangerous reading for young people because, in them, the crowned heads of Europe, "no matter how illustrious," are not "sheltered from calumnies" (160, 251).

The new novel founded in the 1670s proved such a durable power that, over the next half-century, it forced a confrontation with the most venerable prose genre, history. This confrontation is confirmed by the semantic drift whereby, at the dawn of the Enlightenment, "histoire" had been so contaminated from contact with "galante" that critics from opposing camps like Bayle and Jacquin were united in their suggestion that the State should intervene to regulate the new historical fiction. As part of the same process, the adjective yoked to "histoire" underwent its own semantic transformation. Throughout the seventeenth century, "galant" and "galanterie" are part of the core vocabulary of women writers; indeed, this may be the only terminology used heavily by all three generations. Initially, their connotations are exclusively positive. Scudéry uses the terms almost obsessively to indicate the domain under female control. As a result of her usage, by the second half of the century the primary meaning of "galant" was "worldly": someone was "galant" when he or she had, in Furetière's expression, "the air of the Court." A man could also be "galant" by "trying to please women" (*le beau sexe*). A "galant" was sensitive to the code of living and loving properly dictated by women in the salons, had assimilated from women's conversation the lessons of "galanterie," and thus belonged to that parallel intellectual aristocracy of those who acted nobly whether or not they were of noble birth, and who were considered worthy of assimilation into the official aristocracy through marriage.

In Scudéry's writing, however, a pejorative note occasionally invades this vocabulary, as if she had not fully succeeded in banishing from the semantic usage she was dictating a sixteenth-century origin, when "galant" inevitably referred to a "vert galant," a young man with the physical endowments that made him a natural for "galanteries," sexual liaisons.[18] This is the connotation that became reconnected with "galant" as soon as the new novel chose as its preferred historical terrain the late sixteenth century, the period when *galant* was primarily sexual and *galanteries* were presumed to be under male control. In the vocabulary's final seventeenth-century incarnation, it is tied to sexuality: rather than indicating "worldly commerce" and "salon encounters," *galanterie* becomes a synonym for "sexual liaisons."[19]

This should not be taken as a sign that the century's last generation of women writers chose to distance themselves from *préciosité* once it became fashionable to mock it, or that it was they who set the French novel on the course that culminated in *Les Liaisons dangereuses*. On the contrary, when the notorious women writers revive *galanterie*'s sixteenth-century meaning, they do not abandon their allegiance to Scudéry in the process. In their revised map of the land of Tenderness, women no longer feared to venture onto what Scudéry pronounced "unknown lands": sexual liaisons were now portrayed as just as much under female domination as the art of amorous conversation.

This, then, was the double threat of the new version of French history proposed by women writers at a time when the traditional view of French history was losing credibility: that it would convince readers that the great modern heroes were sexually indiscreet, *galants,* and that it would also convince the public that these great men were under female domination. *La Princesse de Clèves* identifies court politics as the reign of *galanterie:* "Ambition and *galanterie* were the soul of this court" (44).[20] In her usage, Lafayette is on the cusp: *galanterie* already connotes "sexual intrigue" but has not yet lost the sense of "knowledge of the court." In the historical fiction that proliferated in her wake—under the name *histoire galante,* but also under those of *histoire secrète, mémoires secrets, nouvelle galante, annales galantes, histoire des amours*—a generation of women writers portrayed *galanterie* as "the soul" of many courts, French courts more or less distant, Italian courts, Spanish courts. In general, following Lafayette's and Villedieu's example, they researched their material so thoroughly that, just as their critics feared might happen, readers sometimes took their volumes for "pure" history.[21]

No critical attack gives a full sense of just how daringly innovative these novelists were with the new turn they gave *galanterie*. Never before (and not often since) have French women writers crafted such sexually explicit plots: it is hard to imagine the shock of their frankness in an age that actively promoted a myth of sexual chastity. The *histoires galantes* are of varying degrees of raciness. Some, for example, Catherine Durand Bédacier's *Les Mémoires secrets de la cour de Charles VII, roi de*

France (1700), portray sexual intrigues similar to those in Lafayette's fiction and are only slightly more explicit in their treatment.[22]

Others are far bolder. Witness *Les Amours du Cardinal de Richelieu* (1687) and the *Histoire des amours de Grégoire VII* (1700), also by Durand Bédacier. Exposés of the sexual liaisons of powerful men are even more indiscreet when they are prelates of the Church, as the author recognizes in a preface to the 1700 volume. She justifies her subject matter by proclaiming that "the truth must be made public" (n.pag.). These *histoires* are both more explicitly *galantes* than their precursors and openly anticlerical: Durand Bédacier had discovered a fictional blend that eighteenth-century readers found irresistible.

Certain of these fictions are more sexually explicit than even eighteenth-century libertine fiction. Madame de Tenain's *Histoire du comte de Clare, nouvelle galante* (1696) may well be the raciest work by any early woman writer: it contains scenes of lovemaking recounted far more graphically than anything in Crébillon (for example, 57–58, 26). However, this novelty should not cause us to lose sight of the fact that the new novelists, Tenain included, never limit the *histoire galante*'s subversiveness to its sexual frankness: *galanteries* become more explicit to undermine more effectively the foundation of the French national estate. Tenain's family history recounts the ruin of a marriage (despite her husband's suspicions, the marquise maintains a long-term adultery with the Comte de Clare) and ultimately the unraveling of two family plots. The marquise has the comte's son while married to the marquis; upon the marquis's sudden death, the boy becomes his heir; the marquise and the comte marry, but he is soon killed in battle. The comte's family tries to break his will that names the boy they think is another man's son his heir, calling it "against all the laws" (204), but his widow wins her countersuit. The novel, which initially seems only a titillating tale of illicit sex, by its conclusion has become a *chassé-croisé,* not of lovers, but of heirs: the comte's family believes that its estate has become the property of another man's son; the marquis's family, sure that its wealth has been properly transmitted, has in reality handed over its estate to a child of adultery.

These tales of *galanterie* highlight the potential threat to families of marriages initially arranged to favor their financial and political well-being: illegitimate children are passed off as legitimate, and "foreign" blood thereby enters a line; illegitimate offspring of royal liaisons are married, often by force, into "honorable" families. We cannot know if these stories had a basis in reality. But surely fictions so successful at the game of history that they convinced readers of royal indiscretions could have persuaded them of the contamination of bloodlines and therefore of the mistransmission of estates? Such a plot, after all, merely feeds off an obsession of the age: contemporary legal scholars constantly stress that, whereas maternity could be established, no proof of paternity existed.

It was not likely that writers who repeatedly cast suspicion on the purity of noble bloodlines would escape with their own reputations intact. This must be the origin of the insinuation that they saw *galanterie* everywhere in France's past because they were themselves so *galantes*. Jacquin, for example, pronounces "calumnies" the stories of queens of France that Charlotte-Rose de La Force called "histoires secrètes" or "anecdotes galantes," then concludes that this is about what one would expect from the "trop tendre Mlle de la Force" (251), turning the adjective Scudéry used to designate a fictional land under female domination into an allegation of a woman writer's personal sexual impropriety.

PUBLIC SCANDALS

> Où est le roman, dans lequel l'héroïne ... ne commande en maître à l'amant, qui se trouve encore trop heureux d'obéir en esclave. Où sont les mémoires secrets, dans lesquels la maîtresse d'un Prince ne gouverne pas, au gré de son caprice, tout un Royaume? Où est l'aventure galante, dans laquelle de petites Bergères, de simples Paysannes n'ayent pas droit d'aspirer à l'alliance des plus grands Seigneurs, après en avoir fait autant d'esclaves de leur beauté?
>
> Abbé Jacquin,
> *Entretiens sur les romans*

IT IS hardly surprising that anxiety about the consolidation of estates would have been high in the final decades of Louis XIV's reign, when so many forces must have seemed to be conspiring to end an era of prosperity. The last peace treaty that brought the country substantial new territorial gain was signed in 1678, the year of *La Princesse de Clèves*'s publication. From then on, the national estate was consistently eroded, as the aging monarch lost territories conquered when he was still the rising Sun King.[23] Family estates were squandered to maintain the ostentatious pomp that was de rigueur at Versailles. And money was drained from all coffers to finance the enormous expense of an endless series of disastrous wars, wars that made many women like the Comtesse de Clare widows when they were still young enough to renegotiate their legacies.

The novel Lafayette published on the brink of this national decline had a dual posterity. It is ironic that Jacquin cast doubt on the personal morality of a writer of historical fiction, La Force, for those who exploited Lafayette's other legacy seem to have gone out of their way to provide a more logical target. This second group of writers developed Lafayette's plot of unhappy marriage into epistolary and memoir novels that are the first true precursors of the numerous eighteenth-century novels taking those forms: in their hands, the novel of marriage realizes its potential to become the novel of adultery. Adultery, legal separation, illegitimate births, even custody battles—any cause for public scandal is dwelled on in loving detail. No longer do novelists distance their accounts by setting them in a historical past: for the first time, the novel is set exclusively in contemporary France. These are the first-person accounts of women who, like the Princesse de Clèves, seem designed to make their readers compare their behavior with the conduct they would expect from someone they knew. In short, everything about these novels would seem to guarantee that their authors would be identified with their scandalous heroines. And they were.

My goal is not to proclaim the notorious women innocent of "crimes" with which they have been charged but simply to point out the complexity of a situation hitherto read far too literally. The heroines of these works—despite their obvious similarities with their creators—are not autobiographical projections: like Villedieu's, the biographies of these women writers have been corrupted, but enough remains to make this much certain. These new heroines have a distinctive trait in common with Henriette-Sylvie de Molière: they present their narratives as open to diverse interpretations. Like the narrators of autobiographies, they ask us to sit in judgment on their lives. However, their works are unique because they make the process of judgment, and especially the act of condemnation, so explicit. When we compile the guilty verdicts at the conclusion of each episode (each an account of crimes with which the heroine is charged by her persecutors), the resulting portrait in every case is nearly identical to the biography that subsequent commentators present as that of the novel's creator—a reconstruction that, these novels teach us, is absolutely predictable. Fin-de-siècle women writers turn the novel into a notoriety trial. In their fiction they show the grounds on which actual women were proclaimed notorious and the consequences of this verdict. Their texts are all the more powerful because they are situated in the realm of the phantasm rather than in the domain of autobiography. Instead of the story of an individual woman, each work projects a powerful construction of gender, a period's obsession with the alleged proliferation of women judged notorious because they threatened the ruin of families.

Literary historians through the centuries who proclaim these novels unworthy because of their, and their authors', immorality have deprived readers of novels of real merit. I will present briefly the two I feel would most readily find a public today: the first, by an aristocrat, features the question of adultery; the second, by a bourgeoise, the plight of the children of a broken marriage. Both suggest that, on the eve of the Enlightenment, the institution of marriage was widely believed to be in crisis.

My involvement with these texts began with an interdiction pronounced with the full authority of Antoine Adam, the individual who was seen and who surely saw himself as the principal architect of our current vision of seventeenth-century French literary history. Researching the *Mémoires de Madame la comtesse de M**** (1697) by Henriette de Castelnau, Comtesse de Murat, I turned to Adam's *Histoire de la littérature française du dix-septième siècle;* there I found no genuine commentary but reckless claims worthy of tabloid journalism: the comtesse, Adam contends, was imprisoned because of her "public scandals" (*scandales éclatantes*). He mocks the "exertions" of her previous biographer in defense of her virtue; the (nameless) scholar was ignorant of the proof of her criminality, a lesbian sonnet that demonstrates that "it was just as dangerous to leave her in the company of women as in that of men" (5:317 n.2). He dismisses her novel categorically: "No one would dream of reading it now"—and immediately offers a count's narrative as substitute for the "dangerous" countess', the *Mémoires de la vie du comte de Gramont* (1713) by Anthony Hamilton, which "remains even today a work justly admired" (5:317).[24] Only those who know that Adam is not usually given to such overt critical hostility will understand how intensely my curiosity was piqued by his attempt, reminiscent of Boileau's in the *Dialogue des héros de roman,* to guarantee the exclusion of a work to which he had experienced a powerful reaction.

The work fully justifies both the strength of his reaction and my curiosity. The *Mémoires de Madame la comtesse de M**** is a crisply written, fast-paced, extended novelization of Woman's struggle to preserve her reputation. I say "Woman's" advisedly, for the narrator frequently reminds her reader that she is going public with her private life to call attention to an issue of general importance for her female contemporaries, the desire to believe that women live their lives for *galanterie*. Some of the work's early editions have a second title page, which is headed "The Defense of Women." Together, the two titles convey perfectly the novel's point of view, according to which "the faithful account of my life's adventures" demonstrates that "most often there is more misfortune than dissoluteness in the conduct of the women whose reputation the public delights in destroying" (5).

The narrator recounts her own life to explain why her behavior is decried publicly. At an early age she is forced by her father to marry an older man to whom he owes money; he in effect sells her to pay off his debt. Her husband, apparently with some cause, is constantly jealous and mistreats her.[25] She flees to a convent and writes her father and her husband to request a separation. She is persuaded to return home but, when she finds herself pregnant, her husband declares publicly that the child is not his and renews his abuse. She again flees. When she learns that her mother is conspiring with her husband and his family to have her locked up, she attempts, in the manner of the Princesse de Clèves, to regularize her irregular situation in the hope of recovering control over her life. Having put herself under the protection of a magistrate, she discloses the details of her husband's mistreatment and asks for an official separation. When her mother, speaking on her husband's behalf, tries to force her to accept a private agreement that would require her to leave Paris, she refuses. She will not accept the exile that would save the family's honor at the expense of her freedom and her reputation: "I had been too abused to content myself with a private agreement, when I wanted public justification" (158–59). When her husband dies just in time to spare both families the disgrace of divorce proceedings, she has recourse to the only "public justification" still left her and publishes these memoirs, which conclude with the threat to continue her literary scandal by editing the memoirs of other women who have been "as harshly treated as she" (276).[26]

The comtesse has no illusions about her ability to rewrite the now public history of her private life: she knows that "a reputation for *galanterie* once [having been] acquired" by a woman, the public will

[marginal notes:]
Mémoires de Madame la comtesse de M (Murat)

= defense of ♀

misfortune ⁊ dissoluteness

(plot)

reputation for galanterie cannot be erased

always think her guilty of this "propensity" (276). Nor does she have faith in the solutions of her precursors, as her vocabulary shows: "on veut qu'elle conserve encore dans la retraite cette inclination" (276)— the recourse of a previous generation, the "apparently sad" compromise of "retirement" is no longer open to a woman once she has gone public with her refusal to accept the familial design on her person.[27]

documents general attempts to obtain divorce for failed marriages

With the *Mémoires de Madame la comtesse de M****, Murat made the novel acknowledge the story latent behind *La Princesse de Clèves*'s brilliant historical façade, the story of Woman's attempt to obtain the divorce that would end an unhappy marriage. I say "Woman's" once again because the text suggests—through references to other ill-treated women and to women who had already publicized their memoirs of unhappy marriages—that the comtesse's tale documents the existence of a social phenomenon bigger than this case history, that this account is a response to history. It is also possible, as we will see, that the novel played a part in shaping history—and not just literary history's depiction of Murat herself (as any reader could predict) as a notorious *femme galante*.[28]

refuses legal limits

Murat's heroine is aware of her legal rights and especially of their limitations. She realizes that "the treatment of which I was accusing my husband was not dangerous enough to authorize my separation" and that her husband is within his rights when he "threatens to keep [her] locked up in his château" (47).[29] Thus the ultimate scandal of her conduct is that it is just as innovative as the Princesse de Clèves's *aveu:* she refuses to accept these legal limits, just as she refuses to accept the private "accommodation" her mother offers her. She holds out for a

wants public justification

"public justification," the official recognition by the State and by the families that were "its foundation" that a husband unhappily married was not allowed to act out his displeasure in violence to his wife's person and that a wife could refuse to remain a prisoner of her husband's suspicions. The *Mémoires* demonstrates that female notoriety is really not an affair of *galanterie* (and this explains why the question of the heroine's guilt or innocence is treated so playfully, its evocation cloaked in innuendo that makes it impossible ever to know what really hap-

crime = request for legal change

pened) but an affair of publicity and legality. The comtesse's real crime is her request, "in defense of [all] women," for legal change.[30]

The 1690s witnessed a reevaluation of the new conception of marriage formulated in the 1670s. The second wave of divorce treatises then produced reflects a certain hesitation regarding what earlier texts present as an absolute distinction (power to the Church or power to the State). In part, this tendency toward accommodation results from a perception that may also be evident in Murat's *Mémoires:* the State was harsher than the Church had been in dealing with women, such as the Comtesse de M*** (and perhaps the Comtesse de Murat), who put their private interests over the public good. Two decades after *La Princesse de Clèves,* the conflict latent in that story, between the new official definition of marriage as contract and the emerging conception of marriage as a means to personal fulfillment, was finally being publicly displayed.

An equally striking illustration of this conflict is provided by a most curious set of paired memoirs, the *Mémoires de Madame Du Noyer écrits par elle-même* (1709–1710) by Anne-Marguerite Du Noyer and the *Mémoires de Mr. Des N*** écrits par lui-même,* presumably by her husband, Guillaume Du Noyer.[31] The identification between author and narrator established by the titles of these memoirs suggests that they be read as nonfiction. However, in the case of the woman's narrative, the presentation of the narrator's life has far more in common with Murat's fiction than with contemporary autobiographical texts. Du Noyer's memoirs repeat the pattern, established by Murat's, whereby the notorious woman makes her life public, thereby establishing her own notoriety, in a form of self-defense that is primarily a defense of all women who are victims of abusive husbands and unjust laws. Like Murat's, Du Noyer's memoirs cross the border between fiction and nonfiction more clearly in their depiction of the situation of Woman at the end of Louis XIV's reign than in their depiction of individual lives.

The status of their companion text, "Des Noyer's" refutation (the memoir allegedly written by Du Noyer's actual husband), is harder to determine: the work seems too polished to have been written by a professional soldier with no known intellectual aspirations. In view of the highly polemical issue that is the focus of Du Noyer's consideration of marriage—intermarriage between Protestants and Catholics in the aftermath of the revocation of the Edict of Nantes—these counterme- moirs could have been composed by a pro-Catholic faction.[32] The bla- tantly controversial stance Du Noyer adopts in all her production sug- gests a second theory: the countermemoirs were also her work, an essential part of both her attempt to portray the destruction of a wom- an's reputation and her attempt to paint a full picture of religion's effects on marriage.[33]

Du Noyer's incipit parallels Murat's: she is "presenting herself as a

[margin notes: nb. State was more harsh than Church had been!; Mémoires de Mme + M. Du Noyer; could be read as 'non-fiction' but prob shouldn't; defense of ♀s who are victims of abusive ♂/laws; "his" refutation prob not written by him; ? of conflict Cath/Protestant → could be Catholic author OR could be Mme's doing]

public spectacle" in a *general,* rather than a personal, defense, "to give a fair idea of myself at a time when calumny is trying to disfigure people" (6:1). The personal history that follows, like Murat's, is full of misfortune, only in this case misfortune that is divorced from sexual innuendo. The narrator loses her mother at an early age; her father literally sells her to her mother's childless sister by means of a contract "unique of its kind" (6:8). She is destined to be well married, when her adopted father gambles away all their money and the marriage contract is broken (6:8).[34] This broken contract sets her on the road to notoriety: she finds herself, a strict Protestant, without protection during the persecutions that surrounded the revocation of the Edict of Nantes (6:16–17). She recounts in great detail the victimization of French Protestants and their diaspora (6:60–64, 76–77, 89–90, 112). She herself escapes the country, disguised as a young man (6:116)—for the first time, a seventeenth-century amazon rides off without fanfare and theatricality.

Upon her return to France she is imprisoned to obtain a forced conversion; she is released when she marries a Catholic. Her orthodoxy, however, is only apparent, for the public marriage contract is founded on the type of private contract that the Princesse de Clèves imagined only too late, in this case her husband's written promise never to use his authority to force her to renounce practices dictated by her religion. The marriage works until her husband violates both contracts, the public one by gambling away her inheritance (6:388), and the private one by refusing (after she has once again left the country to escape religious persecution) to allow their daughters to marry Protestants. In the face of his efforts to force her to return their children to him, she flees to Holland, then to England, where her memoirs culminate in her symbolic reception into the Protestant state: when she takes leave of her reader, she is in Westminster Abbey awaiting the coronation of a queen.

Without the countermemoirs, "written by Mr. Des N*** himself," Du Noyer's heroine would not seem to belong to the class of notorious women. However, the husband's text, presented as "the key that unlocks" his wife's memoirs (5:162), develops the negative vision that Murat's heroine integrates into her own story. When these texts are read together, one woman's private history becomes indicative of a larger, public menace.[35] In his account, "Des Noyers" occupies the position of orthodoxy, political and religious: his orthodoxy is established by various outside authorities called in to confirm his view of his wife's life. First, the anonymous author of the preface tells us that the husband was always a model of patience, controlling his "just anger" at behavior so "dangerous and mad" that it merited a public flogging.[36] The preface is paralleled by the anonymous text used to conclude the countermemoirs, a comedy in three acts, *Le Mariage précipité,* said to have been staged in Utrecht in 1713 as a satire on his wife: the alleged stand-in for Anne-Marguerite Du Noyer is ridiculed because of her outrageous efforts to trap a rich Protestant for her daughter.

In between these predictable proofs that Catholic (men) and Protestant (men) alike were scandalized by "the she-devil's" conduct (1:160), the narrator presents evidence that startles, even in the context of a text as basely mudslinging as this, a "Memoir by my daughter Constantin" (5:256–81). This document indicates the true nature of these paired memoirs: together, they function as a custody trial, at which readers are asked to sit in judgment. Which parent deserves to raise these daughters or, rather, to arrange their marriages: the father who claims to have respected a private marital agreement and supervised their Catholic upbringing? Or the mother who, according to the father, has broken that contract and abducted the daughters "from the arms of idolatry to lead them on the way to heaven" (5:238), that is, to lead them on the journey from Catholicism to Protestantism? This elaborately staged family drama—perhaps the first true precursor of the bloody custody battles in today's divorce proceedings, including the child's statement explaining why he or she wishes to live with a certain parent—is without precedent at this period and is far more vivid than the earliest examples of the parallel legal genre, the custody hearings of the first French divorce trials in the 1790s. Actual legal proceedings, recorded in the third person, lack the immediacy of these "personal" appeals.[37] However, it is hard to reconcile this immediacy with their authors' distanced chronological perspective on these proceedings. Neither of the paired memoirs informs us about their outcome: we can only make assumptions based on the placement of the daughter's account. She is looking back on events that took place some years before; she is writing "because [her father] orders her to do so," and her narrative of their "retreat" (*refuge*) to Protestant countries exactly corroborates his version of those years. From these details we may deduce that the father wins out, and that she therefore ends up a Catholic.

This family docudrama—how fictive, how staged, we will never know—calls our attention to the big picture in which all these tales of female notoriety must be understood. The *Mémoires de Madame Du*

Noyer defines female notoriety as the woman's decision to challenge the State and its official religion in the person of the individual to whom they have delegated authority over her. The memoirs reveal important consequences for the French nation if notorious women are allowed to infiltrate Catholic families: the loss of capital (the narrator demands that her husband return her dowry, which she claims he is squandering) and the loss of children as loyal citizens. In his revenge, "Mr. Des Noyers" becomes the spokesman for all those who fear the public cost of women's personal freedom.[38] Nowhere was this fear more evident than in the abundant contemporaneous commentary about marriage and its dissolution.

MODERN MARRIAGE

> [Les romans] nous apprennent à mépriser les pratiques les mieux établies de la Religion, et les règles les plus respectables de la société, en insinuant que *l'essence du mariage ne consiste pas dans une vaine cérémonie, mais dans le don du cœur et dans les sentiments qui l'accompagnent.*
>
> Abbé Jacquin, *Entretiens sur les romans* (1755)[39]

HENRI COULET is no more given to diatribes in his generally excellent history of the early French novel than is Antoine Adam in his literary history. But the novels of notorious women also make him lose his critical sangfroid:

> In the last third of the century, noble passion . . . is replaced by guilty and degrading passion. . . . The status of the married woman had not changed since 1640: already at that time, girls were married very young and without consulting their hearts; but greatness of soul now seems difficult. (1:212)

Coulet's incursion into the reality of the feminine condition, like Adam's, culminates in an *ad feminam* attack:

> While Madame de Lafayette . . . portrays the failure of heroism, Madame de Villedieu portrays creatures without heroism, a prey to their weaknesses. . . . Her experience, since she adduces it, is more that of an adventuress than that of a lady of the court. (1:267)[40]

At the end of the seventeenth century, it is true, "girls were [still] married very young and without consulting their hearts," but did this mean that "the status of the married woman had not changed since 1640"? I think not. At the very least, we have to admit that women's .expectations about the life of a married woman had changed; despite its evident "greatness of soul," *La Princesse de Clèves* already attests to a new interest in the potential cost to the woman married off without regard for her feelings; it also shows a desire to explore concrete solutions to an officially unrecognized dilemma. This interest was more intense, the solutions proposed more concrete, in fin-de-siècle women's writing: the difference between subsequent fictions of married women and Lafayette's inaugural fiction is thus one of degree, rather than a total change of moral register. In addition, the next generation of novelists had to position their fiction in response to an image of married women that was probably unheard of, or at most dimly visible, when Lafayette was creating her novels. For the image that so scandalizes Coulet, married women "prey to their weaknesses," "without heroism," is not of their creation: it is already on the existential horizon by the time the novels of "adventuresses" began to appear.

What was its origin in reality? In all likelihood, this female plague ("pestilence," in Father Porée's words, 51) was largely phantasm, like all the most powerful fictions of female desire, from the prostitute with the heart of gold to the lesbian *femme fatale*—part wish fulfillment and part dreaded occurrence. This image—of the adulterous woman seeking a "divorce" (legal separation) that would destabilize the genealogical and the financial order of honorable families—becomes so ubiquitous in a variety of texts both legal and literary that it is easy to sympathize with the (feigned?) bewilderment of literary commentator François Granet who, in his response to Porée's diatribe against women and novels, wondered if "secret marriages, divorces, and abductions have really become today such common events" (118). One may legitimately wonder, as Granet did, if the State's "foundations" could really have been threatened by the conduct of a few women no longer willing to accommodate themselves to bad marriages.

It is possible that the threat of upheaval represented by the adulterous woman in search of a legal settlement was useful to the State since, by the 1690s, the complex legal machinery put in place around what was called divorce seems suspiciously like a legal fiction. On the most obvious level, I have in mind the discrepancy, noted by Granet, between the tightening of legal restrictions on women (which continued to make it almost impossible for them to find legal solutions to the most disastrous marriages) and the popular perception, evidenced by an entry in

Furetière's *Dictionnaire universel,* that, aided by cooperative authorities, women were having their own way and making their own law. Furetière's entry reads: *"Separation:* Women begin *separation* proceedings against their husbands in order to live as libertines (*dans le libertinage).*"[41] It was not their living in sin that caused concern but the possibility that women could be "libertine" in the sense of "femme sans aveu," woman answering to no one, woman as legal "adventuress."[42]

On a less obvious level, I refer to French divorce speculation as a legal fiction because the treatises that continued to argue for the definition of marriage as contract, justifying state control over the institution, also continued to encourage the belief that it was possible to dissolve a marriage; in this way they indirectly promoted the desire for a new kind of marriage, the so-called modern marriage. Nowhere is this situation clearer than in Pierre Le Ridant's 1753 treatise, *Examens de deux questions importantes sur le mariage,* perhaps the culmination of contract theory (and certainly the most accessible of the early divorce commentaries). True, neither the subject matter nor the approach had changed radically since the treatises of the 1670s: Le Ridant—the most sweeping early contract theorist, who would make marriage a civil matter entirely outside ecclesiastical jurisdiction—considers only the question of annulment and lists only traditionally accepted grounds for it. Nevertheless, widespread public discussion of annulment and separation—along with the 1670s, the mid-eighteenth century is the period of most intense debate concerning the nature of marriage[43]—surely encouraged the perception that marriage could, according to Le Ridant's favorite expression, "be broken." In addition, general acceptance of marriage as a contract and as a sacrament solely once the contract is valid could only have diminished the institution's moral authority. Divorce historians present this period as the point of no return: the Revolution's divorce decree was but a logical next step (Basdevant 58, 190–91). They have also noted that the vocabulary of "happiness" begins to enter contemporary definitions of marriage in the 1760s, immediately after this new wave of divorce commentary (Dessertine, chapter 1). At the same time, for those unhappily married and seeking a legal solution, all talk of "breaking marriages" was but a tantalizing mirage, a legal fiction that surely made reality all the harsher.

The accommodation that explains how contract theory continued to develop without being as harshly attacked as in the 1670s was worked out in the 1690s. The decade of the notorious women saw the publication of a pair of treatises, one from each camp, although it is easy to confuse their ideological grounding when reading them. In his 1691 *Traité des empêchements du mariage,* the man of the cloth, Father Jacques Boilèau (brother of the poet with the same name), gives concessions to the State and is sympathetic to the civil position. In his 1698 *Traité du pouvoir de l'église et des princes sur les empêchements du mariage,* Jean Gerbais (also an ecclesiastic, but writing in his capacity as "the king's professor at the Royal College of France") yields ground to the Church by arguing that "marriage was not a purely civil contract" (259). In my puzzlement over these shifting legal sands, the sole clue to understanding this moment of compromise, an apparent setback in contract theory's rise to domination, came from Jacques Boileau's only other publication, *L'Abus des nudités de gorge* (1675), a 110–page diatribe against the contemporary fashion for women of uncovering their arms and throat. In this text Boileau lives up to his family name and reveals himself a strict hard-liner: Woman is depicted as virtually the devil's agent. Was it possible, I wondered, that the man of the cloth was prepared to yield to civil authority because he realized that its rule would be harsher on those dangerous women?[44]

This interpretation is supported by the findings of marital historians: when they compare the jurisdiction of Church and State in the early modern period, almost all agree that ecclesiastical courts were far more favorable to women than their civil counterparts. On occasion, family historians such as Lottin warn against an interpretation of the Church's position as in any way "feminist": it allowed the termination of certain marriages judged unsalvageable, in particular, cases in which the conduct of one or both spouses was considered scandalous, but only in order to protect a sacrament whose sanctity was threatened by such behavior ("Vie et mort" 77–78). Whatever its motivation, the Church had permitted certain marriages to "be broken": it was surely this tendency that the lawyers Abraham and Gomont had in mind when they recommended to Louis XIV that the State step in to stop the "abuses" made possible by "the laxness of ecclesiastical jurisdiction" (Lottin, "Vie et mort" 60). Once the State, its usurpation justified by the contract theory of marriage, had done so, royal courts, according to Traer, "gave legal sanction to a double standard of sexual conduct": the husband's adultery was no longer grounds for separation, while the wife's was cause not only for separation but for her prolonged confinement (40, see also Lepointe 340). This advancement of the husband's rights was accompanied, as Dessertine has shown (21), by a promotion of his authority. Whereas canon law, following the guidelines of the Council of Trent, had defended the authority of the *father*, royal justice defined as its mission the protection of the *husband*'s authority in marriage.[45]

This double evolution culminates, in the mid-eighteenth century, in the twin treatises of the influential teacher and legal scholar, Robert-Joseph Pothier, generally considered the definitive statements on the French contract theory of marriage. In particular, Pothier's work makes clear the ultimate ancien régime position on separation. Whereas canon law had allowed women to file for separation on various grounds— including adultery, but also serious injury, corruption of morals, and so forth (Traer 40)—French royal law considered only one reason serious enough, mismanagement of an estate. A wife could be granted a separation only if she could prove that her husband had already squandered his own inheritance and that his bad handling of their affairs had now put her dowry in danger (Lepointe 386, Dessertine 22). An illusion of continuity was guaranteed by the fact that the wife still alleged physical and mental suffering in her testimony, but this was now purely to maintain the appearance of humanitarian concern. Pothier is categorical: a wife "must consider her husband's mistreatment as taking place on God's order as a cross that he is sending her for the expiation of her sins" (*Traité du contrat de mariage* 5:290). A wife's adultery is grounds for separation, but not a husband's, because "adultery committed by the woman is infinitely more contrary to the well-being of civil society because it despoils families by handing over their possessions to adulterous children who are foreign to them" (5:293). Pothier is the first to formulate explicitly a latent guideline of contract law: the clear delimitation and the protection of the wealth of individual families directed royal jurisdiction over marriage. Marriage was an affair of property; the woman whose conduct threatened in any way the correct transmission of that property must be marginalized before her scandalous conduct could spread.

As the fictions of the notorious women make clear, the State was hardening its stand on separation at the same time as the perception was becoming popular that husband and wife have a right to personal dignity, if not happiness, in marriage. The conflict between these views was bound to continue to produce collisions, even after the taste for allegedly indiscreet female scandal literature died out in the early decades of the eighteenth century. The posterity of the seventeenth century

female tradition is nowhere more evident than in the actual and fictional
confrontations of eighteenth-century women writers with the double
legal standard that gave husbands virtual license to deal with their wives
at their whim. In their private lives, eighteenth-century women writers
act out the stages of the continuing struggle for divorce legislation, from
legal separation (Riccoboni, Graffigny) to divorce in the modern sense
of the term (Staël). None of these writers left more vivid testimony, in
life as in fiction, to the force of these collisions between legal thinking
and popular perception than Françoise de Graffigny. Together, her
fictional speculation about marital injustice and the surviving evidence
about her personal experience with this phenomenon provide eloquent
confirmation of the conflict between the two simultaneously developing
notions of a modern marriage, whose union would eventually culminate
in the law allowing divorce.

The legal records—from the plaintiff's statement to the testimony of
witnesses—of Graffigny's separation proceedings read like a textbook
case for the theories of recent historians such as Dessertine and Traer.
These documents, along with the relevant letters from the beginning of
Graffigny's correspondence, prove her understanding of the consequences for the individual of the State's elaborately maintained legal
fiction.[46] Like her recent precursors Ferrand and Murat, Graffigny first
tries to win her family's support: in 1716 she writes her father begging
him to have her sent for "because I am in great danger and am aching
all over (*brisée*) from beatings" (*Correspondance* 1:1). Some months later
she renews her request, but this time she seems to understand the
foundation of the new French marital law because she no longer pleads
her case on personal grounds: their financial situation is dramatic, but
she is unable to sell property since potential buyers are afraid it is
"mortgaged." "Mr de Graffigny must be sent away, and I must be given
a *procuration* [legal authorization to take action concerning his property
in his name] to do in his absence all I think needs to be done concerning
possessions" (*Correspondance* 1:1–2).[47]

The separation hearings confirm Graffigny's intuition about the hy-
pocrisy of women's legal status. Numbers of witnesses testify to the
existence of marital abuse: one young woman had been able to hear
Graffigny screaming for mercy "more than eighty paces away from her
house"; another had seen the husband throw his wife to the ground and
hold her down "with his knee on her stomach." However, in a society
generally ready to accept Pothier's position, a wife would never be

granted a separation because of "a cross God sent her to expiate her sins," but only if the family's financial well-being was threatened. Graffigny was luckier than her precursors Ferrand and Murat, because the second condition was in fact the case: the husband was a gambler; when his profligacy had dissipated his own estate and was menacing her dowry, her family finally intervened and fought for the separation hearings.[48]

Like her notorious precursors, Graffigny became a writer; like them, she composed a first-person novel in which any information related to her own experience is subordinated to a general "defense of women." However, her *Lettres d'une Péruvienne* (1747) contains passages in which the hard edge of the personal still resists that generalization. These passages suggest a vision in the spirit of Scudéry and her co-*salonnières,* whose egalitarian instincts inspired them to infiltrate the highest rank of French society with those whose "natural" nobility made them partisans of equal rights for women. Graffigny's Peruvian heroine Zilia comes to realize that, without legal rights, French women are really outside the class system, outcasts.[49] Her characterization supports Scudéry's view of marriage as "long slavery" for women:

> How could [women] not revolt against the injustice of laws that tolerate men's license . . .? A husband can display repulsive behavior toward his wife without fearing punishment; he can squander with a lavishness as criminal as it is excessive not only his wealth and that of his children but even that of the victim that he leaves moaning in near indigence because of his avarice over reasonable expenses. . . . It seems that in France the marriage bonds are only reciprocal at the time of the ceremony, and that afterwards only women are bound by them. (345)

How can men be surprised if women "revolt," if their behavior appears notorious whenever it threatens society's unjust laws? The only other solution, chosen by Graffigny to conclude the adventures of her outcast heroine, is what the women writers of the post-Fronde years called a "triumph of indifference": Zilia refuses the marriage Graffigny's readers ardently desired for her in favor of "the pleasure of being. . . . Renounce all tumultuous feelings, those imperceptible ravagers of our being" (362). We leave Zilia in a life of legal luxury impossible for a woman in her creator's real world: in a legal triumph more spectacular than the Princesse de Clèves's, Zilia governs, on her own authority alone, her estate and her considerable personal wealth.

The classical French tradition of female literary notoriety extends
beyond Graffigny. A similar spirit motivates Claire de Duras to conclude the *précieuse* questioning of the foundations of French ancien
régime society. In *Ourika* (1823), she takes their interrogation beyond
rank and religion to race and portrays miscegenation as the ultimate
threat to the well-being of the "pillar" of the State, the family. In
addition, she adds race to gender to offer a double explanation for her
heroine's final "retreat" (*isolement volontaire*) (63). The exemplary French
novel of divorce, finally in the full modern sense of the term, was
imagined by the last true *précieuse* and the last true notorious woman in
the ancien régime mode, Germaine de Staël. In *Delphine* (1802), Staël
takes up the challenge of the *Carte de Tendre* and portrays *mariage
d'inclination* in opposition to the right of fathers (and their sons) to rule
with absolute authority over the distribution of property.[50]

It is only logical that Staël would make a questioning of woman's
legal rights central to her novels: in the section entitled "De l'esprit
général de la littérature chez les modernes" of *De la littérature* (1800)—
the first major work of literary theory by a French woman writer and
the volume that, had the female tradition known a glorious future in
the nineteenth century, could have made Staël the new Boileau—Staël
accounts for the novel's evolution from Lafayette's day until the Revolution. Initially, she repeats the conclusions first proposed by seventeenth-century theoreticians—the novel is the modern art form par
excellence; women defined the new genre's scope. However, she concludes that women were only able to define a new genre because they
had been given new rights: "One notes on every page ideas that would
never have occurred to anyone before women were accorded a type of
civil equality" (1:151). They had used this "type of civil equality" to
redefine virtue: in their fiction, virtue is no longer solely synonymous
with "l'amour de la patrie" (1:151). By thus equating female literary
invention with women's legal rights, Staël prepares the way for the
ultimate maxim on women and intellectual achievement offered by her
theory of literature: by limiting women's participation in the uprising
that completed the Fronde, and by relegating them to second-class legal
status, the Revolution decreed the end of the female literary tradition in
France. "Since the Revolution, men have decided that it was politically
and ethically useful to reduce women to the most absurd mediocrity"
(2:335)—an evaluation with which the next generation of women writers, notably those who felt obliged to hide their gender behind male

pseudonyms, such as George Sand and Daniel Stern, would certainly have concurred. Without at least "une sorte d'égalité civile," women could no longer have new literary ideas.[51]

DANGEROUS LIAISONS

> D'abord tu la verras, ainsi que dans
> *Clélie,*
> Recevoir ses Amants sous le doux
> nom d'Amis,
> Puis, bientôt en grande eau sur le
> fleuve de Tendre,
> Naviguer à souhait, tout dire, et tout
> entendre.
>
> Nicolas Boileau, tenth satire

VALINCOUR WAS right—there was a conspiracy—although he certainly did not guess its dimensions. Only one critic took the early novel as seriously as it deserved. To try to stop these women from using the novel as a public forum for such dangerous ideas as a wife's equality with her husband, Boileau was prepared to go to great lengths, even to recontour his own oeuvre.

His satires were a pillar of Boileau's reputation; originally there were nine, written and published between 1657 and 1674. Everything indicates that he intended to stop the series there. Then, in a 1692 letter, Racine announces his hope of seeing "the satire on women" soon.[52] The production of the satires had begun before *Clélie*'s publication had ended. Boileau evidently did not see immediately that Scudéry would be so influential; it took her heirs in Lafayette's generation to prompt him to begin his attack; it took her subsequent heirs, the scandalous women of the 1690s, to push him to complete and make public his strongest allegations.

The tenth satire is most often referred to by the title Racine uses, "Satire on Women"; in it Boileau takes the particular example of Scudéry's text as the springboard for a generalization about the dangerous behavior of a new race of women. The satire is addressed to a young man about to marry; it is a warning about the conduct that *Clélie* promotes in its female readers. The novel's "enchanting discourse" will put his future wife "on the edge of a precipice." How "can she continue to walk without her foot slipping" when all around her "everything is being said, and heard"? What begins only as "the affair of a novel" easily becomes "a début in crime." The end is then in sight: "One fall always leads to another." By the end, the chaste fiancée, fused with Scudéry's chaste heroine, has become the most notorious *femme galante* of the 1690s: Boileau ends his phantasmagoria of the novel's contagion with Clélie as the new Phèdre, the new Messalina, bringing about the "ruin" of twenty men, "a woman without restraint and without law given up to vice" (67).[53] *Clélie* was making women wild; Boileau hoped to convince a new race of husbands to take the law into their own hands and put an end to the "ruin" of families, specifically the bleeding of their resources to finance the libertine excesses of these adventuresses.

Since Boileau was Boileau, "lawmaker of Parnassus" and royal historiographer, this fantastic exaggeration was sure to win allegiance. The claims on which his argument is founded become critical principles, accepted facts of literary life that a commentator might repeat without offering proof: novels corrupted their female readers; novels were responsible for the decadence of French society; they were a threat to marriage and to the financial stability of families. Commentators who wished to curry favor with the regime had the orthodox line thus neatly traced for them.

This was certainly the case with Father Porée, whose only published specimens of his oratorical eloquence are his fire-and-brimstone condemnation of the plague of novels and his funeral oration for Louis XIV.[54] In his denunciation of novels, Porée repeats Boileau's movement from literary threat to civic menace: novels cannot be dismissed as affecting "only the republic of letters"; their "contagion," their "pestilence," is just as real in the "civil republic," whose foundations they weaken by spreading "idleness" among its citizens and discouraging the noble virtues with whose promotion works such as the *Chanson de Roland* had served the State so well (8). Subsequent men of the cloth such as the Abbé Jacquin must have found a sudden vocation for literary criticism because they understood the potential political benefits of this stance: in his tirade against "the danger of novels," Jacquin simply makes Boileau's and Porée's suggestions more explicit.[55]

The work of Boileau and his followers had two major consequences: women were more harshly treated in the theory and the practice of marital law; and the condemnation of the novel as the genre able to set

[marginal notes:] warning to a man about to marry-- · novels make women wild · novels corrupt, are threat to financial stability of families · Porée's denunciation of novels · consequences: 1) women were more harshly treated 2) novel condemned

158

DIVORCE, DESIRE, AND THE NOVEL

women on the road to scandal was sealed. In addition, the appearance of the vocabulary of contagious disease in the fin-de-siècle call to arms against women may well signal an important shift in the civil attitude toward women. This could be the transitional moment between the simple control of marriage and what Foucault terms a "technology" of sexuality.[56] The fantastic outpourings against the scourge of novels could be one inspiration for the images of all-engulfing female sexuality that so obsessed nineteenth-century sexologists and would-be "regulators" of sexuality, who, during the most recent fin-de-siècle, once again made recurrent the association between Woman and contagious disease.

We should remember that Boileau never mentions the notorious women of the 1690s, even though it is evident that he had them in mind. We should also remember that, following Boileau's example, commentators never presented them as solely, or even principally, a literary threat: they were not novelists but "adventuresses," devouring fortunes as they devoured men. Perhaps out of critical prudence, the early historians of the female tradition, who otherwise sin in the direction of overinclusiveness, generally exclude these scandalous figures.[57] Their deletion from literary history might have been complete, without the efforts of twentieth-century critics to recover a fuller picture of the seventeenth century. These women had published so extensively that scholars such as Adam and Coulet could not have excluded them from their accounts.

However, with inclusion like this, writers hardly need exclusion. Coulet dismisses them, one after another, explaining why there is no point in reading them: he mocks the "futility" of Bédacier's presentation of history, the "ponderousness" of La Force's argumentation (1:290). And Adam . . . For Adam, Murat was a shocking lesbian, La Force both sexually and politically "compromised," d'Aulnoy (in a plot worthy of Alexandre Dumas) a would-be husband-killer.[58] In his eyes, these women were dangerous acquaintances, not fit to keep company with the great men who make seventeenth-century French literature an uplifting experience, and perhaps—who knows?—still a source of contagion for women readers.

5

The Origin of Novels: Gender, Class, and the Writing of French Literary History

TRADITIONAL LITERARY history is commonly perceived to be a genre written by, about, and for men. In addition, this genre is generally thought of as monolithic: we seldom imagine that the dominant vision of a period that has come down to us may have been, at the time of its original formulation, but one side of the story, competing, along with opposing views, for acceptance as the true story. It may not be possible, in the case of every national literary tradition, to recover a sense of what was at stake—not only in literary but also in political and social terms —in the primal critical scene. For the French tradition, however, much of the debate that surrounded the establishment of the first canon of French literature was carried out in published exchanges. When we return to that source, it becomes evident that, at this formative period, literary history does not correspond to its traditional image.

The most significant evidence to be gleaned from these archives indicates that gender was a major issue in the controversies at the origin of French literary history. Furthermore, whenever the inclusion of women writers became a possibility for literary history, class inevitably either openly became an issue in the debate or can now be inferred as an explanation for opposing stances on gender. The debates at the foundation of French literature thereby provide historical confirmation of a theory proposed by Teresa de Lauretis on semantic evidence alone: gender is class (4–5).

To conclude this study of female authorship during the ancien régime, I will contrast the two principal versions of the period's literary history proposed by contemporary critics and commentators. I will first

[margin annotations: "literary history — by and for men"; "but early on: gender = a major issue"; "considerations of class"]

present the individuals responsible for the initial formulation of each opposing view, Nicolas Boileau and Pierre-Daniel Huet. I will then consider the fate of the version forgotten by posterity, that of Huet, in an attempt to understand what was at stake in the authorization of Boileau's history rather than his. For this second demonstration, I will highlight the most significant role ever played by French literary critics, who developed a program and a methodology for the national educational system. This system was finally established in the nineteenth century, but its foundation was laid long before, at the time when the opposing literary histories I will describe here were still vying for supremacy.

The two original views of the French tradition and the female novel were contemporary developments. It seems likely that the inaugural impetus for French literary history was provided by the formation of a female literary tradition. Even though the chief proponents on whom I will first focus were both men, in the beginning literary history was not written exclusively by men.[1] It was, however, exclusively written by bourgeois. Yet when we examine the conclusions initially proposed, we realize that the politics of early French literary history are often too complex to permit facile explanations based on a critic's sex or class.

Huet and his followers, both male and female, are partisans of women's right to literary authority; in addition, these bourgeois are more or less vocal proponents of the destabilization of social stratification, a project then commonly associated with women's writing. Boileau and his followers, all men, seek to repress the female literary tradition and to preserve in its purest form the contemporary social system, even though it allowed them, as bourgeois, only limited privileges. When bourgeois such as Boileau adopted a stance more aristocratic than that of such aristocrats as the Duc de La Rochefoucauld and the Comtesse de Lafayette, they surely did so in the hope of preserving the system of royal patronage that guaranteed their authorial status and that of the authors, such as Molière and Racine, whom they promoted most vigorously. In their criticism, arguments developed to serve their own self-interest were portrayed as essential for the good of the French national estate: in the critical line Boileau inspired, women's writing was judged on literary grounds only in passing; it was condemned above all as a threat to the political system designed to guarantee the absolute monarchy's survival. Boileau's reasoning was carefully reproduced in the founding rhetoric of the French pedagogical system: in a repeated gesture of cultural schizophrenia, pedagogue-critics continued—long after the Revolution and under all the regimes that succeeded the monarchy—to proclaim as the goal of French national education the inculcation of the very values that Boileau had hoped would guarantee the survival of the absolute monarchy and the absolute dominance of the aristocracy.

THE CLASS OF AUTHORSHIP

> Les hommes qui assignent les rangs dans la littérature, puisqu'ils en dispensent les honneurs et en distribuent les places, dont toutes les femmes sont exclues, donnent souvent de la célébrité à des talents fort médiocres.
>
> Stéphanie de Genlis,
> *De l'influence des femmes sur la*
> *littérature française*

RECENT AMERICAN experiments with canon revision frequently remind us of a basic pedagogical truth: women authors are granted authoritative status only when they can be considered exceptional, beyond their sex, and when they can be integrated into educational programs and reading lists without disturbing the traditional literary landscape. (Lafayette, Jane Austen, George Eliot, and Virginia Woolf are the writers today most frequently included in this manner.) This process of naturalizing women writers, of simultaneously conferring privileges on them and denying their alien (female) qualities, has been most dramatically operative in literary traditions, like the French tradition, in which powerful literary women played an inaugural role, in which generic origins could therefore be seen as inherently female. At the origin of French literary history in the mid-seventeenth century, we find an illustration of a second basic pedagogical truth: female literary communities and traditions pose a threat to canons, a threat to which those who formulate canonic structures and values may react with critical violence.

Only one woman novelist, Lafayette, has been included in every successive canon of French literature.[2] The original price of her reception into the Academy of classic authors (as opposed to the Académie Française) was a loss of stature for French women writers in general: the exclusion of the women novelists who had preceded her and the suppression of the female tradition that had established the modern French novel.

In 1697, as what was already being called the Golden Age of French literature was drawing to a close, Pierre Bayle provided in his *Dictionnaire historique et critique* an authoritative formulation of a critical commonplace: "Our best French novels have for some time been written by ... women" (446). However, when the tradition of encyclopedic dictionaries that Bayle helped inaugurate culminated just fifty years later in the *Dictionnaire raisonné des sciences, des arts, et des métiers* that we now refer to by its shorter title, *Encyclopédie* (1751–1766), the canonical status of women writers had apparently disappeared. The article "novel" (*roman*), written by Jaucourt about 1762 and included in the fourteenth volume of the *Encyclopédie* (1765), supplies a new, equally authoritative critical cliché: "Mme la Comtesse de Lafayette made the public sick of the ridiculous nonsense we have just discussed (*dégouta le public des fadaises ridicules*)." "Ridiculous nonsense" signifies explicitly the multivolume *romans* written before Lafayette's appearance on the literary scene, but it also implies a more sweeping dismissal of the production of the many women writers whose names were elided when Lafayette was accepted as the only first-class female citizen of the republic of letters. Those who established the version of French literary history that the *Encyclopédie* promotes were willing to acknowledge a woman writer as the originator of the literary form whose eventual domination of the French literary tradition was becoming increasingly clear by the mid-eighteenth century. Lafayette won this recognition, however, on the condition that she be singled out from the female literary community with which her own century had associated her, and that Bayle's maxim, which portrays the French novel as a literary form perfected by many women writers, be overturned. Thus rendered exceptional, Lafayette could be held up as the cause of the female tradition's extermination: her (male) perfection "made the public sick of" the "ridiculous nonsense" (of women writers).

How can we explain the antithetical critical positions enshrined in Bayle's *Dictionnaire historique* and Diderot and D'Alembert's *Dictionnaire raisonné*? In the following pages I will attempt to reverse previous thinking on this issue in order to suggest that the myth of Lafayette as unique (woman) writer, whose greatness eradicated a female literary community, was created by the French critical forces inspired by Boileau to distract attention from the true motivation for their project. Before attempting this demonstration, however, let me sketch out the more obvious explanation for the conflicting positions on the importance of early women writers.

To date, scholars of French literature have interpreted the evolution of the French novel as essentially identical to the trajectory that Ian Watt successfully imposed for decades as the dominant view of the genre's development in England, as a "rise" from lowliness to prominence. Witness the image proposed by Georges May in the study that, more than any other, put the early French novel on the critical map, *Le Dilemme du roman au XVIIIe siècle* (1963): "From the pariah that it was, here it is, all of a sudden, newly successful (*parvenu*) and elevated to noble rank" (3). May describes the novel's acquisition of *titres de noblesse* as having taken place roughly during the period that elapsed between Bayle's pronouncement and that of Jaucourt.[3] According to this view, women writers played a significant role in the evolution of French prose fiction only as long as the novel could be considered, in May's words, "a disinherited genre, which men had more or less consciously abandoned [to women], a bit like a great lady hands over an outmoded hat to her maid" (225). The long-term relation between gender and the rise of the novel thus would seem to have been a casebook study in appropriation: men of letters co-opted the genre as soon as it achieved prominence. For example, in a 1779 eulogy of Voltaire, whose place in the Académie Française he was taking, Jean-François Durcis said of his predecessor that he had "taken the empire of the novel from women" (13).

The theory of the French novel's rise to literary power during the first half of the eighteenth century provides a convenient solution to the conflict of opinion between Bayle and Jaucourt. It implies that the early female tradition produced nothing of value and that the novel came into its own only when men of letters took it in hand and provided the "upstart" (*parvenu*) genre with the masterpieces that would guarantee its standing. It implies that the key decade for the novel's seventeenth-century evolution was the 1670s, the period that witnessed the production of its initial masterpiece, *La Princesse de Clèves*. The theory also implies that the 1670s witnessed what has come to be accepted as *the* crucial early shift in the reading public's taste; the concomitant sudden "disgust" with the voluminous models for prose fiction that had found favor until then and the infatuation with a new, decidedly more concise fictional form. All aspects of this literary history originate with the testimony of Boileau, the individual who, more than any other, succeeded in imposing his vision of the seventeenth-century literary scene on posterity.

What if this long-accepted history, which offers such a convincing explanation for one (token) literary woman's replacement of a female tradition, were founded on several carefully constructed, well-planted myths? This hypothesis is not as farfetched as it might at first appear. From the beginning of the seventeenth century, as texts such as Richelieu's *Testament politique* demonstrate, Woman is defined by the architects of the modern French State as the origin of revolution, of the cabals and intrigues that threaten the State's foundation. Time and again, seventeenth-century French women writers took inspiration from their involvement in the body politic to invent new forms of political fiction. From the violence of the attacks that they inspired, we can infer that the most threatening of these novels were produced by Madeleine de Scudéry. The link between the desire to obliterate fiction subversive to the goals of the increasingly absolute State and the myth of the French reading public's sudden "disgust" with that fiction can be exposed if we center our investigation no longer on the 1670s, the decade during which Jaucourt in the *Encyclopédie* pinpoints the crucial change of taste, but on the previous decade.

Already during the 1660s, *before,* that is, Lafayette's new model was available to win instant acclamation, the exclusion of Scudéry's fiction had been decreed. Antoine Adam provides a lengthy, detailed account of "the devious paths [by which] Despréaux raised himself to the position of regent of Parnassus" ("L'Ecole de 1660" 249). During the mid- to late 1660s, Boileau explored "devious paths" in search of absolute literary authority, an authority he would win in the 1670s with his *L'Art poétique* (1674) and his selection to serve with Racine as royal historiographer (1677). (Note that the two events that solidified his power took place before the appearance of *La Princesse de Clèves*.) In the 1660s, as part of his quest for a prominent role in the codification of Louis the Great's official story, Boileau set himself up as Richelieu's counterpart in the literary domain: he who exposes women as the originators of all plots that threaten national security. It is to the events of the 1660s that I will now turn, to the self-serving critical work that was subsequently covered up when Lafayette was canonized in her uniqueness.

Boileau's brother Gilles was elected to the Académie Française in 1659, whereas not until 1684 did Boileau himself gain much-desired admission (and then only on the strength of the king's intervention). In

1662 neither brother appeared in the list of writers granted royal pensions, pensions they had been expecting: Nicolas was voted a pension only in 1674. In the years during which he was working to obtain official financial and professional recognition, Boileau promoted a vision of great art as governed by the principles ("verisimilitude," "propriety") and as corresponding to the stylistic values ("purity," "simplicity") that, from his day to ours, have been associated with neoclassicism, a literary model coming into prominence at this time and now recognized by French literary history as the dominant form and the literary glory of Louis XIV's mature reign. At the same time, Boileau waged war against the stylistic principles and values of rival literary models, in particular the (female) novel. Boileau never sought to detach political and social values from literary ones: although he wrote only of bourgeois writers (Molière and Racine are particularly highly promoted), he always advised authors to avoid "the popular" and instead to write "nobly" (for example, *O.c.* 178).

As his initial "path" toward what Adam terms "the regen[cy] of Parnassus," Boileau elected a decidedly "devious" route. On the basis of its allusions to contemporary events, editors place the composition of his *Dialogue des héros de roman* in 1664–1666, shortly after Boileau had been denied the official patronage to which he aspired. At that time the enormous success of Scudéry's most popular novels, *Artamène* (1649–1653) and *Clélie* (1654–1660), was far from over (for example, *Artamène*'s fifth edition dates from 1656, *Clélie*'s fourth from 1662), and Lafayette had not yet arrived on the literary scene. However, Boileau consistently presented a version of the parodic dialogue's history that is designed to obscure the date of its composition. Initially, he decided not to publish it ("for reasons that remain obscure," a recent editor concludes [eds. Adam and Escal 1089]). Perhaps on the basis of manuscipts compiled when Boileau gave a series of public readings, the dialogue was published twice (1688, 1693) in allegedly unauthorized editions whose existence Boileau officially ignored. The author claimed to have consented to its publication only in 1710. At that time he added a preface in which he presents the official story: until then, he had not even committed the dialogue to paper, he contends, but had preserved it "in [his] memory" (445).[4]

As Boileau explains in the conclusion to his preface, this unusual compositional strategy was employed to avoid "distressing a girl [*une fille,* in this case an unmarried woman] who, after all, had a great deal of merit" (445). The "girl" in question is identified as "Mlle de Scudéry, sister of the author with the same name" (444), as though her merits were purely personal rather than literary. In similar fashion, the literary production of this worthy woman, the two novels (*Artamène* and *Clélie*) that are the parody's primary targets, is dismissed as already "fallen into oblivion" (*tombé dans l'oubli*) (446). In fact, Boileau coyly adds, "Since they are hardly read anymore, I doubt that my dialogue ... will attract the same applause it received earlier (*autrefois*) during the frequent readings of it I was *obliged* to make" (446; my emphasis). This contorted chronological placement thus completed, Boileau concludes his preface on a mysterious note: "What I do not doubt is that all people of intelligence and *true virtue* will realize ... that I am giving them here perhaps the least frivolous work produced by my pen" (446, my emphasis). What could have inspired Boileau finally to release a work for official publication some forty-five years after its composition and to draw it to the attention of "truly virtuous" readers as his most serious production?

In the decades after Boileau received the recognition he was seeking when he composed the dialogue (admission into the Académie, a royal pension) and prior to its publication, his principal critical activity was tied up with the most significant literary quarrel of a century that had known its share of such disputes, the *Querelle des Anciens et des Modernes.* In this battle, which in the long run essentially determined both the official canon of seventeenth-century French literature and the original French pedagogical canon, Boileau immediately assumed the role played in the most recent reincarnation of "the battle of the books" by Allan Bloom, that of defender of classic, eternal values. The *Querelle* is far too complex to be retraced here: I will evoke only its initial skirmish, the 1687 reading by Charles Perrault before the Académie Française of his *Siècle de Louis le Grand.* In this work Perrault offers a politically clever justification for his defense of modern literature over its classical precursors: literary moderns are second to none because they are protected by the greatest ruler of all time. At the same time, however, Perrault defends modern stylistic merits (often those then associated with women's writing) and the new values (especially progress and the value of individual worth) also promoted by the salons. Because of Perrault's advocacy of what we would term interdisciplinarity and his implicit fracturing of the boundary between high and low culture, the vision of literature presented in his numerous contributions to the *Querelle* is far more diverse than the portrayal of timeless, virile standards that is Boileau's image of the ancients and the canon dictated by fidelity to their ideals.

Not surprisingly, Boileau jumped into the fray: he interrupted Perrault's reading of his poem with numerous loud outbursts about the "falseness" of his judgments and public promises of a response in writing (*O.c.* 1043, n.257). A few months later he mysteriously lost his voice. He left to take the waters; he returned in full voice, although Adam contends that "the waters had had no part in his recovery" (*O.c.* xxxviii). What may have cured him of the symptom, which Boileau's modern editor at least implies was hysterical, was the forthcoming publication of the Dutch edition (1688) of the *Dialogue des héros de roman,* an edition Boileau always denounced, but whose publication in this context was, to say the least, convenient. Boileau and Perrault continued to do battle over the relative merits of ancient and modern literature; gender was always just as present in their debates as was class. In particular, Perrault composed his most open defense of women's contribution to modern literature, *Apologie des femmes* (1694), in response to Boileau's tenth satire, *Contre les femmes.* Even a brief reading of the work that gave Boileau his voice back indicates that it was certainly still another round in his battle with Perrault over women's place in the republic of letters.[5] It may also have been Boileau's promised attack on the value of literary modernity, with the novel chosen to represent all that Boileau opposed.

The man who by 1710 was accepted as the arbiter of classicism asks his readers to believe that he had finally consented to the publication of his attack on the novel only after the death of Madeleine de Scudéry—"now that death has removed her from the ranks of humans" (445). Significantly, however, his *Dialogue des héros de roman* can be seen as driven toward the symbolic recreation of Scudéry's death or, more precisely, her ritual murder. In the dialogue, Boileau's counterparts in the afterlife, the judges of the underworld Pluto and Minos, condemn Scudéry's most successful characters on a charge of usurpation: her pale imitations of the great heroes of antiquity have taken on the names and the trappings of illustrious dead men no longer able to defend themselves against such defamations.[6] The parody culminates in an elaborately staged ritual killing. The shades of Scudéry's ersatz heroes are first "stripped" (a word Boileau repeats four times) of their deceptive clothing, "whipped," and then plunged "head first" into "the deepest part of the river Lethe" (486–87). "The mountains of ridiculous paper on which their stories are written" are tossed in after them. Lest their function as stand-ins be missed, moreover, the heroes cry out "in chorus" as they are led to their second death, "Ah! Scudéry!" (488). Boileau could have avoided inscribing the name of his adversary in his text—as he did in *L'Art poétique* (1674), when he ridiculed *Artamène* and *Clélie* without naming their author (171)—for he had already made the status of the heroes clear by calling them "phantoms" (217). Like the straw effigies (known as "fantômes") used in the seventeenth century to carry out symbolic executions when the criminal could not be found, Boileau chose for the shades the fate he had hoped thereby to decree, if not for their author, for her literary production.[7]

As Georges May points out, Boileau's claim that the novels he parodied in the dialogue were already "forgotten" by the time of its publication was blatantly erroneous: "Everything indicates on the contrary that these novels still held on, for many years, to an enthusiastic readership" (21).[8] The decree prematurely consigning Scudéry's works to the river of oblivion that closes Boileau's dialogue betrays his goal in finally authorizing its publication. The novelist had been dead since 1701; had Boileau simply been waiting until she was no longer able to defend herself, the parody could have appeared much sooner. Boileau's scornful attack in *L'Art poétique* had not eliminated her name from the annals of French literature. A premonition of his own impending death the following year (1711) may have prompted an eleventh-hour renewed attempt to revise the official presentation of the novel's early history. The myth of Scudéry's premature literary demise was thus invented by Boileau on his critical deathbed. His eighteenth-century followers wished her into oblivion even more prematurely: in his *Observations sur les écrits modernes* (1737), the conservative journalist Abbé Desfontaines proclaimed that Boileau's initial readings of the dialogue had awakened "the public's disgust" and thereby "abolished" Scudéry's model for prose fiction (1:72–73). The stage was thus set for Jaucourt's *Encyclopédie* entry and its influential literary "history" of the immediate public disgust with Scudéry when Lafayette appeared on the scene a few years after Boileau's dialogue began to circulate.

The terms of Boileau's death decree were similarly influential. He directed his "least frivolous" work to "truly virtuous" readers because the crimes for which he condemned Scudéry were less literary than civic. In particular, he accused her of having invented a model for heroism that threatened to weaken the male fiber on which the State relied: "And by what right would [her characters] call themselves heroes, if they were not in love? Is not love today the measure of heroic virtue?" (475–76). Rather than models for manly action, Scudéry created heroes so "effeminate" (*dameret*) that their "lack of vigor," their "flabbiness" (*mollesse*), was "written all over their faces" (452, 476). Instead of "an ambitious prince who wanted the entire earth under his domination," Scudéry portrayed Cyrus the Great as dominated by an "unrelenting" mistress (454, 456).

In Boileau's eyes, Scudéry granted love absolute power in her fictional universe in order to blur the distinction between aristocrat and bourgeois. Her novels attempt to "ennoble" (*annoblir*) her fictional creations. Furthermore, when Scudéry proposes that love serve to define class as well as heroism, according to Boileau, she "makes into bourgeois" (*firent des bourgeois*) those who should be seen as most noble (444). Boileau set himself up as the champion simultaneously of classic literary values and of aristocratic values; he sought to defend them against the challenge of writers who elected a more subversive authorial role. More than a decade before Louis XIV appointed him to write the history of his reign, Boileau was already championing what he would proclaim the official values of those years, and was attempting to eliminate novels that, by portraying warriors under female control and by blurring social stratification, provided a challenge to the foundations of the absolute monarchy. The myth of the novel as civic menace, as the literary counterpart of the scheming women against whom Richelieu warned Louis XIII, was thus established in 1665, early in the reign of his son, Louis XIV.[9]

The countermyth was not far behind. The audience for one of Boileau's early recitals of his dialogue must have contained a leading literary authority of the day, the future Bishop of Avranches, Pierre Daniel Huet.[10] Like Boileau, Huet waited ·(until 1670) to make his text public; like Boileau, he presented his commentary in a format so deceptive that it calls attention to the work's unusual compositional history. *Traité de l'origine des romans* first appeared as a preface to a novel, *Zayde, histoire espagnole,* a preface in the form of a letter addressed to the man named on the title page as the novel's author, Segrais, in response to his "curiosity" about the "origin" of the art form he had "perfected" (3).

Huet framed his history of the novel as a classic literary history: a man-to-man discourse, a story between men and about male literary endeavors.

[margin: ".man-to-man dialogue"]

However, the traditional appearance of Huet's literary history was only a cover: the male origin Huet assigned the French novelistic logos was really a fiction fabricated by these two men. As both Huet and Segrais would subsequently admit in their memoirs (Huet 2:6, *Segraisiana* 10), the novel to which Huet's text stood in a pretextual relationship was actually written by a woman, Lafayette. In Huet's presentation of the novel's history, he declares that travesties are recurrent and contends that one must always try to understand their purpose in order to distinguish between "those who use an innocent artifice to disguise and mask themselves for their own amusement and that of others and those scoundrels who, taking the name and the clothing of those dead or absent, under cover of a certain resemblance, usurp their property" (10–11).[11]

[margin: "but nb: novel was actually written by LF"]

This case of disguise may well have been designed for the amusement of the public, male and female, bourgeois and aristocratic, that did not share Boileau's view of literary history as man-to-man discourse. Boileau ends his dialogue with the ritual murder of the most criminal novelist, Scudéry; Huet concludes his search for a genealogy and a pedigree for the fledgling French novel with a eulogy of what he presents as the finest achievement of contemporary prose fiction, the novels of the same writer, Scudéry.[12] He presents his tribute as a righting of wrongs: Scudéry, Huet contends, "deprived herself of the glory that was her due" by allowing her novels to appear "under a borrowed name" (97). Huet explains Scudéry's self-effacement for the profit of her brother Georges (whose name appeared on the title page of her novels) as a desire to exempt men in general from the humiliation of not having realized the same degree of literary accomplishment: "When she worked for the glory of our nation, she wanted to spare our sex this humiliation."

[margin: "Huet ends w/praise of Scudéry"]

[margin: "said she let Georges sign her novels so men wouldn't be humiliated by not shining in the field"]

With this tribute, Huet enacts the initial public inscription of Scudéry's name in the ranks of the modern authors to be included in French literature's first canon, different versions of which were being proposed by his contemporaries. (Prior to his treatise, Madeleine de Scudéry's authorship was common knowledge in seventeenth-century literary circles, but had not yet been acknowledged in a professional critical context.) Huet praises Scudéry in terms that seem calculated to provoke Boileau's wrath. Rather than as a threat to national security, he portrays her novels as a contribution to "the glory of our nation." He then evokes the issue one cannot help but see as the inspiration for Boileau's attack: the degree to which female literary accomplishments and their public recognition can be viewed as bringing "humiliation" upon "our" sex.[13]

The knowledge that France was enjoying its finest hour on the world stage (a view promoted throughout the *Querelle des Anciens et des Modernes*) just when women were attaining previously unheard-of intellectual prominence must often have proved unsettling for contemporary commentators. Huet suggests that the motivations inspiring the opposing views of literary history were complex and that the stakes for each proponent were far from negligible. His treatise reveals a desire on the part of some men to live under female rule, in the sense of learning the ways of the world according to women. His remark about "the glory of our nation" and male "humiliation" raises the specter of what such a desire must have represented for those in the opposing camp, their belief that, thus feminized, the French would no longer make up a glorious nation.

For the second edition of *Zayde* (Amsterdam, 1671), Romeyn de Hoogue designed a frontispiece on two levels that illustrates both Huet's treatise and Lafayette's novel: he stages the importance of female literary authority in literary history (figure 8). In the background, a drama with many characters is being acted out in an open-air theater surmounted by the title "Zayde." In the foreground, a scene entitled "the origin of novels" depicts a group of women gathered in a semicircle. Only one of them is fully clothed; two are naked; and the two on whom the spectator's attention is focused are half-dressed, tied together in a bizarre exchange of garments. The costume and accessories of the woman fully attired—her plumed helmet, her modified breastplate, the miniature Doric column cradled in one arm—identify her in seventeenth-century terms as a representative of classical tradition. She is handing over a scepter, sign of her authority, to the female figure at the center of the scene, who also wears a breastplate indicative of her allegiance to this tradition. This woman is even more intimately linked to the figure to her right by the clothing they share. Over one shoulder is tied a drapery that partially covers the armor of antiquity. The drapery once fully clothed a female figure who now sits half-exposed as her garment is being stripped away to complete the younger woman's motley attire. In

FIGURE 8

Romeyn de Hoogue, etching, frontispiece, Marie-Madeleine Pioche de
La Vergne, Comtesse de Lafayette, *Zayde* (1671). Reprinted by
permission of the Bibliothèque Nationale, Paris. Photo. Bibl. Nat. Paris.

a final provocative gesture, a naked woman covers the mouth of the woman taking over another's clothes, as if to prevent her from disclosing the source of her trappings—or to remind her that, even in her newly usurped garb, her own authority will not be freely revealed.

It was reported in Lafayette's circle that she and her literary advisers found that the hardest part of *Zayde*'s composition was the task of limiting Scudéry's stylistic influence. According to Segrais, Montpensier's literary assistant during the composition of the *Nouvelles françaises,* who was serving Lafayette in the same capacity when *Zayde* was being produced by salon writing, the beginning of volume 1 was rewritten *seven* times in an attempt to establish "a tone different from that of Scudéry's novels."[14] We will be unlikely to interpret this project of establishing a separate stylistic personality as those who accept Boileau's vision of literary history would, that is, as an effort by Lafayette to set herself apart from a fictional model already inspiring public "disgust," if we remember that the treatise that originally preceded *Zayde*'s frequently rewritten first pages was an extended defense of the fictional model Scudéry had created.

Henri Coulet, like all critics who defend the currently accepted version of the novel's development in France and thereby reaffirm Boileau's authority, dismisses Huet as an outmoded critic: "[Huet's] apology ... came too late: [Scudéry's novels] had gone out of style" (*étaient passés de mode*) (1:181–82). In classic fashion, Coulet is able to admit Lafayette's appearance only on the condition of Scudéry's disappearance. However, if we overturn the assumptions on which this literary history is founded, beginning with the assumption that Scudéry had already lost her readership by the 1660s, we can reassess both Huet's critical authority and the opposing views of the novel's development. We can imagine that Huet was not a retrograde critic and that, on the contrary, it was he, rather than Boileau, who best represented the state of the novelistic art in 1670, at the time of Lafayette's arrival on the literary scene. (Contemporary intellectuals appear to have valued his authority more highly than Boileau's; Huet was elected to the Académie Française in 1674, a full decade before his opponent in the battle of the novel.) If Huet's critical authority is restored, then his treatise's pretextual relation to the work in which Lafayette freed herself from Scudéry's influence cannot be used to implicate Lafayette in an act of "usurpation," in a plot to strip Scudéry of her literary mantle. Rather, we can understand both Lafayette's authorial "disguise" and Segrais's as an attempt to force readers to reflect on the extent to which, in a republic of letters governed by Boileau's standards, women writers might be obliged to cross-dress in order to win literary authority. We may also see a realization on the part of those involved in this "amusing masquerade" that, in the wake of Boileau's attack and in an era of rising royal absolutism, the novel had to be made less overtly reminiscent of Scudéry.

Just before his eulogy of Scudéry, Huet provides the most astute contemporary account of the seventeenth-century French novel, a description that defines the novelistic "clothing" passed on from novelist to novelist. He contends that the seventeenth-century novel was superior to its counterparts in other European countries because of the greater "freedom" that characterized the commerce between men and women in France. Elsewhere, men were forced to overcome the physical "obstacles"—from duennas to locked doors—that separated them from the opposite sex, whereas in France women had forced a change of conduct: "Having no other defense but their own heart, women made it into a rampart stronger and more secure than all the vigilance of duennas. Men were therefore obliged to lay siege to this rampart in proper fashion" (*par les formes*) (92). The "forms" were verbal, the language of "politeness," the linguistic code devised by women in the salons and carried over by Scudéry into the novel. The French, Huet contends, had become experts in "this art almost unknown to other peoples." Huet indicates what he terms a uniquely French genius, the art of conversation, as the origin of the French novel and of its success: "This art distinguishes French novels from other novels and makes the reading of them so delicious" (91). At the origin of what he describes as the most significant modern articulation of an art form whose genealogy he traces back to antiquity, Huet inscribes a form of verbal artistry developed by women and only acquired secondhand by men, who were able to learn the discourse dictated by women but not to invent a language of their own.[15]

Huet characterizes the modern French novel as a civilizing genre, and he defines civilization as under female influence, that is, defined by gender rather than by class. This role is radically different from what Boileau sees as the principal social function of literature: for Boileau, civilization is purely an affair of social stratification, and literature's purpose is to make everyone imitate the ways of the aristocracy. (*L'Art poétique*'s third canto, which contains his renewed attack on Scudéry, leaves writers with this command: "Study the Court, and be familiar with the City," that is, learn the ways of the places then synonymous with aristocratic power.) For Huet, rather than an effort to make French civilization synonymous with aristocratic civilization, the novel's civilizing mission should be to enrich French society by making it receptive to otherness—other discourses, other customs, other classes, even other peoples. On this point alone, Huet may be said to agree with Boileau: he admits that the (woman's) novel poses a threat to the demarcations of French society. However, he feels that French society should welcome destabilization.

In his view of the novel's history, Huet returns twice to what he presents as a primal scene, an image that illustrates perfectly the difference between his position on social stratification and Boileau's: the setting is medieval Provence, where "thrilled with pleasure" at a troubadour's recital, a great lord "strips himself of his garments in order to dress [the troubadour] in them" (71). Boileau exposes the novel's threat to the social order of his day by "stripping off" (*dépouiller*) the garments that would allow bourgeois to pass for aristocrats. Huet indicates that novelists (working "for the glory of our nation") should be recognized, as their precursors were, by a gift of the finest garments, royal robes.[16] He implies that the true aristocrat would not care about the class of person wearing his clothes, would want to "strip" himself (also *dépouiller*) in order to "ennoble" the great storyteller, and would see that talent had already conferred nobility upon the artist.

Huet returns to this scene in order to broaden its implications. The practice of royal "stripping," it turns out, was not unique to French lords, but was performed by their Arab contemporaries, the kings of Fez (77). Huet raises the possibility that the French royal habit could have been an Arab influence, only to dismiss it (78). Instead, he uses the image of multinational royal divestment to represent his theory of the novel's transnational origin, its simultaneous rise in Spain and in Arab countries as well as in France. The novel, he suggests, is a genre that takes advantage of permeable frontiers: its practitioners travel freely and take on the nationality of the king who gives them his clothes, and this acceptance of otherness benefits the assimilating society. ("Our art was enriched by the commerce that the proximity with Spain ... gave us" [77–78].)

It is hard to imagine visions of national (literary) identity more radically at odds than those of Boileau and Huet. *L'Art poétique* culminates in a vision of frontiers as obstacles to be conquered, barriers to the Sun King's absolute glory that were falling one after another: "How many ramparts have been destroyed! How many cities forced to yield!" (185). Boileau celebrates conquest by the master race, followed by the imposition of rigid frontiers and an untainted social system in which literature has a nationalistic role to play—"What happy author in another *Aeneid* /.../ Will sing of Batavia lost in the storm, /.../ In terrifying assaults watched over by the Sun?" (185).[17] The decisive military expansionism would, as we have seen, be followed up with an official policy of enforced assimilation, both cultural and racial; the newly conquered would be made over as French. To this politicoliterary vision of conquest and assimilation, Huet opposes a scene of transvestism, complex images of cross-dressing across social, sexual, and political lines.[18] Huet imagines a political system that, rather than enforcing the conversion of the foreign, would profit from the peaceful coexistence of those in various degrees of cross-dressing and find in a multinational heritage a source of strength. Moreover, the novel, Huet suggests, points the way to a meritocracy: it is the means by which all writers—foreign, female, bourgeois—working for "the glory of our nation" can find a place in its system.

Huet suggests that the criteria adopted by other critics may be inadequate to define the genre that French women writers were revitalizing. Huet, who appreciates the French novel for its contemporaneousness, its accurate recreation of a modern style, refuses to evaluate it according to the allegedly timeless values of *vraisemblance* (plausibility) and *bienséance* (propriety), the yardsticks by which Boileau measured literary value. (Under the name of realism, twentieth-century critics have consistently used *vraisemblance* as an indicator of a novel's modernity and of the genre's rise.) Huet is not obliged to identify a rupture between Scudéry and Lafayette because he defines the French novel in terms of its style and its politics. He presents it as an entity unaffected by the formal evolution from an ample, looser format that would now be termed "romance" to a more concise model that would today be identified as "novel."

This undoubtedly explains the new language that Boileau introduced for his second attack on Scudéry's fiction in his manual of neoclassicism, *L'Art poétique,* published in 1674, four years after Huet's preface. In the section of the third canto devoted to "truth" and "the plausible" (*le vrai* and *e vraisemblable*), alongside criticisms familiar from the *Dialogue des héros de roman* (for example, "love should be painted as a weakness and not as a virtue" 171), a new justification for censorship of the novel appears. The lawgiver of Parnassus issues the following dictate to novelists: "Study the mores of [different] centuries and countries. / Avoid attributing, as happens in *Clélie*, / French manners and wit to ancient Italy" (171). The imperative mode of *L'Art poétique* should not blind us to the accusation of ignorance: Scudéry's historical novels are insufficiently documented and therefore implausible.[19] The only evocation of a woman writer in the work that, more than any other, has dictated the canon of early French literature concludes with a more general warning: only those who want to produce "frivolous novels" should imitate Scudéry; writers concerned with the higher values of "rigor" and "strict propriety" (*l'étroite bienséance*) should look elsewhere for a model (171–72).[20]

Even these sweeping pronouncements did not immediately accomplish the goal Boileau had first assigned the *Dialogue des héros de roman* of depriving Scudéry of her contemporary readership. But they may have achieved just this end in the long-term struggle over the canon of French literature. For his attack in *L'Art poétique*, Boileau invented the terms that his eighteenth-century followers would adopt to justify Scudéry's exclusion when they drew up the first pedagogical manuals and programs of French literature: judged according to the allegedly timeless canonical standards of plausibility and propriety, her novels never measured up.

The severing of the bond between Scudéry and Lafayette was an (inevitable) next step. The twenty years that followed the publication of Boileau's dialogue witnessed the creation of Lafayette's official authorial signature. Prior to that time, the authorship of her works was hotly debated: *Zayde* was attributed at least as often to Segrais as to Lafayette, while *La Princesse de Clèves* was often ascribed to La Rochefoucauld. Before the middle of the eighteenth century, however, this debate was more or less closed—although no reason was ever given for its resolution. For the first time, *La Princesse de Montpensier*, *Zayde*, and *La Princesse de Clèves* were published under Lafayette's name. In addition, other works were attributed to Lafayette—*L'Histoire de Madame Henriette d'Angleterre* in 1720, *La Comtesse de Tende* in 1724, and *Mémoires de la cour de France* in 1731—until she had acquired the status of an official literary commodity with a *nom d'auteur*. Once Lafayette had been given her literary "clothes," she became the only woman novelist

—and, along with her friend Sévigné, the only woman writer—granted status as a classic and accorded a major role in the French educational system.

By 1674, four years before the publication of *La Princesse de Clèves* and well before the important new model for (women's) historical fiction announced by Lafayette had begun to make its mark, the battle lines had been drawn and the critical positions that would be evoked to judge all early women's writing had been established. However, Boileau's victory was far from immediate. He did not silence Huet, any more than Lafayette made Scudéry's readers "disgusted" with her fiction. Two parallel theories of the novel and its importance to French letters continued to develop throughout the eighteenth century. Every bit as much as their original formulations by Boileau and Huet, these theories are evaluations of the role of women writers in the French tradition. For more than a century, the battle between Huet and Boileau continued to be waged. None of their followers possessed their critical stature. However, these imitators are in one way more important than the theories' creators: they kept their ideas alive throughout the period during which the foundations were laid both for the modern French pedagogical system and for the image of French literature that was still being promoted, even in this country, when most of those teaching and writing today were educated.

A brief comparison of two of these eighteenth-century men of letters can illustrate this hundred-year war over the origin of novels. From the outset, the Abbé Nicolas Lenglet-Dufresnoy advertises his 1734 *De l'usage des romans* as a "continuation" of Huet's treatise. In the 1755 *Entretiens sur les romans,* the Abbé Armand-Pierre Jacquin, on the other hand, evaluates "the origin of novels" from an orthodox Boileauian perspective. Each pushes his master's position to a theoretical extreme.

In the central chapter of his study, Lenglet-Dufresnoy makes the link between woman and the novel posited by Huet an absolute law: he seldom considers that a novelist could be male. Indeed, he develops an elaborate justification for the genre's usefulness principally in terms of its documentary value, proving thereby that Scudéry's new realism was still recognized in his day: the novel provides an indispensable means of learning about the lives of women and therefore fills in an area passed over in silence by historians. "The imperfection of history should make us value novels. Even though they are the essential driving forces (*mobiles*) of the affairs of state, women hardly appear in histories" (53).

Because history has limited itself to the militaristic vision Boileau sanctioned—"You only see in it sieges, battles, forced marches, and attacks
on fortified places" (111)—it has abandoned to the novel total control
over the unofficial story, the more private details that help us under-   *fills in personal details*
stand the big picture, the personal reasons that explain the decisions
leaders make (66, 68). Readers who use novels to complete their historical vision could not help but conclude, according to Lenglet-Dufresnoy,
that women "are the absolute rulers of all courts" (85).

Lenglet-Dufresnoy repeats all the lavish praise of the novel and the
women writers who perfected the form that is a commonplace of the
critical tradition formed in Huet's wake.[21] In addition, his study's central thesis, on "the imperfection of history," highlights the historical
fiction that women writers had developed in the decades just prior to
his treatise. In so doing, Lenglet-Dufresnoy first exposes what Boileau
must have seen as the real danger of the novel's broad commercial
appeal. Huet's heir presents the novel as far more than mere fiction,   *novel = revisionist history*
instead as revisionist history, the true inside story of European political
history. He ups the ante again when he intimates that the French novel
was intended as a subversion of more than written history: "I would
like to be free to form a new government . . . ; royal authority would
only be in the hands of women" (95). According to Lenglet-Dufresnoy's
theory of "the usefulness of novels," they would serve as the blueprint   *could → restructuring fr polit system*
for a radical restructuring of the French political system, even indicating
a new basis for the determination of nobility: "the womb alone would
ennoble" (*le ventre seul annoblirait*) (95). With its projected revival of the
by then archaic practice of "uterine nobility," *De l'usage des romans*
revives Boileau's worst fear of what might happen if salon society
contaminated court society with its beliefs.[22] It proves that the subversiveness of the *frondeuses* was still linked to the novel a century after
their rebellion. It also bears responsibility for a renewed attack on the
novel, best represented by Jacquin's text, perhaps the most violent
antinovel polemic ever.

Entretiens sur les romans is subtitled *Ouvrage moral et critique*. True to   *Jacquin:*
its name, the work is devoted above all to highlighting the moral
grounds that were, from Boileau on, the cornerstone of the novel's   *novel condemned on moral grounds*
condemnation. Jacquin renews Boileau's attack on the novel, in Boi-
leau's very terms.[23] However, the wide-ranging defense articulated by
Huet and his followers, in particular Lenglet-Dufresnoy, had necessitated two crucial tactical changes. Rather than attack Scudéry alone,

condemns *writers;*
novel = threat
to historical
writing

Jacquin condemns women writers in general. Rather than brand the novel as a threat to society alone, he labels it a menace to historical writing as well.

novel = P =
tyrant of ♂
via love

Jacquin defines as the novel's founding dictate, "the origin of novels," the code of amorous conduct that gave women absolute control: "Novels make [women] the tyrant of men, . . . the mistress who rules as a master over her lover" (339–40). During the first century of this code's exis-

social order↓

tence, he contends, "novels have tended not only to *trouble the peace of families* but to *overturn the order on which society depends for its preservation*" (339, my emphasis). Among the socially malignant messages taught by novels, Jacquin singles out "scorn for the most established practices of religion and the most respectable rules of society" and "the insinuation that the essence of marriage consists not in an empty ceremony but in the gift of the heart and the feelings that accompany it" (337, 338). According to Jacquin, the novel owes its threatening impact on society precisely to those portrayals of history that Lenglet-Dufresnoy praises as

♀ govern via
governing ♂

proof of the superiority of its historical vision: "Where are [the novels] in which the mistress of a prince is not able to govern, at her whim, an entire kingdom?" (340).

Thus, in the minds of literary commentators both hostile and sympathetic, in the mid-eighteenth century the novel still retained the essence of the images bestowed upon it by Boileau nearly a century before. As the genre that depicted "the apotheosis of women" (Jacquin 341), it was proclaimed, according to the political beliefs of the critic pronouncing judgment, either a threat to society or a monument to the nation's glory.

The French women's novel survived the new round of attacks led by Jacquin, too. We find in writers' memoirs evidence that, throughout the eighteenth century, the major figures of the French tradition continued to read the works Boileau and his followers portrayed as a threat to

nb. ♀s continue
to be
read

Church and State. For example, in the *Confessions* Jean-Jacques Rousseau traces his "uninterrupted sense of [him]self" to the years early in the century when he and his father would stay up through the night reading the novels in his dead mother's library. From his first literary language, his mother's tongue, Rousseau claims to have acquired "a knowledge of emotions (*les passions*) unique at my age" (8–9). For the

eg Rousseau

creator of *Julie,* the eighteenth century's most celebrated feminocentric fiction, novels were the maternal literary example, the female (reader's) tradition, and Scudéry's writing—*Artamène* is one of the three novels he mentions—was a foundation of what he terms his "novelistic [*ro-*

manesque] vision of human existence" (8). From the *Mémoires d'outre-tombe* of Chateaubriand, Rousseau's heir and one of the formative voices *eg Chateau-briand* of nineteenth-century French prose, we learn that the situation was still the same in the 1770s: "My mother, gifted with great intelligence (*esprit*) and with a prodigious imagination, . . . knew all of [Scudéry's] *Cyrus* by heart" (1:26–27).

Why is it that critics have continued simply to ignore the massive evidence contradicting Boileau's views, and to propose as literary fact one of the "myths formed in the eighteenth and nineteenth centuries on the basis of a legend forged by [Boileau]?" (Adam, "L'Ecole de 1660" 249). Anyone who doubts that the personal beliefs of a single individual could have played a formative role in determining the shape of a canon and the fate of a female tradition should bear in mind that Antoine *A. Adam* Adam will undoubtedly be known as the most influential interpreter of seventeenth-century French literature of the twentieth century, and remember that his repeated efforts at denouncing Boileau's role have gone unheeded.[24]

For the first century of its existence, the modern French novel was *early novel = outcast,* often an outcast, a genre deprived of the status many had initially *not pariah* granted it whenever the authority of the individual known as "the arbiter of literary taste" was respected, but it was never a pariah, a low-caste genre. Its early history, therefore, is far more complex than the paradigm of a steady rise to prominence that is generally still promoted *evolution:* as the novel's official story: from an initial position of prominence, the novel was brought low, only to rise again to eminence, more than a century after it had first attained this position. That Boileau went to such lengths to humble the novel cannot be explained by the reasons he persistently offered—that the novel was antihistorical, and so forth— but by the fact that the most successful first novelists were women, who had turned the early novel into a feminized, and often a feminist and even a feminizing (in the sense of that which promotes its creators' feminocentric values), literary genre.

Throughout his diatribe against novels, Jacquin portrays the threat of the novel as tied to the genre's dangerously rapid proliferation. By the mid-eighteenth century, this heir of Boileau clearly recognized that the ultimate danger of novels was that they would spread their ideological *ultimate danger:* pestilence beyond the aristocracy and throughout the bourgeoisie. By *novels would spread to* 1755, the French novel was largely being written by bourgeois. At that *bourgeoisie* time, as Terry Eagleton and others have recently argued, the genre had become a tool in the formation of a bourgeois identity. Because in France the novel had remained faithful to the ideals of the seventeenth-century aristocrats who had given it its modern formulation, the ultimate danger of the novel was that it would continue to transmit their sexually, socially, and politically subversive ideology, that it would become an agent of ever more widespread contamination.

Teaching Frenchness, or Reading and (Class) Status

> The history of men's opposition to women's emancipation is more interesting perhaps than the story of that emancipation itself. Virginia Woolf, *A Room of One's Own*

DESPITE BOILEAU's repeated efforts and despite his growing authority in the republic of letters, his vision did not immediately win out. During the declining years of Louis XIV's reign the vitality of the view of French culture that promoted women's achievements was evident. Witness the example of the monument to literary and musical genius, "the French Parnassus," conceived by Titon du Tillet in 1708. In an intriguing reversal of the habitual gendering of the origin of genius, the nine muses are all men—Corneille, Racine, Molière, La Fontaine, Boileau, Segrais, Racan, Chapelle, and Lully. Scudéry, Deshoulières, and La Suze play the role of the three graces (Colton 21). As far as male writers were concerned, the artist made a fairly accurate prediction of the canon to come; however, the women who at the dawn of the Enlightenment seemed just as clearly destined for immortality have all but disappeared from that record of the cultural past.

Both their disappearance and the ultimate victory of Boileau's authority can be understood only by retracing the politics of the most significant moment of canon formation in French history, the moment at which French literature was shaped for the first time into a curriculum of authors to be taught to schoolchildren. In the course of this process, the ideals and the practice that continued to inform the French pedagogical system as recently as the early twentieth century were formulated. Once this process was initiated, the fate of women writers was sealed: commentators became determined that they should play no role in the training of French schoolchildren, that no one should ever be educated into Frenchness on the basis of their example.[25]

The founding moment of canon formation in France begins in the late seventeenth century and continues until the middle of the eighteenth century: at that time, two related developments were transforming the meaning of "classic" in French. In the first place, modern (French) authors were granted equal footing with their ancient precursors as models for pedagogical instruction, becoming therefore "classic" according to standard usage, the primary sense of the term attested in seventeenth-century dictionaries ("author who is taught in classes, in the schools"). In the second place, selected authors of the second half of the seventeenth century (the period that baptized itself France's Golden Age) gradually became accepted as "classic" in another sense of the word, one particular to the French language and included only in modern dictionaries: "that which pertains to the great authors of the seventeenth century and their period, considered as expressing an ideal" (*Robert Dictionary*).[26]

In the course of the semantic drift that eventually allowed seventeenth-century French authors to be considered the modern equals of the great writers of antiquity, these two meanings of classic were often seen as synonymous; after a certain point it was almost universally understood that "the great authors of the seventeenth century" were alone worthy to be taught in the schools. At the same time and as part of the same evolution of linguistic usage and pedagogical practice, the most influential women writers of the Golden Age were pronounced unworthy of membership in the class of "great authors of the seventeenth century" because the "ideal" their works express was deemed unfit to be proposed to schoolchildren as a model. However, these women writers were still proposed as models as long as the original canon of French literature, a canon, as we will see, for adult readers rather than schoolchildren, still survived (roughly until the beginning of the nineteenth century). To explain the exclusion of women writers from classic status, I will contrast the two pedagogical programs available from the late seventeenth century until shortly after the Revolution, what I have just referred to as the canon for adults and the first canon for schoolchildren to include modern authors.

In the closing decades of the seventeenth century, French writers begin to draw up lists of their precursors and then to edit anthologies of their representative works. The best known of these is the five-volume *Recueil des plus belles pièces des poètes français,* published anonymously in 1692 and considered the work of either Fontenelle, a man of letters

sympathetic to women writers, or Marie-Catherine d'Aulnoy.[27] This
compilation is in many ways a model for the major early tradition of
anthologizing. It is devoted exclusively to French authors and almost
exclusively to seventeenth-century writers. Its editor makes no claim to
be a literary arbiter: all authors are included who have acquired a
certain "reputation," whether or not they can be considered "great"
authors. The editor makes no attempt to dictate literary taste but tries
simply to give a sense of the field.

Readers today think of anthologies exclusively as works intended to
introduce schoolchildren to literature. However, in France for over a
century until just after the Revolution, almost all these volumes were
compiled for adults who wished to keep abreast of the literary scene.
The principle of inclusion on which the Fontenelle/d'Aulnoy anthology
is based makes it clear that this anthology, like the dozens that imitated
it throughout the eighteenth century, was destined for a precise public,
the adults who frequented milieus such as the salons, in which literature
was a major topic of discussion and who wished to have a sense of the
range of modern literature, a subject not yet part of the curriculum at
the time of their official education. These early anthologies are therefore
pedagogical in a sense close to the recent usage "continuing education."
In the vision of literary production they propose, the canon is made up
of works read by an adult public active in the world rather than a public
isolated in an educational establishment, a pedagogical role for literature
promoted actively at least until the early nineteenth century. Indeed,
prior to the mid-eighteenth century, the only canonical status to which
French authors could aspire was inclusion in worldly anthologies compiled for adults, a canonical status that was never officially legitimated.
Only under the most exceptional circumstances did a new work become
canonical in the original French sense of literature introduced into the
classroom as a model for students. Prior to the mid-eighteenth century,
the classics, the works taught in the *collèges,* were all Greek and Latin,
whereas modern works could become influential only by appealing to
the worldly adult public.

The view of the literary scene found in the continuing-education
anthologies of the late seventeenth and early eighteenth centuries is
remarkably different from the vision of that era presented in today's
manuals. Perhaps the most striking difference concerns the presence of
women writers. In anthologies devoted to writers in general, women
writers are admitted in numbers far more important than at any time

nb. great numbered women writers

since. In addition, between the late seventeenth and the late eighteenth century, at least a dozen literary anthologies devoted exclusively to women writers were published.[28] Before presenting the canonical revision that was the end result of the Enlightenment's new literary pedagogy, I will consider very briefly two of these continuing-education anthologies, one near the beginning of the tradition and one at its end, in order to suggest the magnitude of the options sacrificed to the remodeled classical ideology.

revision < Enlightenm't

Marguerite Buffet's *Nouvelles observations sur la langue française, avec l'éloge des illustres savantes tant anciennes que modernes* (1668), among the first such anthologies, is a fascinating critical hybrid. Buffet's volume is the clearest demonstration of the genre's goal of continuing adult education: its first half is a French grammar and a treatise on correct usage and orthography destined for a general audience and in particular for female readers who had been denied formal linguistic training. These grammatical considerations are joined to a portrait gallery of literary women in which Buffet broadens the definition of the literary to include demonstrations of the linguistic excellence, oral as well as written, she defines in her grammatical treatise. She is thereby able to record accomplishments, such as conversational brilliance, otherwise excluded from the domain of literary criticism. Volumes like Buffet's—as well as those of her contemporaries Jean de La Forge, Jacquette Guillaume, and Claude de Vertron—provide information on numbers of influential seventeenth-century literary women who have been virtually lost to readers since the demise of the worldly canon after the Revolution.[29]

M. Buffet grammar + gallery of literary women

Early anthologies like Buffet's have none of the pedagogical qualities of the eighteenth-century compilations whose techniques we will analyze. They are often closer to collections of eulogies than to literary manuals from which a potential student of any age could obtain information on what an individual author actually wrote, much less on what that literary production was like.[30] By the end of the worldly anthology tradition, however, editors had made great progress in the pedagogical presentation of material, having learned from their predecessors (almost every compilation contains references to precursor volumes) as much as from the rival tradition of manuals for classroom instruction. Both the most eloquent and the most pedagogical of the worldly anthologies would clearly have realized the genre's potential, had it not become still another victim of 1789.

more like eulogies

later - would evolve into classroom manuals

The fourteen existing volumes of Louise Keralio Robert's *Collection*

Keralio's Collection (margin note)

des meilleurs ouvrages français composés par des femmes (1786–1789) stand as a monument to the tradition's potential for growth. Furthermore, as she makes clear in the preface to volume 1, Keralio had initially planned a venture far more vast, "about thirty-six volumes" that would have presented a panorama of French literary history from the Middle Ages through the end of the eighteenth century, with the lion's share devoted to the "classical age" of French women's writing, the seventeenth century (1:i–ii). Had Keralio completed her anthology, she would have provided an alternative history of French literature until the Revolution, a narrative demonstrating the deficiency of any French literary history that omits the contributions of women to every period, a history challenging the adequacy of the notions of periodization then commonly accepted—many of which are still accepted today—to account for the production of women writers. But Keralio did not nearly finish her history. After the initial five volumes devoted to the Middle Ages and the Renaissance (Christine de Pizan alone is allotted two volumes), she jumps ahead to Scudéry. She then skips over volumes 7 and 8, which she leaves blank in the hope of returning some day to fill in the gaps, and proceeds directly to Sévigné. It is easy to explain Keralio's failure to complete the ambitious contract she initially offered her readers: the last volumes of her collection appeared in 1789, an inauspicious date, as Germaine de Staël would soon observe, both for feminist writing in general and for the until then often aristocratic tradition of French women's literature in particular. No one would ever fill in the gaps in Keralio's history, although the tradition she represents was killed off by a movement that began long before 1789, and one that was hardly revolutionary in its politics.

The volumes Keralio did complete are astonishingly well researched and put together and could easily be used today as the basis for a curriculum in French women's writing. Her format is highly pedagogical: biography followed by selections from major works, with an important innovation found in no other early anthology. Keralio understood that the best literary history presents an overview, a framework in which individual pieces can be situated. Thus she alternates her treatment of women authors from a given period with a history of French literature, presented in segments from its origins (the time of the Gauls), always integrating the women writers she is about to discuss in the general literary context of their day. And Keralio's volumes are the logical culmination of the movement that begins with Buffet and her contemporaries. An examination of early French literary histories shows that, until the dawn of the nineteenth century, women writers were almost as likely as their male counterparts to be included in canonical compilations. However, at the same time as the editors of worldly anthologies were learning to make their case more forcefully, the countertradition was developing that would in the long run become so influential that it would succeed in establishing its program of French literary classics as the only vision possible of the early history of French literature.

No sooner had the first anthologists established the existence of a French tradition (by the early eighteenth century) than the power of the pedagogical canon began to be recognized. Historians have traced the movement whereby, from the sixteenth to the eighteenth century, the family gradually turned over to the *collège* a boy's preparation for professional life. Yet, despite the fact that a student was supposed to enter a profession directly upon leaving the *collège,* schools continued throughout the eighteenth century to rely almost exclusively on literary texts to teach all subjects. In the course of the century, theorists began increasingly to call for a "national" education, a "uniform" education that would replace "provincial prejudices" with "homogeneous ideas of civic and religious virtue" (Chartier et al. 209). Contemporaneous with the development of the desire to standardize the teaching of Frenchness, to develop on a national scale the process of assimilation through education initially conceived in the 1660s with the Collège des Quatre Nations, is the movement to give French authors at least equal importance in the curriculum that was to perform this new pedagogical mission. In a standardized, national educational program whose primary goal was to use the teaching of literature to form model Frenchmen, educators realized that the newly recognized French literary tradition should play a major role. Under these circumstances, pedagogical authorities initiated the process of teaching teachers how the works of literary moderns could be held up as models of Frenchness.

This project for the ideological packaging of literature took shape over the first half of the eighteenth century. Scholars gradually developed the anthology into a full-scale literary program: in 1740, for example, Goujet produced an eighteen-volume *Histoire de la littérature française* still directed at a post-*collège* public, but no longer governed by the principle of the worldly anthologies—that is, an author should be included if he or she is being talked about. On the contrary, Goujet's aim was strictly judgmental: "I want to lead my readers by the hand through our literary riches, to teach them what we have in each literary domain, to show them what they should choose and reject" (1:ii). Goujet transforms the worldly anthology into the arm by which critics could police the reading habits of the "honnête homme" and thereby shape both his taste and his national prejudices. Such a project would in effect be a form of reeducation, an undoing of the vision of the contemporary literary scene spread by the worldly anthologies. Note that the new vision Goujet promotes is inextricably linked to a redefinition of the public for whom the anthology is destined: from this point on, all anthologies that seek to undermine the worldly tradition are intended solely for male readers. Goujet concludes his "preliminary discourse" with a call for a similar effort on the part of pedagogues, who should be adapting the texts of literary moderns the better to accomplish their task of making their young charges, always, it is understood, male, into "good Christians . . . useful to civil society" (xli).

Pedagogues quickly heeded his call to arms. The ancestor of the modern system of national exams, the *concours général des collèges parisiens,* at its inception in 1747 had a double prize, *amplification française* side by side with *amplification latine.* At this crucial juncture, Parisian professors of rhetoric "categorically" demanded that French poets and orators be introduced into the curriculum and that students begin to write *in* French about French authors (Chartier et al. 199). At the time that the system of *concours* was being founded, the philosophy and even the pedagogical tools that are still used to prepare students for the national exams were given their original formulation. The Abbé Charles Batteux's companion volumes *Les Beaux arts réduits à un seul principe* of 1746 and his *Cours de belles-lettres* of 1747 were designed to provide teachers with both what we know from the manual most familiar today, Lagarde and Michard, as a *"program* of *great* French authors" and the techniques for using these authors to teach Frenchness, most notably through the reduction of works deemed masterpieces to *morceaux choisis* made pedagogical through the tool now known as *explication de texte.* The canon that can be assembled on the basis of the worldly anthologies is quite different from the program for the study of seventeenth-century French literature generally proposed today. The ancestor of the manuals in which those of us currently teaching received our first ideas of the period is Batteux: the "reduced" canon he proposes is remarkably close to what, for better or for worse, we think of as the classic French canon.

Batteux threw his considerable authority as holder of the chair of Greek and Latin philosophy at the Collège de France behind a program for the study of the French tradition that aims to eliminate all literature deemed dangerous to civic virtue, especially the women writers who figure so prominently in the nonpedagogical anthology tradition. Before taking up the question of women writers and the case Batteux builds against them, however, I will first discuss the strategy on which Batteux's pedagogy is founded.

Batteux

For his reform, Batteux calls on pedagogues to follow the new scientific model, "to collect data as the basis for a system that reduces their findings to common principles" (1:126). In *Les Beaux arts réduits,* Batteux defines the nature and the origin of the unique artistic principle he claims to have unearthed, and he also demonstrates the ideological goal of this method of literary and critical reduction. Let me outline the reasoning on which Batteux's model pedagogical system is founded. Good taste is unique: "there is only one good taste, that of nature" (1:127). There is, however, progress in the spread of good taste because the public "allows itself, without noticing it, to be taken in (*se laisser prendre*) by the examples [it encounters in literature]. . . . One shapes oneself unconsciously on that which one has seen." Since moderns have the advantage of access to a greater number of authors, it is logical that good taste has become more widespread and that modern taste provides the definitive guide to classical status. On the basis of these two rules, Batteux constructs the following scenario: there is only one "natural" taste. The great artists are those who have "exposed" the natural design in their works. An educated public is able immediately to appreciate and to "approve" this greatness and then, instinctively and without even realizing it, to form itself according to the standards proposed by the classic literary texts. As a matter of course, the model esthete becomes a model citizen: "One wishes to seem good, simple, direct; in other words, the complete citizen will be revealed" (1:145). The ideal citizen, furthermore, is also a perfect Christian, and the artistic manifestations of good taste inspire both civic virtue and Christian ideals (1:146).

sought common principles

eg. ?of taste

Batteux's logic, which he calls "simple, straightforward," is based on a premise never clearly exposed in his initial treatise: good taste may be unique and innate, but it must also be taught, for only an educated public immediately understands great literature. The implied conclusion of Batteux's theory of universal taste and esthetic progress is that the French educational system should use its power to create the ideals and

↓ ideals and standards of Frenchness

the standards of Frenchness. This service Batteux himself provides in the companion volume to his reductionist theory, in which he selects the precise examples that should be imposed upon the minds of those to be made into model Christian citizens, to mold them, without their knowledge, into the recognition of socially correct greatness. In his *Cours de belles-lettres,* he provides the outline for the teaching of literature designed to produce educated French male Christians. He gives examples from Greek, Latin, and French literature, although "of course French letters will occupy the first rank" (2:9). Both his volume's organization and his description of it are resolutely direct:

> We will cover all the genres in succession, beginning with the simplest. We will give a summary presentation of the nature, the parts, and the rules of each of them; we will briefly trace its history; after which we will apply the rules to the most famous works in each genre, which will be analyzed both in terms of their content and in terms of their form. (2:9–10)

In the three volumes of his curriculum, Batteux proceeds genre by genre, giving first general history and principles, followed by a short biography of each author, and finally selected passages from each author's work, passages which—and this is his work's major long-term innovation—he then analyzes. In the *Cours de belles-lettres,* anthologizing is always accompanied by a demonstration of literature's role in the classroom. The *Cours de belles-lettres* is the first example in France of what we call a literary manual.

When Batteux begins the course itself, it quickly becomes apparent that "our" taste simply singles out again and again those works that conform to "our" preconceived notions of what a work on a specific subject should say. For his presentation of La Fontaine, Batteux lays out the foundation of his method, a method with a prodigious future in the French pedagogical tradition. His technique—"which presupposes real genius"—"consists in the comparison of a work with nature itself or, *that which amounts to the same thing, with the ideas that we have about what one can, and what one must, say about the chosen subject*" (2:61; my emphasis). He illustrates his method with a reading of La Fontaine's "Le Chêne et le Roseau" that is a classic of the critical-pedagogical genre known as *explication de texte.*

Before examining the text, however, Batteux shows why it deserves to be singled out as an exemplary work: "Before reading it, let us try to see for ourselves what ideas nature would present us on this subject" (2:61). He then shows how the major elements in La Fontaine's fable correspond to "our" preestablished ideas of what they should be. In his *explication de texte,* furthermore, Batteux goes on to demonstrate that "our" expectations, when properly fulfilled, produce a work that is the perfect embodiment of all the stylistic and formal qualities previously characterized as the highest literary values. The great work, the classic, is the work that contains no surprises for the educated critic-reader and the work that conforms perfectly to the French male Christian's ideas of (human) nature. All "we" have to do to explicate literature properly is to articulate "our" prejudices and proclaim as classics those works that best exemplify "our" vision of what the world should be.

Thus Batteux's program reveals that the teaching of literature in France has been founded from its origin on the phenomenon that Thiesse and Mathieu refer to as "l'histoire littéraire par les textes" [literary history through texts] ("The Decline" 214). Just as in the nineteenth-century process whose unfolding Thiesse and Mathieu retrace, in Batteux's original formulation of "l'histoire littéraire par les textes" works are initially singled out allegedly for their value as examples, that is, for the extent to which they lend themselves to the techniques of *explication de texte.* Yet the overall implication of his work, and of the nineteenth-century program that follows his example, is that literary history can be written solely on the basis of the works thus isolated.

Batteux's program is also a monument to the official exclusion from the pages of literary history of the novel and therefore of the women writers who were until then its most illustrious practitioners. Self-styled Boileau of his age (his collected works appeared in 1774 to coincide with the centenary of *L'Art poétique*), Batteux continues his precursor's battle against prose fiction. Boileau, however, had at least discussed the novel, if only to dismiss it. Batteux's resolute avoidance of the novel could well have been a new tactic for eliminating the genre that for decades had proved stubbornly resistant to the decree denying it classic status.[31] Since Batteux does not allude to the genre's existence, even in the volume he devotes to prose forms, it might be possible to explain his omission on the grounds that the novel was perhaps the mode least malleable to the demands of *explication de texte.* However, this explanation is invalidated by the terms on which Batteux judges the two women writers he chooses to include.

In the volume Batteux devotes to prose genres, he concludes with a discussion of the letter, for which his representative modern author is Sévigné. However, the goal of the *explications de texte* he performs on her epistles is to point out their defects, to prove that she is not a suitable pedagogical model. Her letters are so full of "dead time" (*longueurs*) that they frequently "languish" (355–56). Her arguments are "without body" (356). Her style, in short, is an appropriate model only for "overly tender mothers" (354), and it is unworthy of exemplary status because it is too "risky (*hasardé*) for anyone but her, and especially for a man of letters" (354–55; my emphasis).

This reasoning becomes even clearer in Batteux's treatment of De-shoulières. (She was, in 1671, the winner of the first prize for poetry awarded by the Académie Française, and she is the ideal example of the woman writer always part of the worldly adult canon, but since eliminated, following the judgment of Batteux's followers, from their canon for children.) Her pastoral poetry is judged "the most delicate," "the *softest* possible," but

> unfortunately, the doctrine—the "esprit de mollesse," the "essence of flabbiness or pliancy"—that her poetry fosters is conducive to a weakening of moral fiber, and turns it into a sort of epicurianism entirely opposed, not only to Christian morality, but also to that vigor of the soul, to that *male force,* that is the foundation and the support of true integrity. (2:188; my emphasis)

Thus Deshoulières, like Sévigné, seems to have been included in the first pedagogical canon of French literature the better to justify the exclusion of women's writing in general. These token women achieve exemplary status above all as illustrations of the threat to "vigorous" male Christian standards represented by the "softening" and "languishing" tendencies of female literary models. Women writers, Batteux warns, had to be eliminated from the curriculum because they were a direct threat to Church and State.

Classicists have long been sensitive to the central role in the preservation of Greek literary texts played by the anthologies edited for schoolboys in antiquity. For example, of the forty to forty-four comedies of Aristophanes known to the ancients, we know only the eleven edited by a grammarian as "selected theater" for classes. Similarly, all that has come down to us of the vast production of Aeschylus and Sophocles are the plays selected for the curriculum (Marrou 225). In the case of French literature, one cannot, of course, speak of a phenomenon as dramatic as the permanent destruction of works. Nevertheless, for nearly two centuries it has been as if the works of most of the French women writers included in the early canon for adults no longer existed. Once modern writers had entered the pedagogical curriculum, within decades the anthologies for a cultivated adult public ceased to be compiled, and the other canon thus kept alive began to be forgotten. Increasingly, the modern writers who continued to be read were only those who could be promoted as French classics, that is, those who could be packaged in a national, and a nationalistic, literary program. The educators entrusted with the creation of a literary model for the exclusively male public of the *collèges* followed Batteux's lead and excluded the "dangerous," the "inimitable," as Lafayette would have it, examples of virtue provided by women writers.[32]

The terms in which Batteux eliminated women writers were frequently repeated as the original French pedagogical canon was set in place. I will cite one example from another pedagogue-critic of the day because the importance of repetition in canon formation should never be underestimated. Pedagogue-critics most often reiterate the judgments of others. "[Villedieu's] works are little read today, and I dare say that they are still read too much, considering the danger that young men, above all, cannot fail to encounter from their reading" (Goujet 18:138). When women writers are evoked by any of the eighteenth century's literary pedagogues, it is almost always simply to explain in summary fashion why their works should no longer be read. Often, Batteux's argument about their threat to the nation's male fiber is restated. Just as often, the pedagogue turns to the argument Boileau used, so prematurely, about Scudéry: "She is no longer read." Their pronouncements are as premature as their master's—Villedieu, for example, continued to be reedited throughout the eighteenth century—but that is not the point. Women writers were so threatening to the ideology of the developing pedagogical canon that their elimination had to be reimposed until the new curriculum was firmly established.

Thus, in the sixteen-volume compilation that may best represent the view of the canon that the nineteenth century inherited from the eighteenth, *Lycée ou cours de littérature ancienne et moderne* (1797–1803), the Voltaire disciple and longtime journalist La Harpe uses the customary argument, virtually without exception, whenever he evokes a woman

writer. He mentions eleven seventeenth-century women, not an unim-
pressive list, but for all but Lafayette and Sévigné the entry is limited to
the phrases "her boring novels, plays, and so forth, have been forgotten,"
or "her works are no longer read." La Harpe devotes fully half of the
Lycée's volumes to the literature of his own, not quite finished, century.
In these eight volumes he includes only four women writers: Tencin, de
Beaumont, Riccoboni, Graffigny. La Harpe's compilation demonstrates
that the flowering of the pedagogical tradition brought about the termination of its worldly counterpart. Contrary to what might be thought,
his *Lycée* is intended not for the formation of schoolchildren but as "a
supplement to [the studies they have already done] for people of the
world who do not have the time to begin new studies" (1:vi). (The *Lycée*
is, in fact, the record of La Harpe's lectures at what has been described
as a worldly Sorbonne with an elegant public.) This is the first work of
adult education to be a work of *reeducation:* La Harpe is trying to
destroy the influence of the tradition of worldly anthologies, to make
over the vision of the canon proposed for adult readers in the image of
the pedagogical canon drawn up for schoolchildren. In the worldly
anthology thus brought into the nationalistic line, women writers were
virtual nonentities.

La Harpe concludes the preface to his *Lycée* by paying homage to the
role played by the salons in fostering the cultivation of literature and
taste: "Our nation can be proud of having known better than others the
advantages of sociability" (1:31). He presents his volumes as a permanent
continuation of the salon tradition: "[Our nation] will have a place of
assembly where amateurs will gather to study the masterpieces of human intelligence." La Harpe's project does not ignore the place of
women: "We would not exclude the sex which, with its presence alone,
covers all shared impressions with charm." However, his work is clearly
premised on a complete redefinition of the salons' role, for the *Lycée* is
described as a means of "conversing with the great men of all ages from
Homer to Voltaire" (1:31). In post-Revolutionary literary assemblies,
women—as producers and consumers of, and commentators on, literature—are to be relegated to the role of charming accessories to an
exclusively male cultural exchange.

The pedagogical movement represented by Batteux and La Harpe
was at least partly responsible for one of the major realignments of
power in French cultural history. Within decades of La Harpe's blueprint for the salons' redefinition, the institution recognized for two

centuries as fundamental to French culture bore but a faint resemblance to its original configuration and was on the road to extinction. In *Salons célèbres* (1837), the first work to celebrate the salon tradition as a completed entity, Sophie Gay announced that "the empire of the salons ended along with that of women" (3).[33] In the early nineteenth century we finally witness the victory of the institution whose historical domination of French cultural life is too readily accepted today, the academies, in particular the Académie Française. Until that time, the two distinct institutions in which literary matters were subject to collective, oral legislation (the salon and the academy) had been rivals for preeminence for the two centuries since their nearly simultaneous establishment in France. Richelieu's creation of the Académie Française as an integral component of his project for an officially imposed vision of national unity was undoubtedly at least in part, as I suggested early in this study, a response to the menace of the salons' existence on the literary scene. The cardinal promoted State supervision of literary life in an effort to check the influence of what Sophie Gay termed exactly two centuries later "the empire of women."

Académie triumphs over salon

In the course of the history that separated the first true witness to the salons' influence from the last, "empire" acquired a literal meaning in French. The individual who introduced France to this image of the State was in many ways Richelieu's true heir. Like the visionary cardinal, Napoleon I sought official control over what Bayle had termed the republic of letters (at a time when its government was in fact far less tyrannical than in the early nineteenth century). The principal instrument of France's first imperial literary regime was the national educational system, a pedagogical institution that the French have since then continued to perfect.[34]

Napoleon + national education system

That institution received its definitive shape in the early nineteenth century, just when the modern vocabulary of nationalism was being forged. However, the founding rhetoric of modern French pedagogy is surprisingly free of contamination from this contemporary political vocabulary. It has far more in common with pre-Revolutionary pedagogical rhetoric. It would be a mistake to explain away this similarity through reference to the political conservatism of those critics who formulate pedagogical programs. (La Harpe, for example, refers to the Revolution as "the bad days" [I:vii].) The common vocabulary indicates the values common to the French pedagogical establishment under all regimes, from the most absolute to the most democratic.

Consider, if only briefly, the example that interests us here, that of women writers. The obvious urgency of their desire (finally) to carry out Boileau's decree consigning these writers to oblivion caused post-Revolutionary French pedagogue-critics to overlook major ideological inconsistencies in their packaging of literary texts for educational purposes. I cannot pretend to have mastered the vast archival resources left by the practice of pedagogy in nineteenth-century France. However, examples from two small corners of a field currently the object of active inquiry are sufficient to demonstrate my point: the pedagogical editions of Sévigné's letters that are produced at regular intervals throughout the nineteenth century, and the fin-de-siècle anthologies that best represent the canon of French literature that was the nineteenth century's legacy to the twentieth.

The significant role played by Sévigné's letters in modern French pedagogy is inaugurated with the publication in 1803 of two editions, each of which was clearly designed for the new educational system.[35] One of these editions bears a subtitle indicating that it had already attained this status ("a work destined for the education of young people and adopted for the lycées and schools of France by Messieurs the government's commissioners"), whereas the other (that published by Charaux) has a subtitle that reveals only the hope of such recognition ("an edition destined for young people and for educational establishments"). Both these editions are pedagogical in Batteux's manner: they present only selected letters, *lettres choisies,* often only fragments of letters, *morceaux choisis.* In their prefaces, both these editions justify the role assigned Sévigné in terms that hardly conform to any standard image of the pedagogical ideology useful to "Messieurs the government's commissioners" of a nation just emerging from revolution and on the eve of its reconstitution as an empire.

Lévizac, editor of the Dufour edition, pronounces Sévigné's letters the highest model of the epistolary style (xv), that style being, "of all the styles, that in which it is most essential to receive early training" (ix). His justification for his choice of letters makes it clear that the epistolary style is "essential" above all as a *class* marker: "This style's merit comes from the progress that society has made in France, where it has created a language known well only by those who have spent considerable time in good company" (xvii). To this end he includes, above all, Sévigné's letters describing Louis XIV's court. The other 1803 edition, whose editor is not named, is premised on a similar nostalgia for "French urbanity of former times" and on a similar desire to preserve every trace of ancien régime court life, "these anecdotes that are disappearing from the memory of good company" (v, vi).[36]

"Urbanity," "good company"—this is typical of the rhetoric that, throughout the nineteenth century, is used to justify Sévigné's remarkable promotion, to the virtual exclusion of all other women writers of the ancien régime, as pedagogical model.[37] Long after the Revolution, French pedagogue-critics continued to preach aristocratic values. This means that the canon they proposed was composed solely of authors who, regardless of their social rank, glorified the monarchy and never sought political or social upheaval, and of authors who, like Sévigné, could be portrayed as having taken these positions. These pedagogue-critics were heavily invested in what had already been a central endeavor for the architects of Louis XIV's absolutism, the promotion of the myth of a Golden Age for French letters, with a set of classic authors who defended the values Boileau so curiously termed "Republican." Time and again, those values proved useful in the construction of a spirit of nationalism that could be put at the service of any regime in power—from an empire, to a restored monarchy, to a (finally a real one) republic.

No nineteenth-century regime felt the need to make a place for women writers. Since for most of the century the developing national educational system was still dedicated almost exclusively to the education of male children, it was easy for pedagogues to repeat the argument devised by their ancien régime precursors about the threat posed by women's writing to stable social values and manly virtue. Only in the fin-de-siècle, after the passage of the Camille Sée law in December 1880, did the development of a national eductional system for women finally begin in earnest. As part of that process, educators for the first time developed literary anthologies with schoolgirls in mind. These anthologies are of two kinds: some editors, such as Albert Cahen, reach out to the new market with gender-specific versions of the same manual, one for boys and one for girls; others, such as Paul Jacquinet, create a text exclusively for female education.

The two versions of Cahen's *Morceaux choisis des auteurs français* ("for the secondary education of girls," 1889; for that of boys, 1892) give essentially the same vision of the canon of French literature. In his version of French literary history for girls, Cahen includes a few additional women writers, as well as selections from women writers only *includes some p. writers...*

mentioned in the boys' counterpart. He in no way, however, modifies his stance on women's writing, a stance that seems the logical culmination of a century and a half of French pedagogical speculation. Cahen

but...

has so perfectly internalized the warnings about "the danger of novels" that he mentions virtually no women novelists, only two from the seventeenth century, and even those included are presented as if their

only as portraits

contribution to literary history had taken other forms. Thus, Scudéry is represented by a portrait (that of Cléomire, allegedly the Marquise de Rambouillet, from *Artamène*), and Lafayette by her portrait of Sévigné and by a short selection from *La Princesse de Clèves* that he entitles "Mlle de Chartres," as though it, too, were a portrait. According to Cahen's influential vision—the Bibliothèque Nationale catalogue lists frequent reeditions of his manuals during a formative period in French pedagogy—women writers of the ancien régime wrote *mémoires* (from which he always reproduces portraits of famous individuals), portraits, letters, and occasionally works on education. The goals of his presentation are obvious: to recuperate a small number of women writers either because of the moral significance of their writing or, more often, because their

portraits illustrate aristocratic values of court

works can be held up as illustrations of the aristocratic values of court society (hence Cahen's valorization of the portrait, a genre he views as a window onto the life of "worldly society" [1:165]).

Jacquinet's *Les Femmes de France, poètes et prosateurs* (1886) is among the few examples of the pedagogical anthology devised solely for schoolgirls. The preface opens with the complaint that for too long women writers have been represented in such manuals solely by Sévigné. However, Jacquinet, identified on the title page as an "honorary inspector general of public education," ends up by justifying the long-enforced exclusion of women from French literary history: "Because their intellectual temperament (*tempérament d'esprit*) is sensitive and animated rather than powerful, it is difficult for women ... to reach ... that perfect harmony between reason and imagination ... which alone can guarantee literary excellence" (vii). Given this deficiency, the best he has been able to do has been to unearth "enough pleasing pages ... to provide examples for literary classes" (vii). He believes that his anthology for girls proposes models less perfect than those to which they have been accustomed, but he feels that this lack of quality can be justified:

P's writing mediocre, but is more accessible to weak female brains

women's writing, however mediocre, "is more accessible for girls, more appropriate for their ability, and therefore far more encouraging [for them]" (viii).

Jacquinet's experiment, like Cahen's, seems to have been short-lived. After having gone through four reeditions in rapid succession, his attempt to use mediocrity to "encourage" schoolgirls fell by pedagogy's wayside. The spread of coeducation in France effectively ended attempts to return to women writers the canonic status that critics and pedagogues from Boileau to Batteux had succeeded in denying them. From its beginning, the French educational system has made it clear that women writers can never be used to educate men. Only with women in isolation could educators run the risk of introducing more than a minimal dose of literature produced by women and, even then, only if that writing could be promoted as a worthy reflection of the aristocratic values that have been tirelessly promoted by all those, from Boileau to Cahen, whose vision has shaped the national educational system in France.[38]

"The Republic of Letters," "The Empire of Women"—in a nation that does not practice the separation of State and University, can we imagine a regime, old or new, under which not only will women be active producers and consumers of literature but women's writing will become truly classic, held up, in all its social and cultural subversiveness, as a pedagogical model? Will women's writing ever be considered a worthy vision of Frenchness? Will Francophone women's writing ever be considered truly French?

APPENDIX

ℭℑ

Bibliography of Women Writers, 1640–1715

I INCLUDE here all women who appear in the early histories of French women's writing listed in chronological order at the end of this bibliography. (References to these histories appear in brackets at the end of a specific author's entry.) Not all of these women would be described as authors by today's standards. Some appear not to have published their works but only to have circulated them in manuscript. Others were celebrated for their conversational brilliance rather than for written production. The late ancien régime definition of a woman writer was dictated by the concerns of the salons rather than by those of the academies. I consulted only those seventeenth-century compilations on women that deal with contemporary literary developments.

U.S. locations are given according to the NUC listings. When a work is available in five or more U.S. libraries, no locations are given. For works not available in the United States, the call number of the Bibliothèque Nationale (B.N.) or that of the Arsenal Library is listed. If the information contained in an early literary history might be easily overlooked, a volume number is also given. Authors about whom information is easily available (Lafayette, Sévigné, and so forth) do not receive a complete entry; early literary histories in which they are discussed are listed. N.B.: when looking for an entry in an early literary history, all possible systems of alphabetization should be checked (for example, Lafayette, Fayette, Vergne). Unless otherwise noted, all books were published in Paris.

* means attributed or contested authorship.

** indicates an especially important entry.

ℭℑ

Alerac, Mademoiselle de La Tour d'. b. 1645. Known for her erudition and her poetry.

Amelot, Présidente d'. Known as a good judge of literary works. [La Croix, Vertron].

Armançais, Madame d' (also: Armançay). Wrote occasional verse. See, for example, *Le Mercure galant,* July 1684. [La Croix, La Porte, Vertron].

Arnauld, Jacqueline-Marie-Angélique de Sainte-Madeleine. 1591–1661. *Relations écrites ... de ce qui est arrivé de plus considérable dans Port Royal,* 1716, later editions widely available; *Entretiens ou conférences de la révérende mère Marie-Angélique Arnauld, abbesse et réformatrice de Port Royal,* 1757; various collections of her letters available.

Arnauld, Jeanne-Catherine-Agnès de Saint-Paul. d. 1671. Religious at Port-Royal. *Le Chapelet secret du Saint-Sacrement; L'Image de la Religieuse parfaite* (B.N.: D.23786). [La Croix].

Auchy, Charlotte des Ursins, Vicomtesse d' (also: Ochy, Oulchy). 1570–1646. Wrote "Paraphrases des Epîtres de Saint Paul." In 1638 founded a salon. [Guillaume, La Forge, Vertron].

Aulnoy, Marie-Catherine Le Jumel de Barneville, Comtesse d' (also: Jumelle de Berneville, Aunoy, Anois). d. 1705, age 55. *Nouvelles d'Elisabeth, reyne d'Angleterre,* 1674; *Histoire d'Hypolite, Comte de Duglas,* 1690; *Mémoires de la Cour d'Espagne,* 1690; *Relation du voyage d'Espagne,* 1691; *Histoire de Jean de Bourbon, Prince de Carency,* 1692; *Histoire nouvelle de la Cour d'Espagne,* 1692; *Mémoires des avantures singulières de la Cour de France,* 1692; *Nouvelles espagnolles,* 1692; *Mémoires de la Cour d'Angleterre,* 1695; *Les Contes des Fées,* 1696; *Mémoires secrets de Mr. L.D.D.O. ou les avantures comiques de plusieurs grands Princes de la Cour de France,* 1696; *Contes nouveaux ou les fées à la mode,* 1698. La Porte also cites *Le Comte de Warwick,* novel, 1703? [Alletz, La Croix, La Porte, Vertron].

Aumale, Marie-Jeanne d'. 1683–1756. Biographer of Françoise d'Aubigné, Marquise de Maintenon; known for her letters, see, for example, "Quelques lettres inédites d'Anne d'Osmond, Marquise d'Havrincourt, et de Marie-Jeanne d'Aumale, 1721–1724, ed. Alfred Asselin (Arras, 1875).

Auneuil, Louise de Bossigny, Comtesse d'. *L'Inconstance punie, nouvelles du temps,* 1702 (B.N.: Y2.43416). *Nouvelles diverses du temps. La Princesse des Pretintailles,* 1702 (B.N.: Rés.Y2.2676); *La Tyrannie des fées détruite,* 1702 (B.N.: Y2.8809, also later editions); *Les Chevaliers errans et le Génie familier,* 1709 (B.N.: Y2.8812).

Autreval, Mademoiselle d'. Letters in *La Nouvelle Pandore* (ed. Vertron) and *Le Mercure galant.* [La Croix, La Porte, Vertron].

Barbier, Marie Anne. 1670?-1742? Tragedies: *Cornélie, mère des Gracques,* 1703 (PU, PPULC); *Thomyris,* 1707 (ICRL, ICU); *La Mort de César,* 1710 (MH, OCU, ICRL); *Arrie et Petus,* 1713 (ICRL). Comedies: *Le Faucon,* 1719 (ICRL); one-act comedy *La Petite Soeur* (published 1892) (CU, NN). Began to publish a periodical, *Saisons Littéraires, ou Mélange de Poésie, d'Histoire, et de Critique,* 1714 (DLC), with poetry, stories, and literary criticism. Collection of stories: *Le Théâtre de l'Amour et de la Fortune.* Theater collection published 1719 (IU, CU, IEN, also later editions). Operas: **Les Fêtes de l'été* (staged 1716); **Le Jugement de Paris* (staged 1718); **Les Plaisirs de la campagne* (staged 1719). [Alletz, La Croix, La Porte].

Bédacier, Catherine (née Durand). Known professionally as Madame Durand. d. ca. 1712. *Les Amours du Cardinal de Richelieu,* 1687; *La Comtesse de Mortane,* 1699 (ICN, CtY, NjP, DLC); *Les Petits soupers de l'été,* 1699 (PMB, PPULC); *Les Mémoires secrets de la cour de Charles VII, roy de France,* 1700 (NNC, DLC-P4, CtY, MWelC); *Histoire des amours de Grégoire VII, du Cardinal de Richelieu, de la Princesse de Condé, et de la Marquise d'Urfé,* 1700 (MH); *Les Avantures galantes du Chevalier de Themicour,* 1701 (ICU) (1706, TxU, MH, NjP); *Anecdotes galans,* 1702; *Le Comte de Cardonne,* 1702; *Les Belles Grecques,* 1712 (DLC, CtY, ICN, NcD); *Henri, duc des Vandales,* 1714 (ICN); *Louis III, roi de Sicile.* Her collected works also include poetry and comedies-in-proverbs, which were staged. [La Croix, La Porte].

Beringhen, Olimpe de, Abbess of Farmoutier en Brie. Famous for her erudition. (B.N. lists an "Acte" of 1734, presented by the Abbesse to Cardinal Bissy, opposing *Unigenitus.*) [La Croix, La Porte, Vertron].

Bernard, Mademoiselle (*not* Catherine Bernard). "Panégyrique de Sainte Catherine" delivered to the Recteurs de la Charité générale de Lyon in 1694. [La Porte, Vertron].

Bernard, Catherine. 1663–1712. Member of the Académie des Ricovrati. Wrote novels, verse plays, and other poetry. Novels: *Frédéric de Sicile,* 1680; *Les Malheurs de l'amour. Première nouvelle. Eléonore d'Yvrée,* 1687 (DLC, ICN) (reprinted 1979); *Le Comte d'Amboise, Nouvelle galante,* 1689 (CtY, ICN, MH, DLC, CLU-C); *Histoire de la rupture d'Abenamar et de Fatime,* 1696; *Inès de Cordoue, nouvelle espagnole,* 1696 (MH, ICU, NN, DLC) (reprinted 1979). Theater: *Laodamie,* tragedy; *Brutus,* tragedy, 1691 (MiU, CtY, OCU, MH). "L'Imagination et le Bonheur," fable in verse; "Requête en vers" addressed to Louis XIV; madrigals. Won prizes and was published in collections by both the Académie Française and the Jeux Floraux de Toulouse. B.N. lists "Relation de l'île de Bornéo," also attributed to Fontenelle, Rés. Lb44.1020. [Alletz, La Croix, La Porte, Vertron].

Béthune d'Orval, Anne-Eléonore de. 1658–1733. Abbess of Notre Dame du Val-de-Gif. *L'Idée de la perfection chrétienne et religieuse,* 1719 (B.N.: D.19889 and D.20047). *Réflexion sur les Evangiles. Réglements de l'abbaye de Gif.* [La Croix].

Blémur, Madame de. See Bouette de Blémur, Jacqueline de.

Boissangers, Mademoiselle de. Known for her enigmas. [La Porte, Vertron].

Bonnevaut, Madame de (also: Bonneveau). Studied philosophy, held Cartesian salon. [Buffet, La Croix, La Forge, Vertron].

Boudin, Madame. *La Fameuse Comédienne, ou Histoire de la Guérin, auparavant femme et veuve de Molière, 1688.

Bouette de Blémur, Jacqueline de, Bénédictine du Très-Saint-Sacrement. 1618–1696. Her elegy and the catalogue of her works appeared in the Journal des Savants, June 18, 1696. See B.N. for listing of her religious and historical/biographical writings. [La Croix, Vertron].

Bourgeois, Louise, known as Bourcier. Observations diverses sur la stérilité, perte de fruits, fécondité, accouchement et maladies des femmes et enfants nouveaux nés, 1609. More complete eds. 1626, 1642. B.N.: Td122.2. Récit véritable de la naissance des messeigneurs et dames les enfants de France, 1625. B.N.: T21.729. Apologie de Louyse Bourgeois, sage-femme de la reine mère du roi et de feue Madame, contre le rapport des médecins, 1627. B.N.: Ln27.2766. Receuil des secrets de Louyse Bourgeois, 1635. B.N.: Te18.69.

Bourignon, Antoinette. 1616–1680. Mystic evangelist. Her voluminous religious writings are widely available. Autobiographical writings include La Parole de Dieu; La Lumière du monde, 1679–1681; La Vie de Damoiselle Antoinette Bourignon, in collaboration with Pierre Poiret (Amsterdam, 1683).

Bourneaus, Madame de. Known for her knowledge of languages and for her witty writing. [La Forge].

Brassac, Catherine de Sainte-Maure, Comtesse de. Assembled private portrait gallery of French royal family. Lady-in-waiting to Anne of Austria. [Vertron].

Bregy, Anne-Marie de Flécelles de. d. 1684. Historical/biographical writing, mainly about her religious order, Port-Royal, and her relatives. "Modèle de foi ... ou, Vie de la Mère Marie des Anges" (published 1754; CtY, MH, ICU). Additional titles listed in NUC and B.N.

Bregy, Charlotte (Saumaise de Chazan) de Flécelles, Comtesse de (also: Bregis). 1619–1693. Her works include a volume of letters. Praised in Le Mercure galant, April 1677, October 1689, and March 1695. Lettres et poésies, 1666 (DLC, PPULC, CtY); Les Oeuvres galantes de ..., 1666 (MB-B). [Billardon de Sauvigny, La Croix, La Forge, Vertron].

Bretonvilliers, Présidente de. Known as "l'Admirable." Elected to Académie des Ricovrati. Wrote a comedy-in-proverbs, stories, poetry. [La Porte, Vertron].

Brinon, Madame. Mother Superieur of Saint-Cyr. [La Porte].

Briquet, Soeur Magdeleine de Sainte-Christine. Letters, narratives, and Actes relating to captivity and persecution at Port-Royal. (See B.N. catalogue.).

Buffet, Marguerite. Observations sur la Langue Françoise, avec les Eloges des Dames Sçavantes, tant Anciennes que Modernes, 1668 (DLC, CU, MH). [La Croix, Vertron].

Bussières, Mademoiselle de. d. 1730. Edited Jean Hérault de Gourville, Mém-

oires . . . concernant les affaires auxquelles il a été employé par la Cour depuis 1642 jusqu'en 1698, 1782. B.N.: Lb 37.162. [La Croix].

Bussy, Madame de, Religieuse. [La Porte].

Calanges, Marie de Pech, Dame de. *Judith, ou la Délivrance de Béthulie, poème saint,* 1660. B.N.: Ye.1277. [Billardon de Sauvigny].

Canu, Mademoiselle. Poet; perhaps never published. [La Forge].

Castelnault, Mademoiselle de. [La Porte].

Castille, Mademoiselle de. Verse translation of Horace's ninth Ode appeared in *Le Mercure galant,* also poem on the "Comète de l'année 1680." See her elegy in *Le Mercure galant,* tome 53. [La Croix, La Porte, Vertron].

Caumont de la Force, Charlotte Rose de. See La Force.

Caylus, Marthe-Marguerite Le Valois de Villette de Murçay, Comtesse de. 1673–1729. *Les Souvenirs,* published posthumously by Voltaire. Corresponded with Françoise d'Aubigné, Marquise de Maintenon (see *Lettres de Mme de Maintenon*). [Alletz, La Croix, La Porte].

Certain, Mademoiselle de. *Nouvelles poésies, ou Diverses pièces choisies, tant en vers qu'en prose,* 1665. B.N.: Ye.11438. [La Croix].

Chandiot, Madame de. From Besançon. [La Porte].

Chate, Madame de. See Villedieu. [Vertron].

Chaune, Madame de, Abbess of Saint-Pierre de Lyon. Influential teacher. [Buffet, La Porte].

Chavigny, Anne Phelippeaux (or Phélypeaux), Comtesse de. Directed a salon. [La Forge].

Chéron, Elisabeth Sophie. 1648–1711. Associate of Académie Royale de Peinture et de Sculpture. In 1699 elected to Académie des Ricovrati. Known for her drawing and painting as well as her poetry (she illustrated some of her writings). "Pierres antiques gravées tirées des principaux cabinets de la France," 1706 (NN, DI-GS, NjP). Translated Psalms into French verse: "La Paraphrase des Pseaumes, accompagnée de Figures," 1694 (MH). Translated some of Horace's odes. Also translation of the Latin ode by the Abbé Boutard, containing a description of the Trianon. Poetry: "Les Cerises renversées, poème héroïque," 1717?; poem in response to Molière, "La Coupe du Val de Grace." [Alletz, Billardon de Sauvigny, Du Pin, La Croix, La Porte].

Chétardie, Françoise Trotti de La. d. 1687. Abbess of Effey. Known for her erudite conversation and for her letters. [La Croix].

Chevry, Madame de. Religieuse de Saint Pierre de Lyon. Wrote poem praising Louis XIV, published in *La Nouvelle Pandore* (ed. Vertron). [La Croix, La Porte].

Clapisson, Madame de. Sonnet on "Les Reclus du Mont-Valérien." [La Porte].

Clérambault, Louise-Françoise Bouthillier, Maréchale de. [La Porte].

206

Colletet, Claudine. *Sur la mort de Mme de Mancini, sonnet,* 1656 (B.N.: Ye.1250). *Sur le trépas de Mr. René Michel de La Rochemaillet, poésies,* n.d. (B.N.: Fb.19857). [La Forge, Billardon de Sauvigny].

Comeige, Madame de. "Mahomet," tragedy. [La Porte, Vertron].

Conti, Louise Marguerite de Lorraine, Princesse de (also: Conty). 1574–1631. *Romant royal,* 1620, in collaboration with Nicolas Piloust (Arsenal: 8°BL 22557); *Les Advantures de la Cour de Perse,* 1629, in collaboration with Jean Baudouin (Arsenal: 8°BL 1850b); *Histoire des Amours du grand Alcandre,* 1651 (MH, ICN). [Buffet, La Croix, La Forge].

Cornuel, Anne Bigot. 1603–1693. Known for her wit. [La Croix].

Cosnard, Marthe. *Le Martyre de St. Eustache, tragédie,* 1643 (B.N.: Yf.4835); *Le Martyre de Ste. Catherine, tragédie,* 1649 (B.N.: Yf.4836); *Les Chastes martyrs, tragédie chrétienne,* 1650 (MH; B.N.: Yf.4837), later editions available. [La Croix, La Forge, Robert VI].

Coulanges, Marie Angélique du Gué. Known for her letters.

Courtin, Madame. [La Croix, Vertron].

Dacier, Anne Le Fèvre. 1654?–1720. [Alletz, Du Pin, La Croix, La Platière, La Porte].

Dalet, Comtesse de. "La Calomnie confondue," poem. [La Croix, La Porte, Vertron].

Darquier, Madame (also: Dorquier). Poetry appeared in the "Triomphe de l'Eglantine," ed. M. Dader. [La Croix, La Porte, Vertron].

Descartes, Catherine. d. 1706. "Relation de la mort de Descartes," "L'Ombre de Descartes." See the collections of *Chansons* and *Vers choisis* by M. de Coulange. *Lettres de . . . Mlle Descartes,* published in the Collection Epistolaire (Collin, 1806). [Billardon de Sauvigny, La Croix, La Porte, Vertron].

Deshoulières, Antoinette du Ligier de La Garde. 1638–1694. Recipient of the first prize for poetry awarded by the Académie Française (in 1671). Pastoral, lyric, political, and occasional poetry. Published first in *Le Mercure galant.* Editions of her poetry widely available. Tragedies: *Genséric,* 1680 (B.N.: 8°Yth.7885); *Jule-Antoine.* Opera: *Zoroastre. Réflexions morales sur l'envie immodérée qu'on a de faire passer son nom à la postérité,* 1693 (B.N.: Ye.1446). [Alletz, Billardon de Sauvigny, Du Pin, La Croix, La Forge, La Porte, Vertron].

Deshoulières Antoinette-Thérèse (daughter). 1659–1718. Recipient of the Académie Française's prize for poetry (in 1688: Fontenelle was runner-up). Member of the Académie des Ricovrati and the Académie Royale d'Arles. Wrote epistles, songs, madrigals, and a burlesque tragedy, *La Mort de Cochon.* Her poetry first included in editions of her mother's works in 1695. See *Le Mercure galant,* February 1694. (Aublet de Maubuy, Billardon de Sauvigny, Du Pin, La Croix, La Porte, Vertron].

Desjardins, Marie Catherine. See Villedieu.

207

APPENDIX

Desloges, Marie (née Bruneau). d. 1641, age 70. Organized salon, praised for her wit and erudition. [La Porte].

Despinasse, Mademoiselle. Known for her linguistic ability and her knowledge of natural philosophy. [Buffet].

Desvaux, Mademoiselle de. Poet. [La Forge].

Dorieux, Madame. Religieuse. "Réflexions sur les sept Pseaumes de la Pénitence." [La Croix, La Porte, Vertron].

Dorquier, Madame. See Darquier.

Dourlens, Madame Houlier, and Dourlens, Mademoiselle de Chance (daughter). Wrote salon poetry. [La Croix, La Porte].

Dreuillet, Elisabeth de Monlaur, Présidente. 1656–1730. Held salon. Wrote poem, "Epithalame," and much unpublished poetry. Fairy tale, "Le Phénix," in *Nouveaux contes de fées allégoriques,* 1735 (B.N.: Y2.8816). [La Croix, La Porte].

Dufresnoy, Mademoiselle (also: Du Fremoy). Member of the Congrégation of the Filles de la Croix, Paris. Wrote poetry, including poem in *Recueil de l'Académie Française,* 1691. [Billardon de Sauvigny, La Croix, La Porte, Vertron].

Du Hallay, Madame. Wrote poetry. [La Porte].

Duhamel, Mademoiselle. Prose piece, "La Métamorphose d'Acante en Oranger" (probably not published), addressed to Madeleine de Scudéry. Known for her knowledge of languages and modern philosophy. [La Croix, La Porte, Vertron].

Dumée, Jeanne. Astronomer. *Entretiens sur l'opinion de Copernic touchant la mobilité de la terre,* 1680. [La Croix].

Du Noyer, Anne-Marguerite Petit. 1663?–1720. *Mémoires,* 1710 (CLU-C, later editions available); *Lettres Historiques et Galantes,* 1713 (later editions widely available). *Oeuvres meslées,* 1711 (B.N.: Z.24394). Periodical, *La Quintessence des nouvelles,* 1711. See *Le Mercure galant,* August 1697. Her works are widely available in various editions. [**La Platière, La Porte, Vertron].

Du Plessis Bellière, Suzanne de Bruc, Marquise de. "Sonnets en Bouts rimés" published in collection edited by Sercy. [Vertron].

Du Plexis, Comtesse de. Known as eloquent conversationalist. [Buffet].

Dupré, Marie. Wrote verse and prose. Studied Greek, Latin, Italian, and Cartesian philosophy. *Lettres de ... Mademoiselle Dupré,* published in the Collection Epistolaire (Collin, 1806). [La Croix, La Forge, La Porte, Vertron].

Durand. See Bédacier.

Dutort, Madame. d. 1720. Occasional prose and poetry for *Le Mercure galant.* [La Croix].

Duval, Mademoiselle. Wrote salon poetry. [La Porte, Vertron].

Encausse Berat, Madame d'. From Toulouse. Occasional verse published in various collections, including the "Triomphe du Souci," ed. M. de Sironis. [La Croix, La Porte, Vertron].

Esche, Louise de Vassy, Dame d' Her poetry quoted by Madeleine de Scudéry.

Favart, Madame. Poet, excelled in enigmas. [La Croix, La Porte, Vertron].

Ferrand, Anne de Bellinzani, Présidente. 1657–1740. *Histoire nouvelle des Amours de la jeune Bélise et de Cléante,* 1689; *Lettres galantes de Madame,* 1691. Later editions of collected works widely available. [La Porte].

Ferrières, Madame de. Her poetry appears in *Les Amusemens du Coeur et de l'Esprit.* [La Porte].

Feuillet, Marie-Madeleine. Pious works include: *L'Ame chrétienne soumise à l'esprit de Dieu,* 1701, *Concordance des Prophéties* . . . ; *Les Quatre fins de l'homme, Sentimens chrétiens.* . . . Translated religious works (all available at B.N.). See *Journal des Savants,* July 1690. [La Croix, La Porte, Vertron].

Fiesque, Anne Le Veneur, Comtesse de (also: Fieschi). *Histoire de Jeanne Lambert d'Herbigny, Marquise de Fouquesolle* (collaborative volume of satirical poetry), 1653. (B.N.: Rés. Ln27.7813.) [La Forge].

Flexelles, Mademoiselle. From Amiens. Excelled in anagrams. [La Croix, La Porte, Vertron].

Fontaines, Marie Louise Charlotte de Peland de Givry, Comtesse de. d. 1730. Novels: *Amenophis, Prince de Libye,* 1725 (CLU-C, MiU, later editions available) and *Histoire de la Comtesse de Savoie,* 1726 (IU, ICN, NNC, later editions widely available). [La Croix, La Porte].

Fouquesolle, Jeanne Lambert d'Herbigny, Marquise de. *Histoire de Jeanne Lambert d'Herbigny, Marquise de Fouquesolle* (collaborative volume of satirical poetry), 1653. (B.N.: Rés. Ln27.7813.) [La Forge].

Fredine, Mademoiselle de (also: Fredinie). From Pontoise. Wrote salon poetry; see *Le Mercure galant,* April 1679. [La Porte, Vertron].

Frontenac, Comtesse de. *Histoire de Jeanne Lambert d'Herbigny, Marquise de Fouquesolle* (collaborative volume of satirical poetry), 1653. (B.N.: Rés. Ln27.7813.) [La Forge].

Gillot de Beaucour, Louise-Geneviève Gomès de Vasconcellos. Mother of Louise de Saintonge. Novels: *Le Mari jaloux, nouvelle,* 1688 (B.N.: Y2.7798); *Le Galant nouvelliste, histoire du temps,* 1693; *Le Courier d'amour,* 1697; *Les Egaremens des passions et les chagrins qui les suivent représentez par plusieurs avantures du temps,* 1697; *Les mémoires de Raversant.* Abbreviated translation of Ludovico Ariosto, *L'Arioste moderne, ou le Roland Furieux,* 1685 (B.N.: Rés.Yd.852–856). See *Le Mercure galant,* December 1684, January and February 1696. [La Porte, Vertron].

Gomès de Vasconcellos, Geneviève. See Gillot de Beaucour.

Gomez, Madeleine Angélique Poisson, Dame Gabriel de. 1684–1767? Fiction includes: *Les Journées amusantes,* 1723–1731 (NIC, later editions widely available); *L'Histoire secrète de la Conquête de Grenade,* 1723 (CU-S, later

209

APPENDIX

editions MH, MiU); *Crémentine, Reine de Sanga, histoire indienne*, 1727 (later edition CtY); *Les Anecdotes Persanes*, 1727 (NjP, later edition DLC); *Les Cent novelles nouvelles*, 1733–1739; *La jeune Alcidiane*, 1733, continues Gomberville's (1651) unfinished work with same title; *L'Histoire d'Osman, premier du nom, dix neuvième Empereur des Turcs*, 1734 (WU, NN); *L'Histoire du Comte d'Oxfort*, published with *Eustache de St Pierre, au Siège de Calais*, 1737 (NjP, CtY, later editions ICN, RPB). Brochure: *Le Triomphe de l'Eloquence*, 1730 (B.N.). *Oeuvres mêlées*, 1724 (B.N.), also contains tragedies: *Habis*, 1714; *Marsidie, reine des Cimbres; Sémiramis*, 1716; *Cléarque, Tyran d'Héraclée*, 1733; a ballet, *Les Epreuves*, 1737?; and poetry, including "Les Entretiens nocturnes de Mercure et de la Renommée." (Most of the plays are available in the United States in separate and/or later editions.) Attributed works include *Jean de Calais*, n.d.; B.N. lists others. [La Porte].

Gournay, Marie de Jars de. 1566–1645. *Le proumenoir de M. de Montaigne, par sa fille d'alliance*, 1594 (MH; later editions available); *Adieu de l'âme du roi de France et de Navarre Henry le Grand à la reine* (Lyon, 1610) (MH, ICN, other editions available); "Egalité des hommes et des femmes" (followed by Latin and French poetry) 1622 (B.N.: Rp. 1513); *Les Advis ou les Présens de la demoiselle de Gournay*, 1634 (MH; expanded ed. 1641); occasional verse and translations of Latin poetry available at B.N. Various essays and verse are reprinted in Mario L. Schiff, *La Fille d'alliance de Montaigne*, 1910.

Gredeville, Madame de. Noted conversationalist. Follower of Descartes. Studied literature, mathematics, astrology, philosophy, geography, history, and languages. [Buffet, La Forge].

Grignan, Françoise de Sévigné, Comtesse de. 1645–1705. Her letters are published in collections of those of her mother, the Marquise de Sévigné, and of the Comte de Bussy. [La Forge, Vertron].

Guillaume, Jacquette. *Les Dames illustres, où par bonnes et fortes raisons il se prouve que le sexe féminin surpasse en toutes sortes de genres le sexe masculin*, 1665 (NcD). [Buffet].

Guyette, Madame de. (Probably Catherine Meurdrac, Madame de La Guette.) [Vertron].

Guyon, Jeanne Marie Bouvières de la Motte. 1648–1717. A controversial Quietist figure, imprisoned. Wrote religious poetry. Many editions of her collected works available. *Moyen court et très facile pour l'oraison . . .*, 1685 (later editions available); *Opuscules spirituels*, 1704–1712 (later editions widely available); *Lettres chrétiennes et spirituelles*, 1717–1718; *L'Ame amante de son Dieu*, 1717 (CU, later editions widely available); *Le Cantique des cantiques de Salomon*, 1688 (later edition, DLC, NNUT, CU); *Poésies et cantiques spirituels*, 1722 (MdBP, CU); other religious writings listed in NUC and B.N. [La Croix, La Porte].

Harlay, Louise Françoise de, Marquise de Vielbourg. Wrote "Catalogue des livres," list of books in her extensive private collection. [La Porte].

Héere, Madame de. Daughter of the Comtesse d'Aulnoy. Wrote prose and verse. [La Croix, La Porte, Vertron].

Heliot, Marie (née Herinx). 1644–1681. [La Croix, Vertron].

Hommecour. Follower of Descartes. [La Forge].

Hommertz Patin, Madeleine; and her two daughters, Gabrielle and Catherine-Charlotte. See Patin.

Hooghart, Mademoiselle de. *Lettres anti-poétiques* (Amsterdam: Jean Pauli, 1726). Systematic attack on Boileau's *L'Art poétique*.

Itier, Mademoiselle. Wrote verse on the taking of Ath and Barcelona. [Vertron].

Jeanne des Anges, Mère (née Jeanne de Belcier). 1602–1665. Mother superior of the Ursulines de Loudun.. See her autobiographical writings, ed. Drs. Gabriel Legué and Gilles de La Tourette, *Autobiographie d'une hystérique possédée, d'après le manuscrit inédit de Tours*, with preface by Professor Charcot, widely available.

La Calprenède, Madeleine de Lyée. *Les Nouvelles, ou Les Divertissements de la Princesse Alcidiane*, 1661 (B.N.: Y2.20631). [La Forge].

La Chaise, Mademoiselle de. Poet. [Billardon de Sauvigny].

La Charce, Mademoiselle d'Alerac de. Elder sister of Mlle d'Alerac.. Wrote poem celebrating the taking of Ghent. [Du Pin, La Porte, Vertron].

La Charce, Philis de. Poet, mid-seventeenth century. La Croix cites titles of her compositions. [La Croix].

Lafayette, Marie Madeleine Pioche de la Vergne, Comtesse de. 1634–1693. [Alletz, Du Pin, La Croix, La Platière, La Porte, Vertron].

La Force, Charlotte-Rose de Caumont de. 1646?-1724. Fiction: *Histoire secrète de Bourgogne*, 1694 (ICN, NjP, HM, IU); *Histoire secrète de Henry IV, roy de Castille*, 1695 (MH, ICN, NjP, McDB, later editions widely available); *Histoire de Marguerite de Valois, reine de Navarre, soeur de François I*, 1696 (later editions widely available); *Gustave Vasa, Histoire de Suède*, 1697–1698 (later editions CtY, DLC); *Les Contes des contes*, 1698 (CoU, later editions widely available); *Les Jeux d'Esprit, ou la promenade de la Princesse de Conti à Eu*, 1701 (later editions widely available); *Anecdocte galante et secrète de Catherine de Bourbon, duchesse de Bar . . .*, 1703 (ICN, MH, DFo). Attributed fairy tales appear in later collected works. "Epitre à Madame de Maintenon." See *Le Mercure galant*, March 1684, July 1695, and February 1697. [La Croix, La Porte, Vertron].

La Forteresse, Mademoiselle de. Studied Latin and Italian. [Vertron].

La Guette, Catherine Meurdrac de. 1613–1676. *Mémoires*, 1681 (reprinted 1982).

La Marche, Marguerite de. *Instruction familière et utile aux sages-femmes, pour bien pratiquer les accouchements*, 1710. B.N.: Te121.21 (text originally published in the 1600s).

Lambert, Anne-Thérèse de Marguenat de Courcelles, Marquise de. 1647–1733. Editions of her collected works widely available, which include: "Avis d'une mère à son fils," "Avis d'une mère à sa fille," "Psyché," "Traité de l'Amitié," "Portraits de Messieurs de Fontenelle et de la Motte," "Traité de la Vieillesse," "Réflexions sur les femmes" (original title: "Métaphysique d'amour"), "Discours sur la délicatesse de l'esprit et du sentiment," "Sur le goût," "Sur les richesses," "L'Histoire de la femme hermite," "Alexandre et Diogène, Dialogue." *Réflexions nouvelles sur les femmes* (1727?) (MH, later editions widely available). [Alletz, Du Pin, La Croix, La Porte].

La Mothe, Louise de Prie, Maréchale de. Governess of the Dauphin. [Buffet].

La Roche-Guilhem, Anne de (also: La Roche-Guilhen). 1644?–1707. *Almanzaïde, nouvelle,* 1674 (FU, later editions available); *Arioviste, histoire romaine,* 1674 (later edition ICN); *Astérie ou Tamerlan,* 1675; *Journal amoureux d'Espagne,* 1675 (DLC); *Le Grand Scanderberg, nouvelle,* 1688; *Les Intrigues amoureuses de quelques anciens grecs,* 1690; *Zingis, histoire tartare,* 1691 (later edition TNJ); *Les Nouvelles historiques, contenant Gaston Phébus, comte de Foix . . .,* 1692; *Amours de Néron,* 1695 (MH, NjP); *Histoire des favorites, contenant ce qui s'est passé de plus remarquable sous plusieurs règnes,* 1697 (NIC, MH, CtY, later editions widely available). Translation: *Histoire des guerres civiles de Grenade,* 1683 (B.N.: 8°Ob.61A). *Oeuvres diverses,* 1711 (B.N.: 8°.Y2/61716). Various editions of collected works widely available. Other attributed works listed in B.N. [La Croix, La Porte].

La Sablière, Marguerite Hessein de Rambouillet de. 1640?–1693. Led important salon frequented by literary and scientific figures. Her *Maximes chrétiennes* are included in La Rochefoucauld: *Les Pensées, réflexions morales . . .* (Pissot, 1777) (DLC, CSt, NIC, MB). [Vertron].

La Suze, Henriette de Coligny, Comtesse de (also: La Suse). 1618–1673. Poet. For a bibliography of collective volumes in which her poetry appears, see Emile Magne's *Madame de la Suze,* 1907, pp. 290–319. [Alletz, Billardon de Sauvigny, La Croix, La Forge, La Porte].

La Valière, Madame de. Carmélite, Paris. "Réflexions sur la Miséricorde de Dieu." [La Porte, Vertron].

La Vigne, Anne de. 1634–1684. Her poetry was published in various collective volumes. See selection of her verse in Billardon de Sauvigny, volume 5. [Billardon de Sauvigny, La Croix, Vertron].

Le Camus de Melfons, Charlotte. d. 1702. Her occasional verse appeared in various collections. Member of the Académie des Ricovrati. [La Croix, La Porte].

Le Givre de Richebourg, Madame. *Les Avantures de Zelim et de Damsine, histoire afriquaine,* 1735 (NN, IEN); *Les Aventures de Dom Ramire de Roxas et de Dona Léonor de Mendoce,* 1737 (B.N.); *Persile et Sigismonde.* Translated from Spanish: *Les Aventures de Flore et de Blanche-Fleur; Les Aventures de*

Clamadès et de Clarmonde, 1733 (B.N.); and **La Veuve en puissance de Mari,* which contains a comedy entitled *Le Caprice de l'Amour.* [La Porte, Vertron].
Le Marchand, Madame. *Le Conte de Boca* and unpublished works. [La Croix].
Le Sauvage, Mademoiselle. Poet; often entered competitions of the Académie des Lanternistes de Toulouse. [La Porte, Vertron].
L'Esclache, Madame de. Eloquent public speaker, studied philosophy. [Buffet].
Lesdiguières, Anne de la Magdeleine de Ragny, Duchesse de. Admired for her literary discrimination. [Vertron].
Le Vieux, Mademoiselle. [La Porte, Vertron].
L'Héritier de Villandon, Marie-Jeanne. 1664–1734. Niece of Charles Perrault. *Oeuvres meslées,* 1695 (1696 edition ICN, MH, CoU), includes poems: "Le Triomphe de Madame Deshoulières," 1694; "Apothéose de Mlle de Scudéry," 1702; "La Pompe Dauphine," "Le Tombeau de M. le Dauphin, Duc de Bourgogne"; a verse translation of Ovid's *Epîtres héroïques,* 1730; and prose fiction: *La Tour ténébreuse,* 1705 (ICN, OCl, CoU, later editions widely available), *Les Caprices du Destin,* 1718 (CLC, NcD, IU). and *Bigarures ingénieuses, ou Recueil de diverses pièces galantes en prose et en vers,* 1696 (DLC, PSt). Her "L'Adroite Princesse" is included in some editions of Perrault's fairy tales. She also edited the *Mémoires de Madame la Duchesse de Nemours,* 1719. See her eulogy in *Le Mercure galant,* September 1692. [La Croix, La Porte, Vertron].
Liancourt, Jeanne de Schomberg, Duchesse de (also: Liencourt). 1600–1674. Poet. See collection of *Vers choisis.* Various editions of her "Reglement donné par une dame de haute qualité [la Duchesse de Liancourt], à M*** [la Princesse de Marsillac], sa petite-fille pour sa conduite et pour celle de sa maison, avec un autre Reglement que cette dame avait dressé pour elle-même," 1698, are widely available. [Billardon de Sauvigny, La Croix, La Porte, Vertron].
Liborel, Mademoiselle Wrote salon poetry. [La Croix, La Porte, Vertron].
Louvencourt, Marie de. 1680–1712. Wrote occasional poetry; several "Cantares" set to music by Bourgeois; Clérambault wrote music for "L'Amour piqué par une Abeille," "Médée," "Alphée et Arethuse," "Léandre et Héro," "La Musette," "Pigmalion," and "Pyrame et Thisbé." Her poetry included in Madeleine de Scudéry's *Entretiens de morale.* [Billardon de Sauvigny, La Croix, La Porte, Vertron].
Loyac, Mademoiselle de. Poet, perhaps not published. [La Forge].
Loynes, Mademoiselle de. Sonnets to Louis XIV and the Duc de Saint Aignan. [La Croix, La Porte].
Lussan, Marguerite de. 1682–1758. **L'Histoire de la Comtesse de Gondez,* 1725 (CLSU, ICN, CtY, later editions available); **Anecdotes de la Cour de Philippe Auguste,* 1733–1739; **Anecdotes de la cour de Childeric, roi de France* (B.N.); *Les Mémoires secrets et intrigues de la Cour de France sous Charles VII; Les*

213

Anecdotes de la Cour de François I, 1748; *Marie d'Angleterre, Reine Duchesse*, 1749 (DFo, DLC, PPL, NjP); *Les Annales galantes de la Cour d'Henri II*, 1749 (DLC, FU, MdBP, NjP); *Mourat et Turquia, Histoire Africaine*; **L'Histoire de la vie et du règne de Charles VI, Roi de France*, 1753 (NN); **L'Histoire du régne de Louis XI*; **L'Histoire de la Révolution du Royaume de Naples dans les années 1647–1648*, 1757 (ICN); *La Vie de Louis Balbe-Berton de Crillon, surnommé le brave*, 1757 (ICN, MnU, NjP, later editions available); **Veillées de Thessalie*, 1761 (NjP, later edition available). [Alletz, La Croix, La Porte].

Maintenon, Françoise d'Aubigné, Marquise de. 1635–1719. Correspondence, memoirs, pedagogical treatises for young women, maxims, proverbs. [Alletz, Aublet de Maubuy, Du Pin, La Croix, La Forge].

Mal-Enfant, Présidente de. Known for her poetry and her letters, printed in *Le Mercure galant*. [La Croix, La Porte, Vertron].

Marcé, Baronne de (also: Marsé). Novel: *Cléobuline, ou La Veuve inconnue*, 1658 (B.N.: Y2.23195 and Rés.Y2.3028). [La Forge].

Mareschal, Mademoiselle de. Poet, perhaps not published. [La Forge].

Masquière, Françoise de. d. 1728. Wrote poetry included in *Les Amusemens du Coeur et de l'Esprit, Nouveau Choix de poésies* (La Haye, 1715), and various other collected works. Principal poems: "Description de la Galerie de Saint-Cloud," "L'Origine du luth," "Ode sur le Martyre." [La Croix, La Porte].

Maure, Anne Doni d'Attichy, Comtesse de. 1600–1663. Held salon. *Correspondance*, ed. Barthélemy (1863). [La Forge].

Mazarin, Hortense Mancini de La Porte, Duchesse de. 1646–1699. **Les illustres avanturières dans les cours des Princes d'Italie, de France, d'Espagne et d'Angleterre, ou Mémoires de D.M.L.D* . . . , 1706? (MH, IU, CLU, later editions widely available). [La Croix, Vertrun].

Mazel, Madame. Court poetry. [La Porte].

Meurdrac, Marie. Wrote on alchemy for women, *La Chimie charitable et facile en faveur des Dames*, 1666.

Miramion, Marie Bonneau, Dame de. 1629–1696. Superior, Filles de la Visitation. Illustrious charity worker who founded, ca. 1660, a group known as "Miraminionnes." [La Croix].

Miramminy, Madame de. Wrote poetry, apparently not published. [Buffet].

Monglat, Anne-Victoire de Clermont. 1647–1686. Poet, known for her knowledge of languages. Later abbess of Notre-Dame du Val-de-Gif. [La Croix].

Montbron, Catherine de. "Extrait de deux lettres qu'une dame de qualité laissa escrites et cachetées pour estre rendues à son mary, après sa mort," 1650 (B.N.: 4°Ln27.14586).

Montbrun, Cornélie de. Letters, published in Gédéon Pontier's *Le Cabinet, ou la bibliothèque des grands*, 1681–1682 (CU, later edition NNC). [La Croix, La Porte, Vertron].

Montmorency, Isabelle de Harville, Comtesse de. 1629–1712. Known for her letters, published in the Collection Epistolaire (Collin, 1806).

Montmort, Anne Habert de. *Dialogues;* a prose comedy entitled *Héraclite et Démocrite;* a novel, *Relation de l'Isle de Borneo.* [La Croix, Vertron].

Montpensier, Anne-Marie-Louise-Henriette d'Orléans, Duchesse de (called "La Grande Mademoiselle"). Her *Mémoires,* published posthumously, is available in many editions. *Histoire de Jeanne Lambert d'Herbigny, Marquise de Fouquesolle,* 1653 (B.N.: Rés.Ln.27.7813); *Divers portraits* ..., 1659 (B.N.: Rés.Lb37.187); *Recueil des portraits et éloges en vers et en prose,* 1659 (1663 ed. IU, nineteenth-century editions, not always reliable, widely available); **La Relation de l'isle imaginaire,* 1659 (B.N.: Rés.8°Lb37.3299); pious writings include "Réflexions Morales et Chrétiennes sur le premier Livre de l'Imitation de J.C."; *Lettres de Mlle de Montpensier* ... in the Collection Epistolaire (Collin, 1806). B.N. lists other attributed works. [Alletz, La Croix, La Forge, Vertron].

Mortemard, Madame de. See Rochechouart de Mortemart.

Morville de Champclos. *L'Oiseau du Trianon,* 1698 (Arsenal: 8°BL22382 and 8°BL19509).

Motteville, Françoise Bertaut, Dame de. 1615–1689. Her *Mémoires,* published posthumously, is available in several editions. [Alletz, La Croix].

Moussart, Mademoiselle de. Several poems published in *Le Mercure galant.* [La Croix, La Porte, Vertron].

Murat, Henriette-Julie de Castelnau, Comtesse de. 1670–1716. Memoirs, novels, and fairy tales. Member of the Académie des Ricovrati. *Mémoires de Madame la Comtesse de M***,* 1697 (CtY, later editions widely available); *Contes de Fées,* 1698 (CoU, later edition MB); *Histoires sublimes et allégoriques,* 1699 (CoU); *Les Nouveaux contes des fées,* 1698 (MdBP); *Voyage de campagne,* 1699 (later editions widely available); *Les Lutins du Château de Kernosi,* 1710 (COU, later editions widely available); [La Croix, La Porte, Vertron].

Nemours, Marie d'Orléans-Longueville, Duchesse de. 1625–1707. *Mémoires de M.L.D.D.N.,* 1709, ed. Marie-Jeanne L'Héritier de Villandon (later editions widely available). [La Croix].

Nervèze, Suzanne de. fl. 1644–63. Wrote poetry to commemorate a variety of political occasions between 1644 and 1650 (mainly concerning events of 1649). See B.N. catalogue. [La Forge].

Nouvellon, Mademoiselle. Wrote poetry; probably not published. [La Porte].

Orval, Anne-Eléonore de Béthune d'. See Béthune d'Orval.

Outresale, Madame de. Follower of Descartes. [La Forge].

Ouvrier, Mademoiselle d'. A collection of her poetry was published in Toulouse. [La Croix, La Porte].

Pascal, Françoise. *L'Amoureux extravagant* and *L'Amoureuse vaine et ridicule* (extracts from her *Diverses poésies,* 1657 (CU); *Endymion,* tragedy, 1657;

Sesostris, 1661 (MWiW-C); *Le Vieillard amoureux,* comedy, 1664; *La Grande bible renouvellée, ou Noëls nouveaux,* ca. 1690. [La Croix, La Porte, Vertron].

Pascal, Jacqueline. 1625–1661. Poet. Collaborated on "Les Constitutions du monastère de Port Royal . . . ," 1665 (B.N.). See *Lettres, opuscules et mémoires de Madame Périer et de Jacqueline, soeurs de Pascal, et de Marguerite Périer, sa nièce,* ed. Faugère, 1845. [La Porte, Vertron].

Paschal, Mademoiselle de. Wrote poetry, probably not published. [La Forge].

Patin, Madeleine; and her two daughters, Gabrielle and Catherine-Charlotte. Madeleine wrote a collection of moral reflections. Catherine-Charlotte published *Tabellae Selectae, et explicatae à C. C. Patina, Pad. Acad. Gabriele,* 1691 (B.N.: V.2665), a commentary on famous paintings; she gave public orations in Latin and wrote *Mitra, ou la Démone mariée,* 1745 (B.N.: Y2.63395). Gabrielle wrote "Panégyrique de Louis XIV," 1685, and other occasional verse. All three women lived in Padua and were members of the Académie des Ricovrati. [La Croix, La Porte].

Pauper, Marcelline. b. 1663. Autobiography, *Vie de Marcelline Pauper, de la congrégation des soeurs de la Charité de Nevers* (Nevers, 1871).

Périer, Françoise-Gilberte Pascal, Dame. 1620–1685.. Wrote a biography of her brother, which appears in various editions of his *Pensées* and collected works. Later published separately as *Vie de Blaise Pascal* (MiU, ICN, DLC). [La Porte, Vertron].

Platbuisson, Angélique de. Poem on birth of Duc de Bourgogne appeared in various collections. Madeleine de Scudéry quotes some of Platbuisson's poetry in her works. [Billardon de Sauvigny, La Croix, La Porte, Vertron].

Pringy, Madame de Marenville de (also: Pringis). Fiction: *Les Différens caractères de l'amour,* 1685; *L'Amour à la mode, satyre historique,* 1695; *Les Amours de la belle Junie, ou les sentimens romains,* 1695 (later edition FU); *Le monde renversé, ou Dialogues des génies differens qui renversent le monde,* 1708. Nonfiction: *Les Caractères des femmes du siècle, avec la Description de l'amour-propre,* 1694; *Critique contre la prévention,* 1702 (B.N.: R.19544); *La Vie du Père Bourdaloue,* 1705 (4°Ln.27.2727); *Traité des vrais malheurs de l'homme,* 1707 (Rz.2802). Also occasional poetry, some published in *Le Mercure galant.* [La Croix, La Porte, Vertron].

Puismirol de Saint-Martin, Mademoiselle de. *Recueil de Poésies,* published in Toulouse. [La Croix, La Porte].

Racine, Agnés. In religious life, Mère Agnès de Sainte-Thécle. Aunt of Jean Racine. 1625–1700. Known for her letters.

Rambouillet, Catherine de Vivonne-Savelli, Marquise de. 1588?–1665. The first noted seventeenth-century salon woman. [La Forge].

Rambouillet, Julie d'Angennes, Duchesse de Montauzier. 1605–1671. Noted salon figure.

216

APPENDIX

Ramiez, Mademoiselle. Translated Horace's odes. Praised in *Le Mercure galant,* March 1681. [La Croix, La Porte, Vertron].

Razilli, Marie de (also: Razilly). 1620–1704. Her poetry appeared in various collections, for example, the *Recueil de quelques pièces nouvelles et galantes* (1667). Poems: "Placet au Roi," "Stances à Mr. le Duc de Noailles." [La Croix, La Porte, Vertron].

Ricart, Mademoiselle. Late seventeenth century. Poems addressed to the Queen of Spain. [La Croix, La Porte, Vertron].

Richebourg, Madame de la Garde de. See Le Givre de Richebourg.

Rochechouart de Mortemart, Louise-Françoise de, Abbess of Fontevrault. See *Lettres et vers inédits . . . ,* ed. L.-G. Pélissier, 1899 (B.N.: 8°.Pièce.1118). Also circular announcing death of Marie-Magdeleine-Gabrielle de Rochechouart de Mortemart, September 15, 1704 (B.N.: 4°Ln27.14892).

Rochechouart de Mortemart, Marie-Madeleine-*Gabrielle*-Adelaïde de, Abbess of Fontevrault. d. 1704, age 59. "Question sur la politesse . . ." (B.N.: R.19217); "Ordonnances . . . au chapitre de son ordre," 1687 (B.N.: E.3133). Collaborated on translation of Plato's *Symposium* (B.N.). See Pierre Clément, *Une abbesse de Fontevrault au XVIIe siècle,* 1869. [Buffet, La Porte].

Rochefort, Madeleine-Ursule des Porcellets, Comtesse de. Kept domestic journal, reproduced in part (May 17, 1689–December 31, 1690) in Charles de Ribbe's *Une Grande Dame dans son ménage au temps de Louis XIV,* 1889.

Rohan, Marie-Eléonore de, Abbess of Malnoüe. Paraphrased preface that Madeleine de Scudéry added to *La Morale de Salomon;* also wrote "Paraphrase des Sept Psaumes de la Pénitence" and "Constitutions sur la Règle de Saint Benoist." Other works listed in B.N. Her letters also published in collection of poetry by Anne de Rohan (B.N.: Rés.Ye.4737). [Vertron].

Rohan-Soubise, Anne de. 1584–1646. *Poésies d'Anne de Rohan-Soubise et lettres d'Eléonore,* ed. Barthélémy, 1862. Other editions of her poetry listed in B.N. catalogue.

Roland, Mademoiselle. Known for the quality of her mind. [La Porte, Vertron].

Roland, Mademoiselle. Poem on the revocation of the Edict of Nantes. [La Croix, La Porte, Vertron].

Roque-Montrousse, Madame de. Translated into Latin verse a dialogue on the first conquests of M. le Dauphin; also wrote occasional verse, in particular a poem on the death of Antoinette Deshoulières. Some of her French-to-Latin translations appeared in *Le Mercure galant* (see February 1682), as well as her translations into French verse of some of Horace's odes. Studied modern philosophy, geometry, literature, and Latin. [La Croix, La Porte, Vertron].

Sablé, Madeleine de Souvré, Marquise de. 1599–1678. *Maximes,* 1678, 1870 (NN, IU, MH, MiU, NIC, ICN). N. Ivanoff, *La Marquise de Sablé et son salon,* 1927. [La Forge, Vertron].

Saint-André, Mademoiselle de. Verse description of the chapel of Sceaux, and "L'Hiver de Versailles." [La Croix, La Porte].

Saint-Balmon, Alberte-Barbe d'Ernecourt, Comtesse de (also: Baslemont, Belmon, and Balmont). 1607–1650. Two tragedies: *Les Jumeaux martyrs*, 1650 (MH, DLC); and *La Fille généreuse*, 1650 (only in manuscript, at the B.N., reproduction available DLC). Jean-Marie de Vernon, *L'Amazone chrétienne, ou les avantures de Madame de Saint-Balmon*, 1678. [La Croix, La Forge, Robert VI, Vertron].

Saint Jean, Mademoiselle de. Poet. [Vertron].

Saint-Martin, Marie-Madeleine Germain, Dame de. Unfinished novel, *Daumalinde, reyne de Lusitanie*, 1681. See *Le Mercure galant*, July 1681. [La Croix, La Porte, Vertron].

Saint-Mayolle, Comtesse de. Translated *La République de Naples* from Italian into French. [La Croix, La Porte, Vertron].

Saint-Quentin, Mademoiselle de. Late seventeenth century. "Traité sur la possibilité de l'immortalité corporelle," with a "Réponse aux Objections." Knowledgeable in Roman law and modern philosophy. [La Croix, La Porte, Vertron].

Sainte-Héleine, Comtesse de (née de Longuevue). [La Croix, La Porte, Vertron].

Saintonge, Louise-Geneviève Gillot, Dame de (also: Sainctonge). 1650–1718. Daughter of Geneviève Gillot. Novel: *Histoire secrète de Dom Antoine, roy de Portugal*, 1696 (DLC, CtY, MH). Plays: *Le Ballet des Saisons, L'Intrigue des Concerts, Griselde ou la Princesse de Saluces*. Operas: *Didon*, 1693 (Rés.Yf.1096); *Circe*, 1694 (B.N.: Rés.Yf.1169). Translated Montemayor's *Diane*, 1699 (in 1733 collection, Y2.75930). *Poésies galantes*, 1696 (DLC); *Poésies diverses*, 1714 (MH, CtY, CLU). See *Le Mercure galant*, January and February 1696. [La Croix, La Porte, Vertron].

Salvan de Saliez, Antoinette, Comtesse de. 1638–1730. Admitted to the Académie des Ricovrati, 1689. Founded Société des Chevaliers et des Chevalières de la bonne foi in 1704. *La Comtesse d'Isembourg*, 1678 (1680 edition, ICN). *Lettres de Mesdames ... de Salvan de Saliez ...*, published in the Collection Epistolaire (Collin, 1806). Other printed works include "Réflexions Chrétiennes," "Paraphrases sur les Pseaumes de la Pénitence," and various letters and poems. [La Croix, La Porte, Vertron].

Schomberg, Marie de, née Hautefort. 1616–1691. Known for her letters.

Scudéry, Madeleine de. 1607–1701. Member of the Académie des Ricovrati. Awarded first prize for eloquence given by the Académie Française in 1670. [Alletz, Billardon de Sauvigny, Du Pin, Guillaume, La Croix, La Forge, La Porte, Robert].

Scudéry, Marie Françoise de Martin-Vast de. Wife of Georges de Scudéry.

1627–1711. Wrote letters, in particular to Bussy-Rabutin. *Lettres de Mesdames de Scudéry* ..., published in the Collection Epistolaire (Collin, 1806). [La Porte, Vertron].

Sénecterre, Madeleine de (also: Saint-Nectaire, Seneterre). Novel, *Orasie,* 1646, in collaboration with the historian Mézeray. *La Suite et Conclusion d'Orasie,* 1648, is by an anonymous continuator. [La Croix, La Porte].

Serment, Louise Anastasie. 1640–1692. Wrote court poetry; published in Vertron's *La Nouvelle Pandore.* [La Croix, La Porte].

Sévigné, Marie de Rabutin-Chantal, Marquise de. 1626–1696. [Alletz, Du Pin, La Croix, La Forge, La Porte, **Robert].

Sibut, Mademoiselle. From Lyon. Wrote occasional poetry. [La Porte, Vertron].

Simiane, Pauline de Grignan, Marquise de. 1674–1737. Main contributor to *Porte-feuille de Madame ***, Contenant diverses odes, idyles et sonnets* ..., 1715 (many editions available). Her letters appear in *Lettres nouvelles de la Marquise de Sévigné et de la Marquise de Simiane, sa petite-fille* ... (Lacombe, 1773) (B.N.); and *Lettres de ... Madame la Marquise de Simiane,* published in the Collection Epistolaire (Collin, 1806). Verse and letters appear in *Les Amusemens du Coeur et de l'Esprit.* [La Porte].

Staal de Launay, Marguerite Jeanne Cordier, Baronne de. 1684–1750. *Mémoires;* two comedies in prose, *L'Engoûment* and *La Mode;* satirical poetry. Her letters are published in the Collection Epistolaire (Collin, 1806). [Alletz, Du Pin, La Croix, La Porte].

Suchon, Gabrielle, Religieuse de Semur. *Du Célibat volontaire, ou la Vie sans engagement,* 1700 (DLC, NNUT); *"Traité de la morale et de la politique divisé en trois parties, savoir, la liberté, la science, et l'autorité, où l'on voit que les personnes du sexe, pour en être privées, ne laissent pas d'avoir une capacité naturelle, qui les en peut rendre participantes; avec un petit traité de la faiblesse, de la légèreté et de l'inconstance qu'on leur attribue mal à propos" (Lyon, 1693) (B.N.: R.6220).

Tenain, Madame de. *Histoire du Comte de Clare, nouvelle galante,* 1696 (CtY, MH).

Tencin, Claudine-Alexandrine Guérin, Marquise de. 1681–1749. Attributed or collaborative author of *Le Comte de Comminge,* 1735; *Le Siège de Calais,* 1739; *Les Malheurs de l'Amour,* 1747. *Oeuvres* published 1786. All widely available. Her letters to the duc de Richelieu are published in the Collection Epistolaire (Collin, 1806). [Alletz, Du Pin, La Croix, La Porte].

Ussé, Madame d'. Verse and letters appear in *Les Amusemens du Coeur et de l'Esprit.* [La Porte].

Vandeuvre, Mademoiselle de. Wrote poetry, including a sonnet in prayer form to the glory of Louis XIV. [La Porte, Vertron].

Van Schurman, Anna. 1607–1678. Dutch. *Question célèbre s'il est nécessaire que les filles soient savantes ou non,* 1646, translated from the Latin (B.N.: R.24049). [Buffet, Guillaume, La Croix, La Forge].

Vatry, Louise-Marguerite Buttet. 1682–1752. Wrote poetry; included in the collective volume, *Les Amusemens du Coeur et de l'Esprit.* [La Porte].

Verdier, Mademoiselle de. Some of her poems appear in a collection, ed. Robert Toussain, *Triomphe de la Violette.* [La Croix, La Porte, Vertron].

Vilaine, Marquise de. Directed a salon. [La Forge].

Villars, Marie Gigault de Bellefonds, Marquise de. 1627–1706. Known for her letters.

Villedieu. Desjardins, Marie-Catherine. Known as Madame de Villedieu. 1640–1683. [Alletz, La Croix, La Forge, La Porte, **Richelet].

Early Works Dealing Exclusively with Women Writers, 1663–1811

La Forge, Jean de (signed M. De L. F.). *Le Cercle des femmes savantes* (J.-B. Loyson, 1663). Late sixteenth to mid-seventeenth century. (B.N.: Ye.35571 and Rés.Yf.3743.)

Guillaume, Jacquette. *Histoire des Dames illustres, où par bonnes et fortes raisons, il se prouve que le sexe féminin surpasse en toute sorte de genres le sexe masculin* (Thomas Jolly, 1665). Mainly a late *Querelle des femmes* treatise, but some information on mid-seventeenthth-century writers, although much of it is *à clef* and no *clef* is provided. (Duke.)

Buffet, Marguerite. *Nouvelles observations sur la langue française, avec l'éloge des illustres savantes tant anciennes que modernes* (Jean Cusson, 1668). Microfiche available from B.N. Library of Congress, University of California at Berkeley, Harvard. Mainly contemporary women; some information on pre-seventeenth-century women.

Vertron, Claude-Charles Guionet, Seigneur de. *La Nouvelle Pandore ou les Femmes illustres du siècle de Louis le Grand,* 2 vols. (Veuve Mazuel, 1698), pp. 470–510, 2 catalogues: "Dames illustres mortes" and "Dames illustres vivantes." (Folger Shakespeare Library.) Contemporary women and women recently deceased.

Aublet de Maubuy (Jean Zorobabel). *Les Vies des femmes illustres de la France,* 6 vols. (Duchesne, 1762–1768). Almost entirely devoted to political women, but a few long biographies of literary women. (B.N.: Ln17.1.)

Alletz, Pons-Augustin, *L'Esprit des femmes célèbres du siècle de Louis XIV et de celui de Louis XV,* 2 vols. (Pissot, 1768). Biography, plot summaries, some short selections (Boston Public Library.)

[La Croix, Jean François de.] *Dictionnaire portatif des femmes célèbres, contenant l'histoire des femmes savantes, des actrices, et généralement des dames qui se sont rendues fameuses de tous les siècles par leurs aventures, les talents, l'esprit et le courage,* 2 vols. (Belin, 1788, plus 1–vol. supplement, also 1788) (1st ed. 1769). Biography. (Library of Congress.)

[La Porte, Joseph de.] (Author identified in B.N. catalogue as Jean de La Croix, chief author of the *Dictionnaire portatif.* The author of the preface explains that it was the result of a collaboration by "une société de gens de lettres.") *Histoire littéraire des femmes françaises, ou lettres historiques et critiques,* 5 vols. (Lacombe, 1769). Biography and detailed plot summaries of works and remarks on their critical reception. Medieval to eighteenth century. (DLC, CLU, CtY, ICJ, MB, NjP.)

Thomas, Antoine Léonard. *Essai sur le caractère, les moeurs et l'esprit des femmes dans les différents siècles,* vol. 4 of his *Oeuvres,* 4 vols. (Moutard, 1773) (1st ed. 1772). Survey of women's political and literary accomplishments from the Greeks to his contemporaries. Widely available.

Billardon de Sauvigny. *Le Parnasse des Dames,* 5 vols. (Rualt, 1773). *Only on women poets*—includes Greek, Latin, Italian, and English poets, as well as French poets from the Middle Ages to the eighteenth century. Biography and an anthology of selections from some of the poets. (Harvard, Boston Public Library.) (Note: Billardon de Sauvigny's 1–vol. 1821 work with the same title is not a reprint of his 1773 compilation.).

Robert, Louise-Félicité Guinemet de Keralio, Dame. *Collection des meilleurs ouvrages français, composés par des femmes* (Lagrange, 1786–1788). 12 vols., vols. 1–6 and 9–14; vols. 7 and 8 apparently never appeared. Middle Ages through Scudéry, then skips to Sévigné. Biographies and lengthy selections. Project never completed (her prospectus announces grander plans), undoubtedly because of the Revolution. (Harvard, B.N.: Z.28209–28220.)

[Rivarol, Antoine, Comte de.]. (According to B.N. catalogue, the attribution is erroneous.) *Le Petit almanach de nos grandes femmes* (London, 1789). Information on eighteenth-century women writers.

Briquet, Marguerite-Ursule-Fortunée Bernier. *Dictionnaire historique, littéraire et bibliographique des françaises et des étrangères naturalisées en France, connues par leurs écrits ou par la protection qu'elles ont accordée aux gens de lettres, depuis l'établissement de la monarchie jusqu'à nos jours* (Treuttel and Würtz, 1804). (Library of Congress, University of Florida at Gainesville, Duke, Boston Public Library, University of California at Berkeley.)

Genlis, Stéphanie Félicité Ducrest de Saint-Aubin, Comtesse de (afterwards Marquise de Sillery). *De l'influence des femmes sur la littérature française* (Maradan, 1811). General treatise, widely available.

DuPin, Antoinette. *La France illustrée par ses femmes, ou Beaux exemples d'amour filial, de tendresse maternelle, de dévouement conjugal, de modestie, de traits d'esprit, amour de l'étude, mérite littéraire, des femmes qui se sont distinguées en France par leurs talents et leurs vertus* (Librairie de l'Enfance et de la Jeunesse, 1833). (Title varies in later editions.) General treatise, widely available.

Early Works Dealing with Both Male and Female Writers

Richelet, Pierre. *Dictionnaire.* In some early eighteenth-century editions of Richelet's dictionary, a "liste des auteurs et des livres cités dans ce dictionnaire" is included. There is some information on women writers in this catalogue.

Sabatier de Castres, Abbé Antoine. *Les Trois siècles de notre littérature, ou Tableau de l'esprit de nos écrivains depuis François I, jusqu'en 1772* (a second edition goes up to 1801), 3 vols. (Gueffier, 1772).

La Platière, Imbert de. *Galerie universelle des hommes qui se sont illustrés dans l'empire.* 6 vols. (1787–1788). Lengthy biographies, selections.

Notes

Introduction

1. I do not intend to imply any similarity of political climate or onomastic stakes between classical France and modern America by referring to Geraldine Ferraro. I merely want to indicate that such systems are always both less rigid and less coherently justified than we might imagine.

2. The catalogue of the Biblioteca Medicea in Florence contains three separate entries for Scudéry: "Scudéry, Madeleine de," "Scudéry, Mademoiselle de," and "Sapho" (the name by which Scudéry was known in her circle).

3. In the following pages I will initially give the full title, however cumbersome, of each woman writer. All onomastic information available about women intellectuals active between 1640 and 1715 is included in an appendix, which also lists their activities, their publications, the availability of their works, and sources of biographical information. In this appendix, when I have not been able to recover a woman's first name, she is listed as "Mademoiselle" or "Madame." Women writers of the ancien régime used a variety of signatures. For example, at about the same period when Lafayette wrote Ménage, an old friend who knew her before her marriage, and signed her maiden name simply "De La Vergne," she signed a letter to Charles-René d'Hozier "La Comtesse de Lafayette." Sévigné almost always kept personal identity (her first name) separate from her title and her husband's family name: she signed either "M[arie] de Rabutin Chantal" or "La M[arquise] de Sévigné." At the end of the ancien régime, Germaine de Staël signed all her letters "Louise Necker" until her marriage in 1786. Thereafter, she most frequently used "Necker, baronne de Staël-Holstein" and "Anne-Louise Germaine Necker-Staël de Holstein." She occasionally shortened this last signature to "Necker Staël." I give these examples to show that much variety existed, that no one ever chose "Madame de," and that it would be impossible to establish a single standard form that would account for the range of ancien régime usage. See Sandra Gilbert and Susan Gubar on what they term the woman writer's "fundamental alienation" from the name that is her own

yet not her own, because it is also that of a family, most often not her own family (555).

4. On the importance of the signature for women's writing and for feminist criticism, see Nancy K. Miller's *Subject to Change.*

5. The woman writer's relation to a family name was far more complicated in the pre-Revolutionary context in which "family" still retained its older meaning of "line" or "lineage" and had not yet completely acquired its modern sense of "nuclear family." (Nowhere is this shift better illustrated than in the first part of *La Princesse de Clèves:* the abrupt transition from the prologue, dominated by a sense of genealogy, to the heroine's story, dominated by revised definitions of the bonds between mother and daughter and husband and wife, figures this changing definition of "family.") Sand was sensitive to the new politics of the family (name): "What is a name in our revolutionized and revolutionary world? A number for those who do nothing, a sign ... for those who work" (1:140). On Villedieu's signature and its influence on subsequent women writers, see Micheline Cuénin, *Roman et société* 1:715; see also her edition of Villedieu's *Les Désordres de l'amour* (lxiv) on Villedieu's use of "M. de Villedieu." Note that Madeleine de Scudéry, though unmarried, was able to devise a similarly ambiguous signature, "M. de Scudéry," because her brother Georges was also a writer.

6. I begin in 1640 with the period of political unrest that culminates in civil war; I close at the end of Louis XIV's reign. It seems possible that the limited implementation of this code in English (Mrs. Gaskell and so forth) was originally inspired by French usage.

7. Similarly, many colleagues appear to find the code I adopt here more annoying than any other aspect of this project.

8. I will discuss the novel's development only in a French context. However, because of the enormous influence of the early French novelists, especially Scudéry, on the emerging tradition of English prose fiction, it seems impossible that the feminist ideology everywhere visible at the origin of the French novel was lost in translation. For information on Scudéry's influence in England, see Thomas Haviland and Michael McKeon. I intend the following pages as an outline, one that I hope others will fill in. I have long delayed completing this study because everywhere I turn I find new information on the accomplishments of seventeenth-century women. Future research in this field will surely produce rich results.

9. For an additional reading of female literary power in seventeenth-century France, see Timothy Reiss, *The Meaning of Literature.*

10. It seems likely that the history of English women's writing would be revised if the earlier development in France of both the novel and a tradition of women's writing were taken into account, on the model of McKeon's suggested revision of the novel's rise.

11. For an account of the gradual loss of prominence by the seventeenth-century women intellectuals interested in the development of scientific discourse, see Erica Harth's "Classical Discourse."

12. This is not a study to which feminist criticism's current concerns, in partic-

ular the focus on class and race as well as gender, could easily have been applied. In ancien régime France, literary creation was an elitist enterprise; women who were not highborn left essentially no written records. In addition, the categories on which we now base our evaluations are not always applicable without adjustment to seventeenth-century material. For example, the notion of class may be problematic for a society that, while it was clearly moving toward stratification along what we consider class lines, was not yet detached from what Roland Mousnier terms "a society of orders."

13. The newly annexed provinces were Alsace, Roussillon, Piedmont, and Artois. Construction on the Collège des Quatre Nations was begun in 1663; it opened in 1688, and closed in 1790. In 1806 Napoleon—a worthy (and also foreign-born) heir to Mazarin's project of cultural nationalization—had the Institut de France moved into the collège's buildings. The Académie Française—throughout the history (as opposed to the existence) of the French tradition the guiding force in the elimination of cultural difference—was thereby symbolically annexed to Mazarin's project for pedagogical assimilation.

14. I am aware that the vocabulary of "nationalism" is anachronistic in this context, as are those of "class" and "race." However, women's writing of the ancien régime often foreshadowed semantic drift. The vocabulary of "nationalism" is first displayed prominently in the work of Germaine de Staël and of writers at her salon-in-exile at Coppet. The first clear appearance of "class" in the modern sense that I have noted is in Françoise de Graffigny's *Lettres d'une Péruvienne* (304), published in 1747, decades before this usage allegedly first evolved (see Raymond Williams 51–59). To measure women writers' semantic innovativeness, I rely heavily in this study on the first French dictionaries, especially the 1690 *Dictionnaire universel* of Antoine Furetière, the early lexicographer most sensitive to class issues. I am not using semantics to imply that modern class analysis can be applied unproblematically to early modern France, that we may completely disregard Mousnier's evaluation of privilege and rank as social regulators. (See Beik for a comparison of Mousnier's concept of a "society of orders" with a "society of classes" [6–9].) However, I agree with Beik that such an evaluation, which minimizes the importance of economic factors in social stratification, is "implicitly an apolog[y] for seventeenth-century society [which] accepts the justifications for its social structure … put forth by the very persons who dominated it," as well as "an attempt to sidestep the issue of conflicts deriving from unequal social relations" (8). It is precisely those conflicts that I want to stress, since they seem to explode whenever women's writing becomes an important force in early modern France. Underlying my assumptions about social stratification is what may be my most controversial assumption: I refuse to believe that ancien régime (women) writers, even if aristocrats, chose to detach themselves from the economic reality of literary production.

15. Huet defined this origin for the French tradition as the transfer of power from Scudéry to Lafayette and presented Lafayette's *Zayde* (1670), to which his treatise served as a preface, as an allegory of assimilation, a parody of the effortless conversion to sameness. I will return to this reading of Huet's treatise in chapter 5.

16. An early explicit treatment of race occurs at the end of this female tradition, in Claire de Duras's *Ourika* (1823). However, race receives more discreet evocations long before, notably in Graffigny's *Lettres d'une Péruvienne*. With her heroine's recovery of treasures plundered by the Spanish and then stolen from them by the French, Graffigny links Woman's financial and legal independence to the politics of colonialization. Graffigny refuses to allow her heroine's assimilation (Zilia shares the Indian blood of Garcilaso de la Vega, the authority on whom Graffigny based much of her ethnographic material) into a family such as Déterville's—not, however, because Zilia would contaminate their bloodline. For Graffigny, the aristocracy has wasted its inheritances on superficial ostentation; its sons no longer fulfill their moral role as nobles. Zilia's refusal to marry Déterville signifies that degenerate nobles are thereby denied the possibility of recovering their standing across the bodies of the conquered Incas. (Graffigny's decision to found her novel on the immense chronological leap between the Spanish invasion of Peru and eighteenth-century France made this commentary possible.)

17. The terms on which this fiction was either assimilated or excluded suggest both an explanation for Ian Watt's categorical exclusion of the seventeenth-century French novel from his long-definitive *The Rise of the Novel* and the basis for a revision of Watt's history. Watt considers modern novels solely those works that conform to his conception of realism; critics need only turn their attention to those elements seventeenth-century critics judged "outlandish" to pinpoint factors that could be used to justify the modernity (in Watt's terms) of the early French novel.

18. See Pierre Malandain's review of attempts to deny that Lafayette's treatment of history deserves serious study.

19. In the following pages I frequently use Boileau to represent the novel's early detractors. One anecdote, often repeated in studies of Louis XIV's reign, suffices to demonstrate both Boileau's authority and the extent to which he (was believed to have) enjoyed royal support. During a walk in the gardens of Versailles, Louis XIV turns Boileau into the oracle who can predict posterity's judgment: "Who was the greatest writer of my reign?" Boileau replies with characteristic self-assurance: "Molière." To which this monarch answers with uncharacteristic humility: "Really, I'd never have guessed it."

20. The standard work on early criticism of the novel is Georges May's *Dilemme du roman*. While I do not always agree with the history May proposes for the early novel, I am deeply indebted to his pathbreaking erudition in this field.

21. For a particularly virulent attack on the practice of isolating women in history, see Lawrence Stone's review of Antonia Fraser's *The Weaker Vessel* (*New York Review of Books*, April 11, 1985), in which he lists what he calls "the ten commandments which should ... govern the writing of women's history at any time and in any place." The first of Stone's commandments reads: "Thou shalt not write about women except in relation to men and children. Women are not a distinct caste, and their history is a story of complex interactions."

22. I am also convinced that the sentiment so widespread today that almost all these women novelists are second-rate (at best) can be explained by the apologetic

attitude toward the subject of their research maintained by virtually all the nine-teenth- and twentieth-century critics who (paradoxically) devote immense energy to resurrecting the accomplishments of writers whom they evidently do not hold in high esteem. Witness the example of Micheline Cuénin, thanks to whose vast erudition we can now appreciate the impressive achievements of Marie-Catherine Desjardins-Villedieu: "[Readers] may be astonished to see so much interest devoted to a second-, or even third-rate author" (1:11). When I read such statements, I wonder why critics so seldom stop to consider, first, the extent to which the reading process has been redefined since the time when these novels were written, and the extent to which modern readers are therefore at a disadvantage in responding to them; and, second, the extent to which the canon and the standards that largely determine today's reading ideals may have been shaped against these authors and out of a desire to eliminate their works from literary history. I will give two brief examples of what I have in mind. First, these women writers often represent stylistic values that, *because they are opposed to those of classicism,* have been judged "incorrect." Thus, nineteenth-century editions (in many cases, still the only ones available) regularly altered their texts to make them conform to norms considered more acceptable, with no effort to appreciate the works' own stylistic integrity— what Sainte-Beuve, in a comment on the *Mémoires* of the Grande Mademoiselle (the Duchesse de Montpensier) that explains an entire editorial tradition, refers to as "the purity of her natural incorrectness" (16n.). Second, it is especially difficult to evaluate the place of much women's writing in the context of a movement like neoclassicism, which defines literature's domain as that of timeless issues, to the exclusion of those in the domain of what historians now term "private life." For the most part, women's writing of the classical age privileges concerns both of private life (i.e., the definition of a good marriage) and of daily life (i.e., the price of bread in a city under siege). By thus going against the grain of what we now consider the great tradition of their day, women writers guaranteed that their production would be undervalued, and also that it would be misinterpreted, that is, seen as somehow nonfictional (autobiographical, *à clef,* and so forth).

23. I will center two of my chapters on the most prominent early women novelists, Scudéry and Lafayette. I intend each of them to represent the numerous women writers of each of their generations who were largely forgotten once the modern pedagogical canon began to be drawn up in the early nineteenth century (a process I consider in my concluding chapter). Whenever possible, and especially in notes, I will give information on contemporary writers whose projects resemble those of Scudéry and Lafayette. In addition, the appendix includes factual informa-tion on the range of female production. The growing prominence of women's writing in the ancien régime inspired much terminological innovation. The first generic markers were invented to characterize the production of Lafayette's gener-ation, *nouvelle* and *histoire,* genres generally described as a female domain. (See Malandain on the widespread association between women and history; see also Fritz Nies on the definition of the letter as "a feminine genre.") The naming of the new writers was less stable. In 1670 Huet uses "romanciers," a word associated in

seventeenth-century dictionaries only with the authors of ancient and medieval romances. To distinguish the authors of the new novels, both L'Héritier (*L'Apothéose* 89) and Furetière propose a new term, *romaniste* (which Furetière suggests can be either masculine or feminine). The designation "femme auteur" first appears in the eighteenth century; the earliest occurrence I have noted is in Joseph de La Porte's 1769 *Histoire littéraire des femmes françaises*. The feminine of *romancier*, the most widely adopted designation in French today, is a nineteenth-century invention; both the *Littré* and *Robert* dictionaries credit Chateaubriand (in works from the 1840s) with its earliest usage. (Chateaubriand was, as we will see, perhaps the last true amateur of Scudéry.)

1. Women's Places, Women's Spaces

1. See William Beik on the current debate on the seventeenth-century French State, a debate he summarizes in these terms: "Thus historians have moved from viewing the state as a triumphant organizer of society to viewing it as a fragile organism struggling against a vast, turbulent society" (17).

2. For an illustration of historical methodology sensitive to the dialogue between event and culture that I am trying to recreate here, see Sarah Hanley.

3. In *La Société française au XVIIe siècle*, Victor Cousin traces the beginning of Rambouillet's salon, known as the *chambre bleue*, to 1617–1618 (1:271). Dorothy Backer places it as early as 1611 (58), and the authors of the catalogue entries for the Bibliothèque Nationale exposition *Les Salons littéraires au XVIIe siècle* place the inception at 1608 (6). For my work on the period 1610–1652, I am indebted to the painstaking research of Ian Maclean. The absence of an equivalent salon tradition in England surely helps explain the relatively slow development of women's writing there. The English equivalent of the salon, the drawing room, did have certain connotations of a female space, but the drawing room was associated only with less sophisticated artistic and intellectual endeavors (embroidery, reading aloud, gossip as opposed to conversation), unlike the library, the male domain and the locus of serious intellectual activity. On the notion of conversation as "social space," see Elizabeth Goldsmith (2).

4. Jean Lafond believes it is likely that d'Urfé frequented the Hôtel de Rambouillet during the time between the publication of the first two parts of *Astrée* (ed. *Astrée* 395). The influence between reality and fiction may, therefore, have been mutual.

5. To consider only examples from France's then recent past, the Marquise de Rambouillet's activities continued the Renaissance assemblies popular in Italy, in Lyons, and also in the courts of the last Valois kings (Maclean 141), whereas Marie de' Medici looked back to the regency of Catherine de' Medici. The sense of continuity among regencies, of a royal female tradition almost in defiance of the *loi salique*, is the subject of the lawyer Florentin Du Ruau's 700-page *Tableau historique des régences*, published during Marie de' Medici's regency (1615). Du Ruau sought to establish that women had been just as successful as men in leading the country through these difficult liminal periods.

6. As Roger Lathuillère has shown, the first uses of the term *précieuse* and *préciosité* in the fourteenth and fifteenth centuries already reveal a condemnation of the woman who dares to reject love and a fear of the possible consequences of the spread of such behavior (16–17).

7. See Cioranescu 37–38. His reconstruction is not universally accepted. For example, Tallemant attributed both the *Advantures de la cour de Perse* and the *Histoire des amours du grand Alcandre* to the princesse de Conti, whereas Tallemant's modern editor, Adam, accepts the first but not the second attribution (Tallemant, ed. Adam 1:707, n.4). Lever adopts Tallemant's position on attribution to the Princesse; he attributes the *Romant royal* to Piloust. The question of *Alcandre*'s attribution is already highlighted in the preface to its first edition (1651). The editor indicates that the manuscript must have had extensive private circulation before publication when he states that "public opinion" attributed it to the Princesse de Conti. It is impossible to tell how the printed text was presented to its initial public. The only surviving copy, preserved in the Bibliothèque Nationale, is in excellent condition except for its title page, which has been cut after the title; the bottom part has been glued onto another sheet of paper. It is hard to imagine why this would have been done, except to alter some element related to what the editor terms the "tormented" curiosity about the author's identity.

8. With the *Histoire des amours du grand Alcandre,* the Princesse de Conti also introduced the involvement with political sedition characteristic of the tradition of French women's writing. Paulin Pâris calls the first edition in 1651 "a true Mazarinade," and compares it to the political pamphlets then being published; he contends that the novel could only have appeared in print in the chaos of civil war (812–13).

9. Her name is also written Balmon and Balmont. I capitalize "Amazon" when referring to the mythical figures and use lowercase for the seventeenth-century women seen as their reincarnations.

10. Politicomilitary activity by women was relatively rare in France this early in the century. However, Lawrence Stone notes the unprecedented degree of women's political activity in England in the 1640s (337–39). The fact that England moved toward civil war earlier than France may help explain this chronology.

11. See Cuénin's argument for the text's authenticity in the preface to her edition.

12. Pariset describes, for example, the representations of modern amazons in the château of Richelieu (168).

13. The most notable exception is the *Femmes illustres* (1642), a text sometimes attributed to Georges de Scudéry but whose first volume is clearly the work of his sister Madeleine. Scudéry's writing of the early 1640s marks the origin of a seventeenth-century tradition of feminist literature composed by women. Marie de Gournay's "Egalité des hommes et des femmes" (1622) is more closely related to the defenses of the *Querelle des femmes* than to the new literary forms developed in the seventeenth century.

14. I maintain French spelling when referring to historical figures who are used as characters in French works.

15. Maureen Quilligan analyzes late medieval representations of "women worthies," in particular the illustrations to Boccaccio's *De Claris mulieribus* and Christine de Pizan's *Cité des dames*. The most striking difference between these representations and those in the *femmes fortes* collections concerns the sex of the object of violence. In the late medieval tradition, violence is done to the *female* body; Quilligan stresses that to accent female martyrdom is to make possible a visual fixation on female torture. In the seventeenth-century illustrations, however, violence is done to the *male* body. Does this radical shift of focus prove the threat of contemporary militaristic women?

16. See Hepp on the prevalence of discussions of heroism in the 1640s and 1650s (11–13).

17. The propriety of exceptional female behavior was put into question most strikingly during the quarrels that erupted around *Le Cid* and *La Princesse de Clèves*. The yoking of *vraisemblance* (plausibility, verisimilitude) to *bienséance* (propriety), so persistent yet often unacknowledged in seventeenth-century criticism, also resurfaces in those controversies. On this linking, see Genette and Miller's "Emphasis Added."

18. Maclean describes other contemporary evidence of female prestige. In 1644 Desmarets created a pack of playing cards for the Dauphin's instruction, *Jeux des Reines renommées*, each card of which depicted a famous queen (Maclean 212): the young Louis XIV may have played with a toy as prowoman as any imagined by twentieth-century proponents of a feminist pedagogy.

19. As Lougee points out, "The term *précieuse* was commonly applied to all women in Parisian salons" (7). This is the sense in which the word figures in the title of the Romanelli painting, as a synonym for the woman intellectual or literary woman. Salon women do not seem to have used the term autoreferentially; they normally referred to themselves as "femmes savantes," learned women. See Hautecoeur and the Bibliothèque Nationale catalogue of the exhibit *Les Salons littéraires* (49) for the tradition of the painting's interpretation. Other contemporary ceiling paintings—for example, that done for the *cabinet* or study of the Duchesse de la Meilleraye (in today's Arsénal library) by Nöel Quillerier—treat the subject of Apollo surrounded by the muses, but they were not interpreted as *à clef* works.

20. Eloquent testimony to women's intellectual prestige is provided by the rhetoric of the contemporary tracts, studied by Lougee in particular, that sought to denigrate learned women.

21. The parallelism between the Corneillian heroine and the heroines of the Fronde is a perfect example of the type of overdetermined origin I have been describing: "If the Corneillian heroines had an influence on a *frondeuse* like Mademoiselle de Montpensier, isn't Corneille for his part inspired when tracing the portrait of an energetic, ambitious woman by the models that at the time of the Fronde (the period, for example, when *Rodogune* was written) the Court openly offered him?" (Abensour 43). Unless otherwise stated, all translations are mine. For information on the legal status of seventeenth-century women, see Portemer's "La Femme dans la législation royale." Conflicting opinions on Corneille's view of

women have recently been proposed by Reiss ("Corneille and Cornelia") and Mitchell Greenberg. Whereas Greenberg contends that key plays reveal a fear of the female, Reiss uncovers a prowoman bias in many of the same works.

22. As recently as the turn of this century, "fronde"—it came from a word for "slingshot" and was used in a children's game of the day—was still associated with violent irruptions of female self-assertion. According to André Billy, "The *explosion* of feminine literature in 1900 had been preceded at the end of 1897 by an *explosion* of feminine journalism ... named *La Fronde. La Fronde,* a daily political and literary paper, was directed, administered, written, and typeset by women" (230). Nina Gelbart has demonstrated the existence of a *frondeur* tradition of resistance to absolutism until the Revolution, and occasionally even afterwards. She stresses the "*frondeur* alliance of feminism with other causes" (12–13).

23. The Fronde was a far more complex phenomenon than my brief remarks here attempt to suggest. The uprising has provoked heated debate among historians about such fundamental issues as the importance of peasant uprisings (on this point, see the opposing views of Boris Porchnev and Roland Mousnier) and the relative importance of princely and parliamentary opposition (see A. Lloyd Moote). It is not my goal to take a stance on issues basic to our understanding of the Fronde, still the object of contention among prominent historians. One factor that surely helps explain the interpretive dilemma of today's historian is that, for centuries, the Fronde was romanticized and its political impact devalued. (Michelet's and Sainte-Beuve's visions were particularly influential in this process.) Only recently has the civil war begun to receive serious attention. I support Gelbart's belief that the Fronde was undervalued in part because of women's highly visible participation in it (16–17). Gelbart also stresses the "unprecedented blending of classes during this upheaval" (17). The social contamination of the Fronde years is a second likely explanation for the Fronde's persistent devaluation. (As Beik, among others, points out, many commentators have traditionally avoided issues threatening to the official, absolutist vision of social stratification in seventeenth-century France [8].) On the history of the Fronde's interpretation, see the introductions of Beik and Gelbart and Nannerl Keohane (chapter 7). Seventeenth-century commentary on the Fronde (often written by women) makes it clear that, in the course of the conflict, women played roles of previously (and since) unheard-of prominence. I accent that prominence here, to the exclusion, for example, of the peasant revolts, in the same way as historians who feature peasant revolts have generally excluded the role of the *frondeuses.*

24. Ascoli describes contemporary writing on the amazons and discusses the importance of the subject for antifeminist authors (44).

25. See Faith Beasley on all accounts of her exploits, both Montpensier's own *Mémoires* and the memoirs of other participants in the Fronde. See Eliane Viennot's study of the late 1580s, the last years of Henri II's reign, another period during which highborn women—among them, Catherine-Marie de Lorraine, Duchesse de Montpensier, grandmother of the Grande Mademoiselle—wielded political influence both significant and subversive to the monarchy. The events of that period

would have formed part of the context in which those of the Fronde, including the Grande Mademoiselle's imitation of her grandmother's example, would have been interpreted and may have encouraged seventeenth-century observers to view the Fronde as menacing.

26. See Pierre Ronzeaud on the iconography of the Fronde years. Ronzeaud also sees in seventeenth-century political discourse the fear that masculine rule could be subverted.

27. On the importance of female assemblies in literature, see Nina Auerbach's *Communities of Women*.

28. Furthermore, Retz and his companions were not blind to such resemblances at the time. When he returned from skirmishing with Mazarin's troops, Noirmoutier, termed by Retz a "great amateur of *Astrée*," commented to the future author of the *Mémoires:* "I can imagine that we are besieged in Marcilli," and they proceeded to decide which roles from d'Urfé's novel would have been played by those present.

29. Publication information on all of Scudéry's works is in Mongrédien's *Bibliographie*. A third novel, *Orasie* (1646), by Senectaire, lady-in-waiting to Catherine de' Medici and, like the Princesse de Condé, faithful to her in exile, was undoubtedly influential in the *frondeur* camp. The novel features a long intercalated story centered on an Amazon, "la belle Guerrière," and a battle between the Scythians and the Amazons. The Bibliothèque Nationale's copy of *Orasie* bears the Condé arms.

30. The only resolution to this paradox hinted at in her correspondence is the vaguely formulated, impossible dream that Condé would somehow be called on to revitalize the monarchy. "God be willing that M. le Prince one day be able to reestablish [the monarchy]" (March 2, 1651, Rathery and Boutron 244).

31. See Jôuhaud's chapter 6 for a discussion of the level of violence in contemporary *mazarinades;* he situates the apex of this textual intensity in March 1652, at the end of the preparation period for volume 8 of *Artamène* (168).

32. The attraction for Scudéry of financial independence is evident: a bourgeoise living in a world dominated by aristocrats, she was the first French woman writer to depend on her literary productions for her livelihood. Micheline Cuénin claims this distinction for Villedieu, but Scudéry began writing for a living in the early 1640s, some two decades before her successor. Later in life, Scudéry received a modest royal pension, but for most of her adult life she depended, for her support and initially that of her brother Georges as well, on the income from her novels. Her literary production was one of the great financial successes of the century: according to Godenne (11), she made 100,000 *écus* (presumably silver rather than gold *écus*), a princely sum, for her editor Courbé alone (100,000 *écus* equaled 300,000 *livres,* the approximate equivalent of 4 million *francs* today). According to Augiger's 1691 *La Maison réglée,* one could "live nobly" on 4,800 *livres* a year (Cuénin, ed. Villedieu's *Henriette-Sylvie* 79n.).

33. It is difficult to determine the exact beginning of the *samedis*. Lucien Bel-

mont, the last scholar to have access to the complete manuscript (now presumed lost) of the *Chronique des samedis,* an informal record of the proceedings, placed it as early as 1652 because of evidence contained in that manuscript (656). The salon was certainly meeting on the rue de Beauce well before the summer of 1654 when the Scudérys' lease on the apartment there was renewed (Mongrédien, *Madeleine de Scudéry* 222n.). Most critics set the beginning in 1653. Information on other post-Fronde salon activity, including the declining years of the Rambouillet *chambre bleue,* can be obtained in Backer.

34. "*Préciosité* is born of the feminist demands for education of the 1630s and 1640s, but, unlike these, it is a movement instigated and directed by women themselves" (Maclean 269). Previously, educational reform had been sought by men like Du Bosc and Le Moyne, also architects of the *femme forte.*

35. Some have taken de Pure's *La Prétieuse* as a parodic novel, others as a feminist document. See, for example, Romanowski's feminist reading.

36. In 1905, when these women writers were seldom read, Louise Georges-Renard proposed, without developing her observation, that women's literature was born in France after the Fronde when "reality intervened brutally to break the wings of dream" (213–14).

37. Critics generally trace the inception of Retz's *Mémoires* to either 1658 or 1662. La Rochefoucauld probably began work on his memoirs in 1654 during his exile at Verteuil. The first part of his memoirs opens with a reference to the recent events that had given him the leisure necessary for writing, but his shift of creative focus was neither as immediate nor as total as in the case of his female counterparts who attempted not only to give an account of the Fronde but to create new, gender-specific forms.

38. According to her *Mémoires,* Montpensier threw herself into writing as though it were an act of clandestine sedition. She set up a printer in a room of her château "from which he did not leave: it was a deep secret" (2:380).

39. I am not suggesting that the *Nouvelles françaises* be attributed exclusively to Montpensier, although I find the current tendency to attribute the work solely to Segrais equally erroneous. Montpensier's memoirs and her correspondence are sufficient evidence of her literary talent to make Segrais' description of a collaborative effort plausible.

40. In the years after the Fronde, the greatest *frondeuse,* the Duchesse de Longueville, chose a not unrelated form of retreat—to the Carmel convent in the faubourg Saint-Jacques—and divided her life between this female community and a house she had built for herself at the Jansenist monastery, Port-Royal.

41. In France, the written transcription of fairy tales was not totally controlled by men, as was true in other countries. Perrault's female contemporaries such as d'Auloy, Murat, and La Force also published collections of fairy tales.

42. In this respect it is surely significant that, according to the "key" Segrais provides, the character Montpensier used for her self-portrait in a subsequent collaboration, *La Princesse de Paphlagonie* (1659), was the queen of the Amazons

(*Mémoires anecdotiques de Segrais* 146). Montpensier's desire to profit from the lessons of the past in creating a new script for the future was constantly belied by her nostalgia for the glory of heroinism.

43. Godenne documents (and criticizes) this movement toward narrative inertia in Scudéry's novels.

44. Zumthor uses the selections from the *Chronique du samedi* published by Belmont to document both the *Carte de Tendre*'s origin and Scudéry's compositional speed. He contends that Scudéry created the map in her salon on November 8, 1653 (264). The *privilège* for the first two volumes of *Clélie* was granted on June 23, 1654, and the volume appeared on August 31. As soon as the map was a proven success in her salon, Scudéry recreated it in fiction.

45. See Harth (*Ideology and Culture*) on the portrait and the social and poltical motivations of representation, a model that could be enlarged to accommodate gender.

46. Anonymous publications can be identified with the help of Barbier, Drujon, and Lever.

47. The terms of his description reinforce the comparison between the post-Fronde activities of the Grande Mademoiselle's retreat at Saint-Fargeau and those of the religious retreats undertaken by other former *frondeuses*. Montpensier's portraits may be seen as the secular equivalent of the "general confessions" written shortly thereafter in 1661 by the Duchesse de Longueville and the Princesse Palatine when they retired from active life in the world.

48. On the innovations of Scudéry's portraits and on the influence of the salon tradition on her technique, see J. D. Lafond (140, 143). In Jean Rousset's formulation, "one could almost say that [*Clélie*] exists for the conversations" (*Forme et signification* 34).

49. Recently, a number of critics have studied the imprint of the Sun King's absolute rule on French literature. See in particular Jean-Marie Apostolidès, Nicole Ferrier-Caverivière, and Louis Marin, *Le Portrait du roi*.

50. Montpensier and Motteville were the principal women authors of memoirs recounting their experiences during the Fronde years. They wrote from opposing positions, since Motteville remained loyal to the royalist forces. Their 1660 correspondence indicates that female (literary) solidarity had conquered political differences.

51. A long passage from the *Mémoires*, from which this section's epigraph is taken, confirms that Montpensier viewed this retreat into a private space ("chacun chez soi") as the price of the Fronde's failure (1:383–84).

52. In the article on Pellison in his *Remarques sur le dictionnaire de Bayle*, Joly cites Ménage's version of their attempt to feminize the Académie: "A short while ago in the Académie Française were nominated women, women illustrious because of their intelligence (*esprit*) and their knowledge—Mademoiselle de Scudéry, Madame des Houlières, Madame Dacier, and several others—who are perfectly capable of enriching our language with handsome works and who have already produced marvelous ones. Monsieur Charpentier supported this proposal with the

example of the Academies of Padua, where erudite women (*femmes savantes*) are admitted. My treatise, *Mulierum Philosopharum,* could have furnished more ancient examples of marks of distinction granted erudite women. Nevertheless, the proposal made to the Académie produced no results" (2:605). For speculation on the Ménage-Charpentier proposal, see Rathery and Boutron (121) and Robertson (61). See also the collective work, *Les Femmes et l'Académie Française* (10). Since the volumes containing the reports on the first thirty years of the Académie's meetings burned in 1789, it is unlikely that a fuller account of this historic juncture will ever be obtained.

53. In contrast, the name of a woman was not proposed as the subject for the prize for eloquence until 1840, when Amable Tastu's "Eloge de Madame de Sévigné" won the contest. Germaine de Staël's mother, Suzanne Necker, began, but did not complete, a eulogy of Sévigné for the Académie's contest (1798 ed., *Mélanges,* vol. 3). Scudéry was the only woman (of a total of nine) to win the eloquence prize in the seventeenth century, but two women, Antoinette Deshoulières and Catherine Bernard, won the Académie's prize for poetry (in 1687 and 1697). Since Scudéry, Deshoulières, and Bernard would have been three of the principal candidates for membership, all these awards could be seen as consolation prizes.

54. For information on the debate that led the Académie d'Arles to admit first nonaristocrats and then Deshoulières, see A. J. Rance's history of that academy. Rance mentions that the Académie Française had wanted to admit Deshoulières, then adds that the members "did not dare" to do so, but he gives no seventeenth-century source for this scenario of intimidation (3:125). Her candidacy in Arles was successful because of the "insistence" of a "very vocal" member named Vertron (3:125), who was also the editor of *La Nouvelle Pandore,* a compilation on the literary achievements of seventeenth-century women. Vertron cites the "founding letters" of the Arles academy rewritten to allow women to be admitted: "We believe that we should not exclude women, because ... they share in all the riches of the most noble genius" (1:177–78). The Académie d'Arles, founded in 1622, was an ancestor of the definitive French academy and the first assembly to suggest the seventeenth-century model.

55. The same Salvan de Saliez proposed in the 1680s—much as Montpensier had done in 1660—the establishment of "an academy of women" whose founding maxims are almost identical to those devised by Montpensier and also to those devised by Scudéry's Sapho in the land of the Sauromates. If women would reject life in the world and love, they would forge an existence that would make them "famous for centuries to come" (cited in Vertron 2:116, 113).

56. Yates 30–32. For more information on early academies, especially in the provinces, see Storer.

57. Though most of Mazarin's palace has not survived, the gallery with the Romanelli painting is still standing and has been incorporated into another monument of French intellectual life, the Bibliothèque Nationale. The *précieuse* muses now watch over the archives of the French literary tradition. The edifice provided

for in Mazarin's will, part of which now accommodates the meetings of the Académie Française, was originally the Collège des Quatre Nations, intended by its founder to ensure French cultural supremacy.

2. The Politics of Tenderness: Madeleine de Scudéry and the Generation of 1640–1660

1. Shelley was commenting on the practice of placing a blank next to the name of the actor who played the monster in early dramatizations of *Frankenstein* (cited in Gilbert and Gubar 241).

2. See Alice Jardine's notion of the "writing couple" and Wayne Koestenbaum's *Double Talk*.

3. In this chapter I use the terms "salon," "côterie," and "assembly" interchangeably to refer to the literary bodies that were the private equivalent of the official academies. I do so with the following double understanding: first, all these terms are anachronisms, used to replace such contemporary designations as *ruelle;* second, I in no way intend by this standardized usage to underestimate the crucial seventeenth-century evolution in salon politics.

4. Seventeenth-century critics begin this practice of dividing the literary spoils: Marolles said Georges was the author, Ménage defended the opposing viewpoint, and Tallemant assigned each a part in various works (Marolles cited by Ménage, *Ménagiana* 1:207; Tallemant 2:688). More recently, critics assume a partnership and offer an opinion on who wrote what. (See, for example, Cousin 1:28–29; Adam, *Histoire* 2:133; Tallemant, ed. Adam 2:1455–56; Aragonnès 54; Godenne 18, 307–8; Coulet 1:175.)

5. Cousin suggests that Madeleine de Scudéry may on occasion have called on a specialist other than her brother for help; he gives the always handy example of the battle scenes (1:360).

6. Traditionally, critics have contended that Scudéry's novels are historical in appearance only, that no documentation backs up her evocations of antiquity. Only recently have scholars entertained the possibility that one explanation for the staggering success of these novels is their actual historical and documentary content. (This was Scudéry's position: note in particular her discussion of her historical sources in a letter to Huet [Rathery and Boutron 295].) It is not my intention to refute the traditional reading of Scudéry's fiction, but rather to uncover its motivations. In the following pages I will not, therefore, always provide the detailed readings that could change the opinion of those convinced of Scudéry's frivolity. Such readings, however, exist. For example, I have analyzed "The Story of Sapho" (*Artamène,* volume 10) and found it to be so carefully documented, often using sources not readily available and not yet available in a modern language, that it can actually be referred to as the first modern biography of Sappho. (See my *Fictions of Sappho* 103–10.) In order to prove that Scudéry's historical framework is an astute blending of sources, Nicole Aronson analyzes the character Aronce as a composite creation based on numerous classical sources ("L'Histoire romaine dans *Clélie*" 185).

For an interpretation of several episodes of *Artamène* as an allegory of the contemporary political scene, see my "La Fronde romanesque: De l'exploit à la fiction." Existing research indicates that virtually every episode of Scudéry's novels was generated from intricate documentation. In addition, every source study reveals important modifications on Scudéry's part that point to a political interpretation of her fiction.

7. Scudéry herself, orphaned at an early age, received an impressive education for a woman of her day from an uncle who possessed an extensive private library. She was fluent in Italian and Spanish, then the most common foreign languages, but knew no ancient language. Her unmistakable sources for *Artamène* include works not yet translated into any modern language, thereby proving the collaboration of scholars who knew ancient languages. On Scudéry's education, see Conrart 255.

8. See Armine Kotin Mortimer's "La Clôture féminine des *Jeux d'esprit*" for a political reading of La Force's novel. The La Force-Conti identification is underscored by another of La Force's novels, *Anecdote galante, ou histoire secrète de Catherine de Bourbon,* which devotes over one hundred pages to what Cioranescu calls "a novelistic amplification of details recounted in *Les Amours du Grand Alcandre*" (53). The Princesse de Conti and her novelistic production inspired the third *nouvelle* of Villedieu's *Desordres de l'amour* (1675), which relies heavily, as Cuénin's critical edition explains, on *Les Amours du Grand Alcandre*. In addition, Villedieu features an episode from Conti's youth when she tells the (true) story of Givry's unrequited love for the Princesse de Guise and cites the letter he sent her announcing his desire to die in battle (206). Louise-Marguerite de Lorraine, Princesse de Guise, was the future Princesse de Conti. The actual "love letter from M. de Givry ... leaving to fight in the siege of Laon where he was killed" is included in the *Recueil des pièces curieuses* (2:432–33); Villedieu's version reproduces the original with only small changes.

9. Lafayette's first publication appeared anonymously in the 1659 *Recueil des portraits et éloges*. La Rochefoucauld, who also contributed to the *Recueil des portraits*, published the first fragments subsequently included in his *Maximes* in a collective volume, *Recueil de pièces en prose, les plus agréables de ce temps, composés par divers auteurs,* not even assembled by an author but by its publisher, Charles de Sercy.

10. This explanation for anonymous publication seems to have first been advanced by Adrien Baillet, writing in 1685. Baillet's argument can be recognized in virtually every subsequent discussion of the question.

11. As La Force makes plain in her preface (i), the members of Conti's salon gather at her château at Eu after they have incurred Richelieu's wrath by being of Marie de' Medici's party. With her choice of setting for the *Jeux d'esprit,* La Force may also have intended a reference to the next generation of political exiles, the *frondeurs:* Eu was part of the territory that the Grande Mademoiselle was obliged to give to the Duc du Maine, the child of Louis XIV and Montespan, in exchange for the freedom of her husband Lauzun in 1681.

12. On the notion of socially homogeneous groups functioning in effect as states within a state in ancien régime France, see Jouhaud's use of Arlette Farge's concept of "lieux d'opinion" ("Retour aux Mazarinades" 298).

13. This type of authorship was also achieved in less elaborate arrangements. For example, Senecterre's *Orasie* (1646), the most evident precursor of the formula Scudéry developed in *Artamène* and especially in *Clélie*, was apparently produced in collaboration only with the historian François Eudes de Mézeray. Senecterre, lady-in-waiting to Catherine de' Medici, after the Queen's death became a close friend of Henri de Nemours, son of the Duc de Nemours used as the hero of *La Princesse de Clèves* (a novel largely based, as Chamard and Rudler's research demonstrates, on the histories of Senecterre's collaborator, Mézeray). Until her death in 1646, Senecterre was, therefore, a living link with the world Lafayette later recreated. In an unsigned preface, *Orasie* is characterized as "une véritable histoire" rather than a novel, "un tableau de la plus magnifique ... Cour que l'on ait jamais veue, d'une cour où regnaient les vraies civilités et la plus pure politesse" (iii–iv), a description I cite in French so that readers familiar with the famous letter to the Chevalier de Lescheraine in which Lafayette describes her own novel can recognize the important similarities of vocabulary (*Correspondance* 2:62–63). *Orasie* serves as a striking reminder of the too often forgotten proximity between Scudéry and Lafayette.

14. From Lucien Belmont's reconstruction of the now lost "Chronique du samedi," the informal journal of Scudéry's salon, we know that she tried out ideas orally on her salon; she then had a written record of the discussion drawn up, which she recast in her novels. A number of *noms d'auteur* are employed on the title page of works now gathered together to form the Scudéry corpus. Early works, such as *Lettres amoureuses de divers auteurs de ce temps* (1641) and *Ibrahim* (1644), are published anonymously; the fact that the *privilège*, the official permission to publish, was in both cases granted to her brother makes the attribution possible. (On the attribution of *Lettres amoureuses*, see my "La Lettre amoureuse.") The major novels are signed "Mr de Scudéry." Her later works, both short stories and volumes of her collected "conversations," are published anonymously. Editions of the conversations published in Holland, as well as second editions published in France, are marked either "Mademoiselle de Scudéry" or "M. de S. D. R." For comprehensive overviews of Scudéry's career, see the studies by Nicole Aronson and René Godenne.

15. See Nancy K. Miller on the use of "sentimental" by historians of the eighteenth-century novel ("Mémoires, oublis").

16. Critics today have adopted *roman héroïque* as the most common designation for Scudéry's novels. She herself does not appear to have used the term. I have not been able to uncover its usage before the nineteenth century or to discover any trace of its origin. Readers interested in the total production attributed to Georges and Madeleine de Scudéry should consult Mongrédien's bibliography. Readers should also keep in mind that the attributions I am assuming in this chapter are not always universally accepted and remember the sense in which I use the term "author" when speaking of salon writing, to designate the individual who dictated the style and the direction of a literary enterprise. The crucial factor behind my decision to

attribute a work to the brother or to the sister is my conviction that the production supervised by Madeleine de Scudéry is unified by certain common goals.

17. Once again, I have been unable to trace the history of this expression. I suspect that it may have originated in England, where Scudéry's novels immediately knew immense popularity. See Haviland.

18. See in particular Rousset's discussion in *Narcisse romancier* 49–53. See also René Démoris on Jansenist autobiography and Louis Marin on the Jansenist ban on self-portraiture (*La Critique du discours*).

19. We know that Lafayette was sensitive to what she felt to be her proximity to Scudéry: this multiplication of pronouns is the most evident stylistic similarity between them. On the idea that the lack of differentiation among characters in Scudéry's novels is intentional and functions as a "principle of [social] equality," see Goldsmith (43–44).

20. To cite but one example proving the eagerness of Scudéry's readers: at the height of the Fronde and even under siege, the Prince de Condé and the Duchesse de Longueville were always aware of the appearance of a new volume of *Artamène* (Cousin 1:48 and ff.).

21. For more on the *précieuse* critique of the institution of marriage, see the studies by Backer, Maclean, Pelous, and Stanton. Maclean discusses the *précieuse* desire to abolish marriage and the other options explored in the salons (114–17).

22. Among early critics, see in particular Pons-Augustin Alletz (323) and Joseph de La Porte (2:515). More recent critics repeat nearly the same mixture of blame and praise. See, for example, Brunetière (56), Larnac (85), Pizzorusso (115), and Godenne (198–99). See in particular Showalter's description of what he terms her "minute analysis of the human heart" (28–29). In the following chapter I will consider the attacks, initiated by Boileau, on what was presented as Scudéry's dangerous subversion of history. The critical response that praises Scudéry's historical fiction solely because of her knowledge of the human heart seems to have originated in an attempt to countermand this critique. In the process, sympathetic critics may thus have initiated the interpretive tradition that considers Scudéry's fiction to be without ideological content.

23. Rousset's analyses of Lafayette's debt to Scudéry, in particular of *Clélie*'s influence on character development in *Zayde*, testify eloquently to Lafayette's acceptance of Scudéry's psychological system (*Forme et signification*, especially 32–36).

24. In this context, realism is obviously only a useful anachronism. I intend the term to refer to techniques and developments that early commentators on the novel saw as lending credibility to the genre by making it more "natural," more "real-seeming" (*vraisemblable*), the classical vocabulary for what began to be termed in the nineteenth century "realism."

25. Watt cites *La Princesse de Clèves* as his seventeenth-century example of classical French fiction, but his comments aptly sum up modern views of Scudéry's "implausibility." See the attacks on Watt's view of the French tradition by Peter Brooks and Nancy K. Miller ("Men's Reading"). See also Naomi Schor's critique of traditional uses of realism ("Unwriting Lamiel").

26. Scudéry's concept of *inclination* is taken up by virtually all members of the next generation of French women writers, but is perhaps most present in Lafayette's *Zayde*. The last occurrence of the term faithful to Scudéry's usage that I have noted is in Charlotte Brontë's 1853 *Villette*. The classic study of the role of love at first sight in the novel is Jean Rousset's *Leurs Yeux se rencontrèrent*.

27. The earliest examples of "mariage d'inclination" given by the *Robert Dictionary* are from the nineteenth century (Balzac, Barbey d'Aurevilly). The one earlier example that foreshadows the expression to come is cited in the *Littré Dictionary;* it is from Molière's *Avare:* "Un mariage ne saurait être heureux où l'inclination n'est pas" (4:3). It is logical that the expression would only have been forged after the Revolution, after the brief period during which divorce first existed in France: as the women writers of the late seventeenth century whom we will consider in chapter 5 make clear, "inclination" is the first step toward freedom from prearranged marriages and unhappy unions.

28. On the *Carte de Tendre*'s relation to the contemporary tradition of allegorical maps, see, in addition to Filteau, E. P. Mayberry Senter's study of these utopian engravings.

29. The year of the *Carte de Tendre*'s appearance in *Clélie*'s first volume, 1654, marked, according to Pelous, the creation of what Scudéry's contemporaries described as a separate state within the French State, what the Chevalier de Sévigné —Lafayette's stepfather and the brother of Sévigné's father-in-law—termed "the land of the *précieuses*" (Pelous 309–18).

30. It is even possible that the element in *Clélie*'s plot most frequently mocked by critics, the heroine's repeated abduction, could have been intended as another subversion of paternal authority. The phenomenon legally known as "rapt" was especially frequent between the late sixteenth and the mid-seventeenth century; in some cases, it signified "abduction," the kidnapping of a woman against her will, but other instances were clearly "elopements," the most common means of getting around paternal authority elected by couples who wished to marry without their parents' consent. The frequency of these elopements was the principal inspiration for the legal redefinition of marriage whose impact on *La Princesse de Clèves* I will analyze.

31. The persistent republican imagery is among the most bizarre components of the French myth of the Augustan age. Seventeenth-century France was clearly in no way a republic; however, in criticism of the novel at least, the call for "republican values" stands for the desire for literary representations of "manliness" that could countermand the fictions of female influence.

32. Porée is, to my knowledge, the first critic to apply the metaphor of contagious disease to literature; the strategy is perhaps most widely used at the end of the nineteenth century. Porée's influence was such that a large section of his diatribe was quickly translated into French in volume 1 of François Granet's *Réflexions sur les ouvrages de littérature*. The passage in question is on page 100.

33. By concluding this chapter with *Clélie*, I do not intend to undervalue Scudéry's works from the thirty-odd years during which she continued to write.

The volumes of conversations produced in the late 1680s and early 1690s, in particular, testify to Scudéry's continued involvement with constructions of gender and social ideals of female conduct. However, in the history of French women's writing, *Clélie* was destined to remain her most influential work.

34. I take the novels written to protest the 1816 revocation of the 1792 law allowing divorce, especially Sand's early fiction, as the terminus ad quem of Scudéry's tradition of feminist speculation.

3. "What Is an Author?": Lafayette and the Generation of 1660–1680

1. Quoted in the *Segraisiana* 1:31. Her contemporaries all appear to have written "la Fayette" in two words. In his edition of *La Princesse de Clèves,* Adam contends that "autograph signatures prove that the name was constantly written Lafayette" (n.pag.). I follow his lead, despite the fact that my own examination of the signatures does not confirm his conclusion, and despite the fact that the opposite course has been followed in standardizing contemporary names (La Bruyère, La Rochefoucauld, and so forth).

2. In citing the passage from Segrais's volume, I reproduce the original punctuation. However, in the edition I consulted, the passage's punctuation has been modified with handwritten "corrections" so that the passage reads: "Madame de Lafayette said, Monsieur de La Rochefoucauld gave me wit, but I transformed his heart." This reading—which redistributes their roles according to a founding French literary construction of gender that assigns women writers the domain of sentiment and their male counterparts that of reason—is followed in subsequent editions and by all modern scholars. The correct reading of this (apocryphal) passage matters less to me than the knowledge that Lafayette and La Rochefoucauld were immediately assigned (shifting) roles in the division of literary territory along gender lines.

3. Throughout this chapter I refer to the writings produced by the collaborators under Lafayette's direction with her name.

4. At least one other woman writer, Marie-Catherine Desjardins, generally known today by the name she "borrowed" from a man who never got around to respecting the formal promise of marriage he had made her, Villedieu, was simultaneously reinventing the novel along similar lines. Like Lafayette's, her fiction is far shorter than the epic proportions of the heroic novels; like Lafayette, she elects a modern rather than an ancient historical context for her fiction; like Lafayette, she generally avoids the set pieces (the conversation and so forth) of Scudéry's fiction. Villedieu has largely been eliminated from French literary history for a combination of reasons. First, she was responsible for a vast literary production, but she produced no generally acknowledged masterpiece like *La Princesse de Clèves.* She is thus less easily packaged for distribution by literary history. Second, the personal notoriety that, rightly or wrongly, almost immediately became indissociable from her work encouraged (or served as a pretext for) her dismissal from

accounts of the Golden Age of French letters. For more on Villedieu's biography and her oeuvre, see Cuénin's authoritative two-volume study. I will discuss her along with the generation of "notorious" women writers.

5. In the chapter of *De la littérature* entitled "Des Femmes qui cultivent les Lettres," Staël confirmed this intuition by theorizing that monarchies fostered an atmosphere particularly hostile to the public exposure necessary for modern (female) authorship: "In a monarchy, where the sense of conventions is so precisely grasped, any extraordinary action, any attempt to change one's position, immediately appears ridiculous; . . . anything invented without obligation is harshly criticized" (2:333).

6. In the seventeenth century, anonymous publication was not simply the opposite of signed publication. If we were to examine the title pages of all first editions, we would see much less of the open inscription of authorship than we might expect. Title pages are intended to sell books; publishers clearly did not yet believe that authors were the primary market value. And this is true for all writers, male and female, aristocratic and bourgeois. We cannot, therefore, conclude either that anonymity precluded a sense of authorial status or that aristocrats and women were particularly inclined to favor it.

7. I have discussed these pronouncements and my opinion of them at greater length in my "Lafayette's Ellipses." For other views of Lafayette as writer, see Geneviève Mouligneau (who believes that she composed none of the works attributed to her) and Micheline Cuénin's introduction to her edition of *La Princesse de Montpensier* (she sees Lafayette as an aristocrat anxious to avoid an open association with the bourgeois world of publishing), as well as her review of Mouligneau.

8. None of the requests for clarification is based on the information that there was a single author. Correspondents seek to know how many writers collaborated and something about their roles. As far as is known, these requests were all addressed to Lafayette, indicating that she was rumored to have been the director of the enterprise.

9. On the politics of representation in *Zayde*, see John Lyons' "The Dead Center" and my "No Man's Land." In his critique of *La Princesse de Clèves*, Valincour attacked the novel because of the ambiguity produced by Lafayette's Scudérian replacement of proper names with pronouns. (See, for example, his criticism of a passage on page 44 of the novel [Valincour 292]). Another good example of the avoidance of stable referents in the novel is found on page 35.

10. Bussy should have understood the need for protection: he had allowed his *Histoire amoureuse des Gaules* into limited circulation; when a purloined copy was made public, he was rewarded with exile. Bussy mocked Scudéry's literary-personal involvement with Paul Pellisson in similar fashion: "After having seen Mademoiselle de Scudéry inspire a great passion, I believe that anyone can be loved" (cited by Aragonnès 169). Other "wags" spoke with similar scorn of these individuals who refused to have their bond codified in any traditional way. "Guilleragues [the alleged author of the *Lettres portugaises*] said yesterday that Pellisson abused the license granted to men to be ugly," Sévigné reported in 1674 (1:658). Note that no one wastes "wit" on literary women before they become famous. Note also that the

purveyors of this type of what the French call *bons mots* are always novelists aspiring to literary fame in their own right.

11. The house stood at the corner of Vaugirard and Férou, a stone's throw from Saint-Sulpice; the Comte de Lafayette's estate was in a fairly remote part of Auvergne.

12. What we think of today as the classic French marriage of convenience seems to have occurred more frequently in the eighteenth century than in the seventeenth, at least if we can take the portraits found in novels as evidence of historical trends. As far as the early modern period is concerned, we usually cannot afford the luxury of discounting fictional treatments of marriage: more standard historical information is never abundant. In Lafayette's case, her relationship with La Rochefoucauld, which began in the mid-1660s and lasted until his death in 1680, was the subject of gossip, as Bussy's snide comment proves. Since we are dealing with a period in which what Marguerite Yourcenar terms "the convention of chastity" (*Oeuvres romanesques* 1049) was maintained, we cannot hope to understand the precise nature of that relationship.

13. "The plots of women's literature ... are about the plots of literature itself, about the constraints the maxim places on rendering a female life in fiction. Madame de Lafayette ... italicize[s] by the demaximization of [her] heroine's text the difficulty of curing plot of life, and life of certain plots" (Miller, "Emphasis Added" 46).

14. See Pierre Malandain's discussion of the vehemence with which twentieth-century critics have dismissed the possibility that a commentary on history underlies Lafayette's historical recreations. Malandain suggests ways of reading the ideological situation of *La Princesse de Clèves* (see in particular 33–36).

15. Lafayette was a member of a *frondeur* family: her stepfather (and Sévigné's uncle by marriage), the Chevalier de Sévigné, was exiled after the uprising, and she accompanied him in his "retreat," making a detour during the voyage to visit the future Cardinal de Retz in his political imprisonment.

16. Lafayette's "exemption" does not seem to have extended to the intimacy of friendship. The last pronouncement on love in her correspondence is made the year before her death in a letter to Sévigné: "You can believe, my very dear one, that you are the person in the world that I have the most truly loved" (2:218).

17. "*C'est assez que d'être.* C'est un mot de Madame de La Fayette, qui entendait par là que pour être heureux il fallait vivre sans ambition et sans passions, au moins sans passions violentes." Segrais, *Segraisiana* 1:86.

18. Beaunier transcribed the text from a manuscript in the Arsénal Library. His heirs published his transcription posthumously with the note "attributed to Mme de Lafayette." In his introduction (an abbreviated version of his discussion of the work in *La Jeunesse* 84–90), however, Beaunier does not suggest that Lafayette wrote the dialogue, only that she reached the same conclusions about love as its author did (153–54). Beaunier's (anonymous) heirs must, therefore, have added the attribution, perhaps relying on information that Beaunier would have made public had he lived to supervise the text's publication. The narrator remains anonymous,

but the agreement of adjectives and participles reveals her to be a woman; Beaunier concludes from this, and from certain autobiographical qualities, that the work was written by a woman. I agree with his conclusion because the novel's preoccupations are those of post-Fronde women's fiction. The attribution was partially based on the fact that, among the interlocutors' stories of women betrayed by inconstant men, the most detailed is a barely fictionalized version of the life of Louise de Lafayette, sister of the author's husband, referred to as "la pauvre Lafayette" (189–91). I read this rather as a sign that the author knew the future novelist; this story may even have been included to permit the inscription of an anticipated *nom d'auteur*. In that case, the dialogue would have been written not, as Beaunier infers, in 1653 (152–53) but after Lafayette's marriage in 1655. The later date also seems indicated because of the fact that the author cites the story of Brutus and Lucrèce (199–200) not, as Beaunier contends (152), according to ancient sources but according to Scudéry's version in the second volume of *Clélie*, published in 1654.

19. I say "seems to" in view of the fact that is impossible to assign a date to the work she never published, *Histoire de la Comtesse de Tende*. Given the high standards Lafayette always set for her writing, it is also likely that she suppressed some of her early production at least. Numerous works have been attributed to Lafayette at various times, but no attribution has been generally accepted. Lafayette's correspondence, though never abundant, begins early and continues without interruption until shortly before her death. Her first known published work is in the 1659 *Recueil des portraits* (ed. Montpensier and Segrais). The "Portrait of Madame the Marquise de Sévigné by Madame the Comtesse de Lafayette under the name of an unknown [man] (*inconnu*)" might be lost in the contemporary outpouring of verbal portraiture were it not for its title: unlike other portraitists of the day, who always speak in their own name, Lafayette projects the recital of her best friend's charms into the mouth of an anonymous male narrator.

20. Several contemporary male writers, in particular Cèsar de Saint-Réal, authored novels reminiscent of the historical fiction simultaneously imagined by Lafayette and Villedieu. There are, however, important differences that prove that subsequent commentators had only the female variant in mind when they spoke of "*the* novel." Saint-Réal elects foreign settings, whereas women writers prefer to revise French history. His novels have an exclusively homocentric focus; never does he suggest, as women writers always do, that women had always played a crucial role behind the scenes of history.

21. The classic study of this question is Tony Tanner's *Adultery and the Novel.*

22. Except, of course, in the case of *Zayde,* which, true to pure romance tradition, uses marriage to signal closure. This decision thus to reverse her customary plot must have been part of her homage to Scudéry.

23. Mademoiselle de Mézières first attracts the Duc de Guise's attention while she is formally betrothed to his younger brother; they fall in love at this time, and their mutual passion is temporarily displaced but not extinguished when she is married instead to the Prince de Montpensier because "the house of Bourbon . . . ,

realizing the advantage that it would receive from this marriage, resolved to take it away from [the house of Anjou] and to procure it for itself" (44–45).

24. The story is set approximately between the years 1563 and 1572.

25. Micheline Cuénin, who implies that the foreword was added by an actual "libraire" (18), in her edition prints it separately from the novel (32). However, *La Princesse de Clèves* opens with a similar text, and it is always considered part of the novel. If the preface had been composed by a publisher, it would have been out of fear that the (probably imaginary) story of marital infidelity could have been offensive to "Madame" de Montpensier's descendant, Mademoiselle de Montpensier. *La Princesse de Montpensier* is typical of Lafayette's fiction in that it is based on extensive documentation and in that Lafayette seems to have invented as little as possible of her intrigue. See Cuénin's introduction and notes for information on Lafayette's sources.

26. Montpensier began work on her memoirs in 1653–1657, during her post-Fronde exile to another of her family's estates, Saint-Fargeau. She begins her text by recounting her discovery of a great pleasure in the "retreat" she had so dreaded: "solitude" guarantees the time necessary for writing (1:368). Her *Mémoires* returns to what she clearly sees as two related subjects, the study of her genealogy (she is especially proud of an ancestor from another "very illustrious house," Antoine de Chabannes [1:435], an ancestor who may have lent his name to the ill-fated confidant in Lafayette's story of the house of Montpensier), and her fight against what she terms Richelieu's "tyranny" in the form of his destruction of her ancestral estate at Champigny, "a place [full of] the memory of my predecessors" (1:385). In 1655 Montpensier learned that she had won her suit against the Duc de Richelieu, who was ordered to pay for the destruction of the château (2:475). Montpensier's activities during her exile are thus situated at the intersection of women's writing, the study of history in order to authorize present action, and the legal struggle for control over one's estate.

27. In *Artamène*, Richelieu (in *à clef* guise) functions on several occasions as a stand-in for Mazarin. As soon as *La Princesse de Montpensier* was published, Lafayette had six copies handsomely bound; the first she sent to Ménage so that he could present it to Scudéry (*Correspondance* 1:171). The gesture (like her choice of subject matter with respect to the other literary *femme forte* of the 1650s, Montpensier) is a symbolic exchange: during the brief period Lafayette spent away from her own family land (the years just prior to her literary collaborations with Montpensier and then on *La Princesse de Montpensier*), an important number of her letters are addressed to Ménage, pleading requests to have each volume of *Clélie* sent to her as soon as it appeared (*Correspondance* 1:45, 53, 55, 57, 58, 90, 93, 94, 95, 96, 134).

28. *Les Voleuses de langue* (35). On a number of occasions in her pioneering study, Herrmann insists on the central importance of marital abuse for French women writers, an emphasis hardly surprising for a critic whose first published work was her doctoral thesis on *Le Rôle juridique et politique des femmes sous la République romaine*.

29. Because my concerns here are primarily literary, I will present rather quickly often complicated legal and historical material. The most thorough considerations of the legal treatment of marriage during the ancien régime are those of Jules Basdevant and Maurice Covillard. On the history of divorce in particular, see the study by Dominique Dessertine. See also James Traer on the history of marriage and the family and Jean Portemer's articles on the legal status of women in ancien régime France.

30. See Lafayette 38 and Covillard 12–13 for a description of the case. The heiress of this tale was Diane de France, the illegitimate daughter of Henri II (by Diane de Poitiers).

31. The controversy reopened under the new regime with the *loi* Bonald abolishing divorce on May 8, 1816, and continued until divorce was once again made legal by the *loi* Naquet of July 19, 1884. The parallel role in English marital law was played by Henry VIII, who, like numbers of French kings, forced its evolution to serve his personal goals. Note that in *La Princesse de Clèves* Mary Stuart tells the story of his ill-fated union with Anne Boleyn, and evokes Henry VIII's marital history. (On the role he played in English marital law, see René Pillorget 28–32.)

32. Covillard 17–28. Henri II's edict did not annul clandestine marriages, but it did allow parents to disinherit children because of them, thereby protecting the transmission of patrimony. The Council of Trent took up the issue of these marriages at the request of the French ambassador. Debate was inconclusive: the council members were sympathetic with the French position but realized that to annul marriages previously considered valid was to put marriage's status as a sacrament into question. In the course of the debate, the distinction between marriage as sacrament and marriage as contract was first proposed. In the end, the Council of Trent issued the first official proclamation of marriage's sacramentality. However, the debate leading to that proclamation contained the germ of the next great moment of crisis in the 1670s, when contract theory was resurrected. The preparatory phase ends with a 1639 decree that, first, pronounced "rape of seduction" a form of "violent rape," and thereby grounds for annulment of a marriage under canon law; and, second, pronounced all marriages between minors "rapes of seduction." The long-term consequence of the accommodation that at last made Henri II's wish legal fact was that the Gallican Church had cooperated with the State in its desire to oversee all marital transactions involving property: there was to be no turning back.

33. A formal promise of marriage, even between minors, was considered equivalent to marriage under canon law.

34. Lottin's statistics, confirmed by Dessertine's research (22), indicate that separations were almost always initiated by women; men generally had recourse to less formal means, such as confinement to their estates, to deal with troublesome wives (Lottin, "Vie et mort" 65–66; *Désunion* 114). See also Dessertine on divorces initiated by women (161–62).

35. Roderick Phillips has recently asserted the opposing view of the French legal tradition: "What is particularly striking is that the French revolutionary law was

not the culmination of an evolution of divorce legislation in an increasingly liberal direction"; "the French divorce law represented a truly radical break with French legal tradition" (159). French scholars, however, defend the opinion, to which I adhere, that the contract theory of marriage first developed in the 1670s leads directly to the Revolution's treatment of marriage as "civil contract" (Covillard 117, Basdevant 7, and so forth). I want to note my recognition of the wide variety of legal situations in ancien régime France, especially the crucial difference between regions governed by *droit écrit* and those governed *droit coutumier*. Legal codes varied from region to region, even from city to city. I am not trying to generalize but to establish an outline based on the period's major legal texts. I also recognize that these texts are to some extent fictions, that there was often a wide discrepancy between a law as it was on the books and as it was enforced. Major legal treatises stand nevertheless as representative of the desires of different contemporary power groups.

36. The treatise is in manuscript in the Bibliothèque Royale in Brussels. I cite it from Lottin, "Vie et mort" 60. Ariès notes the gradual transfer of importance in the course of the sixteenth and seventeenth centuries from the line (lineage) to the family, which takes on the value previously attributed to the line as "the social cell, the basis of the State, the foundation of the monarchy" (356).

37. As Phillips stresses, the sacramentality of marriage had only been proclaimed canonically by the Council of Trent (27); however, this status had been proposed much earlier, in particular by Augustine. In an interesting and convincing argument, Philippe Ariès suggests that the promotion of contract theory in the seventeenth and eighteenth centuries was not a new development but merely a return to a prior state of affairs: he contends that throughout the Middle Ages "marriage remained simply a contract," and that only in the sixteenth century did the Church begin to realize "the power of sanctification." In Ariès's view, the sixteenth-century position was, therefore, aberrant (356–57). Note that the structure Colbert sought for marriage, civil (ceremony) followed by religious sacrament, is just that finally imposed by modern French law.

38. His examples provide a mini-history of the recent controversy: "The Council of Trent decrees heretics those who say that *marriage* is not a matter for the Church's judges." "When the King annulled clandestine *marriage,* he did not touch the sacrament, but invalidated the civil contract that is its foundation."

39. This argument seems tailor-made for an age when trials to settle legally problematic inheritances proliferated: Lafayette, for example, was often preoccupied during the years between her two novels of French history with lawsuits regarding the settlement of her husband's estate. Basdevant includes numerous citations demonstrating that, in the final decades of the seventeenth century, the civil interpretation of marriage was widely accepted and openly discussed among the political figures frequented by Lafayette and Sevigné (37–38).

40. In this passage, Lafayette's repetition of "inclination" proves her understanding that Scudéry's concept was already generating the desire for a new kind of marriage, what would eventually be known as "marriage d'inclination": the prin-

cesse first says that "she feels she is inclined (*elle sentait son inclination portée*) to marry him," but concludes by stressing that "she had no particular inclination for his person" (50).

41. Traer links the desire for a modern marriage to the pro-divorce movement: "The creation of machinery for divorce signified not disregard for marriage but precisely this new value: that marriage should be a means to happiness" (16). However, he traces the origins of modern marriage only to the Enlightenment, whereas seventeenth-century French women's writing testifies to the development of these desires a half-century earlier. See also Lawrence Stone (especially his chapter on "The Companionate Marriage") and Pillorget on the family in eighteenth-century England and France.

42. As if to indicate that this novel is the continuation of the history of marriage begun in her first *histoire*, Lafayette has Madame de Chartres enter into (unsuccessful) negotiations with the two families central to the marital dilemma in the earlier novel, Guise and Montpensier (she even attempts to marry Mademoiselle de Chartres to the "prince dauphin, fils du duc de Montpensier" [46], the very "character" her earlier heroine does marry sixteen years earlier in Lafayette's oeuvre and some eight years later in Lafayette's version of history). Lafayette portrays Madame de Chartres as a marital speculator: she attempts to broker her daughter's great beauty into a marriage beyond the family's political standing. She is initially unsuccessful because her daughter is not the supreme heiress that Mademoiselle de Mézières is, and because her family is somewhat out of royal favor (41).

43. Presumably because of his critique of *La Princesse de Clèves* (his only production of any note), Valincour was elected to Racine's chair in the Académie Française. He thereby inherited the notes Racine had prepared for his history of Louis XIV's reign; these notes were burned in the fire that destroyed Valincour's summer home in Saint-Cloud. By this quirk of fate, the novel won an important round in its battle with history for control over posterity's view of the seventeenth century. Racine's projected history would have given the most official view possible of the Golden Age, the opposite of the vision of uneasy corruption transmitted by Lafayette's cynical narrator.

44. Valincour's remark testifies to the division, created by the mechanics peculiar to salon writing, into two publics, the inside public that had access to a work in manuscript and the readers who saw only published works. The publication of *La Princesse de Clèves* in March 1678 was the occasion for the first true publicity campaign in the history of French literature. For a review of the novel's promotion, see Maurice Laugaa's excellent anthology. The linchpin of this campaign was the public paper favored by court society, Donneau de Visé's *Le Mercure galant*. Lafayette and Visé were in the same political camp: she maintained close ties with the house of Savoie, which subsidized *Le Mercure galant* (see Beaunier, *L'Amie* 201). I cite *Le Mercure galant*'s original edition, widely available in microfilm.

45. The classical structure of the legal *aveu* was being developed at the time of *La Princesse de Clèves*'s production. (Foucault cites in particular a 1670 ordinance [42–43].) It seems likely that Lafayette had both the legal reference and its literary

implications in mind in choosing a name for her heroine's account. *Phèdre* (1677) is the other contemporary text featuring *aveu* in the sense of a heroine's public admission of already known criminal passion.

46. Prior to *La Princesse de Clèves,* conversation figures in the novel mainly according to Scudéry's salon-inspired formula, whereby characters analyze a topic collectively. Conversation in this usage is abstract, used to present multiple opinions on an issue, rather than intended to reveal individual character.

47. Two convergences of vocabulary should be noted: the torture used to extract the *aveu* was designated as either "ordinary" or "extraordinary"; *Le Mercure galant*'s issues were initially called "ordinaires"—"La Vertu malheureuse" was published in the first issue named an "extraordinaire."

48. See John Lyons' "Narrative Interpretation" on the forms of pedagogy in the novel.

49. As if to make this comparison inevitable, the January 1678 "Extraordinaire" of *Le Mercure galant* in which the publicity campaign for *La Princesse de Clèves* was launched has as its frontispiece a "Carte de l'Empire de la Poésie" that refers unmistakably to the "Carte de Tendre."

50. In order thus to designate the château, Lafayette has recourse to one of her rare (intentional, of course) betrayals of history. In 1659 there was no building at Coulommiers. The château was subsequently erected by a woman, Catherine de Gonzague. Cuénin describes her construction as a "woman's château" and notes the "many statues of illustrious women from fable and history" found in it ("Châteaux" 118). With this anticipated architectural reference, the equivalent of the reconstruction of Champigny in *La Princesse de Montpensier,* Lafayette elects a feminocentric space for her heroine's projected "retirement." Lafayette may also have intended Coulommiers as a political reference. In 1650 that child of the Fronde, Mademoiselle de Longueville, stepdaughter of the Duchesse de Longueville and the duc's daughter, was exiled there during her father's captivity. Her stepmother was ordered to go there, but refused. Just as she had for *La Princesse de Montpensier,* Lafayette carefully documented the historical setting for *La Princesse de Clèves:* very few characters and events are of her invention. On her use of sources, see the articles by Chamard and Rudler.

51. In Brian Stock's description, "The feudal bond originated as a spoken contractual agreement between two individuals . . . to which certain property rights were appended" (49). On the history of this sense of *aveu,* see the examples in the Robert and Littré dictionaries. Lafayette's usage of the term helps us understand the historical setting she elects for a tale of marital independence. As René Démoris explains, "It is no accident that [seventeenth-century] writers choose the subjects of most of their historical fiction in the troubled years of Henri II's reign, at the moment when the power of the feudal lords was able to destabilize royal authority" ("Aux origines" 29–30). The princesse's challenge to her husband's feudal authority thus parallels a historical movement contemporary to the novel's action—and also could have reminded its first readers of the subsequent "destabilizing of royal authority" carried out by feudal lords during the Fronde.

52. "*SEIGN:* The mark at the bottom of an act, of a document, which confirms its tenor by affixing the name written in the hand of the individual who consents to its execution" (Furetière).

53. The scene of course also raises the issue of the relation between production and reproduction: the princesse gives her husband no son to recognize as his heir.

54. Within the tradition of French women's writing from Tencin to Staël, the notion of *aveu* functions as an internal signature, simultaneously indicating the recognition of Lafayette's *nom d'auteur* and the author's own self-inscription as an author. In Tencin's *Les Mémoires du comte de Comminge* (1735), the *aveu* the comte must make to his beloved Adélaïde is his real name: "I am not what you thought me; I am the son of the Comte de Comminge" (30). The name signifies his position in the paternal order as a member of the family fighting hers for the legal right to certain estates. The crime he must "avow," his having burned papers that would have resolved their dispute, is, like Lafayette's *aveu,* a rebellion against the order represented by the *nom du père,* the interests that control the marital freedom of the children of the landed aristocracy. And Tencin stands midway between Lafayette and Staël's *Corinne* (1807), in which the heroine's *aveu* is the account of her unworthiness of a *nom du père* because she has elected literary authority rather than a woman's place in the patriarchal order. All these scenes confirm Paul Pelckmans' attempt to find in the "family imagery" of the eighteenth-century novel prefigurations of Freud's family romance (21). His most convincing early examples of Oedipal sensibility are taken from Tencin and Graffigny (542), additional evidence that the female literary tradition of the ancien régime should be read as a questioning of the patriarchal system.

55. The fact that the prince sends his order in writing proves that he understood his wife's intentions. Catherine Durand Bédacier's "La Princesse de Condé" (the third part of *Histoire des amours,* 1700) contains a tribute to *La Princesse de Clèves* that suggests that the princesse failed by waiting too long to draw up her contract. Just before marrying the Prince de Condé, Mademoiselle de Montmorancy [*sic*] "opens her heart" to her future husband: he knows that she was almost married to Bassompierre; she has not yet completely "removed him from her heart." To her request that he "remove her from the court," this prince, unlike his precursor, "promised [her] all that she wanted" (184).

56. On the history of the ending's interpretation and for a positive reading of the princesse's decision, see the articles by Harriet Allentuch, Jules Brody, and Domna Stanton ("The Ideal").

57. Witness Tallemant des Réaux's portrait of the Marquise de Rambouillet: "She swears that, if she had been left alone until she was twenty, and if she had not been forced to get married, she would have remained single. I believe she would have been capable of this resolve, when I think that, from twenty on, she no longer wanted to go to the Louvre. . . . It was not that she didn't enjoy entertainment, but only in private" (1:442). "Repos," that code word for "indifference" and the choice of private over public space, is recurrent in the princesse's final decision making (in particular, 175, 176).

58. She is sixteen when her mother brings her to court (41); the events of the novel take place over roughly eighteen months.

59. Because the marriage had produced no children, property the prince had received from his family (*propres*) would have reverted to his relatives. Community property such as Coulommiers would have been equally divided, and the princesse would have kept her own *propres*, in particular the "large estate that she owned near the Pyrenees" (178).

60. Her wish was not to be granted: the Mottier de Lafayette family ends in the early eighteenth century with the death in 1729 of her older (unmarried) son, Abbé Louis. Her other son, Armand, died in 1694, leaving only a daughter.

61. In the letter of September 1691, Lafayette uses "avouer," the verb with which her heroine attempts to "legitimate" her desire for a separate estate, for her denegation of authorship (*Correspondance* 2:182).

62. By limiting her placement of the economics of authorship to nonliquid assets, Lafayette defined the link between the marriage plot and the authorial plot in aristocratic terms: ancestral domains were passed down along with the aristocratic *nom (d'auteur)*, whereas the bourgeois (author)'s assets were more likely to be liquid. It is impossible to draw from Lafayette's metaphoric speculation on authorial assets any message regarding the actual commercial involvement of aristocratic authors. Very few documents have survived regarding economic terms—how much an author was paid, for what, and by whom—on which seventeenth-century bourgeois writers made their careers. I know of no such evidence concerning the production of contemporary aristocrats; we do not even know, for example, how the profits from any of the collective publications were divided up between collaborators and publisher. One thing appears certain: it is highly unlikely, at a time when, as Sévigné's correspondence reminds us, aristocrats were increasingly obsessed with the cash flow necessary to maintain the appearance of power de rigeur at the Sun King's court, that a source of liquidity like a best-selling novel would be overlooked.

63. In the 1657 edition of *La Mérite des dames*, Saint-Gabriel calls Lafayette "la nonpareille" (302). Pierre Costar explains that "she was usually called 'l'Incomparable' " (cited by Mouligneau 11–12).

64. Lafayette's homage is far from the only sign that Scudéry's influence was very much alive in the late seventeenth century. From Lafayette's day until the turn of the nineteenth century, a succession of women writers kept alive the more optimistic, less cautious, more openly feminocentric vision Scudéry inaugurated. To cite but a few examples: Vertron records in 1698 the project of a certain Salvan de Saliez (according to her nineteenth-century editor Collin, it became a reality in 1704) to set up a "female academy," the "Chevaliers and Chevalières of Good Faith." In a correspondence with the Marquise de Montpelliat, she establishes guidelines for the project that seem straight out of *Clélie*. Women will serve as lawmakers for the community, since "all reasonable men have judged that they could follow without shame a path shown them by women." Her conclusion (surely even more utopian in the 1680s and 1690s than in the 1650s): "The equality of the

sexes is no longer in dispute among worldly people" (*honnêtes gens*) (*Lettres* 203). (Salvan de Saliez also authored a novel, *La Comtesse d'Isembourg,* a protogothic tale of a young comtesse married to an old, jealous husband who threatens to poison her. She runs away and hides in Paris. Published in 1678, the same year as *La Princesse de Clèves,* this novel may be the first ancestor of the scandalous accounts of bad marriages produced by the next generation of women writers.) At the turn of the century, Marie-Jeanne L'Héritier authored a pair of "triumph" books, *Le Triomphe de Madame Deshoulières, reçue 10e muse au Parnasse* (1694) and *L'Apothéose de Mademoiselle de Scudéry* (1702), celebrations of two of the seventeenth century's great literary women that indicate their places in a feminocentric Parnassus, a sort of pan-*précieuse* salon in the sky. L'Héritier thereby symbolically reverses the exclusion from the Académie on earth of the two seventeenth-century women most often mentioned as candidates: in *L'Apothéose* Scudéry receives her "brevet d'Imortelle," her "commision as an immortal woman" (members of the Académie Française are known as "immortels," 55). L'Héritier also countermands Boileau's literary history: *Le Triomphe* contains a parody of his symbolic execution of Scudéry in the *Dialogue des héros de roman;* this time an anonymous "misanthrope" (clearly identified as Boileau) is condemned by Minos, judge of the underworld, "to receive from Cerberus as many bites as his slanderous tongue had hurled abusive gives against women" (7). The "triumph" tradition forms the bridge between Scudéry and a strain in Staël's fiction most evident in *Corinne* (1807): the coronation of her heroine, for example, recreates the public celebrations of female literary genius staged by Scudéry and L'Héritier. In similar fashion, Salvan de Saliez's academy project is the link between Scudéry's literary academies and that of Staël's mother, Suzanne Curchod (her Académie des Eaux, like Salvan de Saliez's assembly, began as a utopian project overtly reminiscent of Scudéry and was subsequently actualized). (See Haussonville 1:30.)

65. In this passage Valincour was referring in particular to the salon writing devised for *La Princesse de Clèves,* what he termed its "sorry manner of speech" (339).

66. "These novels were the delight of the sex whose whims writers often do not have the strength to resist. History was forgotten. Scorn for learning followed" (286). Jacquin makes it clear that, by the second half of the eighteenth century, a true "writer" could only be male. The lexicographic equality evident in the definitions proposed by that defrocked academician, Furetière, had disappeared. ("We also say of a woman that she has established herself as an author when she has written a book.")

4. Divorce, Desire, and Novel: The Notorious Women of 1690–1715

1. The novels produced by salon writing and therefore presided over by women were more likely to be left unsigned than works composed by a single author.

2. La Roche-Guilhem, of staunch Protestant background—"La Roche" was

added to the family name, Alexandre Calame believes (10), as a reminder of a Huguenot safehold razed during religious persecution in the 1620s—left France after the revocation for London, where she spent the last twenty years of her life. (On her biography, see Calame's study.) In her *Mémoires,* Anne-Marguerite Du Noyer describes graphically the problems of a mixed marriage and recounts her flight into the diaspora. Bernard abjured her Protestant faith shortly after the revocation. (On her biography, see Plusquellec's article.) I am certain that one could read their works as commentary on the evolving politics of religion in France. Du Noyer's *Lettres historiques et galantes* (1713), for example, clearly related to Montesquieu's 1721 *Lettres persanes,* includes many letters on the events of Louis XIV's reign that had caused the diaspora to flourish. This approach could also feature precursors of such explicit religious commentary, in particular Lafayette's historical novels. For example, the fact that *La Princesse de Montpensier's* historical frame culminates in the Saint-Barthélemy massacre surely merits interpretation.

3. Villedieu's biography has probably been reconstructed as thoroughly as is possible, thanks to the efforts of Micheline Cuénin. I am indebted to Cuénin's research, but I take exception to two of the assumptions that direct her presentation of Villedieu. First, Cuénin reads Villedieu's works, in particular the *Mémoires de la vie de Henriette-Sylvie de Molière,* as autobiographical. While her heroine is certainly a free spirit, as the novelist appears to have been, many of Sylvie's adventures are flagrantly fictional; it is difficult to know where to stop once one begins to read pseudomemoirs as factual accounts. Villedieu's early commentators do not consider the novel autobiographical: La Croix, for example, presents it as the biography of someone with that name (2:69). Second, Cuénin argues that Villedieu never sought to participate in the contemporary female tradition, that she was probably an antifeminist. She states that she took a pro-Boileau, anti-Scudéry line, in particular in an early work, *Récit de la farce des précieuses* (1659), an adaptation of Molière's satire on salon women, *Les Précieuses ridicules* (1:106, 168). Villedieu certainly did not participate assiduously in salon society, but evidence of her hostility is counterbalanced by evidence of a certain degree of collaboration. For example, in the same year as she published her recreation of Molière, she also composed her self-portrait for the *Recueil des portraits,* the collective volume edited by Montpensier and Segrais in which Lafayette made her literary début with a portrait of Sévigné. Villedieu may have stood apart from the female tradition as her career developed because she was a different kind of writer, already announcing the anti-collaborative stance of the next generation. Villedieu defended the same political positions as women writers who made the transition from militancy to literature after the Fronde. Like Scudéry and Sévigné, she fictionalized her loyalty to Louis XIV's minister, Fouquet (in a 1664 play, *Le Favory;* see Cuénin's discussion of it, 1:122–25). In certain of her novels, in particular *Les Désordres de l'amour* (1675), critics see meditations on the politics of the Fronde and the early years of Louis XIV's reign. (See Coulet 1:265, Cuénin 1:12.) The only reference used to situate Henriette-Sylvie's chronology is Louis XIV's marriage, that crucial date for the precious decade.

4. Villedieu's birthdate is disputed. She begins her self-portrait by contradicting a founding tenet of *précieuse* literary psychology, that self-portraiture is impossible because one sees others more clearly than oneself: "It seems natural to know oneself more perfectly than one can be known by the rest of the world" (*Recueil des portraits* 224). The portrait that follows is remarkably detailed (she provides with regard to physical appearance the type of facts rarely included in contemporary verbal portraiture) and carefully avoids the eulogy basic to *précieuse* portraiture. The young woman stresses her compassion for the poor and the fact that she has frequently "complained that her social rank is not elevated enough" to allow her to do something about their misery (225). Villedieu, with Scudéry one of the two great bourgeois women writers of her age, provides thereby the only moment of social critique, even of social commentary, in the vast collective volume. It is extraordinary that she dared to speak openly of the century's most important literary taboo (from all seventeenth-century literary texts combined, one would hardly guess that anyone had suffered during the monarchy's rise to absolutism), and that she foregrounded her implicit critique of the aristocracy's lack of generosity by making place for it in an autobiographical presentation three pages long.

5. Villedieu and Scudéry were the only seventeenth-century literary women to receive royal pensions. Like Scudéry, Villedieu was well paid by her editor (in her case, Claude Barbin), who knew what she was worth to him. Her decision to strike out on her own seems to have been inspired by just those marriage-related issues that provoked the first wave of French legal treatises on the institution some twenty years later. Cuénin recounts that, when the future Villedieu was thirteen or fifteen, she made a secret promise to marry. When her father learned of it, he broke off the engagement and had the young man imprisoned. Apparently in part because of her anger at her husband's behavior, Villedieu's mother obtained a legal separation and went to live in Paris with her daughters. The future writer moved out on her own shortly thereafter (Cuénin 1:29–31).

6. The story of the writer's self-baptism remains obscure and was certainly extremely complicated. Cuénin maintains that she took the name "with the approval of the Villedieu family," indicating the sort of private oral agreement as replacement of an official legal contract that the Princesse de Clèves tries to establish. The young man was conveniently killed in battle; his "widow" 's presence at Villedieu family functions is attested after his death (Cuénin 1:52).

7. I am grateful to Laurent Bray for his help in tracking down this biography.

8. The article "Jardins" is not in the original 1695 edition of Bayle's *Dictionnaire historique et critique* but was added in a reedition after the publication of Richelet's text. Villedieu came from a family of Huguenot supporters. For an additional sympathetic contemporary portrait of Villedieu, see her obituary in *Le Mercure galant:* Donneau de Visé describes her success as a writer and gives no hint of scandal surrounding her person. His view is counterbalanced by Tallement's lewd dismissal of Villedieu as "that kind of woman" (2:896).

9. René Démoris contends that her work is without precedent, since Villedieu could not have known the only directly related contemporary production, the

memoires of the women who participated in the Fronde, because these were published only in the early eighteenth century (*Le Roman à la première personne* 134). However, most of these memoirs had already been composed by the time of Villedieu's novel, and she could have had access to the accounts in manuscript, in particular the Grande Mademoiselle's first-person chronicle of her exploits. Montpensier was working on her memoirs in the late 1650s at the time of the production of the *Recueil des portraits* to which Villedieu contributed. (However, Villedieu could not have known the contemporary work most like the *Mémoires de la vie de Henriette-Sylvie de Molière*, the pseudomemoirs of La Guette, published only in 1681.) Françoise de Motteville began turning the notes she had taken during her years in Anne of Austria's service into memoirs when she left the court after the former Queen Regent's death in 1666. She frequented Lafayette and Sévigné at the time of their composition (*Mémoires* 36:305). Her memoirs, with the spectator's rather than the participant's view of history, are more likely to have influenced Lafayette's brand of historical fiction than the defiant mode of the *Mémoires de la vie de Henriette-Sylvie de Molière*. So many works circulated in manuscript in the salon milieu that the composition date rather than the publication date is often the moment to be determined. These memoirs were published only after all those mentioned in them were dead. The Duchesse de Nemours left her manuscript with L'Héritier, who published it in 1709. Motteville's memoirs were first published in 1723, Montpensier's in 1729. The knowledge alone that women had begun to write autobiographical accounts of their lives on the world stage could have prompted Villedieu and the women writers of the notorious generation to exploit the pseudo-memoir form. The existence of this developing tradition of women's writing could also have inspired critics to believe that all first-person accounts of a woman's adventures were autobiographical.

10. The Marquise de Castellane, by marriage the Marquise de Ganges, was murdered in 1667. Her story (under her married name) was recounted in greater detail by the Marquis de Sade.

11. For example, Fern Farnham recounts the rumors of Anne Lefèvre Dacier's alleged personal irregularities, which, at the very time when Villedieu's biography was rewritten, began to serve as a pretext for the dismissal of Dacier's work as the most celebrated Hellenist of her day and the most famous French female Hellenist of all time (Farnham 92). See also the public defense of Dacier by one of the notorious literary women, Anne Ferrand.

12. For more on the opposition between general (public) history and particular (private) history and on women writers' involvement with the latter, see the study by Faith Beasley.

13. Because of my desire to show the development of a lengthy tradition of women's writing, I will not discuss the other genre in vogue in the late seventeenth century that lends itself to a political reading, the fairy tale. French literary history has portrayed Charles Perrault as virtually the sole practitioner of this genre; however, the fairy tale was first given written form and directed to an adult public by a number of writers, of whom Perrault was the only man. Perrault's niece

L'Héritier was a well-known writer of fairy tales, and a number of the notorious women (De La Force, d'Aulnoy, and Murat) also contributed to the genre's development. Fairy tales are often subversive in the same manner as the *histoires galantes* I discuss in this section: both forms return obsessively to the possibility of misalliances. In both, in particular, beautiful young women of more humble birth can hope to marry a prince of royal blood.

14. Charnes' book-length response to Valincour is generally considered, like the campaign in *Le Mercure galant,* to have been officially authorized by Lafayette and her collaborators.

15. The most sensible response to the accusation originated by Bayle then widely repeated, that the novel was dangerous because it would cause confusion about what had actually happened in French history, was formulated by the critic François Granet in the late 1730s. Granet argues that historians can take care of themselves; surely they would check out any information in a novel before repeating it, thereby preventing the spread of invented stories. He further argues that, since historians certainly do not give a complete picture, the novel may well render "an important service" to history (111).

16. In an earlier fantasy of the policing of the new genre, Bayle suggested that it "would be wise to oblige novelists to create imaginary heroes or to take those furnished by antiquity" (*Nouvelles de la République de Lettres* 316).

17. For more on the late seventeenth-century critique of history, see chapter 2 of Paul Hazard's *La Crise de la conscience européenne.*

18. *Artamène*'s Sapho is the ultimate "femme galante" in Scudéry's sense of the term, a woman who, in conversation in a salon setting, lays down a code of conduct for men (10:380). The "Histoire de Sapho" contains Scudéry's clearest illustration of the ways of *galanterie,* especially in a long discussion later reprinted in her *Conversations nouvelles sur divers sujets* (1684) as a final attempt to impose her vision of commerce between the sexes at a time when that of the notorious generation was winning out (*Conversations* 1:368). This conversation contains reminders of the usage Scudéry had eliminated: for example, Sapho distinguishes "true" *galanterie* from "false"; at times, a "femme galante" is a coquette (*Artamène* 10:522, 398). Cuénin discusses this vocabulary's sixteenth-century origins and its evolution in the first half of the seventeenth century (*Roman et société* 1:329–44). See also Viala on the shifting usage of "galant" (170). See Stone on the parallel contemporary evolution of "gallantry" in English (329). The ultimate tribute to this vocabulary's pervasiveness is provided by Donneau de Visé: in *Le Mercure galant*'s first issue in 1672, he defines "livres de galanteries" as all those *not* concerning "the arts and the sciences" (8). Cuénin points out that, by the end of the precious decade, *galanterie* according to Scudéry's usage was mocked in the same terms as *préciosité* (*Roman et société* 1:340). By the turn of the century, the vocabulary of *galanterie* was used with extreme precaution. Thus, in her *Sapho, ou l'heureuse inconstance* (1695), La Roche-Guilhem notes that the women of Lesbos "appeared *galantes* without endangering their virtue" (6).

19. This final vision of "galanterie" was not dictated exclusively by women. After an initial period during which it was most prominently displayed by a woman (Villedieu, author of *Annales galantes* [1670] and *Galanteries grenadines* [1673]) and a male champion of female literary influence (Donneau de Visé, author of *Nouvelles galantes* [1669] and editor of *Le Mercure galant*), the vocabulary had a double life. On the one hand, it was used by male writers seeking to titillate—for instance, François de Chavigny de La Bretonnière, *La Galante Hermaphrodite* (1683). On the other hand, it was used by the women I am about to discuss, most often as part of their commentary on "galanterie" 's dangers for women. The adjective acquired a particular connotation when it was applied to women writers themselves; whereas male authors of "galant" works were never considered personally "galant," their female counterparts always were.

20. The better-known maxim about the way of this world is pronounced by Madame de Chartres in the same paragraph: "Love was always intermingled with *affaires* and *affaires* with love" (45). Norbert Elias defines "affaires" in a courtly context as "disputes over rank and favor" (271).

21. The Comtesse d'Aulnoy's two works on the courts of Spain, *Mémoires de la cour d'Espagne* (1690) and *Relation du voyage d'Espagne* (1691), are the most famous examples of such deception. Readers were so fooled by her display of erudition and local color that the works were long held to result from personal experience during actual travel in Spain. (Victor Hugo consulted d'Aulnoy's volumes as his principal historical documentation for *Ruy Blas*.) It was only in 1926 that her sources were exposed and the extensive research that had made her works so convincing was revealed. For the history of the debate on her works' status, see Percy Adams' *Travelers and Travel Liars* (97–99).

22. Durand Bédacier signed her novels "Madame D***." Her story of Charles VII's court features a Comte de Lafayette, a true disciple of Lafayette's Duc de Nemours, who recounts his amorous exploits in the first person (2:44–109). Such reminders of Lafayette's inaugural fiction are frequent in these historical novels. (See in particular the beginning and the end of Catherine Bernard's 1689 *Le Comte d'Amboise, histoire galante,* open homages to *La Princesse de Clèves.*)

23. The failure of peace negotiations and the damaging effects of war on the population left behind are recurrent motifs in the *histoires galantes*. Nicole Ferrier-Caverivière has studied the evolution of literary images of Louis XIV.

24. On the practice of what Nancy K. Miller calls "reading in pairs," juxtaposing a novel by a woman writer with a work by a male contemporary in order to establish male superiority, see her "Men's Reading, Women's Writing." See also Margaret Switten and Elissa Gelfand's outline for a gendered history of the rise of the French novel.

25. Especially when she is fleeing her husband, but virtually at all times, the heroine depicts herself as pursued by *galants*. It is impossible to judge if she gave her husband reason to be jealous. She portrays herself in these episodes as an innocent victim of circumstances, but at the same time she shows how those

circumstances were misinterpreted by a public eager to find her a scheming *femme galante;* that second demonstration inevitably gives those interested in this issue cause to doubt her innocence.

26. I provide an abridged version of the novel's plot. In particular, I omit the heroine's life after her husband's death, when she remarries. The novel ends with this husband's death and details of the elaborate funeral the ex-comtesse arranges for him. This final homage to the patriarchal order seems unimportant in view of the novel's flagrant challenge to the laws by which that order confines women. In the unabridged version, the novel's plot bears a strong resemblance to Anne Ferrand's *Histoire des amours de Cléante et de Bélise* (1689), another allegedly autobiographical work by a notorious woman. This resemblance would seem to cast doubt on the autobiographical nature of both works.

27. Note also Murat's use in this context of Scudéry's word for love's power to encourage women to reject arranged marriages, *inclination,* thereby perhaps indicating her realization that her precursor's fictional incitement to legal rebellion had been read as an encouragement of sexual licentiousness, *galanterie.*

28. Murat even includes an episode that indicates she was aware of the accusation of lesbianism that Adam contends is proved by the existence of certain letters describing her conduct. While her heroine is seeking a separation, a jealous wife of one of her suitors writes letters accusing her of an improper involvement with a lifelong female friend (155). The heroine clearly realizes that lesbianism would be the ne plus ultra of female sexual scandal for a critic like Adam.

29. "The division of capital that occurred if a wife legally withdrew her dowry spelled disaster for the household. Time and again, therefore, husbands who suspected wives of contemplating separation suits stalled such moves by initiating charges of adultery, fabricated or not" (Hanley 24). The 1670 treatise drawn up for Louis XIV by Abraham and Gomont specifies that only a man can bring charges for adultery, not a woman: "In punishment, the woman is locked up in a monastery and her dowry is given to her husband" (Lottin, "Vie et mort" 76). However, Murat's heroine was also correct in thinking that, without a legal separation, her situation would never be regularized, a fact confirmed by early treatises. (See in particular the *Encyclopédie* article "Séparation": "Since a wife is under her husband's rule, she cannot legally [*regulièrement*] leave him without the court's authorization.") Finally, Murat's heroine accurately evaluated the amount of physical abuse required for a separation: the trial proceedings of the eighteenth-century novelist Françoise de Graffigny that we will consider shortly prove that the husband had to be accused of a high level of violence.

30. For another reading of marriage history in early modern France, see Hanley's theory of "the Family-State compact" (8–9), whose reinforcement of the patriarchal order she documents. See also her analysis of the "counterfeit culture" fashioned by women to manipulate to their advantage the structures of this patriarchal compact (21).

31. I cannot explain why the husband's name is written "Des Noyers" throughout the memoirs he allegedly authored but "Du Noyer" in his wife's text and in

entries in biographical dictionaries. Such entries, that in the usually excellent *Dictionnaire de biographie française,* for example, in general simply repeat the husband's view of her life and discount the version found in her memoirs. The husband's response to have been added to the wife's text for the first time in the 1720 edition, the first edition published after her death.

32. This idea was suggested to me by the countermemoirs: the author of their preface claims that Anne Du Noyer wrote "with the assistance of a defrocked monk" (5:162). Pillorget discusses the repercussions of the revocation of the Edict of Nantes on marriage laws. His juxtaposition of two contemporary laws suggests that the threat of mixed marriage was then considered as serious as the threat of miscegenation: "In January 1685, the French are forbidden to marry abroad without royal authorization—a decision related to the impending revocation of the Edict of Nantes. Article 6 of the *code noir,* which was published in March of that year, forbade white men in the French colonies to marry black women, and naturally white women to marry black men" (40).

33. I have already described Du Noyer's *Lettres historiques et galantes* (1713) as a precursor of the *Lettres persanes* because of her presentation of philosophical and historical matters in a literary format. In that work she is particularly attentive to the full range of contemporary religious perspectives (Jansenist, Protestant, and so forth). For information on Du Noyer's journalism, see Gelbart.

34. Du Noyer consistently notes, to a degree virtually unheard-of in contemporary French prose and reminiscent of contemporary English fiction, financial and legal details. These memoirs are a rich source of the information sought by historians of private life: for example, the yearly rental cost for a house; details, including the price of bread, about the Paris famine of 1695 (6:332).

35. Editions of Du Noyer's collected works print the countermemoirs before the memoirs. In the 1739 edition they begin in the middle of volume 5, at the conclusion of the *Lettres historiques et galantes;* since they are not announced on the title page, the reader is surprised to come upon this acerbic attack so thoroughly integrated into the production of the author it seeks to undermine. When speaking of the account allegedly written by the husband, I give his name as it appears in the text, "Des Noyers."

36. "He should have made his wife perform her duty by beating her with sticks, with a bull's pizzle (*nerfs*), with belts" (5:161). Note that this imaginary beating of a woman writer is fantasized shortly after the publication of Boileau's symbolic torture and execution of Scudéry in the *Dialogue des héros de roman.*

37. Isabelle Vissière's anthology reproduces legal proceedings of eighteenth-century trials on women's issues such as domestic violence.

38. The *Mémoires de Mr. Des N**** is but one example of the male revenge novel that attempts to counter the pseudomemoirs of notorious women. This tradition, too, originates with Villedieu. Cuénin has established that the 1668 volume *Lettres et billets galants,* previously thought to be an anonymous early epistolary novel, is in fact a collection of the novelist's actual love letters, published against her wishes by their recipient, her former lover, Villedieu (see her edition of the text). Villedieu's

motives, other than financial, are not known, but the novelist's only evident crime against him was her unauthorized use of his name. The most interesting revenge fiction is the revised version of Anne Ferrand's *Histoire des amours de Cléante et de Bélise* (1689). Ferrand is the best-known notorious woman, but her biography deserves reexamination because of the complicated double standard that then governed marital conduct. The current view makes her biography into what could be seen as the pattern from which Murat's memoir-novel was cut. (See René Godenne's preface to her novel.) During the exile her husband obtained from Louis XIV by charging her with adultery, she wrote the *Histoire,* generally considered at least partly autobiographical (Coulet 1:213). The first two parts portray the heroine, Bélise, as a woman born too "tender" (*sensible;* Hazard believes that the novel foreshadows the eighteenth-century reign of *sensibilité,* 353), and so fatally attracted to love, but nevertheless faithful to the man to whom she is first drawn. On the contract, part 3, added for the second edition (1691), depicts Bélise as a "deceitful," "criminal" (70, 73) woman, who pretends to be an innocent victim but really manipulates all men, and betrays her lover in particular. To account for this reversal, Godenne accepts the thesis that the last part was written by Ferrand's former lover, Nicolas Le Tonnelier, Baron de Bréteuil, to tell his side of their story (v-vii). However, this thesis seems suspiciously facile when we consider the complicated trajectory of such scandal-and-defense fictions in Ferrand's wake. For still another fiction of the desiring woman's revolt against the family order, see Ferrand's *Lettres galantes de Madame *** (1691).

39. The passage in italics is a citation from the *Histoire de M. Cleveland* (1731), by the Abbé Prévost, along with Pierre Carlet de Marivaux one of the eighteenth-century male novelists most influenced by early eighteenth-century salon society, which was often presided over by women who had frequented the final assemblies of the seventeenth-century tradition.

40. Since Coulet's judgment suggests that the difference between Lafayette's treatment of marriage and Villedieu's can be explained by the class difference between them, I repeat that the majority of the notorious women were "ladies of the court."

41. Furetière's entry also reveals the extent to which separation was threatening because of its financial consequences. He quickly defines "separation" as "division, distribution." His first example—"For this inheritance the *separation* of property was made in several portions"—slants the reading of his second example, on women and separation. In reality, a wife could not hope to obtain a separation unless her husband's betrayals were scandalously public and had disastrous consequences: the Marquise de Sablé—La Rochefoucauld's literary collaborator, author of *Maximes* (1678), dropped from the literary history that glorifies his—was able to separate from her husband only after he had had twenty liaisons and had caused her financial "ruin" (Adam 1:273). Other legal separations were obtained by *husbands,* who used this means to put away wives declared adulterous.

42. This notion of "libertinage" provides the link between the demands of the

notorious women and the concept of "vagabondage" that Colette develops in *La Vagabonde.* "Libertinage" initially referred to the conduct of those vagabonds who chose to be locked out of city-states like Geneva at night in order to roam the countryside without constraint (see Marcel Raymond 159).

43. During a fifteen-year period in the middle of the eighteenth century, at least a half-dozen treatises about the nature of marriage and jurisdiction over its annulment appeared. The most important of these, along with Le Ridant's, are Paul-Charles Lorry's 1760 *Essai de dissertation, ou Recherches sur le mariage, en sa qualité de contrat et de sacrement* and the works of the century's most influential legal scholar, Robert-Joseph Pothier, *Traité du contrat de mariage* (1768) and *Traité de la puissance du mari* (1769). Pothier's works are always cited today from the numerous nineteenth-century editions of his collected works; according to M. Dupin, the editor of the 1824 collection, these treatises were written somewhat before their publication.

44. For a different view of this compromise over marriage between Church and State, see Basdevant (37–38): he sees the treatises of the 1690s simply in practical terms, as a temporary working solution developed to avert conflict.

45. This shift in focus from father to husband is further proof that, while contract theory continued to pronounce annulment its explicit object of consideration, it is increasingly obvious that the true center of ancien régime marital legislation is separation. See Ariès (356) and P. Petitot (195) on the gradual strengthening of the husband's power over his wife beginning in the late Middle Ages.

46. I am grateful to English Showalter, one of the editors of Graffigny's correspondence, for having generously loaned me copies of unpublished documents from her separation hearing. Her attempt to win a separation prompts Graffigny's coming to writing: her correspondence begins with her pleas to her father to save her from what she portrays as a disastrous marriage.

47. These letters are dated approximately "about 1716" and 1717 or 1718. The date of Graffigny's legal separation is not known, but it was finalized sometime before she became a widow in 1725. The only available record of the proceedings is not the official legal account but a copy that Graffigny had made for herself and kept with her papers.

48. Despite her victory, Graffigny was in litigation for years with her husband's family to settle his estate. Even when a woman obtained a separation, her legal powers were extremely limited. Pothier stresses, for example, that, after a separation, a wife could neither sell nor mortgage her *propres,* the property *she* had brought into the union, "without her [ex-]husband's consent" (*Traité de la puissance du mari sur la personne et les biens de la femme* 6:39); see also Diefendorf on the history of this concept (223).

49. Before extending this realization to women in general, Zilia makes it on a personal level: "I have neither gold, nor land, nor commerce (*industrie*), I am one of the citizens of this city. Heavens! In what class must I put myself?" (304). Graffigny displays one of the great semantic innovations in the French women's tradition in

order to suggest Zilia's new awareness: some four decades before "classe" allegedly began to be used in the modern sense of the term, Zilia chooses it for her self-(dis)placement, rather than the then standard term, "condition."

50. On the influence of Scudéry on Staël's fiction, see Helen Borowitz. *Ourika* and the last portrayal of female notoriety under the ancien régime, Staël's *Delphine*, are among the earliest novels in a Revolutionary setting. Both portray graphically the disintegration of French society, even the events of the Terror, as a backdrop to their narrative of Woman's confrontation with family and with marital law. Sand's *Indiana* (1832), a novel roughly contemporaneous with *Ourika*, serves as an endpoint for the ancien régime tradition of the novel of divorce at the same time as it inaugurates the modern phase of this tradition—novels written after the repeal of the law allowing divorce and therefore from the radically new perspective of those who had briefly known legal freedom, only to lose it.

51. Another novel by a woman writer with links to Staël and to Staël's mother, Suzanne Curchod Necker (on the nature of those links, see Madelyn Gutwirth's biography of Staël), Isabelle de Charrière's *Lettres de Lausanne* (1785), contains a vision of ancien régime politics related to those in *Lettres d'une Péruvienne* and *Delphine*. The novel's third letter is a critique of the malfunctioning of the French class system in the form of a utopian vision ("si j'étais roi," 32) of the nobility once again worthy of its privileges. And to tie up one last loose end: Staël's pro-divorce polemic in *Delphine* was also a contribution to the final round of the original divorce controversy. As soon as the Revolution legalized divorce, and during the period when her own daughter, Staël, was trying to take advantage of the new law to end her unhappy arranged marriage, Suzanne Necker began work on her *Réflexions sur le divorce* (1794). She argues that indissoluble unions are "the foundation of the *patrie*" (5), thereby recasting the absolute monarchy's argument in the vocabulary of the day. With a series of tableaux worthy of Diderot's *drame bourgeois* or Greuze's painting, she illustrates divorce's disastrous consequences for society— how can a mother teach her children filial piety if she has left her husband?, and so forth. Curchod Necker's volume is the sentimental counterpart to the definitive antidivorce tract, whose author lent his name to the 1816 law abolishing divorce. As his title indicates, Louis de Bonald's *Du Divorce considéré au XIXe siècle relativement à l'état public de société* (1801) reaffirms a by then classic position: "The fate of the family, of religion, and of the State depends in France and everywhere on the indissolubility of the conjugal bond" (5). He tries to terrify a country just emerging from the Revolution with the thought that divorce will bring about "the second revolution" (5, 193). Bonald confirms the success of the notorious women's efforts when he traces the impetus for a divorce law to the spread of a "modern" idea, that "a wife is her husband's equal" (xlix). Bonald echoes Porée's fin-de-siècle ravings about the novel as a contagious disease spread by women he offers wild descriptions (not confirmed by Dessertine's statistics) of divorce as a plague being carried through France by women (116–17).

52. Boileau, *Oeuvres* 926. Adam and Escal indicate evidence that the satire was begun in the early 1670s (926), which would make it a work, like the *Dialogue des*

héros de roman, which I will discuss in the next chapter, whose bile simmered for decades.

53. Boileau promotes this vision of *Clélie*'s dangerous attraction at a time when in the *Dialogue des héros de roman,* as I will indicate, he argues that the novel's influence was already over.

54. In a preface to this funeral oration, the future novel-killer explains that this is his first published work (3). Porée pronounced the oration at the Collège Royal de Louis le Grand, which suggests that he was already in favor at court. His subsequent diatribe against novels could, therefore, have been officially commissioned.

55. Jacquin seems to have shared Porée's obsession with contagious disease: his only other published work, *Lettres philosophiques et théologiques sur l'innoculation de la petite vérole* (1756), explains why innoculation should be forbidden on religious grounds—an indication that this critical repression of novelistic disease functioned, according to the logic basic to Foucault's *Histoire de la sexualité,* as an incitement to the spread of the literary plague.

56. On the notion of technologies of sexuality, see Foucault's *Histoire de la sexualité,* volume 1, in particular part 2, chapter 2.

57. Pons-Augustin Alletz, for example, who always makes a point of praising writers for their "virtue," includes none of the *femmes galantes* but d'Aulnoy. (He makes no mention of her notoriety.)

58. "Madame d'Aulnoy was born into one of the best families in Normandy. Married to the Baron d'Aulnoy, she wanted to get rid of him and, with her mother's help, she plotted a scheme destined to have him condemned to death for high treason. But he was acquitted, and the two women's accomplices were executed. The novelist retired to a convent" (5:315n.). The same note contains a similarly wild account of La Force's "adventures," also ending with her forced "retirement" to a convent. Adam offers no corroborating evidence in support of these charges, a gesture that would have been appreciated by those aware of the frequency with which wild accusations of this kind were made at the end of Louis XIV's reign.

5. The Origin of Novels: Gender, Class, and the Writing of French Literary History

1. For example, several of the early volumes devoted to women writers, which are listed at the end of the bibliography I include as an appendix to this study, were compiled by women.

2. See Anne-Marie Thiesse and Hélène Mathieu's history of an essential modern canonic barometer, the reading lists for the French doctoral exam, the *agrégation.* See also Daniel Milo's work on the formation of the French pedagogical canon. Sévigné has played almost as important a role as her best friend, Lafayette, in the canon of French literature; I will return in my concluding remarks to the terms of her inclusion. However, because she is associated with a genre, the letter, whose fortunes have fluctuated more than those of the novel, which has steadily risen to

pedagogical prominence, her pedagogical fate is less clearly evaluated than that of Lafayette.

3. May is especially concerned with the years between the publication of *Gil Blas* (1715) and that of *La Nouvelle Héloïse* (1761). The characterization of the novel's early history in France as a "rise" parallel to that ascribed by Watt to the English novel seems to be another instance of a phenomenon to which I have already alluded, the influence of English literary history on the writing of its French counterpart.

4. Unless otherwise noted, all references to Boileau will be to the Adam and Escal edition. I rely on Adam's notes for information on Boileau's management of his career. In his edition, Sylvain Menant contends that the first authorized edition dates from 1710 (2:8), whereas Adam and Escal give 1713 as its date (1090). I am concerned here not with the work's actual history but with Boileau's motivation in inventing, if not a false publication history, at least a false compositional history for the dialogue—it is impossible to believe that, the year before his death at age 75, Boileau was able, as he claimed, simply to "locate in his memory" a text he had stored there for some twenty-five years.

5. Adam traces Boileau's effort throughout his career to combat "female literary influence" and to encourage authors to "have higher ambitions." He considers Boileau's *L'Art poétique* "the perfect fulfillment of this doctrine" ("L'Ecole de 1650" 146).

6. Boileau's dialogue is allegedly also directed against another writer of romance fiction, La Calprenède, but he actually refers very little to this novelist's work, thereby confirming my belief that the novel was viewed as a female creation by early critics. The pretense of attacking a male novelist may be part of a strategy to deflect attention from the gender-specificity of his critical project. Furthermore, in the dialogue Boileau speaks of "Scudéry" and not "Mlle de Scudéry," as though he were parodying the individual he terms "the author" rather than "the sister of the author with the same name." In addition, his title refers only to "the heroes of novels," even though most of the dialogue is devoted to a parody of Scudéry's heroines, notably Sapho from *Artamène,* a character he clearly believed to be autobiographical.

7. On symbolic executions in seventeenth-century France, see the first chapter of Foucault's *Surveiller et punir.* According to the Girardian thesis of the leap into water as a form of death frequently chosen for the scapegoat, the fall into Lethe of Scudéry's phantom figures the elimination of all women writers from the canon dictated by the heroes of classicism. Boileau may well have encouraged others to fight the spread of novels: the first posthumous edition of Boileau's *Oeuvres complètes* (1713) was coedited by Valincour, author of the first attack on *La Princesse de Clèves.*

8. An article on *Clélie* in the *Bibliothèque universelle des romans* in 1777 suggests that Scudéry's readership initially fell off in the 1730s. It states that the 1731 edition was the first to sell poorly (7) and that, until that time, sales had still been excellent. This would mean that there would have been many editions of her novels in private

collections in the eighteenth century and would thus explain her continued reader-ship until many of these collections were dispersed at the time of the Revolution.

9. We should not allow Boileau's literary politics to obscure what could be the more or less officially dictated political explanation for his attack on Scudéry alone among contemporary novelists. In the early 1660s, just before the composition of the *Dialogue des héros de roman,* Scudéry and her circle, especially Pellisson and Huet, had been actively involved on the side of Nicolas Foucquet, the finance minister whose too ostentatious glory proved so irritating to the rising Sun King that he locked up the man and stamped out his memory. Boileau publicly took the opposite side, that of Colbert, in this affair.

10. On the basis of testimony in Huet's *Commentarius de rebus ad eum pertinen-tibus* (Amsterdam: H. du Sauzet, 1718, p. 255n.), Arnaldo Pizzorusso concludes that Huet composed his treatise on the novel in 1666. It is evident that Huet's treatise was designed to respond to Boileau's attack in the *Dialogue des héros de roman.* In 1666 Huet could only have known the dialogue from one of Boileau's recitals or from a manuscript in circulation at the same period. Huet's most recent editor, Fabienne Gégou, agrees with the date of 1666 (9). The treatise was written at the Malnoue convent, whose directress, Marie-Eléonore de Rohan, was herself a woman writer (see the bibliographic appendix). Also according to Gégou, it was written at the request of Segrais, who was then acting as Lafayette's literary assistant, because of her desire for additional information on the form she was exploring in *Zayde* (9). Gégou contends that there was an earlier edition of the work; however, all trace of it has disappeared.

11. It seems likely that the language of Huet's comparison was inspired by Boileau's punishment of Scudéry in the *Dialogue des héros de roman* on the grounds that she had used the clothing of ancient heroes to "ennoble" her bourgeois fops.

12. Huet's treatise is a creative attempt to find ancestors (especially in classical literature, but also in modern traditions, in particular Spanish literature) for the novels being produced in France in his day. Huet was thus forging the most effective response to Boileau's charge that the novel was a literary upstart, without classical precedent to guarantee its status.

13. Boileau's refusal to name Scudéry as author and his reference to the "sister of the author with the same name" in the preface he added in 1710 for his dialogue's publication, as well as his refusal to mention her by name in *L'Art poétique,* can be seen as attempts to countermand Huet's public attribution of authorial status. Huet explains that cases of "innocent disguise" are carried out for the "amusement" of a social circle. The relations that existed between Boileau and the participants in Huet's exchanges of authorial trappings are not always clear, but two factors at least are known: first, Boileau's hostility to women, intellectuals in particular, is well documented and is displayed with particular prominence in his tenth satire (1694); this work contains still another attack on *Clélie,* this time stressing the novel's threat to "honor" (67). Second, near the time of the publication of Huet's treatise and of *Zayde,* at least one member of their circle, Sévigné, had a personal reason to dislike Boileau. Two letters from early 1671 complain that he was using actresses to corrupt

her son, who was then "entre Ninon et [La Champmeslé], Despréaux sur le tout" (1:191, see also 1:206).

14. Niderst, "Traits, notes et remarques de Cideville" 825. Cideville, a friend of Voltaire, reports what he alleges was a remark made by Segrais to Fontenelle.

15. Huet and Boileau discuss precisely the same set of issues. In every case, what Huet praises as a source of the French novel's greatness is for Boileau a proof of the genre's degradation. For example, Huet praises the conversational style as the hallmark of the French novel, while Boileau mocks Scudéry's "vague and frivolous conversations," her "endless empty talk" (*verbiage*) (445). Huet ascribes the superiority he accords the French tradition to the ability to find a literary equivalent for a style developed in contemporary society, whereas Boileau's reference to "the *précieuse* affectation of [Scudéry's] language" (445) indicates a scornful dismissal of this transfer from society to literature. Arpad Steiner provides a convincing discussion of Scudéry's influence on Huet's treatise: "The essential points of Huet's thesis . . . only rework Scudéry's ideas" (183n.). In addition, letters from Scudéry to Huet from the period of the treatise's composition reveal her desire to respond to Boileau's accusations. See in particular her defense of her novels' moral content and their pedagogical value (Rathery and Boutron 294–95). It is possible, therefore, to imagine the treatise as a double case of transvested authority, with Huet as a "ghostwriter" (*fantôme?*) for Scudéry, just as Segrais represented Lafayette.

16. For another interpretation of this sartorial exchange, see Peggy Kamuf.

17. *L'Art poétique*'s final images evoke the Sun King's conquest of the Netherlands, right up to battles fought only days before it went to press.

18. This is also the lesson of *Zayde:* subtitled a "Spanish story," it takes advantage of that permeable frontier indicated by Huet to stage an elaborate drama of the assimilation, through cross-dressing rather than conquest, into the ranks of the civilized (the Greek) of different forms of "barbarian" genius.

19. Boileau's pronouncement that Scudéry's novels contain no knowledge of antiquity has been so generally accepted that, even today, it rarely occurs to specialists of seventeenth-century French literature that they could have been based on documentation.

20. While *L'Art poétique* is filled with proper names, Boileau continues his policy of not mentioning Scudéry by name.

21. The last true representative of this tradition was Louise Keralio Robert; in 1789 she still followed an orthodox Huetian line to present the novel's development.

22. May points out that the critics who continued to defend Huet's thesis in the eighteenth century, like their seventeenth-century precursors, had close associations with contemporary salons, especially the assemblies of Anne-Thérèse de Lambert (who began her career in the last of the great seventeenth-century salons) and Claudine Alexandrine Guérin, Marquise de Tencin (144). "Noblesse utérine," which stipulated that rank was transmitted through the mother, already by the seventeenth century was no more than a practice occasionally noted in provincial France, especially in Brittany. However, it was evoked long afterwards, in moments of utopian speculation, in critical texts such as Lenglet-Dufresnoy's and in literary

ones such as Isabelle de Charrière's 1785 novel, *Lettres écrites de Lausanne* (see the third letter, which begins "If I were king," 32–33).

23. Jacquin also makes it clear that he is taking Boileau's side against Huet. His first section is entitled "Sur l'origine des romans"; it contains numerous refutations of Huet's opinions (for example, 116–17).

24. Boileau's authority to dictate the shape of French literature was repeatedly challenged throughout the last decades of the seventeenth century, often in such a public forum as the Académie Française and by such notable authorities as Charles Perrault, Segrais, and Huet, who, in language that foreshadows Adam's twentieth-century attacks, denounced his ignorance of matters on which he continued to pronounce. (Adam retraces the history of this enmity in many notes in his edition of Boileau: especially 1003, n.20; 1043, n.257; 1072, n.2; 1095.) The first systematic attack on Boileau in print was by a woman, identified only as Mademoiselle Hooghart. Her *Lettres anti-poétiques* (1726) has a pro-Protestant bias and is therefore also an implicit attack on the policies of Louis XIV: "Let us grant the French language, which has been for so long a refugee in our provinces, . . . the freedom . . . that the English and the Dutch languages possess" (66–67).

25. In Jacquin's attack on the novel, his condemnation of the genre becomes most virulent in the section devoted to "the young reader," when he raises the question of the potential corruption of schoolchildren by women's writing (156–62).

26. There is an unusual degree of uncertainty about the origin of this usage. One suggestion, that Voltaire was the first to employ "classic" in this sense, has not been convincingly demonstrated. The *Robert Dictionary* states that this usage was introduced only at the turn of the nineteenth century by Staël, providing still another indication of her often proved sensitivity to semantic innovation.

27. Initially the anthology was generally accepted as d'Aulnoy's. Fontenelle's name was attached to it only later; even though no convincing reason for the change in attribution has ever been offered, it has gained wide acceptance (Reed 40, n.1). Today the compilation is referred to as the Recueil Barbin, after the publisher who signed its dedicatory preface. (He was the publisher of many early women writers.) For a different reading of some of the archival material that I discuss in the following section, see Viala.

28. A listing of the principal early anthologies of French writers is included at the end of the bibliographic appendix.

29. These volumes make it clear that ancien régime authors did not have to publish to obtain recognition of their talent. They also make it clear that literary accomplishments were not necessarily written: numbers of women were recognized as "illustrious," as "intellectuals" (*savantes*), because they spoke brilliantly in the semipublic forum provided by the salons. Witness Buffet's praise for a certain Mademoiselle Despinasse because "when she spoke in public she attracted all Parisian high society to hear her" (237). Such evidence explains my decision to include in the bibliography of women writers both women who never published their writing and those known only for their oral accomplishment.

30. When considering its lack of pedagogical efficiency, it is important to

remember that this genre (the compilation on women writers) was originally inspired, not by any form of literary criticism, but by the volumes, such as Le Moyne's *Les Femmes fortes,* that marked the end of the *Querelle des Femmes.* It is logical, therefore, that these literary compilations would share the defects of those tracts from the 1640s. (See, for example, Ronzeaud on Le Moyne's methodological "inefficiency" [16–17].) The link to the *femmes fortes* collections was maintained throughout the anthology tradition's existence. Thus, in his five-volume compendium published in 1773, Billardon de Sauvigny includes a section devoted to "femmes courageuses" between the sections devoted to Greek women poets and Latin women poets. Even his title, *Le Parnasse des dames,* is reminiscent of those given to both the volumes and the ceiling paintings of the mid-seventeenth century devoted to the praise of women.

31. Subsequently, Boileau's authority was implicitly evoked to authorize this silence with regard to the novel. In the index to La Harpe's 1797 *Lycée,* the only entry for Scudéry sends the reader to 5:479 and indicates what to expect there: "Boileau gave her novels the evaluation they deserve." However, the reader who turns to that page finds that, in fitting homage to Boileau's judgment, Scudéry's name has been suppressed. The entry on the early French novel declares only that, until Boileau's day, those novels had had many admirers, but that "no one dared contest his decree condemning them to nothingness" (*le néant*) (5:479).

32. There were occasional attempts to found a pedagogical canon for schoolgirls, the most celebrated of which was drawn up at St.-Cyr for and by the Marquise de Maintenon. These curricula always made frequent use of women's writing—witness the impressive role played by Scudéry in the curriculum at St.-Cyr. However, given the tiny percentage of girls among the schoolchildren of the day, it is obvious that these alternative pedagogical curricula are largely utopian artifacts. It was only at the turn of the twentieth century that the notion of a curriculum for schoolgirls acquired any true significance. Many of the issues relating to the pedagogical value of these women writers first raised during the ancien régime were brought up again at that time.

33. By all accounts, post-Revolutionary salons became increasingly more political than their pre-Revolutionary counterparts. See, for example, Beth Archer Brombert (80). In the course of their evolution, French salons turned away from the debates on literary and social issues that had originally brought them into existence, until they became almost exclusively concerned with political issues; at the same time, they became ever more dominated by male participation.

34. Richelieu naturally also remembered pedagogy's power to disseminate a unified vision of national culture: he ordered the creation at his visionary city, Richelieu (built in part with the stones from the Grande Mademoiselle's nearby ancestral estate, which he had had razed), of an academy in the sense of a school for boys, a clear model for the Collège des Quatre Nations that Mazarin established soon after Montpensier and her fellow Amazons had challenged the monarchy's rising absolutism. On Richelieu's academy and its program for a standardized, nationalistic education for young noblemen, see Nicolas Le Gras's 1642 project.

35. The preface to the volume published by Dufour states that it is a second edition, but I have found no trace of an earlier publication.

36. The volume's editor might well be the "Mademoiselle Charaux" listed as its publisher. If so, she might have been consciously renewing the onomastic practice of such ancien régime women writers as L'Héritier: the volume's title is *Quelques lettres de Sévigné,* and in its preface the editor consistently writes the author's name with no title. The rhetoric of the preface leaves no doubt that this should not be considered a post-Revolutionary, egalitarian gesture.

37. The Bibliothèque Nationale catalogue contains an impressive list of pedagogical editions of Sévigné's letters from this period.

38. In an attempt to understand why women played no role in the development of secondary education for women during the second half of the nineteenth century, Françoise Mayeur illustrates an argument that supports the theory I have developed in these pages. She explains that female "notoriety" guaranteed women's exclusion from the pedagogical scene in the conservative political climate of 1870–1880, when the glorification of the family was the primary objective (113). She shows that female notoriety was defined as the openness with which women had called for more liberal marriage laws (61–67). Mayeur's examples of politically threatening behavior by women are taken from the late eighteenth and early nineteenth centuries (she speaks of Sand in particular), but surely the period preceding the second law allowing divorce in 1884 provided additional examples of the type of conduct that the *précieuses* originated.

Works Cited

Unless otherwise noted, all books were published in Paris.

Abensour, Léon. *La Femme et le féminisme avant la Révolution.* F. Leroux, 1923.

Adam, Antoine. "L'École de 1650." *Revue d'histoire de la philosophie* (January-March 1942):23–52.

———— "L'École de 1660. Histoire ou légende?" *Revue d'histoire de la philosophie et d'histoire générale de la civilisation* (July-December 1939):215–50.

———— *Histoire de la littérature française au XVIIe siècle.* 5 vols. Del Duca, 1949–1956.

Adams, Percy. *Travelers and Travel Liars, 1660–1800.* Berkeley: University of California Press, 1962.

Allentuch, Harriet. "The Will to Refuse in the *Princesse de Clèves.*" *University of Toronto Quarterly* (1975), 44:185–98.

Alletz, Pons-Augustin. *L'Esprit des femmes célèbres du siècle de Louis XIV et de celui de Louis XV.* 2 vols. Pissot, 1768.

L'Amazone françoise au secours des Parisiens, ou l'Aproche des troupes de Madame la Duchesse de Chevreuse. Jean Henault, 1649.

Apostolidés, Jean-Marie. *Le Roi machine.* Editions de Minuit, 1981.

Aragonnès, Claude. *Madeleine de Scudéry, reine du tendre.* Colin, 1934.

Ariès, Philippe. *Centuries of Childhood: A Social History of Family Life.* Trans. Robert Baldick. New York: Random House, 1962.

Aronson, Nicole. *Mademoiselle de Scudéry.* Boston: Twayne, 1978.

———— "Mademoiselle de Scudéry et l'histoire romaine dans *Clélie.*" *Romanische Forschungen* (1976), 88:165–87.

———— *Mademoiselle de Scudéry, ou, Le Voyage au pays de Tendre.* Fayard, 1986.

Ascoli, Georges. "Essai sur l'histoire des idées féministes en France du XVIe siècle à la Révolution." *Revue de synthèse historique* (1906), 13:25–57, 161–84.

Auerbach, Nina. *Communities of Women.* Cambridge: Harvard University Press, 1978.

——— *Woman and the Demon: The Life of a Victorian Myth.* Cambridge: Harvard University Press, 1982.

Backer, Dorothy. *Precious Women.* New York: Basic Books, 1974.

Baillet, Adrien. *Jugements des savants.* 5 vols. 1725; repr. New York: Olms, 1971.

Balzac, Guez de. *Lettres.* Pierre Rocolet, 1636.

——— *Lettres familières de Monsieur de Balzac à Monsieur Chapelain.* Elzevier, 1661.

Barbier, Antoine-Alexandre. *Dictionnaire des ouvrages anonymes.* 4 vols. and suppl. P. Daffis, 1872–1879.

Basdevant, Jules. *Les Rapports de l'église et de l'état dans la législation du mariage du Concile de Trente au Code Civil.* Société du Recueil général des lois et des arrêts du Journal du Palais, 1900.

Bassy, Alain-Marie. "Supplément au voyage de Tendre." *Bulletin du bibliophile* (1982), 1:13–33.

Batteux, Abbé Charles. *Principes de la littérature.* 1746. Saillant, 1774.

Bayle, Pierre. *Dictionnaire historique et critique.* 1695–1697. Desoer, 1820.

——— *Dictionnaire historique et critique.* 1695–1697. Rotterdam: Michel Bohm, 1720.

——— *Nouvelles de la République de Lettres.* Octobre 1684. "Catalogue de livres nouveaux," vol. 8.

Beasley, Faith. *Revising Memory.* New Brunswick: Rutgers University Press, 1990.

Beaunier, André. *L'Amie de La Rochefoucauld.* Flammarion, 1927.

——— *La Jeunesse de Madame de Lafayette.* Flammarion, 1926.

Bédacier, Catherine Durand. *Histoire des amours de Grégoire VII, du Cardinal de Richelieu, de la princesse de Condé, et de la marquise d'Urfé.* Cologne: Pierre Le Jeune, 1700.

——— *Les Mémoires secrets de la cour de Charles VII, roi de France.* 2 vols. Pierre Ribou, 1700.

Beik, William. *Absolutism and Society in Seventeenth-Century France.* New York: Cambridge University Press, 1985.

Bellour, Raymond. "Un Jour, la castration." *L'Arc* (1978), 71:9–23.

Belmont, Lucien. "Documents inédits sur la société et la littérature précieuses: Extraits de la chronique du samedi publiés d'après le registre original de Pellisson (1652–57)." *Revue d'histoire littéraire de la France* (1902), 9:646–73.

Bibliothèque universelle des romans. Article on Scudéry's *Clélie* (October 2, 1777), pp. 1–214.

Billy, André. *L'Epoque 1900.* Tallandier, 1951.

Boileau, Nicolas. *Oeuvres.* Ed. by S. Menant. 2 vols. Garnier-Flammarion, 1969.

——— *Oeuvres complètes.* Ed. by A. Adam and F. Escal. Gallimard, 1966.

Bonald, Louis de. *Du Divorce considéré au XIXe siècle relativement à l'état domestique et à l'état public de société.* Le Clere, 1801.

Borowitz, Helen O. "The Unconfessed *Précieuse:* Madame de Staël's Debt to Mademoiselle de Scudéry." *Nineteenth-Century French Studies* (1982), pp. 32–59.

Bray, Bernard. *L'Art de la lettre amoureuse: Des manuels aux romans (1550–1700).* La Haye and Paris: Mouton, 1967.

Bray, Bernard, ed. *Romans d'amour par lettres*. Garnier-Flammarion, 1983.

Brody, Jules. "*La Princesse de Clèves* and the Myth of Courtly Love." *University of Toronto Quarterly* (1969), 38:105–35.

Brombert, Beth Archer. *Cristina, Portraits of a Princess*. New York: Knopf, 1977.

Brooks, Peter. *The Novel of Worldliness*. Princeton: Princeton University Press, 1969.

Brunetière, Ferdinand. "L'influence des femmes dans la littérature française." In *Questions de critique*, pp. 23–61. Calmann-Lévy, 1899.

Buffet, Marguerite. *Nouvelles observations sur la langue française, avec l'éloge des illustres savantes tant anciennes que modernes*. Jean Cusson, 1668.

Burney, Fanny. *Cecilia*. London: G. Bell, 1882.

Bussy, Roger de Rabutin, Comte de. *Correspondance*. Ed. Ludovic Lalanne. 6 vols. Charpentier, 1858.

Cahen, Albert. *Morceaux choisis des auteurs français*. Hachette, 1889 and 1892.

Calame, Alexandre. *Anne de La Roche-Guilhem*. Geneva: Droz, 1972.

Chamard, H., and G. Rudler. "Les Sources historiques de *La Princesse de Clèves*. *Revue du XVIe siècle* (1914), 2:92–131, 289–321; (1917–18), 5:1–20.

Charnes, J.-A., Abbé de. *Conversations sur la critique de "La Princesse de Clèves."* Eds. by François Weil et al. Tours: Publications de l'Université François Rabelais, 1973.

Charrière, Isabelle de. *Caliste; Lettres écrites de Lausanne*. Des Femmes, 1979.

Chartier, Roger, M.-M. Compère, and Dominique Julia. *L'Education en France au XVIIe et XVIIIe siècles*. PUF, 1964.

Chateaubriand, François August René, Vicomte de. *Mémoires d'outre-tombe*. Ed. by M. Levaillant. 2 vols. Flammarion, 1964.

Cioranescu, Alexandre. *Les Romans de la Princesse de Conti*. Ecole roumaine en France, 1935–1936.

Cixous, Hélène. *La Venue à l'écriture*. 10/18, 1977.

Colton, Judith. *The "Parnasse François": Titon du Tillet and the Origins of the Monument to Genius*. New Haven: Yale University Press, 1979.

Conrart, Valentin. *Mémoires*. Ed. by L. J. Monmerqué. Geneva: Slatkine Reprints, 1971.

Conti, Louise-Marguerite de Lorraine, Princesse de. *Advantures de la cour de Perse*. Signed by J. D. Baudouin. Pomeray, 1629.

———— *Histoire des amours du Grand Alcandre*. Veuve Guillemot, 1651.

———— *Roman royal*. Signed by Nicolas Piloust. Loyson, 1621.

Coulet, Henri. *Le Roman jusqu'à la révolution*. 2 vols. Colin, 1967.

Cousin, Victor. *La Société française au XVIIe siècle d'après "Le Grand Cyrus" de Mademoiselle de Scudéry*. 2 vols. Didier, 1858.

Covillard, Maurice. *Le Mariage considéré comme contrat civil dans l'histoire du droit français*. Arthur Rousseau, 1899.

Cuénin, Micheline. "Les Pièges de la critique d'attribution." Review of G. Moulig-neau's *Madame de Lafayette, romancière? Revue de Synthèse* (1981), pp. 159–68.

———— *Roman et société sous Louis XIV: Madame de Villedieu (Marie-Catherine Desjardins 1640–1683)*. 2 vols. Honoré Champion, 1979.

Cuénin, Micheline, and Chantal Morlet. "Châteaux et romans au XVIIe siècle." *XVIIe siècle* (1978), pp. 118–119.

Dacier, Anne Lefèvre. *Les Poésies d'Anacréon et de Sapho.* D. Thierry, 1681.

Davis, Natalie Zemon. "'Women's History' in Transition: The European Case." *Feminist Studies* (Spring 1976), 3(3/4):83–103.

DeJean, Joan. *Fictions of Sappho, 1546–1937.* Chicago: University of Chicago Press, 1989.

—— "La Fronde romanesque: De l'exploit à la fiction." In R. Duchêne and P. Ronzeaud, eds., *Actes du dix-huitième colloque du Centre Mériodional de Rencontres sur le XVIIe Siècle,* pp. 181–92. Marseilles, 1989.

—— "Lafayette's Ellipses: The Privileges of Anonymity." *Publications of the Modern Language Association* (October 1984), pp. 884–902.

—— "La Lettre amoureuse revue et corrigée: Un texte oublié de M. de Scudéry." *Revue d'histoire littéraire de la France* (January-February 1988), pp. 17–22.

—— "No Man's Land: The Novel's First Geography." *Yale French Studies* (1987), 73:175–89.

De Lauretis, Teresa. *Technologies of Gender: Essays on Theory, Film, and Fiction.* Bloomington: Indiana University Press, 1987.

Démoris, René. "Aux origines de l'histoire: Le croisement, au dix-septième siècle, du roman et de l'histoire." In P. Ronzeaud, ed., *Le Roman historique. Biblio 17* (1983), 15:23–41.

—— *Le Roman à la première personne.* Colin, 1975.

Desfontaines, Abbé Pierre-François Guyot. *L'Esprit de l'abbé Desfontaines.* 4 vols. London and Paris: Duchesne, 1757.

Dessertine, Dominique. *Divorcer à Lyon sous la Révolution et l'Empire.* Lyons: Presses Universitaires de Lyon, 1981.

Diderot, Denis. *Oeuvres esthétiques.* Ed. P. Vernière. Garnier, 1968.

Diefendorf, Barbara. *Paris City Councillors in the 16th Century.* Princeton: Princeton University Press, 1983.

Doody, Margaret. *Frances Burney: The Life in the Works.* New Brunswick: Rutgers University Press, 1988.

Drujon, Ferdinand. *Les Livres à clef: Étude de bibliographie.* 3 vols. Rouveyre, 1885–1888.

Duchêne, Roger. *Mme de Lafayette: La Romancière aux cent bras.* Fayard, 1988.

Du Noyer, Anne-Marguerite. *Oeuvres complètes.* 10 vols. London: Jean Nourse, 1739.

Du Plaisir. *Sentiments sur les lettres et sur l'histoire avec des scrupules sur le style.* 1683. Ed. Philippe Hourcade. Geneva: Droz, 1975.

Durcis, Jean-François. *Oeuvres.* Nepveu, 1827.

Du Ruau, Florentin. *Tableau historique des régences: Où se voit tout ce qui s'est passé pendant icelles depuis Clotilde jusques à Marie de Médicis—ensemble leurs droicts et prérogatives.* I. Mesnier, 1615.

Elias, Norbert. *Power and Civility.* Trans. E. Jephcott. New York: Pantheon, 1982.

Fagniez, Gustave Charles. *La Femme et la société française dans la première moitié du XVIIe siècle*. Librairie Universitaire J. Gambar, 1929.

Farnham, Fern. *Madame Dacier: Scholar and Humanist*. Monterey, Calif.: Angel Press, 1976.

Fayolle, Roger. *La Critique littéraire en France*. Colin, 1971.

Ferguson, Moira. *First Feminists: British Women Writers, 1578–1799*. Bloomington: Indiana University Press; Old Westbury, N.Y.: Feminist Press, 1985.

Ferrand, Anne Bellinzani. *Histoire des amours de Cléante et de Bélise*. 1689. Ed. René Godenne. Geneva: Slatkine Reprints, 1979.

———— *Lettres galantes de Madame ****. In *Lettres portugaises, Lettres d'une Péruvienne, et autres romans d'amour par lettres*. Ed. B. Bray. Garnier-Flammarion, 1983.

———— "Une Lettre de la présidente Ferrand sur Madame Dacier." *Revue d'histoire littéraire de la France* (1906), 13:326–31.

Ferrier-Caverivière, Nicole. *L'Image de Louis XIV dans la littérature française de 1660 à 1715*. Presses Universitaires de France, 1987.

Filteau, Claude. "Le Pays de Tendre: L'Enjeu d'une carte." *Littérature* (December 1979), 36:37–60.

Foucault, Michel. *Surveiller et punir: Naissance de la prison*. Gallimard, 1975.

———— *The Use of Pleasure*. Trans. Robert Hurley. New York: Pantheon, 1978. Vol. 2 of *The History of Sexuality*. 3 vols.

———— "What Is an Author?" In Paul Rabinow, ed., *The Foucault Reader*, pp. 101–20. New York: Pantheon, 1984.

Fukui, Yoshio. "Une théorie sur l'art épistolaire vers 1625." *Etudes de langue et littérature françaises* (1965), 1:42–48.

Gay, Sophie. *Salons célèbres*. Dumont, 1837.

Gelbart, Nina Rattner. *Feminism and Opposition Journalism in Old Regime France*. Berkeley: University of California Press, 1987.

Genette, Gérard. "Vraisemblance et motivation." In *Figures II*. Seuil, 1969.

Genlis, Stéphanie Félicité Ducrest de Saint-Aubin, Comtesse de. *De l'influence des femmes sur la littérature française*. Maradan, 1811.

Georges-Renard, Louise. "La Femme et l'éducation sous la minorité de Louis XIV." *Revue internationale de l'enseignement* (1905), 49:206–20.

Gerbais, Jean. *Traité du pouvoir de l'église et des princes sur les empêchements du mariage*. Maurice Villery, 1698.

Gilbert, Sandra M. "From *Patria* to *Matria*: Elizabeth Barrett Browning's Risorgimento." *Publications of the Modern Language Association* (March 1984), 99(2):194–211.

Gilbert, Sandra M., and Susan Gubar. *The Madwoman in the Attic*. New Haven: Yale University Press, 1979.

Girard, René. "Generative Violence and the Extinction of Social Order." *Salmagundi* (Spring-Summer 1984), 63–64:204–37.

Givry, Anne d'Anglure, Baron de. "Billet du brave Givry, qui fut tué au siège de

Laon en 1617." *Recueil de pièces curieuses et nouvelles* 2:432–33. La Haye: Moetjens, 1694–1696.

Godenne, René. *Les Romans de Mademoiselle de Scudéry.* Geneva: Droz, 1983.

Goldsmith, Elizabeth C. *Exclusive Conversations: The Art of Interaction in Seventeenth-Century France.* Philadelphia: University of Pennsylvania Press, 1988.

Goujet, Abbé Claude-Pierre. *Bibliothèque française; ou Histoire de la littérature française.* 18 vols. Mariette, 1740–1756.

Graffigny, Françoise de. *Correspondance.* Ed. by English Showalter et al. Oxford: Voltaire Foundation, Taylor Institution, 1985–.

——— *Lettres d'une Péruvienne.* In *Lettres portugaises, Lettres d'une Péruvienne, et autres romans d'amour par lettres.* Ed. B. Bray. Garnier-Flammarion, 1983.

Granet, François. *Réflexions sur les ouvrages de littérature.* 1737–1741. 12 vols. Geneva: Slatkine Reprints, 1968.

Greenberg, Mitchell. *Corneille, Classicism, and the Ruses of Symmetry.* Cambridge: Cambridge University Press, 1986.

Grenaille, François de. *Nouveau Recueil de lettres des dames tant anciennes que modernes.* 2 vols. Toussainct Quinet, 1642.

Gubar, Susan. "*She* in *Herland:* Feminism as Fantasy." In G. Slusser, E. Rabkin, and R. Scholes, eds., *Coordinates: Placing Science Fiction and Fantasy,* pp. 139–49. Carbondale: Southern Illinois University Press, 1983.

Gutwirth, Madelyn. *Madame de Staël, Novelist.* Urbana: University of Illinois Press, 1978.

Hanley, Sarah. "Engendering the State: Family Formation and State Building in Early Modern France." *French Historical Studies* (Spring 1989), 16(1):4–27.

Harth, Erica. "Classical Discourse: Gender and Objectivity." *Continuum* (1989), 1:152–73.

——— *Ideology and Culture in Seventeenth-Century France.* Ithaca: Cornell University Press, 1983.

Haussonville, Gabriel de Cléron, Vicomte de. *Le Salon de Madame Necker.* 2 vols. Calmann-Lévy, 1882.

Hautecoeur, Louis. *L'Histoire des châteaux du Louvre et des Tuileries.* Paris and Brussels: A. Morancé, 1924.

Haviland, Thomas. *The "Roman de longue haleine" on English Soil.* Philadelphia, 1931.

Hazard, Paul. *La Crise de la conscience européenne.* Fayard, 1961.

Hepp, Noémi. "La Notion d'héroïne." In *Onze études sur la femme dans la littérature française du XVIIe siècle.* Ed. W. Leiner. J.-M. Place, 1978.

Herrmann, Claudine. *Les Voleuses de langue.* Des Femmes, 1976.

Hooghart, Mademoiselle. *Lettres anti-poétiques.* Amsterdam: Jean Pauli, 1726.

Huet, Pierre-Daniel. *Memoirs from the Life of Peter Daniel Huet.* Trans. from the Latin by John Aikin. 2 vols. London: Longman, Hurst, and Rees, 1805.

——— *Traité de l'origine des romans.* Claude Barbin, 1670. Published in the first volume of the original edition of Lafayette's *Zayde.*

———— *Traité de l'origine des romans.* Ed. F. Gégou. Nizet, 1971.

L'Illustre conquérante ou la généreuse constance de Madame de Chevreuse. N. Charles, 1649.

Irigaray, Luce. "Ce sexe qui n'en est pas un." Trans. Claudia Reeder. In I. de Courtivron and E. Marks, eds., *New French Feminisms*, pp. 99–110. Amherst: University of Massachusetts Press, 1980.

[Jacquin, Abbé Armand-Pierre.] *Entretiens sur les romans, ouvrage moral et critique.* Duchesne, 1755.

Jacquinet, Paul. *Les Femmes de France, poètes et prosateurs. Morceaux choisis avec une introduction.* Belin, 1886.

Jardine, Alice. "Death Sentences: Writing Couples and Ideology." In Susan Rubin Suleiman, ed., *The Female Body in Western Culture*, pp. 84–98. Cambridge: Harvard University Press, 1986.

Joly, Abbé Philippe-Louis. *Remarques sur le dictionnaire de Bayle.* H.-L. Guerin, 1748.

Jouhaud, Christian. *Mazarinades: La Fronde des mots.* Aubier, 1985.

———— "Retour aux mazarinades: Action politique et production pamphlétaire pendant la Fronde." In R. Duchêne and P. Ronzeaud, eds., *Actes du dix-huitième colloque du Centre Mériodional de Rencontres sur le XVIIe Siècle*, 297–307. Marseilles, 1989.

Kamuf, Peggy. "The Gift of Clothes: Of Madame de Lafayette and the Origin of Novels." *Novel* (1984), 17(3):233–45.

Kany, Charles. *The Beginnings of the Epistolary Novel in France, Italy, and Spain. University of California Publications in Modern Philology* (1937), 21:1–158.

Kelly, Joan. *Women, History, and Theory.* Chicago: University of Chicago Press, 1984.

Keohane, Nannerl. *Philosophy and the State in France.* Princeton: Princeton University Press, 1980.

Keralio (Robert), Louise-Félicité Guinemet de. *Collection des meilleurs ouvrages français composés par des femmes.* 14 vols. Lagrange, 1786–1789.

Koestenbaum, Wayne. *Double Talk: The Erotics of Male Literary Collaboration.* New York: Routledge and Kegan Paul, 1989.

Kotin Mortimer, Armine. "La Clôture féminine des *Jeux d'Esprit.*" In "Women's Writing in Seventeenth-Century France." *L'Esprit créateur* (Summer 1983), 23(2):107–16.

Laclos, Pierre Ambroise François Choderlos de. *Oeuvres complètes.* Ed. L. Versini. Gallimard, 1979.

Lafayette, Marie-Madeleine Pioche de La Vergne, Comtesse de. *Correspondance.* Ed. André Beaunier. 2 vols. Gallimard, 1942.

———— *La Princesse de Clèves.* Ed. A. Adam. Garnier-Flammarion, 1966.

———— *La Princesse de Montpensier.* Ed. M. Cuénin. Geneva: Droz, 1979.

Lafond, J. D. "Les Techniques du portrait dans le *Recueil des portraits et éloges* de 1659." *Cahiers de l'Association Internationale des Etudes françaises* (1966), 18:139–48.

La Force, Charlotte-Rose Caumont de. *Les Jeux d'Esprit ou la Promenade de la Princesse de Conti à Eu.* Ed. M. de La Grange. Aubry, 1862.

La Forge, Jean de. *Le Cercle des femmes sçavantes.* Loyson, 1663.

La Guette, Catherine Meurdrac. *Mémoires de Madame de La Guette (1613–1676).* 1681. Ed. M. Cuénin. Mercure de France, 1982.

La Harpe, Jean-François de. *Lycée, ou Cours de littérature ancienne et moderne.* 1797–1803. 16 vols. Lefèvre, 1816.

La Mesnardière, Jules de. *Poétique.* Sommaville, 1640.

[La Porte, Joseph de.] *Esprit de Mademoiselle de Scudéry.* Amsterdam: Vincent, 1766.

———— *Histoire littéraire des femmes françaises, ou lettres historiques et critiques.* 5 vols. Lacombe, 1769.

Larnac, Jean. *Histoire de la littérature féminine en France.* Editions Kra, 1929.

La Rochefoucauld, François, Duc de. *Maximes, suivies des Réflexions diverses.* Garnier, 1967.

Lathuillère, Roger. *La Préciosité: Etude historique et linguistique.* Geneva: Droz, 1966.

Laugaa, Maurice. *Lectures de Madame de Lafayette.* Colin, 1971.

Launoy, Jean de. *Regia in matrimonia potestas.* 1674. Barrillot and Bosquet, 1731.

Le Gras, Nicolas. *L'Académie royale de Richelieu.* 1642.

Le Moyne, Pierre. *La Gallerie des femmes fortes.* A. de Sommaville, 1647.

[Lenglet-Dufresnoy, Nicolas.] Signed "Gordon du Percel." *De l'usage des romans.* 2 vols. Amsterdam: Veuve Poilras, 1734.

Lepointe, Gabriel. *Droit romain et ancien droit français: Régimes matrimoniaux, libéralités, successions.* Editions Montchrestien, 1958.

Lever, Maurice. *La Fiction narrative en prose au XVIIe siècle.* CNRS, 1976.

L'Héritier, Marie-Jeanne. *Le Triomphe de Madame Deshouilieres, Recue dixième muse au Parnasse.* N.P. 1694.

———— *L'Apothéose de Mademoiselle de Scudéry.* J. Moreau, 1702.

Lorris, Pierre-Georges. *La Fronde.* A. Michel, 1961.

Lorry, Paul-Charles. *Essai de dissertation, ou Recherches sur le mariage, en sa qualité de contrat et de sacrement.* G. Martin, 1760.

Lottin, Alain. "Vie et mort du couple: Difficultés conjugales et divorces dans le nord de la France aux XVIIe et XVIIIe siècles." *Dix-septième siècle* (1974), 102–3:59–78.

Lottin, Alain, and J. R. Machuelle. *La Désunion du couple.* Lille: Editions Universitaires de Lille III, 1975.

Lougee, Carolyn. *Le Paradis des femmes: Women, Salons, and Social Stratification in Seventeenth-Century France.* Princeton: Princeton University Press, 1976.

Lyons, John. "The Dead Center: Desire and Mediation in Lafayette's *Zayde.*" *L'Esprit créateur* (Summer 1983), 23(2):58–69.

———— "Narrative Interpretation and Paradox: *La Princesse de Clèves.*" *Romanic Review* (November 1981), pp. 383–400.

McKeon, Michael. *The Origins of the English Novel 1600–1740.* Baltimore: Johns Hopkins University Press, 1987.

Maclean, Ian. *Woman Triumphant: Feminism in French Literature, 1610–52.* Oxford: Clarendon Press, 1977.

Magendie, Maurice. *Le Roman français au XVIIe siècle de "l'Astrée" au "Grand Cyrus."* Droz, 1932.

Malandain, Pierre. "Ecriture de l'histoire dans *La Princesse de Clèves*." *Littérature* (December 1979), pp. 19–36.

Marin, Louis. *La Critique du discours.* Editions de Minuit, 1975.

—— *Portrait of the King.* Trans. M. Houle. Minneapolis: University of Minnesota Press, 1988.

Marrou, Henri. *Histoire de l'éducation dans l'antiquité.* Seuil, 1948.

May, Georges. *Le Dilemme du roman au XVIIIe siècle.* Paris and New Haven: Presses Universitaires de France and Yale University Press, 1963.

Mayeur, Françoise. *L'Enseignement secondaire des jeunes filles sous la troisième République.* Presses de la Fondation Nationale des Sciences Politiques, 1977.

Ménage, Giles. *Ménagiana.* Pierre Delaune, 1694.

Michelet, Jules. *Richelieu et la Fronde.* Vol. 14 of *Histoire de France.* Calmann-Lévy, 1899.

Miller, Nancy K. "Emphasis Added: Plots and Plausibilities in Women's Fiction." *Publications of the Modern Language Association* (1981), 96:36–48.

—— "Mémoires, oublis, et les pouvoirs du genre." *Cahiers du grif.* Forthcoming.

—— *Subject to Change: Reading Feminist Writing.* New York: Columbia University Press, 1988.

—— "Men's Reading, Women's Writing: Gender and the Rise of the Novel." In J. DeJean and N. K. Miller, eds., *The Politics of Tradition. Yale French Studies* (1988), 75:40–55.

—— "The Text's Heroine: A Feminist Critic and Her Fictions." *Diacritics* (1982), 12:48–53.

Milo, Daniel. "Les Classiques scolaires." In Pierre Nora, ed., *Les Lieux de la Mémoire II: La Nation,* pp. 517–62. Gallimard, 1988.

Moers, Ellen. *Literary Women.* New York: Oxford University Press, 1985.

Mongrédien, Georges. "Bibliographie des oeuvres de Georges et Madeleine de Scudéry." *Revue d'histoire littéraire de la France* (1933), 40:225–36, 413–25, 538–65.

—— *Madeleine de Scudéry et son salon.* Tallendier, 1946.

Montpensier, Anne Marie Louise d'Orléans, Duchesse de. *Galerie des portraits et éloges.* Ed. by E. Barthélemy. Didier, 1860.

—— *Lettres.* Collin, 1806.

—— *Mémoires.* In C. Petitot, ed. *Collection des mémoires relatifs à l'histoire de France.* Foucault, 1819–1829.

Montpensier, Anne Louise d'Orléans, Duchesse de, and Jean Regnauld de Segrais. *Divers portraits.* N.p., 1659.

—— *Recueil des portraits et éloges en vers et en prose.* Charles de Sercy and Barbin, 1659.

Moote, A. Lloyd. *The Revolt of the Judges: The Parlement of Paris and the Fronde.* Princeton: Princeton University Press, 1971.

Motteville, Françoise Bertaut, Dame de. *Mémoires.* In C. Petitot, ed., *Collection des mémoires relatifs à l'histoire de France.* Foucault, 1819–1829.

Mouligneau, Geneviève. *Madame de Lafayette, romancière?* Brussels: Université de Bruxelles, 1980.

Mousnier, Roland. "Recherches sur les soulèvements populaires en France avant la Fronde." *Revue d'histoire moderne et contemporaine* (1958), 5:81–113.

Murat, Henriette de Castelnau, Comtesse de. *Mémoires de Madame la comtesse de M***.* 1697; 1740.

Necker, Jacques. *Oeuvres complètes.* 1821. Darmstadt: Scientia Verlag Aalen, 1971.

Necker, Suzanne Curchod. *Réflexions sur le divorce.* Lausanne and Paris: Aubin and Desenne, 1794.

Niderst, Alain. "Traits, notes, et remarques de Cideville." *Revue d'histoire littéraire de la France* (1969), 69:821–27.

Nies, Fritz. "Un genre féminin?" *Revue d'histoire littéraire de la France* (1978), 78:994–1003.

Ortigue, J. d.' "La Bruyère à l'Académie Française donnant sa voix à Madame Dacier." *Bulletin du Bibliophile* (1862), pp. 1193–96.

Pâris, Paulin. "Notes sur deux romans anecdotiques: *Les Amours d'Alcandre* et les *Advantures de la Cour de Perse.*" *Bulletin du Bibliophile* (1852), pp. 811–27.

Pariset, F. G. "Héroïsme et création artistique." In *Héroïsme et création littéraire sous les règnes d'Henri IV et de Louis XIII.* Klincksieck, 1974.

Payer, Alice de. *Le Féminisme au temps de la Fronde.* Editions Fast, 1922.

Pelckmans, Paul. *Le Sacre du père: Fictions des Lumières et Historicité d'Oedipe 1699–1775.* Amsterdam: Rodopi, 1983.

Pelous, Jean Michel. *Amour précieux, amour galant.* Klincksieck, 1980.

Petot, Pierre. "La Famille en France sous l'Ancien Régime." In *La Sociologie comparée de la famille contemporaine.* Colloques du CNRS, 1955.

Phillips, A. Roderick. *Putting Asunder: A History of Divorce in Western Society.* New York: Cambridge University Press, 1988.

Pillorget, René. *La Tige et le rameau: Familles anglaise et française XVIe-XVIIIe siècle.* Calmann-Lévy, 1979.

Pingaud, Bernard. *Madame de Lafayette par elle-même.* Editions du Seuil, 1959.

Pizzorusso, Arnaldo. "La Concezione dell'arte narrativa nella seconda metà del seicento francese." *Studi mediolatini e volgari* (1955), 3:114–25.

—— *La Poetica del Romanzo in Francia (1660–1685).* Rome: Edizioni Salvatore Sciascia, 1962.

Plusquellec, Catherine. "Qui était Catherine Bernard?" *Revue d'histoire littéraire de la France* (July-August 1985), 85:667–69.

Porchnev, Boris. *Les Soulèvements populaires en France de 1623 à 1648.* S.E.V.P.E.N., 1963.

Porée, Father Charles. *De Libris qui vulgo dicuntur romanenses, oratio.* Bordelet, 1736.

―――― *Oraison funèbre de Louis le Grand.* Joseph Monge, 1726.

Portemer, Jean. "Le Statut de la femme en France depuis la réformation des coutumes jusqu'à la rédaction du code civil." *Recueils de la Société Jean Bodin* (1962), 12:447–97.

―――― "La Femme dans la législation royale des deux derniers siècles de l'ancien régime." In *Etudes d'histoire du droit privé offertes à Pierre Petot,* pp. 441–54. Editions Montchrestien, 1959.

Pothier, Robert-Joseph. *Oeuvres.* Ed. M. Dupin. 11 vols. Bechet ainé, 1824–1825.

Prévost, Abbé Antoine-François. *Le Pour et le contre.* Vol. 1, no. 5. 1735.

Pure, Abbé Michel de. *La Prétieuse ou le mystère des ruelles.* 1656. Ed. E. Magne. 2 vols. Droz, 1938–1939.

Quilligan, Maureen. *The Allegory of Female Authority: Christine de Pizan's "Cité des Dames."* Ithaca: Cornell University Press, 1991.

Rance, A. J. *L'Académie d'Arles au XVIIe siècle.* 3 vols. Librairie de la société bibliographique, 1886–1890.

Rathery and Boutron. *Mademoiselle de Scudéry: Sa vie et sa correspondance.* 1873. Geneva: Slatkine Reprints, 1971.

Raymond, Marcel. *Jean-Jacques Rousseau: La Quête de soi et la rêverie.* Corti, 1962.

Reed, Gervais. *Claude Barbin.* Geneva: Droz, 1974.

Reiss, Timothy J. "Corneille and Cornelia: Reason, Violence, and the Cultural Status of the Feminine." *Renaissance Drama* (February 1988), pp. 3–53.

―――― *The Meaning of Literature.* Ithaca: Cornell University Press. Forthcoming.

Retz, Paul de Gondi, Cardinal de. *Mémoires.* Gallimard, 1956.

Richelet, Pierre. *Les Plus Belles Lettres françaises sur toutes sortes de sujets, tirées des meilleurs auteurs, avec des notes.* La Haye: M. Uytwerf and L. Van Dole, 1699.

Richelieu, Armand Jean du Plessis, Duc de. *Testament politique.* Ed. Louis André. Robert Laffont, 1947.

Richetti, John. *Popular Fiction Before Richardson: Narrative Patterns 1700–1739.* Oxford: Clarendon Press, 1969.

Rilliet-Huber, Catherine. "Notes sur l'enfance de Madame de Staël." *Occident et cahiers staëliens* (June 1933, March 1934), 2(1–2):41–47, 140–46.

Robertson, D. Maclaren. *A History of the French Academy.* London: T. F. Unwin, 1910.

Romanowski, Sylvie. "Un roman féministe du XVIIe siècle: Héroïsme et langage dans *La Prétieuse* de l'abbé de Pure." *Kentucky Romance Quarterly* (Fall 1977), 24(4):461–71.

Ronzeaud, Pierre. "La Femme au pouvoir ou le monde à l'envers." *Dix-Septième Siècle* (1975), 8:9–33.

Rosbottom, Ronald. Review of J. Todd's *Women's Friendship in Literature.* *Comparative Literature* (Spring 1984), 36(2):183–86.

Rousseau, Jean-Jacques. *Oeuvres complètes.* Eds. B. Gagnebin and M. Raymond. 4 vols. Gallimard, 1959–1969.

Rousset, Jean. *Forme et signification: Essais sur les structures littéraires de Corneille à Claudel.* Corti, 1962.

——— *Leurs Yeux se recontrèrent: La Scène de la première vue dans le roman.* Corti, 1981.

——— *Narcisse romancier: Essai sur la première personne dans le roman.* Corti, 1973.

Rues, François des. *Les Fleurs du bien diré.* Lyons: Roche, 1595.

——— *Les Marguerites françaises.* Rouen: Reinsart, 1612.

Sade, Donatien-Alphonse-François, Comte de. "Idée sur les romans." In *Oeuvres complètes,* vol. 10. 16 vols. Cercle du livre précieux, 1964.

Sainte-Beuve, C. A. *Portraits de femmes.* Garnier, 1845.

Saint-Gabriel, Sieur de. *Le Mérite des dames.* Aux despenz de l'auteur, 1657.

Les Salons littéraires au XVIIe siècle, catalogue. Bibliothèque Nationale, 1968.

Salvan de Saliez, Madame de. *Lettres de Mesdames de Scudéry, de Salvan de Saliez, et de Mademoiselle Descartes.* Ed. L. Collin. L. Collin, 1806.

——— "Lettres sur son projet pour une nouvelle secte de philosophes en faveur des dames." In de Vertron, *La Nouvelle Pandore,* 2:111–19. 126–32. 2 vols. Veuve Mazuel, 1698.

Sand, George. *Oeuvres autobiographiques.* Ed. G. Lubin. 2 vols. Gallimard, 1970.

Sarasin, Jean-François. *Les Oeuvres de M. de Sarasin.* Preface by Paul Pellisson. A. Courbé, 1656.

Schor, Naomi. *Reading in Detail: Aesthetics and the Feminine.* New York and London: Methuen, 1987.

——— "Unwriting *Lamiel.*" In *Breaking the Chain: Women, Theory, and French Realist Fiction.* New York: Columbia University Press, 1985.

Scudéry, Madeleine de. *Artamène ou le Grand Cyrus.* 10 vols. Augustin Courbé, 1649–1653.

——— *Clélie, Histoire romaine.* 10 vols. Augustin Courbé, 1654– 1660.

——— *Les Femmes illustres ou les Harangues héroïques.* Antoine de Sommaville and Augustin Courbé, 1642.

——— *Ibrahim, ou l'Illustre Bassa.* 5 vols. Antoine de Sommaville, 1641.

——— *Lettres amoureuses de divers auteurs de ce temps.* Augustin Courbé, 1641.

Segrais, Jean Regnauld de. *Mémoires anecdotes de Monsieur de Segrais.* In *Oeuvres,* vol. 2. 2 vols. Durand, 1755.

——— *Nouvelles françoises.* 2 vols. La Haye: Pierre Paupie, 1741.

——— *Segraisiana.* 2 vols. Amsterdam: Changuion, 1723.

[Senecterre, Mademoiselle de.] *Orasie.* Sommaville, 1646.

Senter, E. P. Mayberry. "Les Cartes allégoriques romanesques du XVIIe siècle: Aperçu des gravures créées autour de l'apparition de la 'Carte de Tendre' de la *Clélie* en 1654." *Gazette des Beaux-Arts* (1977), 89:133–44.

Sévigné, Marie de Rabutin-Chantal, Marquise de. *Correspondance.* Ed. Roger Duchêne. 3 vols. Gallimard, 1972.

——— *Lettres choisies de mesdames de Sévigné et de Maintenon.* Dufour, 1803.

——— *Quelques lettres de Sévigné.* 3 vols. Mademoiselle Charaux, 1803.

Showalter, English. *The Evolution of the French Novel (1641–1782).* Princeton: Princeton University Press, 1972.

283

WORKS CITED

Somaize, Sieur de. *Le Grand Dictionnaire des prétieuses.* Ed. Charles Livet. 2 vols. Jannet, 1861.

Spencer, Jane. *The Rise of the Woman Novelist: From Aphra Behn to Jane Austen.* London: Basil Blackwell, 1986.

Spender, Dale. *Mothers of the Novel: 100 Good Women Authors before Jane Austen.* London; New York: Pandora, 1986.

Staël, Germaine Necker, Baronne de. *De la littérature.* Ed. P. Van Tieghem. 2 vols. Geneva: Droz, 1959.

——— *Journal de jeunesse. Occident et cahiers staëliens* (June 1930, July 1931, October 1932), 1(1–4):75–81, 157–60, 235–42.

——— *Oeuvres complètes.* 17 vols. Strasbourg and London: Treuttel and Würtz, 1820–1821.

Stanton, Domna. "The Fiction of Préciosité and the Fear of Women." *Yale French Studies* (1981), 62:107–34.

——— "The Ideal of 'repos' in 17th-Century French Literature." *L'Esprit créateur* (1975), 15:79–104.

Steiner, Arpad. "Les Idées esthétiques de Mademoiselle de Scudéry." *Romanic Review* (1925), 16:171–90.

Stock, Brian. *The Implications of Literacy.* Princeton: Princeton University Press, 1983.

Stone, Lawrence. *The Family, Sex, and Marriage in England, 1500–1800.* New York: Harper & Row, 1977.

Storer, Mary Elizabeth. "Information Furnished by the *Mercure galant* on the French Provincial Academies in the Seventeenth Century." *Publications of the Modern Language Association* (June 1935), 50(2):444–68.

Switten, Margaret, and Elissa Gelfand. "Gender and the Rise of the Novel." *The French Review* (February 1988), 61(3):443–53.

Tallemant des Réaux, Gédéon. *Historiettes.* Ed. Antoine Adam. 2 vols. Gallimard, 1961.

Tanner, Tony. *Adultery in the Novel: Contract and Transgression.* Baltimore: Johns Hopkins University Press, 1979.

Tastu, Amable. *Prose.* Brussels, 1836.

[Tenain, Madame de.] *Histoire du comte de Clare, nouvelle galante.* Cologne: Jean Lalemand, 1696.

Tencin, Claudine-Alexandrine Guérin, Marquise de. *Mémoires du Comte de Comminge.* Editions Desjonquères, 1985.

Thiesse, Anne-Marie, and Hélène Mathieu. "Déclin de l'âge classique et naissance des classiques." *Littérature* (May 1981), 42:89–108. English trans., "The Decline of the Classical Age and the Birth of the Classics." *Yale French Studies* (1988), 75:208–28.

Thuillier, J., and J. Foucart. *Rubens's Life of Marie de' Medici.* Milan: Rizzoli, 1967.

Traer, James F. *Marriage and the Family in 18th-Century France.* Ithaca and London: Cornell University Press, 1980.

284

WORKS CITED

Le Triomphe de l'indifférence. Ed. André Beaunier. *Mesures* (1937), pp. 155–206.

Urfé, Honoré d.' *Astrée.* Ed. Jean Lafond. Gallimard, 1984.

Valincour, J. B. de. *Lettres à Madame la marquise* * * * *sur le sujet de "La Princesse de Clèves."* 1678. Eds. J. Chupeau et al. Tours: Université François Rabelais, 1972.

Vernon, Jean-Marie de. *L'Amazone chrestienne, ou les avantures de Madame Saint-Balmon.* Gaspar Méturas, 1678.

Versini, Laurent. *Le Roman épistolaire.* PUF, 1979.

Vertron, Claude Charles Guionet, Seigneur de. *La Nouvelle Pandore ou les femmes illustres du siècle de Louis le Grand.* 2 vols. Veuve Mezuel, 1698.

Viala, Alain. *La Naissance de l'écrivain.* Editions de Minuit, 1985.

Viennot, Eliane. "Le Rôle politique des femmes de la famille de Lorraine durant la Ligue, 1587–1598, d'après les témoignages contemporains." *Cahiers du grif.* Forthcoming.

Villedieu. Desjardins, Marie-Catherine, known as Madame de Villedieu. *Les Désordres de l'amour.* Ed. M. Cuénin. Geneva: Droz, 1970.

—— *Lettres et billets galants.* 1668. Ed. Micheline Cuénin. La Société d'Etude du XVIIe Siècle, 1975.

—— *Mémoires de la vie de Henriette-Sylvie de Molière.* Ed. M. Cuénin. Tours: Publications de l'Université François Rabelais, 1977.

Visé, Donneau de. Obituary of Madame de Villedieu. *Le Mercure galant* (November 1683), pp. 267–69.

Vissière, Isabelle, ed. *Procès de femmes au temps des philosophes.* Des Femmes, 1985.

Watt, Ian. *The Rise of the Novel.* Berkeley: University of California Press, 1957.

Williams, Raymond. *Key Words.* New York: Oxford University Press, 1976.

Yates, Frances. *The French Academies of the Sixteenth Century.* London: Warburg Institute, 1947.

Yourcenar, Marguerite. *La Couronne et la lyre.* Gallimard, 1979.

—— *Discours de réception à l'Académie Française.* Gallimard, 1981.

—— *Oeuvres romanesques.* Gallimard, 1982.

Zéraffa, Michel. *Roman et société.* Presses Universitaires de France, 1971.

Zumthor, Paul. "La Carte de Tendre et les Précieux." *Trivium* (1948), 6:263–73.

Index

Abensour, Léon, 6, 38, 230*n*21
Absolutism, French: as developed by
Louis XIV, 16, 42, 108, 253-54*n*4; its
influence on feminism, 63, 97, 111;
its influence on literature, 101; and
the politics of assimilation, 12, 13,
174-76; and the politics of marriage,
112; its use of literature, 13, 41, 96,
169, 176, 197; women's legal status
under, 110-13, 134, 151-54, 157
Académie Française, the, 164, 166, 173,
195, 225*n*13, 235*n*57, 266*n*24; its dictionary, 121; exclusion of women
from, 18, 67-70, 234-35*n*52, 235*n*54,
251-52*n*64; and women's writing,
248*n*43; women writers awarded
prizes by, 67, 192, 235*n*53
Academies: in France, 67, 69, 129, 195,
228*n*5, 235*nn*54 and 56, 236*n*3, 251-
52*n*64; in Italy, 68, 228*n*5; see also
Salon, the
Adam, Antoine, 2, 83, 128, 142, 148,
158, 229*n*7, 257-58*n*28, 263*n*58; on
Boileau, 164, 167, 181, 262*n*52,
263*nn*4-5, 266*n*24
Adams, Percy, 257*n*21
Adultery: charge of, used against
women, 258*n*29; husband's, 260*n*41;
in the novel, 106-7, 141-43, 149,
244*n*21; as threat to bloodlines, 13,
139-40; women's punishment for,

107, 151-52, 259-60*n*38, 260*n*41; *see
also* Divorce; Marriage
Allentuch, Harriet, 250*n*56
Amazon, the: as construction of gender, 10, 229*n*9; during the Fronde,
36-42, 132; iconography of, 26, 29,
229*n*12; literary amazons, 25; male
fear of, 26, 70, 231*n*24; in seventeenth-century French literature, 24,
132, 146, 232*n*29, 233*n*42; seventeenth-century myth of the, 22, 24;
see also Femme forte
Anne of Austria, 26, 42, 254-55*n*9; and
the Fronde, 36-37, 46
Anonymous publication, 3, 15, 59, 75,
95, 98-100, 129, 229*n*7, 237*nn*9 and
10; authors' identified, 234*n*46; benefits of, 101; defined, 98, 242*n*6; and
women writers, 252*n*1; *see also* Author, writers' identity as; Signature
Anthologies, literary: in antiquity, 192-
93; compiled for adults, 184, 185,
187, 194, 267*n*27; compiled for
schoolchildren, 184, 109-10, 197; development of, 185, 186, 187, 196,
267*nn*28-29; devoted exclusively to
women writers, 185, 198, 263*n*1; *Recueil des plus belles pièces des poètes
français*, 183-84, 267*n*27; *see also*
Canon, French pedagogical
Apostolidès, Jean-Marie, 234*n*49

Cabinet, the, as room of one's own, 50, 64, 230*n*19
Cahen, Albert, 197-98
Canon, French pedagogical, 166, 178, 182-83, 227*n*22, 267-68*n*32; and its counterpart for adult readers, 183-85, 192, 194; presence of French authors in, 184, 187, 193; *see also* Anthologies, literary; Education
Canon of French literature: development of, 13, 97, 159, 170, 181, 183-86, 188, 196; elimination of women writers from, 189, 227*n*22, 266-67*n*26; in the nineteenth century, 263*n*2; presence of women writers in, 187, 192, 199; seventeenth-century views of, 182
Carte de Tendre, 55-57, 78, 87-90, 155, 234*n*44, 240*n*29; compared to contemporary allegorical maps, 240*n*28, 249*n*49; *see also Artamène, ou le Grand Cyrus; Clélie;* Scudéry, Madeleine de
Catholic Church: compromise with the State on marriage, 260*n*43; on marriage, 110-11, 112, 151-52
Caverivière, Nicole Ferrier, 66, 234*n*49, 257*n*23
Charnes, Abbé J.-A. de, 135, 255*n*14
Charpentier, Gervais, 67
Charrière, Isabelle de, 2, 261-62*n*51, 266*n*22
Chartier, Roger, 187, 188
Chateaubriand, François René, Vicomte de, 181, 227-28*n*23
Chauveau, François, 29
Chevreuse, Duchesse de, 37, 38
Child custody, in fiction, 141, 142, 147
Le Cid, quarrel of, 230*n*17
Cioranescu, Alexandre, 22, 229*n*7
Cixous, Hélène, 23
Class: blurring of during the Fronde, 231*n*23; as category in ancien régime France, 224-25*n*12, 225*n*14, 261*n*49; importance of in French literary history, 159, 165, 260*n*40; promoted by the French educational system, 195-96, 198, 199; seen as ba-

sis of French civilization, 174; sense of, 13, 76, 117, 137, 253-54*n*4; subversion of in women's writing, 88-89, 92, 115, 154-55, 169, 174-76, 179, 181, 226*n*16, 239*n*19, 261-62*n*51, 265*n*11; vocabulary of, 261*n*49
Classic: authors, 197, 199; in the classroom, 191; meaning of, 183, 266-67*n*26; women writers seen as anti-, 183
Classicism, French neo-: and aristocratic values, 169, 174-75, 198; and the Golden Age of French literature, 69, 183, 197; its stylistic values, 165, 176-77, 227*n*22; *see also* Literary history
Clélie, 55-58, 80, 82-85, 86, 87-93, 234*n*44, 240*n*30; its influence, 240*n*33, 243-44*n*18, 262*n*53; tender geographies in, 18, 55-56, 62, 87-89, 115; *see also* Carte de Tendre; Scudéry, Madeleine de
Code noir, 13, 258*n*32
Colbert, Jean-Baptiste, 112, 247*n*37, 264*n*9
Colette (Sidonie Gabrielle Claudine Colette), 260*n*42
Collaboration, literary, 101, 102, 237*n*7, 237-38*n*13, 241*n*3, 242*n*8; *see also* Salon writing
Coming to writing, 23, 78
Communities of women, 43, 47, 232*n*27; literary, 161, 162, 251-52*n*64; religious, 233*n*40; in women's fiction, 49-50, 53, 62
Condé, Prince de, 36, 45, 48
Conti, Louise-Marie de Lorraine, Princesse de, 22-23, 74, 229*n*7, 237*n*8; and the politics of her salon writing, 229*n*8, 237*n*11
Contract: authorial identity as, 4; in Lafayette's fiction, 120-22, 249*n*51, 250*n*55; in Scudéry's fiction, 89; *see also* Marriage, as contract
Conversation, art of, 47, 50, 228*n*3, 267*n*29; and literary style, 48, 174, 265*n*15; *see also* Salon
Conversation, the, 46-47, 57, 65, 82, 84-

GENDER AND CULTURE

A SERIES OF COLUMBIA UNIVERSITY PRESS

Edited by Carolyn G. Heilbrun and Nancy K. Miller

In Dora's Case: Freud, Hysteria, Feminism
Edited by Charles Bernheimer and Claire Kahane

Breaking the Chain: Women, Theory and French Realist Fiction
Naomi Schor

Between Men: English Literature and Male Homosocial Desire
Eve Kosofsky Sedgwick

Romantic Imprisonment: Women and Other Glorified Outcasts
Nina Auerbach

The Poetics of Gender
Edited by Nancy K. Miller

Reading Woman: Essays in Feminist Criticism
Mary Jacobus

Honey-Mad Women: Emancipatory Strategies in Women's Writing
Patricia Yeager

Subject to Change: Reading Feminist Writing
Nancy K. Miller

Thinking Through the Body
Jane Gallop

Gender and the Politics of History
Joan Wallach Scott

Dialogic and Difference: "An/Other Woman" in Virginia Woolf and Virginia Woolf
Anne Hermann

Plotting Women
Jean Franco

Inspiriting Influences
Michael Awkward

Hamlet's Mother
Carolyn G. Heilbrun

Rape and Representation
Edited by Lynn A. Higgins and Brenda R. Silver

Shifting Scenes: Interviews on Women, Writing, and Politics in Post-68 France
Edited by Alice A. Jardine and Anne M. Menke